AND GOD SAW
THAT IT WAS GOOD

CATHOLIC
THEOLOGY
AND THE
ENVIRONMENT

D1532300

"And God Saw That It Was Good"

Catholic Theology and the Environment

Edited by
Drew Christiansen, SJ,
and
Walter Grazer

United States
Catholic
Conference
Washington, D.C.

In fall 1993, the United States Catholic Conference (USCC) initiated a program on the environment called the Environmental Justice Program. The program is under the direction of the bishops' Domestic and International Policy Committees. The Environmental Justice Program is part of a larger formal ecumenical effort known as the National Religious Partnership for the Environment (NRPE), whose membership includes the National Council of Churches, the Coalition on Jewish Life and the Environment, and the Evangelical Environmental Network. Funding for the program is provided through a special grant from the NRPE. A key element of the overall program is to promote theological study of this issue. The USCC's Environmental Justice Program has hosted several consultations with scholars, and this book represents a collection of the essays and other relevant materials from the second consultation. It is hoped that these essays will spur further interest and research on the Catholic viewpoint on ecology and environmental concerns. *And God Saw That It Was Good* was approved by Most Rev. William S. Skylstad, chairman of the Domestic Policy Committee, and is authorized for publication by the undersigned.

Monsignor Dennis M. Schnurr
General Secretary
NCCB/USCC

"The Sacramentality of Creation and the Role of Creation in Liturgy and Sacraments" by Kevin Irwin, from *Preserving the Creation: Environmental Theology and Ethics,* reprinted with permission from Georgetown University Press.

"Pastoral Letter on the Relationship of Human Beings to Nature" reprinted with permission of the Dominican Episcopal Conference. Translated from the Spanish by Sr. Helen Phillips, MM.

"The Cry for Land: Joint Pastoral Letter by the Guatemalan Bishops' Conference" reprinted with permission of the Guatemalan Bishops' Conference.

"Ecology: The Bishops of Lombardy Address the Community" reprinted with permission of the Archdiocese of Milan. Originally published as "La questione ambientale"; translated by Dr. Howard Limoli, Sr. Ann McBrayer, Gloria Dondero, and Br. Robert de Lucia for the North American Conference on Christianity and Ecology.

"What Is Happening to Our Beautiful Land?: A Pastoral Letter on Ecology from the Catholic Bishops of the Philippines" reprinted with permission of the Catholic Bishops' Conference of the Philippines.

"Christians and Their Duty Towards Nature," reprinted with permission of the Australian Catholic Social Justice Council.

Scripture quotations, unless noted, are taken from the *New American Bible with Revised New Testament,* copyright © 1986 by the Confraternity of Christian Doctrine, Washington, D.C., and are used with permission. All rights reserved. Psalms are taken from *The Revised Psalms of the New American Bible,* copyright © 1991 by the Confraternity of Christian Doctrine, Washington, D.C., and are used with permission. All rights reserved.

ISBN 1-57455-089-6

CONTENTS

PREFACE

As we look to the twenty-first century, a concern for the ecological health of humans and the natural world is likely to emerge as a priority issue. One does not have to be an alarmist or subscribe to apocalyptic environmental scenarios to recognize the serious environmental challenges facing us today and well into the future here and across the globe. While much has been done over the past decades to clean up the environment in the United States, there is much left to do to stop significant soil erosion, clean our water supplies, and solve toxic waste problems. Certainly the poor disproportionately face environmental hazards that affect their communities and the future of their children. Without constant vigilance and active work to prevent or solve environmental problems, our nation could risk its own environmental health.

But the environment is not something contained within national borders. Bad air, polluted water, and industrial waste know no boundaries. Much pollution stems from the industrial waste of the richer nations and now from the developing ones trying to catch up to twenty-first-century economic development. The stakes for the environment as well as social justice are high in crafting public policies that can promote the health and life of human communities and their natural environments.

This ecological challenge invites the Church to take seriously its role in the modern world. Vatican II called the Church to read the "signs of the times" and interpret them in light of the Gospel. Large issues, like global warming, the ozone layer, and natural resource management, and more local problems, like safe drinking water and toxic storage and clean-up, affect how we care for God's creation and promote the flourishing of human communities. In short, as Pope John Paul II says, "The ecological crisis is a moral issue."

While the Church has always addressed theological concerns centered on creation and the natural world, the present environmental challenge requires new theological research and commentary. For the first time, humankind can alter its environment globally for good or ill. This presents new challenges that are not only technological but also moral, affecting individual and collective decisions. The magnitude of these moral challenges led Pope John Paul II and the U.S. Catholic bishops to address ecological concerns through pastoral statements earlier in this decade.

The U.S. Catholic bishops, in their 1991 pastoral statement *Renewing the Earth,* called upon theologians and ethicists to "explore, deepen, and advance the insights of our Catholic tradition and its relation to our environment." This book is part of a larger project to challenge Catholic theologians to heed this call. A series of consultations with Catholic theologians and ethicists have been held to examine our rich theological and ethical tradition and to develop principles to guide us in addressing ecological crises. This book collects the essays and other relevant materials from the second consultation, "Ecology and Catholic Theology: Contribution and Challenge," held at Mount Angel Abbey in Portland, Oregon, in summer 1995. Our hope is that this book will help stimulate additional interest by students and other Catholic scholars to further explore this issue in light of Catholic theology and social teaching.

We thank the bishops' Committees on Domestic and International Policy and the Department of Social Development and World Peace for their overall support, direction, and supervision of the Environmental Justice Program. In particular, we appreciate the support of Bishops Malone, McRaith, Reilly, Ricard, and Skylstad, who have helped us implement this project. We also thank the scholars who have graciously and enthusiastically participated in this project and who continue to remain engaged in further research and writing. We extend our indebtedness to Jill Ortman-

Fouse, program specialist with the Environmental Justice Program; to Anna Minore, who spent long hours helping to prepare the texts for submission; and to the Office for Publishing and Promotion Services at the United States Catholic Conference.

Editors
Drew Christiansen, SJ
Walter E. Grazer

INTRODUCTION

Christians, in particular, realize that their responsibility within creation and their duty towards nature and the Creator are an essential part of their faith.

Pope John Paul II, *The Ecological Crisis: A Common Responsibility,*
1990 World Day of Peace Message

IN 1990, POPE JOHN PAUL II ISSUED HIS WORLD DAY OF PEACE MESSAGE, *The Ecological Crisis: A Common Responsibility,* which was the first Vatican statement devoted entirely to the ecological question.[1] Pope John Paul opens his appeal with the comment that "there is a growing awareness that world peace is threatened not only by the arms race, regional conflicts and continued injustice among peoples and nations, but also by a lack of *due respect for nature.*" He emphasized that "the ecological crisis is a moral issue." Pope John Paul II places this entire concern into a larger perspective, linking care for the poor with care for the earth.

Also in January 1990 in an unrelated effort, thirty-two internationally eminent scientists, including several Nobel laureates, issued an urgent appeal to the religious community to "preserve the environment of the world." As scientists, they openly acknowledged that environmental problems were a significant point of concern to many in the scientific community. More importantly, these scientists recognized that the challenge to take care of the planet meant that "problems of such magnitude, and solutions demanding so broad a perspective, must be recognized from the outset as having a religious as well as scientific dimension."[2]

The Roman Catholic bishops of the United States released their own pastoral statement on the environment in November 1991.[3] Using biblical themes and applying principles from Catholic social teaching, the U.S. bishops establish the environment as an issue worthy of reflection and action on the part of American Catholics. They specifically call upon "theologians, scripture scholars, and ethicists to help explore, deepen, and advance the insights of our Catholic tradition and its relation to the environment."

The appeals by Pope John Paul II, the U.S. Catholic bishops, and other Catholic religious leaders mean that the Catholic community needs to take up the challenge to see environmental concerns not just as emerging political or economic issues, but as concerns intimately related to their faith life.[4] Making this connection invites and advances the Catholic community into a new realm of theological inquiry with practical applications in personal and community morality. To ignore the challenge could risk forfeiting environmental concerns to secular forces or committing a "sin of omission," depending upon the eventual seriousness of environmental damage. History will judge.

Ultimately, the Catholic community is a faith community. Its belief in God and confession of faith in Jesus Christ centers the whole life of the community. Catholicism's rich intellectual tradition helps articulate this faith, a tradition which time and again has been explored for its contributions to pressing problems facing the world. In turn, this tradition and heritage has been enriched by engaging perplexing societal issues. While it is science's task to determine the extent of environmental problems (severity and urgency), it is religion's obligation to discern the meaning of these concerns in light of its belief in God. Both religion and science have a cooperative role in addressing such a serious issue.

This book is a direct response to the U.S. bishops' call to Catholic theologians, ethicists, and scholars to help research and articulate the Catholic contribution to an environmental ethic. It represents the cooperative work of the United States Catholic Conference's Environmental Justice Program, the National Religious Partnership for the Environment, and Catholic scholars open to doing the research and participating in this effort.

The U.S. Bishops' Environment Program and the
National Religious Partnership for the Environment Project

Taking seriously their own pastoral reflection as well as the appeal of Pope John Paul II, the Catholic bishops of the United States have initiated a program called "Renewing the Earth: Environmental Justice Program." As the name suggests, the link between care for the poor and care for the earth is central to the bishops' approach to environmental concerns.

The mission of the U.S. bishops' Environmental Justice Program is to help the Catholic community in the United States make the link between their faith and the environment issue. In doing this, the Church seeks to promote and live a consistent ethic of life. In striving to protect the dignity of every person and promote the common good of the human family, particularly the most vulnerable among us, the Church champions the rights of the unborn, helping to lead the national effort to oppose abortion; it endeavors to bring dignity to the poor and help them become full partners in our society; it works to overcome the scourge of racism and bring everyone to the table of the human family; it welcomes the stranger among us; and in all cases, it promotes the family as the center of human culture and moral development. Now, the Church is recognizing that the web of life and the promotion of human dignity are linked to the protection of God's gift of creation.

The U.S. Catholic bishops are developing their environmental efforts with a distinctively and authentically Catholic approach. This has theological and practical implications. The Church's theological view of creation and the environment is sacramental. Nature reveals the presence of God. This book explores this sacramental view in depth. Practically, the bishops' program is designed to be integrated within the existing framework of daily Catholic life. Consequently, to fulfill its mission, the program has set four program goals. First, since the local diocese and parish are the pastoral heart of the Church's life, the Environmental Justice Program prepares educational materials and provides small grants to dioceses, parishes, and other Catholic organizations to support existing activities and spur new ones. Second, the program devotes significant resources to leadership development. Third, the intersection of environmental public policy and ethics receives increased attention. Finally, the program seeks to ground this entire effort in the Church's theology, spirituality, and social teaching. The combination of these elements hopefully can help craft a genuinely and distinctively Catholic approach to environmental concerns.

While the USCC's own environmental efforts were gaining focus and strength in the late 1980s and early 1990s, the Conference also joined the interfaith and ecumenical effort known as the National Religious Partnership for the Environment. The formal launching of the NRPE in 1993 reflected the emergence of concern in environmental issues by the broader religious community. Certainly, mainline Protestant communities had been addressing this issue for some time with a considerable body of scholarly work. The United States Catholic Conference, the public policy agency of the U.S. Catholic bishops, had an active track record in areas of agriculture, conservation and energy.[5] Increasingly these issues were leading it to broaden its concern to other environmental issues. More recently, Jewish and Evangelical Christians have initiated their own independent environmental efforts.

On June 2-3, 1991, after a series of special briefings by prominent scientists and meetings with Congressional leaders, each of the major faith communities—Catholic, Jewish, and Protestant—committed itself to exploring a more definitive commitment to dealing with environmental issues. An informal survey of local congregations by the faith communities revealed that activity was already occurring at local levels and that a base of support existed for a more formal approach to addressing environmental issues in a sustained way.

After what turned out to be a year of heightened activity by all parties, the scientific and religious leaders met again from May 10-12, 1992. This meeting included not only briefings but testimony before a specially convened congressional committee, followed by more formal arrangements for future collaboration among the communities. On the evening of May 11, 1992, senior leaders of the United States Catholic Conference, the National Council of Churches in Christ, the Evangelical Environmental Network, and the Consultation on the Environment and Jewish Life agreed to establish the National Religious Partnership for the Environment. At this meeting, strategic goals for a three-year program were set. Following this meeting, senior staff from the four communities worked to establish the actual program, which began in the summer of 1993.[6]

The premises for establishing a special project were rooted in the historic moment and the role religious communities have played traditionally in major issues facing society in the United States. The historic moment was the judgment based upon the appeal by scientists of eminent respect that environmental problems were intensifying. Such an appeal could not be summarily dismissed even if the national and international debate over the extent and severity of these problems was and continues to be open to further research.

Traditionally, religious communities have played a pivotal role in a number of major issues facing society. We need not go back too far in history to recall the pivotal role of the religious community in the civil rights, war and peace, and human rights movements. All have benefited from the formal and sustained engagement and leadership of religious communities with these issues. The current debate over the place of religion in society and the role and relationship between state and religion places religious communities at the front in the values debate around abortion, poverty, societal violence, and support for families and children. This may well be the case for the environmental issue.

Religious communities are particularly well suited to engage the issue of the environment. They have theological and teaching resources, geographically and culturally diverse communities, and most importantly, the moral authority needed to address major issues by virtue of their very mission. Creating a sense of the sacred is fundamental to an ethic of respect and care for God's creation, and it is the distinctive mission of the religious community to develop such an ethic. While addressing environmental concerns is clearly a task for the religious community, it will not be easy. The issues are complex with no simple solutions; the diversity of the religious community itself reflects this complexity. However, complexity should never deter the religious community from tackling major societal concerns.

All of the participating religious communities in the NRPE have a shared mission, namely to help their members respond to environmental issues in light of their faith and traditions. This means helping theologians and religious educators uncover new fields for study and religious education; it means lifting up aspects of our liturgical and prayer life that show forth the sacramentality of God's creation; it means connecting people's faith to public policy that promotes a respect for the environment in which they live; and it means defending the poor who so often suffer disproportionately from environmental degradation.

Care for God's creation is an intrinsically religious issue. God is the Creator of our universe. The new *Catechism of the Catholic Church* calls our attention to the fact that "our Creed begins with the creation of heaven and earth, for creation is the beginning and the foundation of all God's works" (no. 198). It further affirms that "all creatures bear a certain resemblance to God, most especially man, created in the image and likeness of God. The manifold perfections of creatures—their truth, their goodness, their beauty,—all reflect the infinite perfection of God" (no. 41). Certainly, the covenant made with Noah, a covenant made with all of creation, reminds us that although humans are unique and special in God's eyes, we share creaturehood with the rest of creation and must exercise a stewardship of care and responsibility for the sake of God's creation and for future generations. Our liturgy and spiritual traditions—the early desert fathers, the Benedictine, and most especially Franciscan—point toward a respect for creation and a view of creation as sacramental, revealing the presence of God.

In a special way, linking justice for creation with justice for those on the margins of society conceptually and practically is an emerging task. It offers the Church as a whole and parishes in particular a unique role and opportunity to join both dimensions of environmental justice—protection of God's creation and care and justice for the poor and vulnerable. For it is in local communities that environmental problems and the struggle for justice so often meet face to face.

As already cited, the practical programs of the USCC and the NRPE have several elements to give shape and life to their mission. There are educational programs for parishes with specially produced materials; efforts to train leaders at the congregational level to help build a network of concern and action; public policy initiatives to help give expression to deeply held moral values as they affect the environment; special efforts to work with seminarians, priests, and clergy to assist them in integrating this concern into their daily ministry; and consultations with scholars and academicians to reflect upon and write about ecological concerns from their disciplines.

All of these program efforts aim to help people of faith see ecological and environmental concerns, as expressed in the words of senior religious leaders in their June 1991 consultation, as "an inescapably religious challenge." While the practical goal is to help people of faith integrate this concern into their daily faith life, it must be stressed that environmental concerns are not meant to be just another issue in a long series of issues, but rather are to be seen from the perspective of what it means to be religious, to be people of faith.

The Need for a Theological Foundation

The ultimate significance of the endeavor to help Catholics link their faith life to environmental concerns rests on its theological foundation. Environmental concerns will be taken seriously as a matter of faith only if Catholics and other faith communities see this concern as deeply rooted in Scripture and theology, spirituality and worship, and moral and ethical norms.

For Catholics, two recent documents provide a basis for a more profound theological study—Pope John Paul II's 1990 World Day of Peace Message and the U.S. bishops' statement *Renewing the Earth*. Pope John Paul II has increasingly referred to environmental concerns in his teaching on social ethics.[7] His most comprehensive statement to date, the 1990 World Day of Peace Message, is organized around several principles. First, environment is linked to our faith life in a fundamental way. "Many ethical values, fundamental to the development of a *peaceful society*, are particularly relevant to the ecological question. The fact that many challenges facing the world today are interdependent confirms the need for carefully coordinated solutions based on a morally coherent world view."

This "order" upon which the universe is based is rooted in the biblical account of creation. Pope John Paul II, who often cites Genesis as a key to a number of theological constructs, begins his statement on the environment by tying the concern directly to the biblical account of creation and its goodness to God's "first self-revelation to humanity. . . . When man turns his back on the Creator's plan, he provokes a disorder which has inevitable repercussions on the rest of created order." Christ's death and resurrection restore the harmony and renew all of creation.

Second, Pope John Paul II calls for respecting the "integrity of creation." In effect, he makes the environment a moral issue. The order and harmony of God's creation must be respected. He cites a variety of abuses and environmental disharmonies that threaten the integrity of creation including such post-modern problems as the "*indiscriminate application* of advances in science and technology," "the lack of respect for life evident in patterns of pollution," "the dominance of economic interests over the dignity of workers and even entire peoples," the "reckless exploitation of natural resources," the "uncontrolled destruction of animal and plant life," and "genetic manipulation." These issues are widened into more global ethical concerns when Pope John Paul places ecology within the wider context of problems of development and structural poverty, lifestyle and consumerism, and even war. The social and environmental imbalance resulting from these problems calls for the virtue of solidarity and a strong role for the state when necessary in redressing the imbalances.

Finally, he calls for a new attitude of appreciating the "*aesthetic value of creation.*" Our contact "with nature should have a deep restorative power: contemplation of its magnificence imparts peace and serenity." Integrating a more spiritual focus on God's creation in the midst of so many practical environmental problems makes the moral duty to care for creation an essential part of faith. It is no wonder that Pope John Paul II has chosen St. Francis, who maintained a lively sense of "fraternity" with all of creation, as the patron saint of the environment and an example for all to emulate.

The U.S. Catholic bishops echo and expand upon the concepts and concern of Pope John Paul for the environment. While the bishops' statement deals extensively with the environment as a moral challenge, they root their commentary in scripture and in the sacramental tradition of the Church. The book of nature is here for everyone to see, believer and nonbeliever, but the sacramental universe makes the world not only humanity's home but one where God dwells with us. Creation reveals the presence, wisdom, and goodness of God. It is this God-centered approach to creation and the environment that calls people to respect and reverence creation as a pathway to union with God. "Dwelling in the presence of God, we begin to experience ourselves as part of creation, as stewards within it, not separate from it."

The bishops' view of the environment requires new thinking and behavior. To really believe that creation is sacramental means that Catholics cannot ignore the effect of their individual or collective actions on the rest of creation. To do so would offend the Creator. Just as Christian charity and justice make a special claim on the Church's concern for the poor, these virtues now make claim on Catholics to exercise a stewardship that "places upon us responsibility for the well-being of all God's creatures."

Pope John Paul's use of language calling for a *"right to a safe environment . . .* that must be included in an updated Charter of Human Rights" and the bishops' theological and ethical view are really an invitation to the Catholic community to integrate environmental concerns into the everyday life of faith. While Pope John Paul II and the U.S. Catholic bishops have provided a vision and the leadership necessary to help propel this issue forward, theologians, scripture scholars, and ethicists also need to play a role in helping Catholics understand the environment in light of their faith. These specialists are specifically called to give more thought in extending the disciplines of systematic theology, scriptural exegesis, liturgical study, and ethical analysis to the concern for creation and ecology.

This particular scholars' project, leading to the publication of this book, is an attempt by the Bishops' Conference to advance a more determined application of theology to the environment and the challenges it poses. The project seeks to provide a solid theological basis for developing a Catholic approach to the entire environmental challenge. Each essay deals with a question or aspect of the environment from the Catholic tradition. This in no way implies indifference to, unawareness of, or exclusion of other Christian or non-Christian perspectives. Some of the essays include insights or commentary from these other rich traditions. Rather, the Catholic approach is meant to examine a critical contemporary issue from the perspective of our own tradition, and one which has recently begun to revisit questions of cosmology, the environment, and nature. As such, this effort represents an invitation to dialogue; it is not a final word but rather an ongoing conversation. The project so defined invites further reflection, critique, and debate.

Catholic Reflections and the Essays on Environment

At Vatican II, the Council in its document *The Pastoral Constitution on the Church in the Modern World* stated that "at all times, the Church carries the responsibility of reading the signs of the times and interpreting them in the light of the Gospel" (no. 4). Today, given the accumulating scientific evidence and increasing public and political concern about environmental and ecological issues, these matters clearly are a "sign of the times." While science has the role of helping to determine the full extent of these problems, religion's role is to help believers and others of good will address these concerns in the context of faith and with moral urgency.

Many people encounter environmental issues as community problems and conflicts. Judgments need to be made about who will reap the benefits and who will

reflective of God but also must include transformative action. Sacrament effects change; consequently, sacrament should be seen as not just revelation but also agency.

Ancient cosmology was pregnant with religious meaning. It was the road to the meaning of human existence. Modern cosmology has to do with a subset of physics—the origin of the universe and its physical structure. Existential religious questions arising from cosmological discoveries dominated ancient cosmology but over the last four hundred years have received a rockier reception. Toolan's conclusion is that the situation has now changed and that modern cosmology offers to theology a rich diet of existential questions. The new discoveries associated with quantum physics and chaos theory and Catholicism's sacramental history offer more compatible grounds for religion and science's dialogue than the earlier history of modern science.

Catholicism's premodern roots of a sacramental view of nature were based in a preliterate world culture given to aural and oral, rather than visual, communication. Humans experienced a God who was close and a God who encompassed all. Our modern culture is visual, allowing us to distance ourselves from nature. The question in Toolan's mind is whether we can go back as a literate urbanized people and whether modern cosmology can be an ally. While we cannot go "home" as in turning back the clock to before the modern era or even should do this, considering all the gains of modernity, Toolan believes that modern physics' view of the world as forces, fields, and energies rather than a static Newtonian world is closer to a Catholic sacramental view of a world where God is Creator and Sustainor.

Irwin and Feiss

Essential to forging a Catholic ecological ethic are liturgy and spirituality. Liturgy, particularly the eucharist, prayer, and spirituality, are the daily avenues we use to grow in our life in Christ. Unless we as believers are touched and transformed by the Spirit in our worship and praise of Christ, we have little hope of developing the deep sense of respect necessary to care for God's creation. Without the sustaining resources that come from a deep prayer and spiritual life, we will be unable to integrate concern for creation into our faith life. It is the transformation in Christ arising from our prayer and liturgical life that makes our pastoral work the natural fruit of the life of Christ among us. Fortunately, Catholic liturgy and spirituality offer rich resources for responding to the Spirit's promptings to witness to and take part in God's work to "renew the face of the earth" (Ps 104:30).

Fr. Kevin Irwin in his commentary on liturgy, "The Sacramentality of Creation and the Role of Creation in Liturgy and Sacraments,"[10] and Fr. Hugh Feiss, OSB, in his examination of the Benedictine contribution, "Watch the Crows: Environmental Responsibility and the Benedictine Tradition," provide entree points for placing a concern for creation at the center of our daily prayer and the routine of Christian living.

Irwin links the traditional formula of *lex orandi*, what we pray; *lex credendi*, what we believe; and *lex vivendi*, what we live with the wider theme of liturgy and creation. The central question he tries to answer is how our worship and prayer and our theology of liturgy relate to the sacramentality of creation and the use of creation in worship. His answer calls us to pay careful attention to the creation motif existent in the liturgical texts. This means having a positive regard for the things of this earth simply because they are used in our liturgical worship.

What is important to Irwin is the use of symbol. Human speech, gesture, and elements of nature that result from human craft—bread and wine from wheat and grapes—and the use of water and oil all serve as a "symbolic rehearsal of salvation." Irwin emphasizes the dynamic nature of liturgy, which leads to transformation of the community. Consequently, to use creation as part of our liturgical worship enables us to show reverence for creation, through which the incarnate God is disclosed and discovered. The work of human hands to transform wheat and grapes into bread and wine which become the body and blood of Christ in the eucharist is at the center of our praise and worship. The use of these elements fosters a harmony between creation theology and the paschal mystery of redemption. Being conscious of and using creation in liturgy in this way help overcome the problem of spiritual/material dualism.

In Irwin's view, a more focused attention on the use of creation in liturgy will help ground the ethical imperative to revere and preserve God's gift of creation. There has to be a living out of our transformation in Christ through our prayer and liturgical life. As Irwin says, "the liturgy could be interpreted properly as the closest we can come here and now to what will only be perfected in the kingdom—the renewal of all things in heaven and earth and their recapitulation in Christ."

If what we pray is what we believe and do, then the Benedictine tradition, which has remained vital for fifteen hundred years, is a living example of the integration of prayer, study, and a life of virtue. Fr. Hugh Feiss, OSB, examines key elements of Benedictine spiritual tradition as it applies to the virtues and attitudes necessary for taking responsibility for the environment. Using the Rule of St. Benedict and the lives of several Benedictines as examples of how to live harmoniously with the rest of creation, Feiss presents the Benedictine tradition as a model for developing a Catholic environmental ethic.

The Rule has implications for the development of specific virtues helpful to an environmental ethic. As a prelude and precondition for developing a virtuous life,

Feiss makes the case that the Rule requires stability of place. This lifelong vow means that monks have the opportunity to get to know their place well. In our modern world, high mobility, while providing cultural enrichment, tends to negate deep knowledge of our physical environment, leading perhaps to negative environmental habits. Feiss refers to specific positive virtues: humility and thus reverence for life; service to others and not control or self-aggrandizement; work, labor, and the good of the physical world; and the sacredness of the ordinary. The practice of these virtues would mean not only a less possessive view of the earth and its resources but, more importantly, a creative interaction with our environment in a way that respects nature and provides for the poor and future generations. Moderation in all things is a hallmark of Christian virtue. St. Benedict's monk formed in light of the Rule would be "out of place in a culture whose measure of success is power and money, which employs maximum technological force to squeeze as much as possible out of the natural world as quickly as possible."

Feiss uses examples from the lives of St. Benedict, Cuthbert of Lindisfarne, Wulstan of Worcester, and Hildegard of Bingen to illustrate that humans are to be at peace with their environment. This is not an artificial or easy peace that diminishes the harshness of nature or the seeming war the medieval world could have with nature. Rather it is the ability of the monastic life to provide its followers with the conditions, discipline, and capacity to listen to God, nature, and others for direction in their lives. Lives of the hermits and early monastics provide rich stories of contact with nature and animals. A great ease exists between these monastics and nature, which often provides a companionship that we moderns tend to look upon with some degree of skepticism, since we are so far removed from nature. As a conclusion, Feiss comments that "the abiding ecological relevance of the Benedictine tradition lies in its emphasis on stability of place, moderation, and humble awareness of God's presence in every place and act and person."

Hinze, Christiansen, and Blake

The fruit of our theological inquiry, prayer and liturgical life, and spiritual development is in our commitment to the Church's social teaching and the virtues that habitually form our life in Christ. Christine Firer Hinze and Fr. Drew Christiansen, SJ, lay the basis for an environmental ethic within the context of Catholic social teaching. Hinze formulates an overall approach by examining Catholic social teaching's contribution from a comprehensive point of view. Christiansen places ecology within the larger context of the Church's concern for the common good. Deborah Blake examines the stress upon virtues within Catholic theology, highlighting those necessary for living in a more ecologically balanced manner.

Hinze examines the potential contribution of the Church's social teaching to an environmental ethic, particularly its stress on fostering human dignity. She initiates her commentary, "Catholic Social Teaching and Ecological Ethics," by reminding us that Catholic social teaching should be understood as "encompassing the beliefs and practices of Christians in relation to their social milieu from scriptural times forward . . . including theology, liturgy, mysticism, and the lives of the saints." It is this broader context, in her judgment, that allows the U.S. bishops to make a strong claim "that modern social teaching is, in fact, fundamentally compatible with religio-moral attention to ecology." She herself makes a more specific claim that a "mutual and interpenetrating" influence between environmental and social concerns must undergird Catholic ethics in the next century.

Hinze structures her argument around three themes. First, she highlights major topics arising from recent official church pronouncements relating social thought and environmental questions; second, she examines concerns about anthropocentrism and the Church's emphasis on fostering and protecting human dignity, which she argues must include an interdependent responsibility for our physical environment; and third, she addresses questions of the economy and work, which she says serve as an intermediary and nexus between environmental realities and humanly constructed social communities. Hinze uses the work of St. Thomas and Msgr. John A. Ryan to support her third thesis.

Fostering and protecting human dignity lies at the heart of the Church's social teachings. Hinze examines this emphasis on human dignity to see whether it serves as a stumbling block or fruitful norm for an environmental ethic. She reminds us that the human person is intimately linked with the surrounding environment, dependent for life on air, water, and land. In her judgment, human dignity can serve as a basis for an environmental ethic which can "champion the good of the earth" while seeking to discern how humans can continue to flourish. Protection of the earth and the human community go hand in hand—a truly classic case of the common good.

Finally, Hinze connects the environment and the economy in Christian theology and modern Catholic social thought. For Hinze, the economy serves as the link between natural and social ecology. Her notion of economy includes "God's wanting to provide for people's livelihoods, an interdependence with nature, God's wanting to establish a reign of justice and peace." Economic justice in this way includes justice for land and justice for people. Catholic social teaching— with its emphasis on the economy serving people, its stress on the rights and obligations of workers and employers, and its new concern for the environment—can serve to integrate these concerns of the economy in a broader environmental ethic.

While Hinze applies Catholic social teaching broadly to the environment, Fr. Drew Christiansen, SJ, focuses on Catholic social teaching's use of and emphasis on the "common good"—a notion that offers a distinctive contribution to the development of an environmental ethic. Christiansen's article, "Ecology and the Common Good: Catholic Social Teaching and Environmental Responsibility," highlights the historical meaning and moral norms comprising elements of the common good both as a principle and as an ideal of Catholic social teaching. He also demonstrates the usefulness of the notion of the common good as a guide to our responses to environmental concerns.

Christiansen begins by making the common good the standard for measuring social health and societal integrity—a standard that demands that all sectors of society including individuals, mediating institutions (family, civic organizations, etc.), and the state promote and work cooperatively for the welfare and well-being of society. He notes that the common good is not a precise concept, but more of a notion and ideal that enables us to adjust competing goods and principles in a new order that serves the good of the entire society.

Christiansen examines several principles from Catholic social teaching that draw out the meaning of common good. The first is authentic development. Authentic development promotes the right of every person to live a fully human life, but it measures that development by a balance of goods, including spiritual goods, and is not limited to economics. The second is moderation. Moderation enables us to counteract the overdevelopment of the West and North with the underdevelopment of the East and South. It requires self-restraint in consumption and in lifestyle. The third is sacrifice. The Church teaches "the universal destination of goods," which requires that everyone has access to sufficient goods for a fully human life and that no one be excluded from the banquet of the Lord. To achieve this means sacrifice on the part of all for the common good.

Each of these public virtues is helpful for achieving the common good as applied to environmental concerns. While the notion of the common good historically was limited to more specific settings, e.g., city-states and nations, popes from John XXIII to the present have extended it to a global notion. As the U.S. bishops point out in their 1991 statement *Renewing the Earth,* a "planetary common good" now must include ecology and the environment. Air, water, soil resources, fish stocks, and safe disposal of toxic waste require collective global action for the sake of the common good of society and the earth itself. The common good as an ethic and as an approach would help transmute adversarial approaches in favor of burden-sharing. It would also foster sustainable development, which can help meet present-day needs without sacrificing the needs of future generations or leading to wanton destruction of the earth.

Christiansen ends with a practical moral lesson that "different moral weights attach to different moral goals." This caution is aimed at those who would like an immediate solution to all environmental problems and those who pursue special-interest solutions. The common good as ideal can, over time, make basic attitudes more favorable to "common-sense solutions" and create a public policy climate more conducive to the flourishing of both human and natural environments.

The final essay, "Toward a Sustainable Ethic: Virtue and the Environment," by Deborah Blake draws the necessary conclusion to the prior essays, namely that the global environmental challenge requires a culture of virtues—one reflecting the good of the global commons and the good of the individual. "Values" and "virtues" are frequently discussed today. Much of the public discourse, while reflecting deep need and genuine longing for a more ordered moral life, is still relatively undefined with "little conformity and consistency in the meaning of virtue and the underlying assumptions of the varied theoretical frameworks." To establish a suitable virtue definition and framework for a Catholic environmental ethic, Blake bases her approach on St. Thomas Aquinas's commentary on virtue. For Blake, a recovery of virtue can provide for a more adequate and sustainable environmental ethic within the Church.

Maintaining a tension and dialectic in her approach, Blake wants to retrieve the virtue tradition of Aquinas and open it to development and application to the challenge of the environmental ethic. Any notion of virtue embodies our conception of the good: "Since every nature desires its being and its own perfection, it is necessary to say that the being and perfection of any nature has the character of goodness" (Summa Theologica I.48.1). While the ultimate good is our desire for union with God, there are intermediate goods that must be properly ordered. This virtue theory of Thomas, which is relational, provides a foundation for considering the necessary virtues for an environmental ethos.

Blake uses the four traditional cardinal virtues of fortitude, temperance, prudence, and justice as the foundation for a virtuous life capable of responding to the environmental crisis. She further suggests tolerance (unity in diversity—a Thomistic principle), love, mercy and humility, relationality and responsibility, and farsightedness and cooperation as corollary virtues to guide us environmentally. Finally, she uses "narrative," a story context that can exemplify concrete actions that display the necessary virtues. She examines a case history, the Hispanic Globeville community of Denver and its struggle to achieve justice in a toxic waste clean-up situation. Blake demonstrates that a community that exercises the virtues the Globeville community displayed—equity, a relational and community vision, co-operation, and farsightedness—can achieve justice for itself and help protect the environment. The values of family, respect, and trust so evident in the structure of the community enabled it to overcome great disadvantages relative to money and political power. Blake concludes that more attention should be given to adequately interpreting and rearticulating the Church's tradition about virtue if we are to promote a sustainable and helpful environmental ethos.

Conclusion

This series of essays represents the opening words of a conversation and not the end. The body of work on theology and the environment is growing and will continue to grow, and the USCC consultations with Catholic theologians and ethicists as a part of the larger effort will also continue. The precise formats may vary, but the goal of engaging Catholic scholars and Catholic centers of higher education remains a key program objective and strategy.

Developing a comprehensive and integrated way of looking at the environment from a Catholic theological perspective will take time and effort. The issues are complex and our tradition needs to be examined more thoroughly. While there is no preset agenda of theological questions to explore, there are several areas that deserve further research and commentary. Certainly, more emphasis should be placed on Christ and the New Testament understanding of the fullness of the reign of God in relationship to creation. In addition, this book begins to explore one tradition of spirituality, namely the Benedictine. However, more research is needed on the contributions of Franciscan, Dominican, Jesuit, and other Catholic traditions of spirituality. Our liturgy as a source of theology and spiritual meaning deserves and needs additional research. Finally, the list of ethical problems associated with the environment is formidable. What does Pope John Paul II's call for a "right to a safe environment" specifically entail? What are the principles and ethical norms to guide us in dealing with a truly intergenerational issue? There is also a larger role for an ecumenical and interfaith approach to environmental questions. While there are no easy answers to these questions, the challenge is to articulate an authentically Catholic approach.

Editors
Drew Christiansen, SJ
Director
Office of International Justice and Peace
United States Catholic Conference

Walter E. Grazer
Director
Environmental Justice Program
United States Catholic Conference

Notes

1. Pope John Paul II, *The Ecological Crisis: A Common Responsibility*, World Day of Peace Message, December 8, 1989. Washington, D.C.: United States Catholic Conference, 1990.

2. "An Open Letter to the Religious Community," by Thirty-two Internationally Eminent Scientists, January 1990. Copies are available from the National Religious Partnership for the Environment.

3. National Conference of Catholic Bishops, *Renewing the Earth: An Invitation to Reflection and Action on the Environment in Light of Catholic Social Teaching*. Washington, D.C.: United States Catholic Conference, 1991.

4. Forty-eight known statements on ecology or the environment have been issued to date by bishops' conferences or individual dioceses around the world, including Australia, Belgium/Walloon, a joint statement by Brazil/Bolivia, Brazil, Burundi, CELAM, Canada, Chile, Dominican Republic, Ecuador, England and Wales, Federation of Asian Bishops' Conferences, Germany, Haiti, Indonesia, Ireland, Italy, Kenya, Korea, the Pacific Region, the Philippines, Portugal, Spain, Thailand, the United States, and Zaire.

5. Statements by the bishops of the United Statements include *Reflections on the Energy Crisis,* a statement by the Committee on Social Development and World Peace, April 2, 1981; *Economic Justice for All: Pastoral Letter on Catholic Social Teaching and the U.S. Economy*, Chapter 3—Food and Agriculture; *Report of the Ad Hoc Task Force on Food, Agriculture, and Rural Concerns*, November 15, 1989; and *Food Policy in a Hungry World: The Links That Bind Us Together: Pastoral Reflections on Food and Agricultural Policy*. Washington, D.C.: United States Catholic Conference.

6 This history relies upon the work of Paul Gorman and Amy Fox, the executive director and former associate director, respectively, of the National Religious Partnership for the Environment.

7. Selected major references on ecology from Pope John Paul II and other Vatican or Church statements include the following: *On Social Concern* (no. 26), Encyclical Letter, December 30, 1987; *On the Hundredth Anniversary of Rerum Novarum* (nos. 30-31, 37), Encyclical Letter, May 1, 1991; *The Gospel of Life* (no. 42), Encyclical Letter, March 25, 1995; *Catechism of the Catholic Church* (particularly the sections on the Creed, nos. 279-301 and Life in Christ, nos. 2415-2418); and *Paths to Peace: A Contribution of the Documents of the Holy See to the International Community* (pp. 54-57, 248-249, 463-493), Permanent Observer Mission of the Holy See to the United States, New York, 1987.

8. Gabriel Daly, "Foundations in Systematics for Ecological Theology," in *Preserving the Creation: Environmental Theology and Ethics*, ed. Kevin W. Irwin and Edmund D. Pellegrino. Washington, D.C.: Georgetown University Press, 1994, 43.

9. See Dennis Edwards, *Jesus the Wisdom of God: An Ecological Theology* (New York: Orbis Books, 1995) for an additional and more detailed examination of Christ as Wisdom and the theological implications for developing an ecological theology.

10. Kevin Irwin, "The Sacramentality of Creation and the Role of Creation in Liturgy and Sacraments," in *Preserving the Creation: Environmental Theology and Ethics*, ed. Kevin Irwin and Edmund Pellegrino. Washington, D.C.: Georgetown University Press, 1994, 67-111. This article is reprinted with the permission of Georgetown University Press.

FOUNDATIONS
FOR A
CATHOLIC ECOLOGICAL
THEOLOGY OF GOD

Anne M. Clifford, CSJ

EVERY YEAR AT THE EASTER VIGIL, THE CATHOLIC COMMUNITY GATHERS with lighted candles in hand in parish churches adorned with lilies to hear an ancient proclamation: "Exalt, all creation. . . . Rejoice, O earth, in shining splendor. . . . Christ has conquered [the forces of death]." In the first reading following the majestic "Exsultet," we hear these words from Genesis: "In the beginning, when God created the heavens and the earth, . . . [God] saw how good it was" (1:1,10). During the night watch for the resurrection of Jesus, the story of the "Days of Creation," itself an ancient liturgical hymn, is the first in a series of readings from both testaments in which we are reminded of God's involvement with creation from its very beginning. This involvement is an unfolding history culminating in Jesus Christ, who, though crucified, "has been raised exactly as he promised" (Mt 28:6). The readings chosen by the Church for the Easter vigil narrate a magnificent chronicle of God active in the world. Beginning with creation, God is continually bringing order out of chaos. The Spirit is always breathing over troubled waters, creating and recreating life.

Today, the survival of God's earthly creation is at risk. We can perceive the fragility of the earth with our own eyes. Environmentalists and ecologists continually draw our attention to the extent of the threat to life on earth.[1] Our waters are indeed troubled: the pollution of surface waters, both fresh and salt, and the contamination of ground water aquifers is always growing. Air quality and the destruction of the ozone layer is another source of distress. Debates rage about the extent and long-term effects of the "greenhouse effect." Warnings about soil erosion, creeping desertification, deforestation, and species' extinction are all too familiar. Clearly, we must change the way we live in order to bring to an end the chaos of ecological destruction.

Pope John Paul II, in his New Year's day message of 1990, stressed the need for recognizing nature as God's creation, thereby, giving it the proper respect.[2] He pointed out that the planet's devastation is the result of people's behavior that disregards the God-given order and harmony of nature. The sins of greed and selfishness—both individual and collective—break the order and diminish the harmony of creation. The pope stressed that the reconciling work of Jesus Christ, who died on the cross and rose from the dead, is not only for the sake of humanity but also for *"all things,* whether on heaven or earth."[3] The saving work of Christ, therefore, has ecological consequences. In this short message, Pope John Paul II brought together two central doctrines of the Christian tradition—creation and redemption—and focused them on the ecological crisis. A major emphasis in this message is the need for "an education in ecological responsibility."[4] An ecological theology of God—one that brings together creation and redemption—is likely to provide a rich theological foundation for such an education.

Although Christianity has very rich and beautiful sources upon which to draw, Christian Churches, including the Roman Catholic Church, have only recently begun to develop ecological theologies. Why is this the case? For many generations theologians have worked under the assumption that a dichotomy existed between humans and the rest of creation. Largely in reaction to modern science and its claim to objectivity about nature, they have emphasized the human subject and the individual's relationship to God, while neglecting or simply ignoring nonhuman nature. Closely related to this first dichotomy is a second—the separation of redemption from creation. This dichotomy represents virtually an exclusive emphasis on human salvation contributing to the neglect of creation theology that encompasses nonhuman creatures. Why do these dichotomies exist in Roman Catholicism? This is the first question I will address. I will then show not only why these dichotomies are unnecessary, but also how classical Christian texts can provide a foundation for an ecological theology that can overcome them.

The Neglect of Creation in Roman Catholic Theology

The most obvious theological link with ecology is creation, because both are concerned with the earth and its many forms of life. The Genesis accounts of creation, along with other biblical creation texts, provide Christianity with a beautiful framework for a vision of God's relationship to the world. In the modern period, however, this vision has focused on God and the *human* world. The doctrine of creation has been interpreted primarily in human-centered terms. As a result, nonhuman nature was denigrated or at least neglected. For much of the twentieth century, nonhuman nature has been treated by Christian theologians as a mere context in which human beings work out their salvation with the help of God's grace. Ecological consciousness makes explicit that nonhuman nature is far more than an external environment for human activity. Moreover, we ignore our interrelation, interconnection, and interdependence with all forms of life and with the earth itself at our own and their peril.

There are historical reasons for the neglect of nonhuman nature by theologians that have a great deal to do with how Christianity responded to the early challenges posed by modern science. Western Christianity, beginning with Galileo's hypothesis of heliocentricism and intensified by Darwin's theory of evolution by natural selection, assumed a defensive posture against science. The positivist tendency of modern science and the challenges it posed, especially to the credibility of the Genesis creation accounts, resulted in theological emphasis on the salvation of humans and the virtual surrender of nature—not just nonhuman earth forms but the entire cosmos—into the hands of scientists. It was less and less to the world and more and more to the human soul that believers turned to find signs of God.

During the height of the controversy over biological evolution in the late nineteenth and early twentieth centuries, Christian Churches tended to develop their own forms of biblical positivism, making creationism common in Roman Catholic theology.[5] Interpreting the first Genesis account of creation literally, creationism proposed that all types of plants and animals were the direct creation of God at the beginning of time. Referred to as "Special Creation," this position maintained that God directly intervened to originate each new species. Obviously, "Special Creation" conflicted with Darwinian evolution, which explained the origin of new and higher species in terms of natural selection and their ability to survive in a struggle of existence. A literal interpretation of Genesis 1 also had the potential of contributing to the exploitation of nonhuman nature. Directives to "subdue" the earth and to have "dominion" over every living creature (Gn 1:28) were applied uncritically to legitimate human domination of nonhuman nature, as if it were a right given to humans by God.[6] I intend to examine this issue further, but first I want to point out a few things about biblical interpretation because of its importance for an ecological theology that recognizes both the interconnectedness of all creatures and the fundamental continuity of creation and redemption.

In time, the basic tenets of the theory of evolution became largely uncontested, at least by the scientific community, and Roman Catholicism came to recognize that creationism was untenable. There is no need for a defensive stance against biological evolution; moreover, this position only impoverishes our theology of creation.[7] The Genesis stories of creation do not conflict with evolution because they were not meant to be scientific accounts. The official Church teachings that influenced biblical scholarship in the formation of this view were *Divino Afflante Spiritu*, an encyclical of Pope Pius XII (1943), and *Dei Verbum*, "The Dogmatic Constitution on Divine Revelation" of the Second Vatican Council (1965).

Appealing for greater use of contemporary biblical scholarship in the interpretation of the Bible, Pius XII stressed the need for biblical scholars to discover and expound the genuine meaning of sacred texts with the aid of ancient language studies and the use of biblical criticism (*Divino Afflante Spiritu*, no. 23).[8] Although the methods of interpretation that Pius XII called for can be traced to Richard Simon, a seventeenth-century Oratorian priest, Simon's research was officially rejected by the Church. His methods of biblical criticism were not adopted by Roman Catholic scholars. As a result, when Pius XII called for scholarship that applied new methods of biblical criticism, Roman Catholic scholars found themselves learning its methods from the Protestant scholars who had already been engaged in it for several generations. Therefore, well-respected Protestant scholars, like Gerhard von Rad, had a considerable impact on Roman Catholic understandings of the Bible. In the 1930s, von Rad argued that creation is ancillary to divine election in the Old Testament; God's offer of salvation is the central and overriding theme.[9] Due largely to von Rad's influence, the most important category for interpreting biblical faith became "the history of [human] salvation."

Overcoming the False Dichotomies

Because of the virtually exclusive emphasis on human redemption, the religious meaning of nonhuman creation was ignored. This neglect of creation overlooks the fact that God's work of creation provides the cosmic purpose behind God's redemptive activity.[10] It disregards what, I believe, is beautifully expressed in the Easter Vigil liturgy and clearly articulated in the 1990 New Year's message of Pope John Paul II cited above. The redemptive activity of God through Jesus Christ, the Word incarnate within creation, is not only for humans but is ultimately for all of creation. For this reason, it is certainly appropriate for the Church to proclaim with one voice that all creatures—not only humans—rejoice in Jesus' rise to a new and transformed life.

In the Second Vatican Council, especially in *Dei Verbum*, it is possible to discern the extent to which biblical criticism has grown in the twenty years since Pius XII's encyclical. *Dei Verbum* stressed that Sacred Scripture, taken together with the Church's Tradition, is the supreme rule of Catholic faith (no. 21).[11] To assist the Church in its understanding of Sacred Scripture, *Dei Verbum* presents three broad principles for interpreting biblical texts:

1. The primary message of any biblical text is the meaning intended by its author(s) (no. 12).[12] To discover the meaning of a text, the language, history, and culture of the Bible must be studied.

2. When a text is being interpreted, it is important to examine its themes in light of how the Bible as a whole treats them. Since the Catholic tradition believes that the Holy Spirit is the ultimate author of the Bible, a single text has meaning in the context of the Bible as a whole.

3. Taking into account the entire tradition of the Church (keeping in mind that throughout history the Church has read biblical texts in communities gathered for worship and instruction), the interpreter should study how a particular passage was used and understood in the earlier life of the Church (no. 12).[13]

The three principles of biblical interpretation of *Dei Verbum* affirm a fundamental characteristic of Roman Catholicism: it is an ever-evolving tradition concerned with illuminating the Catholic community's ever-developing faith in God in response to the changing signs of the times. For more than its two-thousand-year history, the theological tradition of the Church has grown when, under the guidance of the Holy Spirit, its members have explored new ways of thinking in response to urgent needs and questions. Much of this growth has been in response to challenges and criticisms from outside its traditions. Today, part of that challenge is from the earth itself and from environmentalists and ecologists who argue that Christianity is anti-ecological because it has concerned itself with human salvation, apart from and sometimes at the expense of the rest of the inhabitants of the planet.

In service to the development of a Roman Catholic ecological theology, one which overcomes the related dichotomies of human and nonhuman nature and of creation and redemption, I will examine Genesis 1 and 2, mindful of the three broad principles of biblical interpretation in *Dei Verbum*. My purpose is to uncover grounds for an ecological theology of God. My focus on the initial chapters of Genesis is deliberate. As I have already pointed out, environmentalists and ecologists have cited them as a religious license for the exploitation of nonhuman nature by the industrialized West. My concern will be to show that, although this criticism has some validity with respect to the historical record of Western Christian industrial societies, it grossly misrepresents the intended meaning of these texts. In the interest of applying the second principle of biblical criticism, I will then proceed to survey some other biblical texts relevant for an ecological theology of God. Finally, I will focus on some of the theological insights of Thomas Aquinas on creation. I have chosen Aquinas's theology not only because it has played a significant formative role in the development of the Catholic tradition but also because I believe that his theology of creation provides a substantial (though limited) source for a Catholic ecological theology of God.

Creation in Genesis 1–11

Nearly three decades ago, Lynn White Jr. argued that Christianity's doctrine of creation was inimical to the health of the earth.[14] In his judgment, the Genesis stories of creation promote anthropocentricism (human-centered attitudes and values) at the expense of nonhuman nature. He faulted the Bible for its command that humans exercise dominion over every living thing (Gn 1:28) and its directive that the first man name all the animals (Gn 2:19), "thus establishing his dominance over them."[15] These divine charges, he argues, legitimated human exploitation of the earth for human ends. In biblical Christianity, nonhuman creation has no value in and of itself; its sole function is to serve human purposes.

Do Genesis 1:28 and 2:19 legitimate human domination of nonhuman nature, as Lynn White claims? Are these texts hopelessly anthropocentric at the expense of nonhuman creatures? I believe that it is possible to give a negative response to these questions if one examines these texts in their respective historical contexts. White may be overly influenced by what "dominion" implies to the mind of a twentieth-century English speaker, questioning whether "dominion" is the type of control exerted by a ruler over his or her domain.

Before I begin to engage in a critical examination of these texts, I want to stress a fundamental truth about the Bible: from start to finish, it is primarily theocentric.[16] The Bible is not intended to be an anthropocentric book. The Bible, with God as the principal actor in its stories, teaches again and again that it is in God that the origin and ultimate meaning of all creatures are found. It is important to keep this in mind as we examine the creation accounts in Genesis.

I will treat the second account of creation first because it was written much earlier, roughly five centuries before the first chapter of Genesis, and because the argument that it is a directive legitimating humanity's dominance of nonhuman nature is relatively easy to dismiss. Written during the time of David and his successor Solomon (ca. 1010–930 B.C.E.), the ancient story in Genesis 2 is attributed to the Yahwist source. As the tale unfolds, God is the dominant character who forms the first human from the dirt of the earth (v. 7). Clearly, the human person belongs to the earth and is bound to it and all the other creatures that inhabit it. The gift of life-breath that God breathed into the human earthling makes this creature a living being, a person, who must be provided with the means to sustain life. God, therefore, places the first human person in the garden of Eden, a place of plenty, which the human earthling is to cultivate and care for (v. 15). God also creates the animals that the human is directed to name (v. 19). Naming in this context, contrary to Lynn White's assessment, is not an indication of divinely ordained human domination of all the animals. As the biblical scholar Claus Westermann points out, the divine charge for humans to name the animals is not an exercise of human power over the animals, nor is it an indication that animals are to be exploited for human ends. He explains:

> By naming the animals the man opens up, determines and orders his world and incorporates them into his life. The world becomes human only through language.[17]

Put simply, naming is reflective of how human persons establish relationships with other creatures and with God. From an ecological standpoint, the activity of naming is one way in which humans express the bond that they have with nonhuman creatures.

In the first chapter of Genesis we find the story of the "Days of Creation" attributed to the Priestly authors (ca. sixth century B.C.E.). This story has received considerable negative attention from ecologists because of the directive for humans to "subdue" the earth and to have "dominion" over all creatures. These directives are problematic if interpreted literally rather than historically. If one examines the historical context of the formation of this story, one finds it likely that it was composed during the era of the Babylonian exile, a time of crisis for Jews enslaved in a foreign land. In the midst of considerable uncertainty, the authors of the Priestly tradition reasserted their belief in God's power over chaos. They did this by developing their own creation narrative, a narrative that includes among its intentions the praise of God who provides a day of rest for this purpose. The Genesis story's six-day progression has a great deal in common with the structure of the creation story of the Babylonians, *Enuma elish*,[18] which also played a liturgical role in the Babylonian religious community. Both stories have the same general succession of events: chaos at the beginning and then the creation of the firmament, dry land, the heavenly bodies, and finally, people. God's rest, which brings the work of creation to a conclusion, also corresponds to a feast for the Babylonian gods.

What is different about the two stories are their respective elements. In *Enuma elish*, the "stuff" of creation comes from a terrible conflict in which the goddess Tiamat is violently slain in an act of vengeance by a young god named Marduk. It is from her carcass that he makes the world. In contrast, Genesis 1 depicts God creating simply by a word that brings order out of chaos. The Spirit of God, the *rûah* of Yahweh, sweeps over the waters breathing life-giving energy into all of creation.

In Genesis, the sun, the moon, the stars, and the fertility of nature, which the Babylonians worshiped as divine, are believed to be simply creatures. This belief, when compared with the beliefs of their neighbors, was indeed revolutionary. Also revolutionary is the treatment of the creation of the first humans. In the Babylonian creation story, the first human is created from the blood of the most evil of the gods who has been slain by the others. This creature is then commanded to serve the gods.

In Genesis 1:26-27, on the same day on which God created the animals, humankind is made, and this sixth-day's creation is proclaimed by God to be "very good." From an ecological standpoint (obviously not directly intended by the Priestly authors), since humans share the same day of creation with animals, a kinship exists between humankind and the animal species. There is a fundamental connectedness between humans and the rest of creation.

Judaism's understanding of humans is different from the Babylonians on another score—humans, male and female, are created in God's image and likeness. The word "image" is possibly royal in origin; it may echo the language used by ancient Egyptian and Mesopotamian kings, the sovereigns who, in theocratic societies, were regarded as representatives of their gods or as trustees of the gods' possessions.[19] The nobility of being an exiled Jewish person entrusted by God with the privilege of representing God sharply contrasts with and is pointedly critical of the Babylonian enslaver's depiction of humans as created to give service to the cult of Marduk by ministering to the needs of the gods. After declaring humans to be made in the image of God, these words immediately follow:

> God blessed them, saying: "Be fertile and multiply; fill the earth and subdue it. Have dominion over the fish of the sea, the birds of the air, and all the living things that move on the earth" (Gn 1:28).[20]

Light is thrown on the directive for humans to exercise dominion (in Hebrew *radah*) over all animal life if the command is read in the context of *Enuma elish*. The creation of humans is not for the service of demanding gods but rather for the service of living creatures with whom humans share an earthly kinship. Biblical scholar

Richard Clifford's research has led him to conclude that the full meaning of "dominion" cannot be discerned in Genesis 1. It emerges later in Genesis in the story of the Great Flood.[21] In Chapter 6, we find God deeply grieved about the extent of the wickedness of humans, precipitating an ecological disaster of worldwide proportions. Noah and his family alone are found to be righteous in the sight of God and excepted from the great flood that would destroy not only all other humans, but also "the beasts and the creeping things and the birds of the air. . . ." (v. 7). God instructs Noah to build a huge ark, telling him: "Of all kinds of birds, of all kinds of beasts, two of each shall come into the ark to stay alive" (v. 20). God's directive makes the meaning of having dominion clear—it is to see to the survival of the other living creatures. A brief sentence confirms that Noah and his family carried out this commission (v. 22).

After the flood, God indicates that henceforth a reckoning will be required not only from humans but also from every beast (Gn 9:1-4). God establishes a covenant with Noah's family and their descendants and with every living creature—birds, cattle, and wild beasts (vv. 9-11). There is an inherent relational interdependence of humans with the rest of creation in this covenant. The Noachic covenant is a symbol of the unbreakable bond between all creatures and their Creator. The perpetual sign of the covenant is God's "bow in the clouds" (v. 13).

What the story of Noah and the flood illustrates is the recognition by the biblical authors that human offenses potentially imperil the rest of creation. Dominion, enacted by a representative of God in Noachic covenant partnership, clearly rules out an anthropocentricism tolerant of the exploitation of nonhuman nature. As descendants of Noah, with every "bow in the clouds," humans are invited to recall a covenant initiated by God, not only with humankind but also with the earth and all of its inhabitants. Because of the interconnectedness of all of creation articulated in this covenant, I believe that the dominion it implies can be named "ecological."

There is another reference in Genesis 1:28 that is more troublesome than the exercise of dominion—the directive from God for humans to "subdue the earth." The Hebrew word for subdue (kābās) has as a root meaning "to bring into bondage"; this meaning could convey the image of a conqueror ravishing the conquered and, therefore, could be open to a potentially violent and ecologically damaging interpretation. Richard Clifford's examination of "subdue" in other biblical texts, for example, in Numbers 32:21-22, has led him to conclude that subdue means to inhabit the land that God has given as a gift, transforming it into a home where God can be worshiped.[22] In my judgment and in the light of the heartbreaking loss of their homeland and their enslavement in Babylon, "subdue the earth" may simply mean that every exiled Jewish person has the responsibility to reoccupy the "Promised Land." This ancestral home is important because it provided the Jews with a space to freely give Sabbath worship to God as a community of faith. Viewed in the historical context of sixth century B.C.E., subduing the earth cannot be equated with a license to exploit nonhuman creation, as if it was merely an instrument for humans, but rather is a directive to reclaim a divine gift, the original homeland where God could be worshiped. This land is described in Deuteronomy with the imagery of an ecological paradise:

> a good country, a land with streams of water, with springs and fountains welling up in the hills and valleys, a land of wheat and barley, of vines and fig trees and pomegranates, of olive trees and of honey. . . (8: 7-8).

In summary, Genesis 1 confesses a belief in a God whose creation does not originate from cosmic conflict with other deities. Instead this God brings order out of chaos in a nonviolent manner. In this context, the commission given by God to humankind, to those creatures who are made in God's image, is to protect the balance of life that God's ordering word has built into the earth and to promote the continuation of all species having a place in that delicate balance.

Biblical Creation–Redemption Texts

1. The Old Testament

It is not possible to treat all other creation texts in the Bible in this essay; therefore, I will limit my discussion to some selections that challenge the false dichotomy of creation and redemption and have some theological bearing on ecology. My choices will be from the classical prophets, the psalms, and wisdom literature; many of these selections are representative of others that I am unable to address.[23] I will begin with the prophet known as "Second Isaiah" (Chapters 40–50) because this text is thought to have been composed at approximately the same time as Genesis 1. The context of its writing is clearly stated: the unnamed author(s) of Second Isaiah is directed by God to "speak tenderly to Jerusalem [because] her service [as an exile in Babylon] is at an end" (Is 40:1). It is time to return home. In his reflections on the theological significance of the end of the exile and the new exodus to the Promised Land, the prophet makes numerous references that link Yahweh's redemption of Israel and Yahweh's re-creation of the earth. God leads the people through the wilderness to a new occupation of the Promised Land; redemption is God's gift. During this new exodus, valleys are filled in and mountains leveled, not only so that the journey will be easier but also so that the glory of God can be revealed anew (40:4-5); the new creation is God's gift.

Echoing Genesis 1, Second Isaiah encourages a people, destitute and discouraged, to trust in Yahweh:

For thus says the LORD,
The creator of the heavens,
    who is God,
The designer and maker of the earth
    who established it,
Not creating it to be a waste,
    but designing it to be lived in:
I am the LORD, and there is no other (45:18).

The word "waste" (Hebrew word, *tohu*) is an obvious allusion to the beginning of creation when the earth was waste and void (Gn 1:2), and order had not yet been called forth from the primeval chaos by God. For Second Isaiah, creation cannot be limited to God's ordering activity at the beginning. God continues to call order out of chaos through his involvement with all creatures, an involvement that is solicitous for their survival. A few verses later, Second Isaiah, speaking for God, asserts: "Turn to me and be safe, / all you ends of the earth, / for I am God; there is no other" (v. 22). Creation theology enriches the promise of redemptive freedom and makes it all the more hope-filled. Clearly, no dichotomy between creation and redemption exists in Second Isaiah; in fact, the two themes are complementary, in the deepest sense of the word.

The link between creation and redemption is also made by other classical prophets in a negative way. It is the role of the classical prophet to bring to the people a timely message, one which challenges them to attend to the ways in which God is both present and absent in their lives. The "underside" of the connection between creation and redemption is revealed in the way ecological destruction is connected with sin. In the pre-exilic writings of Hosea and Jeremiah,[24] in particular, we see this connection made that resonates with the Genesis story of the Great Flood. Early in Hosea, we find a recollection of the Noachic covenant:

I will make a covenant for them [Israel] on that day,
    with the beasts of the field.
With the birds of the air,
    and with the things that crawl on the ground (2:20).

Later Hosea points out, because of the people's sin, God has a grievance against Israel for violating the covenant, and, therefore, creation suffers:

The land mourns,
> and everything that dwells in it languishes:
The beasts of the field,
> the birds of the air,
> and even the fish of the sea perish (4:3).

This extension of the covenant to the earth is also expressed approximately a century later in the longer prophecy of Jeremiah, in which creation themes abound. For example, he gives what perhaps is the earliest recorded direct "first-person" statement of Yahweh's creation of the universe:

Thus says the Lord of hosts, the God of Israel: It was I who made the earth, and man and beast on the face of the earth, by my great power, with my outstretched arm . . . (27:4-5).

It is perhaps because of his profound sense of God as Creator that Jeremiah stresses that the suffering of the people because they have failed to honor the sacred covenant relationship is not limited to them alone; the land also suffers. He calls for a mournful dirge on behalf of the ravaged land and all that dwell on it:

Over the mountains, break out in cries of lamentation,
> over the pasture lands, intone a dirge:
They are scorched, and no man crosses them,
> unheard is the bleat of the flock;
Birds of the air as well as beasts,
> all have fled, and are gone (Jer 9:9).

The dominant theme of the section in Jeremiah (8:4–10:25) from which these words are drawn is lament over a crisis that Jeremiah maintains the people have brought upon themselves by their own life choices.[25]

These sinful choices also result in the land of Israel falling into the hands of Nebuchadnezzar, king of Babylon (Jer 27:5-6). What God created and what has been reduced to chaos by sin, Jeremiah infers, can be re-created again. He announces a time of a new creation when Nebuchadnezzar's kingdom will collapse (27:7), after Israel's long period of exile (25:11-12; 29:10; 28:1). This new creation, as I have already noted, is the subject of the prophecy of Second Isaiah.

As we turn from prophecy to the Book of Psalms, we find many poems that give praise to Yahweh-Creator. The one that has the most profound and explicit connection to Genesis 1 and allusions to Genesis 2, as well, is Psalm 104, which honors God the Creator, who skillfully transformed rampaging waters and primordial night into a world vibrant with life. A dark and watery chaos is made dry and lit so that creatures may live. In great detail, the psalmist, reacting to the beauty of creation with a profound sense of wonder (24-34), describes God's splendor in the heavens (1-4), how the chaotic waters were tamed to fertilize and feed the world (5-18), and how primordial night was transformed into a gentle time of refreshment (19-23). It is in this context that the creative activity of the *rûaḥ* of Yahweh, the Spirit of God, again appears.

When you hide your face, they are lost.
    When you take away their breath, they perish
    and return to the dust from which they came.
When you send forth your breath, they are created,
    and you renew the face of the earth (vv. 29-30).

These verses appear to presuppose that God always creates in the Spirit, and that the Spirit is poured out on everything that exists, preserving and renewing it. In the Hebrew language *rûaḥ* (spirit/breath) is feminine, so the divine life in creation can be apprehended not only in masculine metaphors but also in feminine ones.

Psalm 104 shows little explicit interest in redemption and salvation history; rather it presents a song of praise for a well-ordered and beautiful world, enlivened by the breath, the energy, of the Spirit. It does, however, end with the hope that sin may not deface God's wonderful work; human-made chaos must not destroy what God has already ordered so well. The theme of the underside of redemption is not ignored: "May sinners vanish from the earth, and the wicked be no more" (35).

In Psalm 146, the first of the five hymns that conclude the Psalter, the unity of the God who creates and redeems is more explicitly expressed.[26] This psalm is a hymn by someone who has learned that there is no other source of salvation (v. 3) than God the Creator—

The maker of heaven and earth,
    the sea and all that is in them ... (v. 6).

It is this same God who

    secures justice for the oppressed,
    gives food to the hungry ...

sets prisoners free . . .

gives sight to the blind . . .

raises up those who are bowed down . . .

protects the stranger, [and]

sustains the orphan and the widow,

but thwarts the way of the wicked (vv. 7-9).

In each activity, God responds to the creatures most in need, offering them the freedom of a redeemed life.

In the wisdom literature, we find the themes of creation and redemption united in wisdom (*Hôkmāh* in Hebrew and *Sophia* in Greek, both feminine nouns). Creation is particularly significant to this body of literature, so much so that Walter Zimmerli has argued that "wisdom theology is creation theology."[27] While this is a bit of an overstatement, his explanation for it lies in his belief that wisdom literature is an outgrowth of Genesis 1:28, especially the divinely ordained dominion relationship of humans to the rest of creation. The pursuit of wisdom represents the human effort to relate to creation as God has intended. The theme of redemption is closely intertwined with creation, because people are forever struggling with the forces of chaos in their lives.

Wisdom texts that directly address creation appear in Job, Sirach, and the Book of Wisdom,[28] but it is in Proverbs that the themes of creation and redemption converge with extraordinary power. In Proverbs 3, the sage boldly declares: "The Lord by wisdom founded the earth" (v. 19). Although the female character of wisdom is not explicit in this text, in other texts wisdom is presented as a female with strong intimations of divinity. For this reason, I will render wisdom as Sophia, the Greek term that makes the female character explicit.[29]

Sophia is often presented as intimately related to the activity of creation; it is she who is the giver of life (Prv 4:23). In chapter eight of Proverbs, Sophia speaks at length in the first person to describe her character and works.

From of old I [Sophia] was poured forth,

at the first, before the earth (v. 23).

Sophia presents herself as the very first of God's works, brought forth before any creation (vv. 22-26). She continues:

When he established the heavens I was there,

when he marked out the vault over the face of the deep;

When he made firm the skies above,

"AND GOD SAW THAT IT WAS GOOD"

when he fixed fast the foundations of the earth;
When he set for the sea its limit . . .
Then was I beside him as his crafts[wo]man,
and I was his delight day by day . . . (vv. 27-30).

Like Psalm 104, the activity of creation is described in picturesque detail. As co-creator with God, Sophia imagery replaces the royal imagery of Genesis 1.[30] Preexistent Sophia, who is beside God as the master craftswoman or designer, is not of the ordinary created order. Instead, she participates in the activity of creation: "When he [Yahweh] fixed fast the foundations of the earth, . . . then was I beside him . . . " (vv. 29-30). In probing Sophia's role in creation, we find that she is the model or exemplar of Yahweh's works. This is what it means for Sophia to be the master craftsperson.[31] She is also the one who executes the creative activity of God—through her creation happens. Further, she continues to take delight in creation.

In Sophia, we also find a connection between creation and its order in a twofold way: she both designs creation and sustains its order by opposing evil for the sake of justice. Earlier in this same chapter of Proverbs, Sophia indicates that she is adamantly on the side of justice and opposed to evil (v. 13). Finally, Sophia bids her followers to obey her instruction. Those who follow them find life, but those who neglect her ways perish (vv. 35-36).

In summary, this survey of Old Testament texts related to Genesis 1 and 2 amply demonstrates that there is no dichotomy between creation and redemption, nor is there a dichotomy between humans and the rest of God's creatures. In Second Isaiah (and in other texts as well), the God who creates is also Redeemer, a God who continues to bring order out of the chaos caused by sin. The creation pattern originating "in the beginning" continues as a "new creation" in the present; it is all the work of a loving God. The Scriptures also present a covenant relationship with God made not only with humans but with all of creation. Long before theories of biological evolution or chemical analysis of elements human bodies share with the rest of creation, the Bible presents humans and earth's other life forms as interconnected and interdependent on religious grounds. Humans are distinct among creatures—they cultivate gardens, name animals, and are said to be created in God's image and likeness—but they are also profoundly related to all creatures. When humans abuse the charge of dominion given to them, taking upon themselves the domination of the rest of creation as their possession, instead of respecting the charge entrusted to them by God, all of creation suffers. There is no biblical basis for justifying this exploitation of the earth and its many forms of plant and animal life. Such behavior breaks God's covenant with creation and is a sin against the Creator. Because of such sin, a mournful dirge is heard throughout the land; all of creation suffers.

Humans need to make a commitment to listen to Sophia, co-creator with God, to heed her instructions, and to make her ways their own. When we follow her ways, we can take delight in creation. Perhaps there are few greater true delights than for humans to take part in the unfolding of God's creation wisely and responsibly. For then, in company with the Spirit, the face of the earth will be renewed.

2. The New Testament

The primary focus of the New Testament is Jesus Christ, whom Christians confess to be the Son of God and Savior of the world. Because of the soteriological nature of so many of its texts, one might argue that Jesus is irrelevant to ecology, or even that Jesus, whose name means "Yahweh saves," contributes to an anti-ecological emphasis on human redemption at the expense of nonhuman creation. Such judgments are not only very simplistic, they are erroneous. They treat the mysteries of creation and redemption in the New Testament as if they were in competition, whereas the New Testament actually presents them as two related aspects of God's one engagement with the world. Put simply, through Jesus' life, death, and resurrection, God's creative activity continues as a work of redemption.

In the New Testament, the belief that God has created and is sustaining the world is not a peripheral theme. What the early Christian community experienced in Jesus is interpreted and understood in terms of creation faith. This is particularly evident in texts that have explicit and profound connections with Genesis 1 and with the Old Testament wisdom tradition, especially Proverbs 8. The Prologue of John's Gospel launches into the story of the good news of Jesus with the very same words as Genesis 1 and proceeds to recall the work of Creator-Sophia and apply them to Jesus, the only Son of God.

> In the beginning was the Word,
> and the Word was with God,
> and the Word was God.
> He was in the beginning with God.
> All things came to be through him,
> and without him nothing came to be.
> What came to be through him was life. . . .
> He was in the world,
> and the world came to be through him. . . .
> And the Word became flesh
> and made his dwelling among us,
> and we saw his glory,
> the glory as of the Father's only Son,
> full of grace and truth (Jn 1:1-14).

In this early Christian hymn, God creates the world through Jesus, who becomes enfleshed in creation. John's identification of Jesus with the Word (Greek *logos*) combines God's dynamic, creative word of Genesis, the personified pre-existent Sophia (craftsperson of creation), and the intelligibility of reality in Greek philosophy. The incarnate Word is a new mode of God's presence: God indwells the world (literally, he pitched his tent among us) and is continuous with it. Through the incarnate Word, God comes into contact with the world in a personal and intimate way, while still remaining distinct from it. This hymn bespeaks a freedom in the relationship of God with the world not found in Greek cosmology and its doctrine of emanation.

A major part of this freedom is embodied by Jesus in his care for creatures. The Gospels are filled with revered memories of Jesus carrying out actions that Psalm 146 attributed to the Creator. In the Lukan introduction to the mission of Jesus, for example, the same things done by Yahweh, "the maker of heaven and earth" (Ps 146:6) are done by Jesus; it is Jesus who brings glad tidings to the poor (the widow and the orphan of Psalm 146), proclaims liberty to prisoners, gives sight to the blind, and secures justice for the oppressed (Lk 4:18). While it is true that these activities are directed to people, the passage ends with a proclamation of a Sabbath Year, a year of favor in which not only were slaves freed and debts canceled, but planting, pruning, and harvesting for storage were forbidden. The earth itself was given sabbath rest in honor of the Creator (Lv 25:2-7 and Dt 15:7-11).

More examples from the Gospels indicating a profound unity of creation and redemption in Jesus' ministry and preaching could be cited. Instead, I will reflect on the closest parallel to the first chapter of John's Gospel: the early christological-creation hymn with which Paul begins Colossians 1:15-20. In this case, Christ (though not mentioned by name) is God's preeminent and supreme agent in creation. The hymn's roots in Genesis 1 and Proverbs 8 are clear.

> He is the image of the invisible God,
> the firstborn of all creation.
> For in him were created all things in heaven and on earth,
> the visible and the invisible,
> whether thrones or dominions or principalities or powers;
> all things were created through him and for him.
> He is before all things,
> and in him all things hold together (1:15-17).

This hymn presents Christ, the perfect image of God, as acting in the role of Creator-Sophia. It is by applying Sophia to interpreting the significance of Jesus that

Jesus Christ is portrayed as the mediator of creation, acting both as God's son and eternal Wisdom.

In this hymn, Jesus is also the mediator of redemption: "to reconcile all things for him, making peace by the blood of his cross" (Col 1:20) The whole cosmos—all things on earth and in heaven—finds reconciliation and peace in Jesus Christ. The saving activity of God in Jesus is the unfolding of God's purpose in creation and the beginning of its transformation in, as the passage continues, "his fleshly body" (v. 22).

Elsewhere, in Romans 5:12-21, Paul gives attention to Genesis 2–3 and the justification of human beings in Christ, the New Adam. Later in Romans, he presents a vision of the future of the earth as intimately bound to the future of humanity. Introducing a theme found in Genesis 6–9, and the texts cited in Hosea and Jeremiah above, Paul describes how "creation awaits with eager expectation the revelation of the children of God; for creation was made subject to futility, not of its own accord but because of the one who subjected it. . . ." (8:19-20). The Greek word translated as "futility" could also be translated as fruitlessness, a fruitlessness due to human sin, a fruitlessness that results in decay (v. 21). He reflects on the effects:

> All creation is groaning in labor pains even until now; and not only that, but we ourselves, who have the firstfruits of the Spirit, we also groan within ourselves as we wait for adoption, the redemption of our bodies (8:22-23).

It is not only creation that groans, but "the Spirit itself intercedes with inexpressible groanings" (8:26). Paul gives Christianity the insight that not only do humans groan inwardly in longing for redemption, but creation as a whole does. In the midst of the groaning of creation, the Spirit that gives life groans in an outpouring of a compassion that extends to all of creation.

Although the New Testament does not provide a developed trinitarian theology (this emerges gradually in the early centuries of the Christian tradition), many of its texts, especially ones that I have cited, offer solid grounds for recognizing an inherent threefoldness in God's relationship to creation. It is one that sustains and redeems not only humans but all creatures. Upon this biblical foundation, a contemporary trinitarian ecological theology can be built. This foundation will be greatly strengthened and enriched, I believe, by some reflection on the creation theology of Thomas Aquinas.

Creation in the Theology of Thomas Aquinas

Mindful that *Dei Verbum's* third principle for interpreting biblical texts calls for attention to how texts have been interpreted over the centuries, in this final section I will examine the rich insights of Thomas Aquinas (ca. 1225-74) to discern what his theology can provide to an ecological theology of God. First, I want to briefly locate his thinking in the context of the history of the Christian tradition. My reason for doing this is to show that the false dichotomies drawn between creation and redemption, and human and nonhuman life, are not due solely to the conflict of theology with modern science and the split between creation and redemption. These supposed dichotomies reflect the presence within Christianity of a latent gnosticism that has long haunted its theology. Christianity has struggled with gnostic dualism since it encountered the Hellenistic world. On the basis of claims to privileged knowledge, gnostics, on the one hand, taught that nature, due to its materiality, was inherently evil. On the other hand, they taught that the human soul was nonmaterial or spiritual and, therefore, good or at least had the capacity for goodness that matter lacked. Because of the hierarchical dualism of spirit over matter, gnostics distinguished between a Supreme Divine Being, who never intended to create a material universe, and a "creator god," envisioned as a demiurge or inferior deity who made the material universe. Since matter was alien to the Supreme God, the spiritual soul needed to be saved from it.

In the second century, there were gnostics within Christianity who drew a line of demarcation between the Creator of the Old Testament and the God of Jesus Christ of the New Testament, who was distinct from the Supreme God only in name, revealing the existence of the invisible world and the identity of its deity. To ensure that Christianity could escape the contamination of this demiurge, Christ was said to only appear to be a fleshy, corporeal being. Irenaeus (ca. 130-200) forcefully argued against positions of the gnostics. He described the faith that the Church received from the apostles in this way:

> Many . . . having salvation written in their hearts by the [Holy] Spirit . . . carefully preserve the ancient tradition of the apostles, believing in One God, the Creator of Heaven and Earth, and in all things therein, by means of Jesus Christ, the Son of God, who because of his surpassing love towards his creation, condescended to be born of a virgin, he himself uniting man through himself to God . . . , the Savior of those who are saved.[32]

In this passage, Irenaeus affirms monotheism and the unity both of the three divine persons and of creation and redemption. Jesus Christ, the Son of God incarnate, is embodied in material creation to redeem humankind. For Irenaeus, who is positive in his assessment of material creation and the human body, the divine plan is for creation as a whole to move toward fulfillment. It is God's plan for all of creation to be redeemed along with humankind.

The unity of God the Creator of the Old Testament and the God of Jesus Christ of the New Testament, addressed by Jesus as "Abba" or Father, was confirmed in the fourth century in the Nicene-Constantinopolitan Creed:

> We believe in one God,
> the Father, the Almighty, maker of heaven and earth,
> of all that is seen and unseen.
>
> We believe in one Lord Jesus Christ, the only Son of God,
> eternally begotten of the Father . . . one in Being with the Father, through him
> all things were made. . . .
>
> We believe in the Holy Spirit, the Lord, the giver of life . . .
> With the Father and the Son he is worshiped and glorified.

The creed begins with a clear statement of belief in monotheism, but professing monotheism was not its primary purpose. Instead, the aim was to elucidate the identity of Jesus and his relationship to God, the Father and Creator. Against Arianism and its assertion that Jesus was a mere creature—although an extraordinary one—the Church confirmed the divinity of Jesus. Rooted in the many creation texts of the Bible, the creed underscores the fact that creation is the work of the divine three in consort and not only the work of the Father. The Son, "consubstantial" with the Father, and by implication the Holy Spirit as well (since the Spirit too is worshiped and glorified), are together involved in creation. By the same token, the divine three are also involved in the saving work revealed in Jesus. By implication, the creed also affirms, against gnosticism, that material creation is inextricably entwined in divine redemption.

Having studied the Bible, the creed, other dogmatic pronouncements on creation by the Church (e.g., the Fourth Lateran Council of 1215), and many Christian theologians who preceded him, Thomas Aquinas developed a theology that flies in the face of the gnostic tendencies of Christianity. Aquinas affirmed the godliness of all of creation, both spiritual and material beings. A major part of Aquinas's legacy to the Roman Catholic tradition is his sacramental view of material creation, which I believe provides a meaningful foundation for an ecological theology. His vision of the godliness of creation is beautifully expressed in the *Summa Theologiae*:

> . . . We should state that the distinctiveness and plurality of things is because the first agent, who is God, intended them. For he brought things into existence so that his goodness might be communicated to creatures, and re-enacted through them. And because one single creature was not enough, he produced many and diverse [creatures], so that what was wanting to one expression of the divine goodness might be supplied by another, for goodness, which in

God is single and uniform, in creatures is multiple and scattered. Hence the whole universe less completely than one [creature] alone shares in and represents the divine goodness.[33]

These words echo Genesis 1's refrain after each day of creation, "It was good," and poignantly draw attention to the sacramental character of every creature. For Aquinas, creation is the overflowing of divine goodness. Each creature, possessing an integrity of its own in its own distinct way, is revelatory of God. In this statement, reverberations of Wisdom 13:5 can also be heard: "For from the greatness and the beauty of created things their original author, by analogy, is seen."

Who is this "original author" for Thomas Aquinas? It is virtually impossible to provide an adequate summary of Aquinas's rich theology of God, so I will highlight only a few major elements. At the core of Aquinas's understanding of God is the insight that God is the Pure Act of Being. His interpretation of Exodus 3:14—"I am who am"—leads him to speak of God as that being whose essence is the sheer act of existence itself.[34] This is what distinguishes God's being from all the beings that God causes to exist. In the treatise on creation, Aquinas identifies God as the efficient, first exemplar and final cause of all things.[35] In causing creation to exist, however, God's agency is unique. As Aquinas points out in the initial questions of the *Summa Theologiae*, God exists in everything.[36] Paradoxically, God, although the efficient cause and therefore distinct from creation, is never really distant from creatures. God is both transcendent over creation and immanently present in each creature. Clearly, no dichotomy exists between God and creatures. This point is also clearly made in the *Summa Contra Gentiles* when Aquinas points out that contemplation of the beauty of creation incites the soul to the love of God's goodness because creatures are good "by a kind of participation" in the divine.[37] In the *Summa Theologiae* Aquinas amplifies this insight in trinitarian terms when he points out that in every single creature "a trace of the Trinity is recognized."[38]

From the standpoint of an ecological theology based on Aquinas's insights, the destruction of our earthly habitat suggests that discernible traces of the Trinity are lost. When species are made extinct, a unique manifestation of the goodness of God is gone forever. From Aquinas, one can also argue that the needless extinction of species due to human behavior jeopardizes the unity of the order of creation which is derived from "the unity of God governing all" and the "unity of the [divine] exemplar after which it [all of creation] is fashioned."[39]

The loss of eco-diversity is distressing not only for these reasons but also for another: the all-good, three-personed God, who brought the earth into existence, also lavishly adorned it with beauty. In his theological reflections on the days of creation, Aquinas calls God's creative process on days four, five, and six "works of adornment."[40] In the rich biodiversity of creation, Aquinas finds tremendous beauty. He professes that birds and fish are called into being by God to embellish creation with beauty.[41] He asserts that land animals exist, not only to move upon the earth, but also to further adorn it.[42] Aquinas's aesthetic sensibility where creation is concerned offers a distinctive standpoint for contemplating the tragedy of reducing pasture land to desert, thoughtlessly destroying the lives of beasts and birds, and needlessly extinguishing plant and animal species. Some of the beauty with which God adorned the earth is forever lost.

For all of the potential for ecological theology that Aquinas offers, his judgment about the order of creation is not without shortcomings. Aquinas ascribes to a hierarchy of beings that is not only of complexity, but also of value. He asserts:

> It is to be said that God's wisdom is the cause of the inequality [of creatures], as it is of distinction. . . . Distinction in form always requires inequality. . . . So among the things in nature an ordered scale is observed; compounds are higher than the elements, and plants than minerals, and animals than plants, and men than other animals, and under each of these headings we find one species more perfect than others. Consequently divine wisdom causes the distinction and inequality of things for the perfection of the universe, which would be lacking were it to display but one level of goodness.[43]

Aquinas's ascending list of inanimate matter—plants, then animals, and finally humans—constitutes a hierarchy in which those beings beneath humans in the chain are regarded to be of lesser perfection and value. Among all of the creatures, the human being is the most spiritual and rational, and therefore for Aquinas the most sublime. The less sublime beings serve the needs of the more perfect. In the development of his hierarchical understanding of creation, Aquinas is influenced by the thinking of Aristotle and other classical thinkers, and, no doubt, also uncritically affected by the rather rigid hierarchy of defined roles in the Church and civil society of his time. The hierarchy to which he ascribes obviously leaves Aquinas's theology open to the critique that it is anthropocentric.

Given Aquinas's emphasis on the inherent goodness and beauty of all of creation, however, I do not believe that his reflection on the hierarchy of beings indicates that Aquinas believed that humans have a God-given right to dominate the "lower" or less complex creatures in an exploitative way. Aquinas can be interpreted this way only if this passage is read in total isolation from other passages in which he affirms the inherent goodness of all creatures as unique manifestations of the Trinity and if his theology is interpreted ahistorically.[44] Living in a preindustrial, agrarian society at a time that antedates the massive exploitation of nonhuman nature, Aquinas's description of the hierarchy of beings reflects a simple fact of life: humans rely on plants and animals for sustenance. In this sense, plants and animals are ordered to human ends. His hierarchy of being, with humans at the top of the chain, is obviously open to abuse. But this fact does not necessarily detract from Aquinas's affirmation of the sacramental character of nonhuman creatures. Plants and animals not only nourish human life but also assist humans in knowing God, inasmuch as a human being can see traces of the Trinity in God's creatures.

Conclusions

The Christian tradition offers a firm foundation for an ecological theology of God. Although the health of the planet has deteriorated to an exponential degree during the era in which the related dichotomies of redemption and creation and human and nonhuman nature were common in Christian theology, these divisions are not constitutive of the Christian tradition. To treat creation as if it were the mere context for human redemption ignores the many biblical texts that underscore the fundamental unity of creation and redemption. Many of these same texts also provide ample reasons for affirming the interconnectedness of humans with the rest of creation. I believe that I have shown that overcoming these unnecessary divisions has ramifications not only for what we believe about the relationship of the doctrines of creation and redemption, but also for how we conceive of our relationship to nonhuman creatures.

Some important steps have been initiated to reverse the ecological crisis, but far more must be done. Our concern must not be limited to what has been widely termed "the environment," as if nonhuman creation was something from which we, as humans, are divorced. Our concern must be truly ecological, which means that we must bring into our consciousness the interconnected relationships that constitute the web of life of which we humans are a part. An ecological theology of God can deepen this consciousness by attending to how our faith in the trinitarian God of Christian revelation bears on our understandings of our relatedness to the whole of creation.

The Bible is unquestionably not anti-ecological. The criticism of the Genesis creation stories, voiced by many environmentalists and ecologists, is based on a simplistic literal reading of them and clearly does not represent the core meaning of these texts. The Bible does not legitimate human exploitation of nonhuman nature, nor is it inherently anthropocentric at the expense of the rest of creation. The Genesis creation texts, read in the context of the time of their formation and in light of other texts on creation in both testaments, present a picture that differs greatly from the domination-exploitation scenario. For humans to live in harmony with all creatures requires us to show the kind of loving care for all of creation revealed to us in the scriptures, especially in the life and teachings of Jesus Christ, the Son of God incarnate in creation.

It is also true, however, that the Bible does not provide an ecological theology, per se. Ecology was not the burning issue that it is today when the biblical texts were being formed. But it is also equally true that the Bible does not present a developed theology of creation, redemption, or, for that matter, the Trinity. Rather, the Bible provides disparate theological perspectives from which theologians have drawn guidance and insights in response to questions and issues as they have arisen. The Bible presents narratives and symbols that give rise to thought and guidance for living, but it does not present theology in a developed, systematic sense.

To further explore the Christian tradition for an ecological theology of God, I have examined some of Aquinas's insights on creation in the context of the Christian tradition. I believe that, in spite of some shortcomings, Aquinas does provide elements that can be applied or adapted in an ecological theology meaningful to our era. In his theology of creation, Aquinas affirms the God-given autonomy and integrity of every species and the fundamental beatitude of the eco-diversity of the planet itself. God's creation is sacramental: every creature is capable of embodying and manifesting something of the divine. According to Aquinas, because of God's goodness, there is an intrinsic value in all that exists. Moreover, from an ecological standpoint, when a living species is needlessly made extinct, a manifestation of the goodness of God and a revelation of the Trinity is lost.

From Aquinas we also receive encouragement to develop an aesthetic relationship to creation. In appreciating creatures, whether the first cry of a newborn infant or the sight of a drop of dew on a delicately woven spider web, we are awed by beauty and are drawn closer to God. Taking aesthetic delight in creation is basic to a contemplative relationship with the Trinity, a relationship which also leads a person to empathize with the pain of other creatures and to grieve their extinction.

Perhaps if we kept these many insights in mind, we would not only refrain from exploiting our fellow inhabitants of the earth, but we would also reverence them earth itself while recognizing that we inhabit a world in which not a single thing exists without God. Neither mountain nor river, neither tree nor flower, neither beast nor bird, neither woman nor man came into existence without the Spirit who gives life, without Jesus Christ who was enfleshed with that life, and without Yahweh God, whom Jesus lovingly addressed as "Abba," ordering that life. All things exist because they have been created by the triune God and are sustained by God's creative and redemptive energy. Each creature manifests something of this mystery, and all of creation exalts in its holy splendor.

Notes

1. In common parlance today, ecological and environmental movements are often spoken of interchangeably. This trend reflects the general fluidity of language and of the evolution that the term "ecology" has undergone in the past twenty-five to thirty years. In the late nineteenth century, the term "ecology" was coined by Ernst Haeckel (1834–1919) to specify the branch of biology that deals with the interactions of living organisms with their environment. Today, the term ecology has a broader usage in reference to the quality of the environment and the biological health of the complex eco-systems of the biosphere. The current meaning emerged in practices different from those of scientific research and theorizing. Today, the term "ecology" is applied not only to nature but also to social and cultural attitudes. What is common in these understandings of ecology is their emphasis on the interconnectedness of the various elements that comprise the world as a whole.

2. Pope John Paul II, "And God Saw That It Was Good" (Message for the World Day of Peace, January 1, 1990) in *The Pope Speaks*, 35 (1990), 200–206. The pope also addressed the ecological crisis in his encyclical *Sollicitudo Rei Socialis* ("On Social Concern"), *Origins* 17 (1988): 641–660. See also the United States bishops' "Renewing the Earth," *Origins* 21 (1991), 426–432, and the *Catechism of the Catholic Church* (Washington, D.C.: United States Catholic Conference, 1994), nos. 2415–2416.

3. Ibid., 201; the emphasis on "all things" is his.

4. Ibid., 206.

5. For an analysis of church documents of this era on the interpretation of Genesis 1–3, see my "Creation," in *Systematic Theology, Roman Catholic Perspectives*, Vol. 1, ed. Francis Schussler Fiorenza and John P. Galvin (Minneapolis: Fortress, 1991), 223–224.

6. Arnold Toynbee, for example, has argued that biblical Christianity contributed to a demystification of nature that rendered it non-sacred and passive; controlling and manipulating it became a human duty. He writes: "Man was licensed [by the Bible] to exploit an environment that was no longer sacrosanct. The salutary respect and awe with which man had originally regarded his environment was thus dispelled by Judaic monotheism in the versions of its Israelite originators and of Christians and Muslims. See Arnold Toynbee, *The Toynbee-Ikeda Dialogue* (Tokyo: Kodansha International, 1976), 39.

7. The Second Vatican Council in *Gaudium et Spes* ("The Pastoral Constitution on the Church in the Modern World") expressed an openness to science, including biological evolution (no. 5); it also stated that science and the faith do not conflict because "both secular things and the realities of faith derive from the same God" (no. 36).

8. *Divino Afflante Spiritu* ("The Most Opportune Way to Promote Biblical Studies"), (September 30, 1943), in *Biblical Interpretation, Official Catholic Teaching*, ed. James J. Megivern (Wilmington, N.C.: A Consortium Book, McGrath Publishing Co., 1978), 327.

9. Later von Rad qualified his views but not before his position had influenced many scholars. Gerhard von Rad, "The Theological Problem of the Old Testament Doctrine of Creation," in *The Problem of the Hexateuch and Other Essays* (New York: McGraw-Hill, 1966), 131–143.

10. For more development of this point, see Terence E. Fretheim, *Exodus: Interpretation, A Bible Commentary for Teaching and Preaching* (Louisville, Ky.: John Knox Press, 1991), 12–14, *passim*.

11. *Dei Verbum, Dogmatic Constitution on Divine Revelation* (1965) in *Vatican Council II, The Conciliar and Post Conciliar Documents*, New Revised Edition, ed. Austin Flannery, OP (Grand Rapids, Mich.: William B. Eerdmans Publishing Co., 1992), 762.

12. In this first principle, *Dei Verbum* is arguing against simplistic literal interpretations of biblical texts and calling for scholarly effort at grasping their meaning. The discovery of the intention of biblical authors cannot be equated with the arrival at certainty about what the authors of particular texts meant. The primary duty of the authors of the Scriptures was to convey God's word in a manner that was intelligible to the people for whom they were writing, in an era far removed from our own. In addition, the authorship of biblical texts is often complex; a text may have not only a substantial writer, but also one or more editors separated by time, outlook and experience.

13. The articulation of these broad principles has opened the door to enormous growth and considerable pluralism in methods for interpreting Sacred Scripture since the Council. See especially ed. Raymond E. Brown, SS, Joseph A. Fitzmyer, SJ, and Roland E. Murphy, OCarm, *The New Jerome Biblical Commentary* (Englewood Cliffs, N.J.: Prentice Hall, 1990), 1083-1174.

14. Lynn White, Jr., "The Historical Roots of our Ecologic Crisis," first published in *Science* 155 (1967), 1203-07; reprinted in *Readings in Ecology and Feminist Theology*, ed. Mary Heather MacKinnon and Moni McIntyre (Kansas City: Sheed and Ward, 1995), 25-35. Interestingly enough, he called for a renewed Franciscan spirituality because Francis "tried to substitute the idea of the equality of all creatures, including man, for the idea of man's limitless rule of creatures" (35).

15. Ibid., 30.

16. The major exception is some of the wisdom literature, e.g., the Proverbs that concern human virtue and righteous living.

17. Claus Westermann, *Genesis 1-11, A Commentary*, trans. John J. Scullion, SJ (Minneapolis: Augsburg Publishing House, 1974), 228-229.

18. *Enuma elish* ["From on High"], in Alexander Heidel, *The Babylonian Genesis Story of Creation* (Chicago: University of Chicago Press, 1951), 18-60.

19. Westermann points out that the Egyptian pharaoh, as the representative of god on earth, is called "his very image." The description of the king as "the very image of god" is attested also in Mesopotamia, *Genesis 1-11*, 153.

20. All biblical citations are from *The New American Bible, The Catholic Study Bible*, ed. Donald Senior (New York: Oxford University Press, 1990).

21. Richard J. Clifford, SJ, "Genesis 1-3: Permission to Exploit Nature?" *Bible Today* (1988): 135. Clifford's interpretation of the creation text, in light of the context of the first eleven chapters of Genesis, reflects a belief, widely shared by Old Testament scholars, that these chapters should not be interpreted in isolation from one another. It is also helpful to keep in mind that the ancient Hebrews did not have dictionary definitions for their words because they did not use dictionaries. They discerned the meaning of words from the patterns of speech in which they were used.

22. Ibid., 136.

23. To complement this section, I recommend Richard J. Clifford, SJ, "The Bible and the Environment," in *Preserving the Creation, Environmental Theology and Ethics*, ed. Kevin W. Irwin and Edmund D. Pellegrino (Washington, D.C.: Georgetown University Press, 1994), 1-26.

24. For my treatment of Hosea and Jeremiah, I am indebted to Carroll Stuhlmueller's essay written jointly with Dianne Bergant, "Creation According to the Old Testament," in *Evolution and Creation,* ed. Ernan McMullin (Notre Dame, Ind.: University of Notre Dame Press, 1985), 165-66.

25. The occasion of this lament is probably Nebuchadnezzar's first campaign against Judah in 597 B.C.E. See Guy P. Couturier, CSC, "Jeremiah," in *The New Jerome Biblical Commentary*, 276.

26. For another psalm that treats the themes of creation and redemption, see Psalm 19.

27. W. Zimmerli, "The Place and the Limit of the Wisdom in the Framework of Old Testament Theology," in *Studies in Ancient Israelite Wisdom*, ed. J. L. Crenshaw (New York: KTAV, 1976), 316.

28. See Job 38–41; Sir 24; Wis 7:17-22, 8:6; and 13:6.

29. For an excellent treatment of "Lady Wisdom" and of wisdom literature as a whole, see Roland E. Murphy, *The Tree of Life* (New York: Doubleday, The Anchor Bible Reference Library, 1990).

30. For a thorough survey of the question of female personification of Wisdom in the book of Proverbs, see Claudia V. Camp, *Wisdom and the Feminine in the Book of Proverbs* (Decatur, Ga.: Almond Press, 1985). For a beautifully written reflection on Sophia as Creator Spirit, I recommend Elizabeth A. Johnson, *Women, Earth, and Creator Spirit* (Mahwah, N.J.: Paulist Press, 1993).

31. The Hebrew term is *'mwn*. Its meaning has been a subject of debate. It has sometimes been rendered as crafts [wo]man, as darling, or even as nursling. See Roland E. Murphy, *The Tree of Life, An Exploration of Biblical Wisdom Literature*, 136. Murphy indicates that in his opinion, *'mwn* of Prv 8:30 is an "artisan or crafts [wo]man, or maker of all. . . ." Thus she is identified with God, 143.

32. Irenaeus, *Against Heresies* ("A Refutation and Subversion of Knowledge Falsely So Called"), Book III, Ch. 4, no. 2, ed. Rev. Alexander Roberts and James Donaldson, *Anti Nicene Christian Library*, Vol. V (Edinburgh: T & T. Clark, 1880), 264-65.

33. *Summa Theologiae* Ia, q. 47, a. 1, trans. Thomas Gilby, OP, Vol. VIII (New York: Blackfriars in conjunction with McGraw Hill Book Co., 1967), 95. All subsequent citations will be taken from this multi-volume edition.

34. ST, Ia, q. 2, a. 3 (Vol. II), 13; q. 3, a. 3 and a. 4 (Vol. II), 29-35.

35. ST, Ia, q. 44, a's. 1-4 (Vol. VIII), 5-24.

36. ST, Ia, q. 8, a. 1 (Vol. II), 111-113.

37. *Summa Contra Gentiles* (*The Truth of the Catholic Faith*), Book Two: Creation, trans. James F. Anderson (Garden City, N.Y.: Doubleday and Co., 1956), Ch. 2, no. 4, 31-32.

38. ST, Ia, q. 45, a. 7 (Vol. VIII), 59. Aquinas chooses his words carefully. Creatures present only traces of the Trinity because they cannot represent their Creator adequately. Through creatures, the Trinity is both manifest and hidden from us.

39. ST, Ia, q. 47, a. 3 (Vol. VIII), 103.

40. ST, Ia, qs. 70-72 (Vol. X), 106-137. The works of adornment are distinguished from works of other days that address [initial] creation and distinction.

41. ST, Ia, q. 71 (Vol. X), 129.

42. ST, Ia, q. 72 (Vol. X), 133.

43. ST, Ia, q. 47, a. 2 (Vol. VIII), 99. In reading this passage, it is helpful to bear in mind the question to which it is a response: "Is the inequality of things from God?" Or, to put it differently, is the hierarchy of being from God or is it the result of sin? His reply is an argument against Origen (ca. 185-254) who claimed that God created all things equal at the beginning of time; inequality entered the world and with it corporeality due to the sin of the first rational creatures. Aquinas argues against this on the grounds that if this were true, then the corporeal universe would be the result of evil and not the imparting of God's goodness to creatures.

44. In regard to my assessment of Aquinas on the hierarchy, I find myself in disagreement with H. Paul Santmire's sweeping negative appraisal of Thomas Aquinas's theology as anti-ecological. See H. Paul Santmire, *The Travail of Nature: The Ambiguous Ecological Promise of Christian Theology* (Philadelphia: Fortress Press, 1985), 91-92.

ECOLOGY
AND
ESCHATOLOGY

John F. Haught

*Then I heard every creature in heaven and on earth
and under the earth and in the sea, everything in the universe, cry out:*

*"To the one who sits on the throne and to the Lamb
be blessing and honor, glory and might, forever and ever."*

*The four living creatures answered, "Amen," and the elders fell down and worshiped.
(Rev 5:13-14)*

ALL OVER THE EARTH AND ESPECIALLY IN THE MOST IMPOVERISHED LANDS, sources of fresh water are diminishing, forests are being destroyed, soil is eroding, deserts are spreading; the land, air, and water are being poisoned, and species are disappearing at an alarming rate. Patterns of excessive consumption and the pressure of increasing human numbers are making these problems even worse in many areas. But the news is not all bad: for example, there has been some reforestation of areas in the eastern United States previously ravaged by bad agricultural practices; some municipal recycling programs are succeeding; industrial polluters are beginning to acknowledge that good business practice is not opposed to sound environmental policy; the quality of water and air in various places is improving; and ecological sensitivity is emerging in many lands.

Still, the picture is far from satisfactory. Pollution, global warming, the thinning of the stratospheric ozone layer, and numerous other ills pose unprecedented dangers to human, plant, and animal life. Holmes Rolston III, one of America's best-known environmental ethicists, writes:

> As a result of human failings, nature is more at peril than at any time in the last two-and-a-half billion years. The sun will rise tomorrow because it rose yesterday and the day before, but nature may no longer be there. Unless in the next millennium, indeed in the next century, we can regulate and control the escalating human devastation of our planet, we may face the end of nature as it has hitherto been known. Several billion years worth of creative toil, several million species of teeming life, have now been handed over to the care of this late-coming species in which mind has flowered and morals have emerged. Science has revealed to us this glorious natural history; and religion invites us to be stewards of it. That could be a glorious future story. But the sole moral and allegedly wise species has so far been able to do little more than use this science to convert whatever we can into resources for our own self-interested and escalating consumption, and we have done even that with great inequity between persons.[1]

A sincere appraisal of the ecological data available today could easily cause us to lose heart. But doesn't realism require an honest pessimism as we ponder the planet's future? Runaway ecological decline has gained such momentum in some regions that many people have already surrendered to the prospect of final catastrophe. For solace they have retreated into their private pleasures, or, if they are religiously inclined, they have taken consolation in their belief that this world was never meant to last anyway. Having set their sights on a better home "beyond" the earth, they remain quite untroubled by ecological problems. Meanwhile, faithful Christians sensitive to the fact that something is radically wrong with their relationship to the natural world cannot always recite convincing theological reasons for taking ecological responsibility seriously.

At least to some extent, this is the fault of those of us who are theologians, since until recently we have attended only superficially to nature. In the early modern period, we virtually handed the natural world over to science, reserving for theology the task of pondering matters such as human freedom, social justice, or "salvation history." So, to a great extent, theology has lost touch with the universe. Today, however, the theology of nature is making a comeback of sorts, and we earth-bound theologians have begun to weigh, perhaps more deliberately than ever before, precisely why the life-systems of the planet are worth saving.

The basis for an ecological theology, we have found, is certainly not lacking in the scriptural and traditional sources. We have discovered anew the relevance to our contemporary crisis of the biblical creation theology, of the theme of God's incarnation in the world, of the Catholic sacramental vision, and of the necessity of practicing the virtues of humility, detachment, compassion, justice, and gratitude. In our theological sources, we can now discern a wealth of ecologically relevant material that had previously escaped our notice.

But have we looked at our sources deeply enough? Without minimizing the ecological significance of the items just mentioned, I shall propose that in our attempts to construct an ecological theology, we need to probe more deliberately than ever into one of our faith tradition's central though often overlooked characteristics, namely, its vision of the universe and the earth as the embodiment of a divine *promise*. Even though Christian faith includes at its very foundation the sense that the world is continually being shaped by promise, theology has yet to draw out explicitly the ecological significance of the so-called "eschatological" vision of reality.

A major reason for this oversight is that eschatological concern, a preoccupation with *future* fulfillment, seems at first sight to be ecologically dangerous. For if we cast our attention toward the future, whether we think of it in a this-worldly or an other-worldly way, will we not thereby discount today's tribulations, averting our eyes from the depressing devastation in nature as presently experienced? Some sensitive religious ecologists are actually embarrassed by the Bible's concern for the future. They see no way of integrating "eschatology" into their ecological vision and ethics.[2] We must ask, though, whether it is appropriate for ecological theology to ignore what many theologians consider the most distinctive feature of our faith.

The term "eschatology" comes from the Greek "*eschaton*," a word that literally means "last." Traditionally, "eschatology" denoted the kind of theological speculation and religious doctrine that deals with the "last things," which meant, at least in Catholic theology, death, heaven, hell, and purgatory. In a wider and more original sense, however, eschatology has to do simply with "what we may hope for." In the Bible, especially in the prophetic traditions, there is an overwhelming sense that the world and its history are defined by God's promise, and so we are encouraged to hope for the fulfillment of this promise.[3] Biblically speaking, then, "eschatology" arouses a hopeful trust in the God who makes promises, who is faithful to these promises, whose "reign" will bring about a "new creation," and who comes to meet us out of an always surprising and ultimately fulfilling future. In the resurrection of Christ, Christian faith discerns the future fulfillment of the whole universe made manifest in advance.[4] Eschatology, then, clearly lies at the heart of our faith. I would ask, then, whether we can ever have a distinctively Christian ecological theology if we leave out this central theme of hope for future fulfillment.

The evangelist Luke pictures Mary as the very model of genuine eschatological faith because she "believed that what was spoken to [her] by the Lord would be fulfilled" (Lk 1:45). Authentic faith, if we follow the spirit of the Bible, is openness to a divine promise that points us in the direction of a fulfillment yet to come. It is an eager anticipation of the arrival of "the reign of God" and of the "new creation." It is the conviction that God's initial creation (*creatio originalis*) continues even now (*creatio continua*) and will be brought to fulfillment in the future (*creatio nova*). Eschatology is the extension into the future of our fundamental faith in the God who is still creating "the heavens and the earth."

However, even though the belief that all of creation is oriented toward future fulfillment in God is fundamental to Christian faith, theology has yet to clarify just how this eschatological thrust can also be the basis of an ecologically responsible theology. Happily, the recent Catholic bishops' pastoral *Renewing the Earth* (1992) refers to "hope" as the fundamental ecological virtue. This felicitous observation implies that eschatology, the biblical anticipation of a future fulfillment of God's promises, is central rather than tangential to the shaping of an ecological theology. The following reflections, then, are an attempt to draw out some implications of the bishops' message.

I.

Ecological theology begins with the question of whether there is an *essential* connection between Christian faith and ecological concern. It asks if there is an inner momentum in the Christian vision of the world that might *intrinsically*, and not just as a historical accident or afterthought, lead us to take special care of the nonhuman natural world.

Some environmentalists doubt that there is. The Australian philosopher John Passmore, for example, states that Christianity is irreformably anti-ecological. Belief in God and the "next world," he argues, removes any serious obligation to safeguard "this world." The best framework for environmental concern is pure naturalism, a philosophy that denies the existence of God and views "this world" as all there is. Only after we have acknowledged that we are all alone in a world devoid of "supernatural" protection will we ourselves begin in earnest to take responsibility for the earth's well-being. Thinking of the earth as our only and final home, Passmore argues, will motivate us to take much better care of it than does Christian optimism.[5]

Occasionally, ecologists issue even more passionate outbursts against religion and especially Christianity. "Religion must die," says one. "It is the fundamental cause of virtually all social, economic, and ecological problems. . . ." Another told Gerald Barney, a Christian environmentalist, "You have done some very important work, but just think of how much more you would have done if your parents had not exposed you to the pernicious influence of Christianity!"[6]

Such statements, however excessive they may be, indicate that Christian tradition has given at least some environmental ethicists the appearance of being ecologically problematic. How then can we expect our theology to convince both unbelievers and believers of Christianity's *essential* support for ecological responsibility? Are there sufficient resources in the tradition for an ecologically responsive theology? My argument will be that we need not look merely toward those biblical texts and traditions that *explicitly* proclaim the goodness and glories of nature, although it is important to seek these out as well. Rather, we may find the core ingredients of an ecologically responsible theology at the very centerpiece of our faith tradition, namely, in the conviction that all of reality exists within the embrace of God's revelatory promise.

There are, of course, other prominent features in scripture and tradition that must enter into the shaping of an ecological theology. For example, there is the creation theology of the Hebrew Scriptures. Not only Genesis but numerous psalms, the Wisdom literature, the cosmic christology of John and Paul, and other segments of the Bible and tradition proclaim creation as a gift deserving of our reverence, wonder, and gratitude. And, of course, there is the biblical ordinance to humans to exercise the role of responsible "stewardship" with respect to nature.

Additionally, the traditional religious (and not just Christian) exhortations to practice the virtues of love, humility, moderation, detachment, justice, and gratitude are perennially relevant. Since human arrogance, greed, injustice, and hunger for power have led us to ruin the blessings of creation, only the practice of true virtue can keep us from further pillaging nature. Thus, to the extent that Christianity shares in the wider religious world's calling to live the virtuous life, it answers the accusations that it is ecologically irrelevant. Environmental abuse is not the fault of Christianity or religion, as Passmore and other secular thinkers would insist, but the consequence of our shared human failure to heed the religious vocation to live the life of virtue.

Another essential ingredient of ecological theology—especially typical of both Eastern Christian and Roman Catholic spirituality—is an emphasis on the "sacramental" character of nature. In a sacramental outlook, nature's beauty and diversity tell us something about what God is like. Nature itself, in other words, is symbolic or revelatory of God. As Michael and Kenneth Himes have written: "The essence of a sacrament is the capacity to reveal grace, the agapic self-gift of God, by being what it is. By being thoroughly itself, a sacrament bodies forth the absolute self-donative love of God that undergirds it and the entirety of creation." Thus, "every creature, human and nonhuman, animate and inanimate, can be a sacrament."[7]

By acknowledging nature's inherent transparency to the divine, sacramentalism keeps us from turning our world into nothing more than raw material for human projects. It gives nature a "sacral" quality, meaning that nature somehow participates in a finite way in the very being and holiness of God. Its sacramental quality, therefore, should shield nature from diminishment at the hands of our exploitative and destructive tendencies. "By its nature," the Himes brothers argue, "a sacrament requires that it be appreciated for what it is and not as a tool to an end. . . ."[8] To them, the sacramental vision of Catholic faith "provides the deepest foundation for reverencing creation."[9]

In summary, creation theology, the injunction to faithful stewardship, the call by Christian spirituality to follow the virtues, and the incarnational-sacramental timbre of Catholic faith all provide substantial resources for an ecological theology. For many ecological theologians these are sufficient to demonstrate the intrinsic connection between faith and ecological ethics. However, in my judgment, while these are all essential to the larger project of formulating a Christian ecological theology, we may unearth an even deeper foundation for ecological sensibility in the future-oriented, promise-filled, hope-inspired quality of biblical faith. A biblically based ecological theology will understand nature's inherent worth to be grounded not only in its sacramental disclosure of God, but also, and no less fundamentally, in its character as a *promise* of the future perfection of creation.

II.

As scholars have rediscovered in this century, "eschatology" means not simply a hope for survival in the "next world," but the conviction that the whole universe is somehow shaped by God's gracious promise. Eschatological faith affirms that the same promise that brought Israel and the Church into being has always encompassed the totality of creation and still enfolds the whole cosmos, as apocalyptic literature in late Judaism and early Christianity already implied. Eschatology, in its deepest and widest meaning, adds up to the very good news that a splendid fulfillment awaits the *entire universe*. The divine promise first announced to Abraham is extended not only to the "people of God" but also, if we listen to St. Paul in Romans 8:22, to the "whole creation." Any ecological theology failing to root itself in this cosmic eschatological vision, that is, in faith's sense that God's promise covers the whole temporal and spatial sweep of creation, is incomplete and only tangentially biblical.

This means that cosmic creation itself is essentially inseparable from promise. Indeed, in a very literal sense it *is* promise. And so, if through faith we can interpret the totality of nature as a great promise, we may learn to treasure it not simply for its sacramental transparency to God, but also because it carries in its present perishable glory the seeds of a final, eschatological flowering. Allowing the embryonic future to perish now at the hands of our own carelessness and selfishness would be not only a violation of nature's sacramental bearing, but also a turning away from the promise that lies embedded in all of creation. Seen in terms of a properly biblical framework, then, our ecological carelessness is fundamentally an expression of despair.

To bring eschatology and ecology together, as I am doing here, may at first sight seem to be an awkward if not unseemly proposal. As I have mentioned above, many ecologists fear that religious concern for a future fulfillment will allow us to tolerate ecological indifference in the present. Hope for a future new creation, their argument goes, causes us to dream so extravagantly of the age to come that we lose interest in this one. If the eyes of faith are trained on the eschatological future—especially if the final future is an otherworldly one—we may be too willing to let this present world slip toward catastrophe. In short, isn't eschatology really quite incompatible with ecology?

We cannot ignore this question. After all, some permutations of biblical expectation, if taken in isolation, are ecologically dangerous. For example, apocalyptic visions, when interpreted too literally and independently of other biblical forms of anticipation, look with enthusiasm toward this world's tumultuous dissolution: "The heavens will pass away with a mighty roar and the elements will be dissolved by fire . . ." (2 Pt 3:10). Moreover, earth-despising brands of supernaturalist optimism seek an acosmic "spiritual" world as our final destiny, thus shrouding our present earthly abode in insignificance. Certain versions of eschatological fervor, in other words, appear to be an ecological menace.

Still, we cannot divorce eschatology from Christian faith. For, as theologian Jürgen Moltmann emphasizes:

> From first to last, and not merely in the epilogue, Christianity is eschatology, is hope, forward looking and forward moving, and therefore also revolutionizing and transforming the present. The eschatological is not one element *of* Christianity, but it is the medium of Christian faith as such, the key in which everything in it is set, the glow that suffuses everything here in the dawn of an expected new day. . . . Hence eschatology cannot really be only a part of Christian doctrine. Rather, the eschatological outlook is characteristic of all Christian proclamation, of every Christian existence and of the whole Church. There is therefore only one real problem in Christian theology . . . : the problem of the future.[10]

A major task of ecological theology, therefore, is to show that our looking toward the future "coming of God" is not an obstacle to ecological responsibility but a condition thereof. Our eucharistic liturgy invites us to say: "We hope to enjoy forever the vision of your glory," but exactly how is this prayer compatible with caring for the present natural world? And when we say with the early Christian Church, "Maranatha; come Lord Jesus," how can this most characteristically Christian petition become for us an incentive to love rather than ignore the natural world? If it is accurate to say that all of Christian theology must be erected on the foundation of hope in the "coming of God" and on God's promise of "new creation," can an ecological theology find nourishment in such a setting?

I believe that it can. For in spite of the fact that the advent of God takes the form of a dramatic reversal of "this present age" (as apocalyptic literature powerfully imagines), the essence of biblical hope is that we may look toward a future *for* the world, not a future completely apart from it. Essentially, eschatology is the hope for the new creation of *this* world, not the expectation of a total substitute for the one we live in now. A complete discontinuity between "this present age" and "the age to come" would hardly be consistent with the good news of the coming of God's reign. It would amount to a denial of the inherent goodness of creation and of God's incarnation in our present world. Just as we can assume some continuity between our personal identities now and our glorified existence in the "age to come," we may also be permitted to assume that the coming of God's reign transforms or transfigures but does not abandon or obliterate the natural world.

The biblical distinction between "this present age" and the "age to come" is not nearly so ecologically problematic as it might at first seem. A problem arises only when we forget the temporal-historical bearing of these expressions and imaginatively translate them respectively into "the natural world" on the one hand and the "supernatural world" on the other. This latter dichotomy could easily suppress the biblical sense that all reality, including the present age and all that pertains to it, is *already* defined by promise. In transfigured status, then, the present cosmos will continue to remain deeply implicated in the world's eventual eschatological fulfillment. Without a hope that nature has such a future, our present ecological commitments might indeed have entirely too flimsy a footing.[11]

Eschatology, I must now make clear, is the basis of ecological concern not only in the sense of encouraging us, as the Bible always does, to hope against hope or to inspire us to make the world ready for the coming of God. Rather, an even deeper reason why eschatological faith can be said to arouse ecological concern is that it invites us to see everything in our experience, including the natural world, as *essentially promise*. The very fact that something is a promise means that it is not just a gift, but that it is a gift that carries the future within itself—brought to us ahead of time, so to speak. Bearing the glow of the future, therefore, nature always has a uniquely precious significance, one that a purely sacramental perspective may not explicitly profess.[12]

Although we may already have thought of nature as a gift, have we thought sufficiently about nature as a promise? I would suggest that our ecological theology must go beyond the bare announcement that nature is a gift. For if we view nature only as a gift and not as promise, it is still too easy for us to think of it as something we may consume or use up. Such a "religious" reading provides too paltry a protection against the complete exhausting of nature's resourcefulness. On the other hand, the intuition that God's gift of nature is at heart the gift of a promise will provide us with deeper and more lasting reasons to preserve our precious resources than would the sacramental vision all by itself. For unless we protect and nourish the natural world, we may lose touch with the future it bears within itself.

In the Bible, there is a close connection between nature and promise. One of the most obvious examples, of course, is in the story of Noah where the miraculous beauty of the rainbow becomes a token of God's eternal fidelity. Likewise, the Abraham stories suggest the experience of precarious green growth in the desert, along with the nomadic anticipation of fresh patches of fertility, may well have provided the original basis of biblical faith in the future. The first sparks of what would eventually flame out into the passionate, prophetic hope for the coming of God could have occurred in our remote biblical ancestors' encounter with the fragile thriving of life at the frontiers of their own wanderings. In addition, the prophetic pictures of the future *shalom* were often framed in pastoral imagery. So, too, for us today the well-being of nature remains an essential condition for arousing our own hope in the future. It is the future already latent in the glories of nature that invites our best efforts at conservation and sustainability.

If we fail to conserve and protect those natural processes in which we experience the faithful emergence of new life, we will eventually lose our native taste for the *final* renewal of all things. To keep hope for new creation alive, we need to secure the integrity of nature here and now. Hope will surely die if our ecosystems disintegrate. Today, as a matter of fact, the hopelessness that many people experience, especially in impoverished and environmentally devastated areas, is a symptom not only of economic injustice, but also of the deeply felt human estrangement from a natural world that often seems itself to be near death. For hope to survive, nature must thrive. Hints of a final renewal of life would be unavailable to us if we divested the natural world here and now of the gift of its vitality. Ecology and eschatology, therefore, form a much tighter fit than either agnostic naturalists or Christian theologians have usually detected.

Thinking about the goodness of nature from the sacramentalist perspective, Thomas Berry is fond of saying that losing the richness of life around us will impoverish our sense of the God whose being is symbolically revealed to us through the extravagant diversity and beauty of nature. Likewise, Jürgen Moltmann's pneumatology has shown how much our sense of the Spirit of Life (the Holy Spirit) depends upon our feeling the power, complexity, and integrity of the biotic levels supporting our own existence here and now.[13] We might also argue, from the *eschatological* perspective, that if we lose touch now with nature's beauty, we also risk losing our sense of the "power of the future," the renewing energy that faith perceives most explicitly in the resurrection of Christ.[14]

III.

There are two additional implications for ecological theology and ethics in interpreting nature as promise. In the first place, an eschatological interpretation of nature helps restrain the strong human temptation to worship or divinize either particular aspects of the natural world or the "cosmic whole." There is a pantheistic yearning in some recent ecological perspectives that may easily attach itself to the sacramental perspective, unless the latter is eschatologically qualified. In the second place, putting nature into an eschatological perspective allows us to realistically accept its limitations, its ambiguity, and finally its perishability, without letting these lead us to despair. Let us examine each of these points in turn.

1) An eschatologically framed ecological vision resists the absolutizing of nature to which an exaggerated sacramentalism may be prone. While some ecologists now understandably highlight the ecological importance of neolithic and native peoples' sacramental approach to nature, an unrestrained resacralization of the world could lead us back to the suffocating bondage to natural objects and occurrences from which the biblical prophets tried valiantly, and often unsuccessfully, to liberate religion. Prophetic faith is distinctive for its awareness that the human spirit cannot find fulfillment in any given state of nature. Resourceful as the natural world is, biblical faith looks beneath it and beyond it for the ultimate wellspring of nature's munificence. It finds the source of this bounty in the transcendent power of a creative, renewing Spirit distinct from nature itself. At the same time, it opens up to us the horizon of a future that draws us out of complete servility to the rhythms and cycles of the seasons.

However, precisely because of this apparent loosening of our ties with cyclical nature, some ecologists think of the Bible as fundamentally hostile to the ecological need to revere nature. They even propose that ecological ethics now demands a return to the prehistoric "paganism" found in the neolithic worship of the "goddess" or in many native peoples' deep reverence for the earth. It was our being exiled into the terrors of history, they argue, that caused us to lose touch with the cosmos, and it is the sense of ourselves as historical rather than natural beings that now renders us oblivious to the needs of nature.

While initially such an accusation may seem persuasive, it overlooks two important points. In the first place, the prophetic-eschatological vision did not abandon nature to insignificance but took it up into the momentous story of the divine promise of a final perfecting, not the abandonment, of creation. This assimilation into a promissory history, instead of cheapening nature, gives it unprecedented significance. Some feasts of Israel, and later of Christianity, inserted what had previously been pure celebrations of nature's beneficence into the broader scheme of

God's promise of new creation. That the earlier celebrations gradually became overlaid with the motif of promise, one could argue, turns out to be ecologically salutary rather than ruinous.

In the second place, even science now agrees that nature and history are inseparable. As Carl Friedrich von Weizsäcker pointed out some years ago, and as an increasing number of scientists now agree, the most significant discovery of modern science is that nature itself is inherently historical, indeed that the cosmos has always had a historical character.[15] To say that nature is historical means that even physical reality seeks to transcend or "go beyond" itself. Not only humanity, but nature too is a self-transcending reality. Evolutionary biology, geology, physics, and now even astronomy have shown that the cosmos is a restless adventure. The irreversibility of the cosmic process stands out decisively in the laws of thermodynamics and in the "big bang" cosmology to which most scientists subscribe today. Science itself dictates that we simply cannot return to the vision of an ahistorical, eternally unchanging cosmos that appealed to earlier generations of philosophers and scientists and which still has a romantic fascination for some ecologists.

In what sense, though, is this historical reading of nature pertinent to our attempts to construct an ecological theology? In answer to this question, it could be argued that because of science's recent discovery of nature's fundamentally historical character, we may, with more confidence than ever, locate *the whole cosmos*, and not just human affairs, within the horizon of the promise that molds the experience of Israel, Jesus, and the Church's life of faith. Envisaging all of nature as participative in this story of divine promise does not require that we ignore the ecologically important notion of nature's sacramentality, which must always be overlaid with eschatology.

Viewing nature both historically and as promise still allows us to attribute to it the special kind of intrinsic value that the sacramental perspective requires. A promise, after all, is something to be treasured and valued. When we receive a promise, we instinctively cherish it as a token of the promiser's fidelity. We do not just throw it away in haste to get to the fulfillment it pledges. Perhaps, then, if we learn once again to experience nature as a great promise, this attitude could give a more specifically biblical slant to our Christian ecological morality. Nature understood as promise would have intrinsic but by no means ultimate value. In gratitude, we might treasure and care for nature in such a way that we would not forget what it betokens; however, we would not have to view it in a naturalistic or pantheistic manner, as though it were our ultimate environment. At the same time, we would realize that if we "trash" nature, we would also lose touch with our Ultimate Environment, the God who comes to meet us out of the future.

Biblical faith, in other words, invites us to relate to nature as we would to any momentous promise. We do not have to embrace it as an end in itself, but we do have to value and nurture it nonetheless. In the absence of such an eschatological perspective, it is too easy to make nature the full and final context of our lives. However, if we see it as essentially promise, we can accept nature realistically as it is, worthy of our veneration but never our prostration. An eschatological faith liberates nature from the burden of having to function as the final fulfillment of our deepest human longings.

2) Viewing nature as promise rather than perfection is especially intolerant of those destructive ecological practices that expect the earth to be limitless in its resourcefulness. Viewing our rich planet as promise rather than paradise allows us, at least in principle, to come to terms with its limitations. Modernity unfortunately has not yet accepted the earth's obvious finitude, and this idolatrous attitude underlies our ecological crisis. An eschatological grounding of ecological theology, on the other hand, allows us to accept the earth's limitations. For in light of our conviction that full perfection lies only in the eschatological future, we do not expect in nature's unfolding to bestow upon us the limitless being toward which hope orients us.

Moreover, our vision of nature as promise allows us to face up not only to nature's inherent limitations, but also to the troubling ambiguity and suffering we find there. Eschatology and hope are broad-minded enough to acknowledge the ugliness and unresolved cruelty in the present world without requiring that we accept these as final. A sense of nature as promise can also reconcile us to the fragility and perishability of natural beauties. For we do not expect perfection from a promise, but only from its fulfillment. And so, living with a sense that nature is promise rather than perfection allows us to tolerate its transiency and its defects, including instances where nature seems indifferent to us.

IV.

My point thus far has been that nature, when seen from a biblical perspective, has the character not just of sacrament but also of promise. More strictly speaking, I would say that a genuinely Christian sacramental outlook must always be colored by eschatology. The cosmos in its present state is neither essentially a testing ground for the hereafter nor a final sacramental epiphany of God's presence. Rather, it is at heart a foretaste of future perfection, "the kingdom which will have no end" that constitutes the good news of our faith. My argument is that if we want our ecological theology to connect deeply with biblical religion, and not just with incidental or tangential aspects of it, then we need to make the notion of nature's promise central to such a theology. An eschatologically transformed ecological vision would still see the natural world around us as sacramental, but nature's sacramentality would be transfigured by the sense of a God whose being is essentially future. God, according to Karl Rahner, is the "Absolute Future,"[16] and according to Moltmann (following Ernst Bloch), "the One whose very essence is Future."[17] No particular present, then, can exhaustively represent the divine infinity. Thus, the natural world deserves neither neglect nor worship but simply the kind of care we would tender toward any significant promise.

However, such a view might still be taken too narrowly and anthropocentrically. For that reason, we must reflect further on what it means to say that the whole cosmic story—and not just human history—is defined by God's promise. The entire universe is heir to God's pledge of fidelity, but if the totality of nature and its long history are God's creation, and not our own, we can assume that it has levels of meaning and value that we humans may never fully grasp. Prior to our own appearance in evolution, for example, the cosmos had already brought forth countless surprising evolutionary developments, most of them having little or nothing to do with our own existence. We need not assume that during that prehuman evolutionary span of fifteen billion years the only meaning the diverse creatures on earth and the stars in the heavens had was to foreshadow the coming of human persons. Nor can we plumb the possible depths of significance the cosmos may have for God as it moves into the future, perhaps even without us. The world may well have a future that, like its past, is not narrowly definable in terms of its being a home for our own species.

Therefore, as the still unfinished creation of the cosmos continues at a time when humans are the dominant species on earth, we have the responsibility not only of ensuring our own species' survival but also of leaving ample room for more incalculable outcomes. Even if these outcomes have little relevance to our own lives and interests at the present moment, a robust creation faith demands that we rejoice in the prospect that other natural beings have a meaning and value to their Creator that may be quite hidden from our human powers of discernment. This universe, it bears constant repeating, is God's creation and not our own. It has taken billions of years for nature to attain the ecological richness that existed prior to our appearance. So, when in our own time we allow pollution, resource exhaustion, and the annual extinction of thousands of species to fray the delicate tissue of life, we are surely aborting the hidden potential for a larger and wider-than-human future creativity that still lurks in the folds of the earth's complex ecosystems.

Since nature's beauty, vitality, and creativity are an irreplaceable intimation of the new creation promised not only to us but, as the citation from Revelation at the beginning of this paper testifies, to the whole universe, we must protect them with all of our moral energy. If we truly hope for the *complete* unfolding of God's vision for the universe, we will take immense delight, here and now, in saving the natural world for the sake of its future in God, even when we see no advantages for ourselves. Those who are sensitive to the element of promise in nature will mourn the poisoning of land, air, streams, and oceans, and the destruction of ecosystems everywhere, not only for the suffering this causes us humans, but also because such negligence amounts to a frustration of God's own creative envisagement of the future of this vast universe. It is not only the human present but also the cosmic future that is diminished by our ecological devastation.

V.

Eschatology, however, refers not only to our collective human destiny and that of the universe, but also to the prospect of our personal survival beyond death. What is the relationship between this aspect of eschatology and an ecological theology?[18] Traditional theology's treatment of personal destiny in terms of the soul's immortality seems, to many at least, to raise serious questions about the possibility of honestly reconciling Christian faith with ecological responsibility. The idea that we have immortal souls destined for a heaven beyond this world seems to imply that the material universe out of which our bodies are composed is itself worthless, at least in the final analysis. The influence of Greek philosophy on Christian thought can easily lead us to think of ourselves as essentially immortal souls exiled in material bodies; this dualistic vision, though perhaps consoling to individual humans, hardly seems good news for the rest of creation. Why should we invest our moral energy in saving a material world if it seems finally superfluous anyway? Is there any reason for "saving the earth" other than to have a training area for working out our personal salvation?

The doctrine of bodily resurrection, as distinct from the idea of "immortality of the soul," implies that the whole physical universe shares in our destiny. It is extremely difficult to imagine how we could completely disassociate any *bodily* form of being from the rest of the physical universe, even eschatologically. But our theology has yet to draw out the ecological implications of the doctrine of bodily resurrection.

To exist in a bodily way means, at the very least, to be bound up with a wider universe in a network of innumerable relationships that all contribute something to our embodied existence. Ecology, biology, physics, and astronomy now convince us that all entities in the cosmos are made up of complex, dynamic interconnections. Indeed, the way things tie together with one another in space and time—and this is as true of humans as of other beings—is what gives them their identity. Reality, as both science and philosophy have recently concluded, is fundamentally relational.[19] For instance, if you take away an atomic particle's surrounding energy field, it vanishes. A living cell removed from its setting in a complex organism composed of other cells is no longer a living cell. Likewise, if you were suddenly torn out of your natural and social environment, your identity would dramatically change. Ecologically speaking, each human person is a deeply relational center dynamically tied into an environment that includes numerous other complex living and nonliving

"AND GOD SAW THAT IT WAS GOOD"

systems. Any changes to that environment inevitably reconfigure the identity of the personal centers interconnected with it.

But what happens to each personal center at death? All efforts to answer such a question are quite speculative, of course, but if we understand human personality ecologically, that is, in terms of its complex relatedness to the wider world, then our dying need not mean a decisive break with the cosmos. Rather, it may be the occasion for entering into an even deeper relationship with it. While this idea may seem novel to many Christians, it is entirely consistent with our hope for bodily resurrection. Theologian Karl Rahner conjectures that in "personal" death, we would not break our bonds with the universe, but instead enter more deeply into relationship with it.

Death, of course, is a *natural* occurrence, and therefore one to which we must passively submit. Yet, from the personal center built up from all the relationships we have had with others and the natural world during our lifetime, we can freely transform our dying into a radically *personal* movement toward deeper participation in the universe.[20] Belief in God's incarnation and the resurrection of the body embolden us to think of death in terms such as these. Since in Christ's incarnation God has already taken on the flesh and materiality of the world, a deeper relationship to the cosmos in death would not be a distancing from, but a movement toward deeper intimacy with, the divine.

Death so conceived could still be a decisive moment of liberation. Apparently, it was the promise of such definitive freedom that made the Greek idea of the soul's immortality so attractive a conceptual scheme in early Christian efforts to unfold the implications of Jesus' redeeming career. But there may now be other ways of understanding our personal participation in the liberation promised by our life in Christ. Understood in a manner consistent with ecological sensitivity and recent science, as well as with the apocalyptic innovation that God's redemption is cosmic in scope, our individual death need not mean a total separation of the self from nature. Hoping for a complete severance of our identities from the natural world that constitutes and nourishes us would be neither good news for us nor for the universe to which we believe God has unreservedly communicated the divine Selfhood. Resurrection, if it is truly *bodily,* could mean a person's being set free from a very limited relationship to nature to take on an even deeper intimacy with it, a relationship that Rahner calls "pancosmic."[21]

A theology of death sensitive to ecology would interpret dying in Christ as a transition from our present relatively shallow associations with the world to an ever deepening solidarity with the entire universe and its future in God. Perhaps one way of understanding the doctrine of the "communion of saints" would be to see it in terms of the deeper presence that those who have already died have left to us through the mediation of the world that gave birth to them and to us.

My point, then, is that ecology is now inviting theology to think of death, and of what may await us beyond death, in a way that allows nature to have some share in our destiny. Or should we not put this another way? Perhaps God's primary concern is that of creating and saving an entire complex *universe*? If so, we should rejoice that we are privileged to be a small part of a much grander and indefinitely wider-than-human story of God's creating and continually renewing the immense cosmos to which we are privileged to belong.

How then can we prepare for our death in a way that helps us to love rather than escape the earth? Saints and philosophers have often advised us that the appropriate way to live our lives is to prepare for death. But does our preparation for death have to mean the detaching of ourselves from nature, as it often has in the past? Cannot preparing for death mean instead the intensifying of our capacity to relate to the world? Such a preparation would not be devoid of its own kind of asceticism. After all, it is not only liberating and enlivening, but quite painful to expand the circle of our relationships. Perhaps the pain of death consists, at least in part, of our undergoing the transition from a relatively narrow range of relationships "in the present age" to the wider web of relations that would pertain to a perfected creation. Such a prospect would fit an ecological spirituality that consists not so much of separating ourselves from the earth as of deepening our sense of being forever a part of it and its future in God.

For Christians, of course, the main paradigm of such widening of relationships is Jesus. The gospel portraits of Jesus picture him as one who constantly sought out deeper connections. He was especially concerned with relating to those who seemed relationless: the sinners, the religiously despised, the sick—and the dead. A central motif of his life was that of embracing those who no longer belonged in accordance with what he took to be God's will. Jesus' life then is the model of our own ecological concern. From a Christian point of view, our ecological sensitivity and action can be seen as a manifestation of the radically inclusive Spirit of Christ extending over the long stream of life—not just over the human species—and calling all creation into the kingdom that will have no end. The Spirit of Life, the Holy Spirit, groans not only in our hearts, but in the depths of the still emerging and unfinished universe as it seeks to be brought into final unity with God in Christ. An ecological theology, as it is conceived in the Christian context, extends Jesus' inclusive compassion for the unincluded toward all of nature, no matter how unintelligible, alien, or forbidding it may seem to our narrow sensibilities.

It is no longer as difficult as it used to be to picture the entire universe as sharing in the "redemption of the children of God." The total cosmic process, as we now understand it with the help of science, is in some very real way interior to our very existence. The rest of the physical world is not just accidental to our being but constitutive of it. Recent astrophysics has even shown that the structuring of matter during the earliest moments of the universe's existence fifteen billion years ago was already so specifically defined as to promise the eventual emergence of living and thinking beings at least somewhere in this vast cosmos.[22] We now realize, much more clearly than did the Greek philosophers who gave our theology its earliest categories, how intimately our mental and spiritual existence meshes with the larger story of the physical universe. The latest scientific thinking no longer pictures our unimaginably immense cosmos as indifferent to life and mind but as actively cooperating in their production. Hence, our own existence is neither cosmic exile nor evolutionary accident. The thrust of much recent science, especially physics and astrophysics, is that we truly belong to the universe.[23] Theologically this would mean that the revelatory promise that gives us our hope extends backward to cosmic beginnings, outward to the most remote galaxies, and forward to the future of creation. And if all of nature shares in the promise, then this should be more than enough reason for our taking care of it here and now as we wait "with joyful hope" for its fulfillment in God's new creation.

Notes

1. Holmes Rolston III, "Science, Religion, and the Future" (unpublished manuscript).

2. For example, Daniel Cowdin writes: "The substantive vision of the end-time, insofar as it is the norm on which we base our actions, undercuts environmental ethics." "Toward an Environmental Ethic," in *Preserving the Creation*, ed. Kevin W. Irwin and Edmund D. Pellegrino (Washington, D.C.: Georgetown University Press, 1994), 143. A similar distrust of the messianic aspects of eschatology can be found in the writings of Thomas Berry, *The Dream of the Earth* (San Francisco: Sierra Club Books, 1988).

3. This is a major theme in the writings of Jürgen Moltmann. See his *The Experiment Hope*, ed., trans. M. Douglas Meeks (Philadelphia: Fortress Press, 1975). It is also a constant motif in the writings of Teilhard de Chardin, Wolfhart Pannenberg, Karl Rahner and their many followers.

4. See Wolfhart Pannenberg, *Jesus, God and Man*, translated by Lewis L. Wilkins and Duane A. Priebe (Philadelphia, Westminster Press, 1968). A readable adaptation of Pannenberg's perspective may be found in Ted Peters, *God, The World's Future* (Minneapolis: Fortress Press, 1993).

5. John Passmore, *Man's Responsibility for Nature* (New York: Scribner, 1974), 184.

6. Cited by Gerald O. Barney, *Global 2000 Revisited* (Arlington, Va.: The Millennium Institute, 1993), xiv-xv.

7. Michael J. Himes and Kenneth R. Himes, "The Sacrament of Creation," *Commonweal*, CXVII (Jan. 12, 1990), 45.

8. Ibid., 46

9. Ibid.

10. Jürgen Moltmann, *Theology of Hope*, trans. James Leitch (New York: Harper & Row, 1967),16.

11. Even the Book of Revelation is ecologically significant in extending the sphere of God's action beyond the history of Israel and to the cosmos as a whole.

12. In fact, sacramentality is a feature that Christianity and biblical religion share with many other religious traditions, especially those of native peoples. Sacramentality, in other words, can exist apart from eschatology. Hence it is all the more important, if we are looking for the distinctive contributions of Christian and Catholic faith to ecological theology, that we highlight the eschatological coloring the Bible gives to our sacramental vision.

13. Jürgen Moltmann, *The Spirit of Life* (Minneapolis: Fortress Press, 1992.)

14. Wolfhart Pannenberg interprets Christ's resurrection as the revelation in history of the "power of the future." Pannenberg's eschatological vision, his theology of revelation, and his interpretation of resurrection can provide the basis for an ecological theology that discovers not only in history,but also in the history of nature, the presence of God's future. See his *Toward a Theology of Nature* (Louisville, Ky.: Westminster/John Knox Press, 1993), 50-122. Moltmann also writes:"[Hope] sees in the resurrection of Christ not the eternity of heaven, but the future of the very earth on which his cross stands." *Theology of Hope*, 21.

15. Carl Friedrich von Weizsäcker, *The History of Nature* (Chicago: University of Chicago Press, 1949). See also Pannenberg, *Toward a Theology of Nature*, 86-98. For further investigation of the ecological implications of our new historical view of nature, see my book *The Promise of Nature* (Mahwah, N.J.: Paulist Press, 1993), 39-65.

16. Karl Rahner, *Theological Investigations*, Vol. VI, trans. Karl H. and Boniface Kruger (Baltimore: Helicon Press, 1969), 59-68.

17. *Theology of Hope*, 16.

18. I have developed a fuller response to this question in *The Promise of Nature*, 113-142.

19. One of the most consistent and thorough treatments of the relationality of things both cosmic and personal is the ecological vision of Alfred North Whitehead, especially *Process and Reality*, corrected edition (New York: The Free Press, 1978).

20. See Karl Rahner, *On the Theology of Death* (New York: Herder and Herder, 1961), especially 18-19.

21. Ibid., 21.

22. For details see my book *Science and Religion: From Conflict to Conversation* (New York: Paulist Press, 1995).

23. See Fritjof Capra and David Stendl-Rast, *Belonging to the Universe* (San Francisco: Harper San Francisco, 1991.)

THE VOICE
OF THE
HURRICANE

COSMOLOGY AND A CATHOLIC
THEOLOGY OF NATURE

David Toolan, SJ

How can we conceive to be at once astonished at the world and yet at home in it?
How can this queer cosmic town . . . give us at once the fascination of a strange town
and the comfort and honour of being our own town?

G. K. Chesterton, *Orthodoxy*

THE QUESTIONS I HAVE BEEN ASKED TO ADDRESS IN THIS CHAPTER ARE
two: (1) What does an earlier Catholic theology of nature—that of Augustine of
Hippo, Francis of Assisi, and Thomas Aquinas—have to contribute to the cosmology
that is currently being developed by physicists who inherit the mantle of Isaac Newton? Or, are theology and physics utterly disparate? (2) What is the relevance and
unique contribution of a sacramental theology to the development of a theology of
nature suitable to address current ecological concerns?

These two questions involve the whole troubled relationship between the
Church and modernity, and in particular our mixed record regarding modern science. The conversation got off to a bad start. Yes, Copernicus was a devout Polish
priest; in our own day, the original theorist of the big bang, Georges Lemaitre, was a
Belgian priest. (As a Jesuit, I also proudly note that some thirty-four craters of the

moon are named after early astronomers of my company.) But all such boasts turn to dust before the image of Galileo Galilei kneeling before the Roman Inquisition in the great hall of the Dominican priory of Santa Maria Sopre Minerva on June 22, 1633, recanting what he'd inferred from his telescope. After more than four hundred years and papal acts of apology, the wound of that event has yet to heal.

The first of these questions, which has to do with the relationship between science and theology, is the simplest and can be disposed of rather easily. Whether early or recent, a Catholic theology of nature, I would say, is largely irrelevant to the "theory of everything" that contemporary physicists and cosmologists are searching for. Theology and physics can be connected, but distinctions between the two must be drawn. The question can also be reversed, asking what contemporary physics has to offer Catholic theology. My answer will be—a lot.

The second question, which deals with the special role of a sacramental consciousness regarding ecology, will require a more elaborate response. A sacramental consciousness declares the earth holy; it prepares the way for an ecological ethic. But in order to define our current situation and our problem, we will have to examine the Western attitude toward nature over different historical periods. What I hope to show in what follows is (1) that the premodern sacramental consciousness of medieval times, while not being ecologically aware (that would be an anachronism), was basically friendly to nature; (2) that our current ecological problems began with the dualistic, adversarial relationship with nature spawned by the seventeenth century's scientific revolution; and (3) that the physics underlying contemporary cosmology intimates something of a "paradigm shift" that supports a cooperative or synergistic relationship to nature. Again, this new attitude toward nature is by no means identical with a premodern, sacramental attitude—too much science and technology has intervened for that to be the case. But the new understanding of nature and of our relationship to nature, I will argue, is basically congruent with a sacramental interpretation of nature. Conversely, a sacramental consciousness that holds that "the heavens and the earth declare the glory of God" can be of great service in promoting a more responsible attitude toward the environment.

Ironically, from an ecological perspective, the Church's resistance to a mechanical worldview and the great nineteenth-century myth of progress (and the assumption that modernity has nothing to learn from its prescientific ancestors) can be seen in a positive light. Part of Catholicism's function in the modern world, I would say, is to preserve the link, notably through its liturgy, with a premodern, essentially oral/audial sense of the world—where people feel a great kinship with nature precisely because they perceive it as animated by the Great Spirit and the spirits of the dead. Should we lose sight of this bridging function, we shall have lost not only our empathy for the traditional societies of the developing world (as well as the oral street culture of our own inner cities), but also our capacity to keep holy the earth—and therewith any ability to contribute to an ecological ethic. In short, so far as an ecological ethic is concerned, the premodern roots of Catholic sacramentalism constitute an advantage.

But will this bring us to a theology of nature suitable to address current ecological concerns? Not quite, I think. What we have to incorporate in any adequate theology today is the legitimate claims of the Western Enlightenment—its assertion of human autonomy and our ability to shape ourselves by the kind of society we build, and accordingly, the uses to which we put science and technology. Of course, human beings are not quite so autonomous as the Enlightenment once dreamed; genetic and cultural inheritance set limits and will not be denied. Even so, that emancipatory dream must be taken into account—and what may still be missing from Catholic sacramental theology is an adequate conception of the role of human agency within nature—and on nature's behalf—that takes the measure of the technological power (for good and ill) that we have accumulated since the rise of modern science. And to put this new power in proper, Christian perspective, we will want to complement our understanding of the sacramentality of nature with an understanding of sacrament as verb, that is, as transformative activity.

In what follows, I shall proceed dialectically, back and forth between the insights of modern science and those of religion. What does Catholic sacramental theology and a sacramental sense of the universe have to do with the new cosmology? That is the overarching question of this paper. At the outset, then, a few clarifications are in order.

I. Catholic Sacrament in Two Senses

The term "sacrament" derives from the Roman soldier's formal promise to serve the emperor. When Christians adopted this term for their own rites of initiation and blessing, it came to mean the mediating human act of giving a sign (e.g., pouring water, rubbing ashes on a forehead, lighting the paschal candle, burning incense, or signing the cross) that confers God's promise and grace. In this sense, sacrament is a verb—a divine-human act.

The term "catholic," from the Greek *katholokos,* is not to be confused with the word "universal," which carries a slightly different connotation (that of a circle about a point, which excludes whatever lies beyond its circumference).[1] Thus universality may seem like a noble aspiration, but it can also imply a pretentiously invidious attitude toward outsiders (a form of imperialism usually). The word catholic means "throughout-the-whole" (combining *kata,* which denotes through or throughout, and *holos,* which means "whole"). Over the centuries of the Church's missionary activity, this word has come to have a largely geographic meaning, though when attached to the word sacrament it implies considerably more—a flow-through of another sort.

Catholicism, if it does its job, keeps us close to bodily experience. Traditionally, it has aimed to be a sensuous faith, and behind its use of earth, air, fire, and water in its rites lies a rich sense of the sacramentality of the universe as a whole. That is, nature in whole or part (*physis/natura* in the original sense of "giving birth") is deemed semiotic, a system of signs (as in the "Book of Nature") signifying the Creator/Life-Giver. At root, this is an experiential matter: God's energy, glory, favor, and promise are perceived to flow throughout the whole of creation much the same way as the sun's radiance pours down upon earth. It is this rampant, life-giving grace, the immanence of the Holy Spirit in nature and culture, to which the Church testifies. As Alfred North Whitehead once put it, in deciding for the direct immanence of the Spirit in the material world, the great fourth-century theologians of Alexandria and Antioch "have the distinction of being the only thinkers who in a fundamental metaphysical doctrine improved upon Plato."[2]

There are thus two kinds of sacramentality here. The first is that of nature's graceful signs, its spendthrift, life-giving abundance, acknowledged with gratitude and contemplated in relative tranquility at moments of Sabbath "rest." The earth and the heavens abound in promise, but inevitably the signs are perceived "through a glass darkly" and remain ambiguous. Oxygen by itself is poisonous; the sun's radiation, but for photosynthesis, is lethal; and life-giving water can turn to devastating flood. Darwinian natural selection highlights the harsh struggle for survival—nature red in tooth and claw. Nature brings death. Nature's signal, then, is not simply of the Abrahamic God of blessing and promise, but always and equally of Shiva, the Hindu Creator/Destroyer.

The second sense of sacrament involves human agency, the making of promising signs—whether they be in the building of a temple, a ritual action, or the building of a civilization. A sacramental consciousness in this second sense does not look backward to what is settled, as science generally does. It focuses on the present and future and asks what we are making of the world of matter and energy and what, energized by God's grace, we shall make of it. I will say more about both kinds of sacrament, but especially the latter—in connection with technology—in the final section of this chapter.

II. Two Different Senses of Cosmology

What is the link between theology and science? What is the difference? As human activities, both are culturally formative; both are shaped and transmitted by myth and transmute into the mythic meanings by which we live. Yet when we speak of ancient and modern cosmology in the same breath, we are mixing questions and answers of a very different sort. Thus, before we can consider the contribution of traditional Catholic thinking about nature and modern cosmology, we must make some distinctions.

At the outset it must be said that "cosmology" is an equivocal term that supposes very different meanings depending on historical context. If we think of the cosmology of premodern times, we have to consider more than a particular way of "saving the appearances" of the heavens—say the Hebrews' disc of earth encompassed by cosmic waters above and below or Ptolemy's heliocentric conception. We must also advert to the fact that these putatively empirical conceptions formed only one element in a larger, religiously based conception of the Creator, creation, and divine providence. For the ancient Hebrew sages and the medievals, the abstract idea of the "merely physical" had not shaken loose. When the Greek philosopher Thales spoke of everything being "water," he was thinking holistically of life-giving rain, rivers, seas, and mystically of the water of life, just as when Jesus of Nazareth uses the single term *pneuma* he meant breath, wind, and spirit altogether (Jn 3:8). Similarly, the word *kosmos* referred to an order that spans the contemporary boundaries of science, philosophy, and religion. As philosopher of science Stephen Toulmin has pointed out, the Greek term for the physical universe is *ouranos*. Strictly speaking, then, contemporary astrophysicists might be considered "ouranologists" rather than "cosmologists" in the broader, ancient definition of the term.[3]

In the ancient or medieval world, then, cosmology was a cultural horizon in the fullest sense. It represented a way of getting at our ultimate meaning and destiny; it located the human drama within the big story—from the Christian perspective, the story of redemption—of the universe as a whole. With the "fall" of human nature, according to this perspective, all of nature falls as well, and conversely, when human beings wake up or are restored to their true meaning, the very stones cry out and the mountains clap their hands.

By contrast, in modern times cosmology refers to a subfield in physics regarding comprehensive theories about the origin, evolution, and present physical structure of the astronomical universe (i.e., the big bang and the formation of galaxies).[4] Accordingly, one can very well maintain, as Alfred North Whitehead did, that Christian belief in the fundamental intelligibility and rationality of God's creation undergirds and furthers the whole scientific enterprise, astrophysics included, and this is a very important connection indeed.[5] For "faith" in the orderliness of things is the unprovable supposition of all science, the *sine qua non* fuel, as it were, upon which it runs.

But to push this supportive and affirming relationship further and say that Catholic theology has anything specific to contribute to the material content, say, of high energy particle physics, would be foolish. Theology and physics deal with different realms of human experience, using distinct methods appropriate to each.

Stephen W. Hawking, for instance, the occupant of Isaac Newton's old chair as the Lucasian Professor of Mathematics at Cambridge University, defines a good scientific theory as "just a model of the universe, or a restricted part of it, and a set of rules that relate quantities in the model to observations that we make. . . . It must make definite predictions about the results of future observations."[6] In other words, it must be empirically falsifiable. Hawking will be disturbed if it turns out, as the latest empirical indications from Hubble Space Telescope imply, that the universe is much younger than the 15 billion years he and most others have thought because it will play havoc with both his numbers and predictions. Augustine would not have cared.

Falsifiability is one of the big differences between scientific cosmology and the visionary cosmology—really an eschatology—elaborated by St. Augustine in *The City of God*. The latter is designed specifically to withstand countervailing empirical evidence (e.g., the fall of Rome or the Visigoths' hostile visit to North Africa in the early sixth century). Obviously St. Augustine's reflections on time in *The Confessions* or *The City of God*—or the opening chapters of the Book of Genesis—had something else in mind than Stephen Hawking does. The biblical author/editors and the fathers of the church surely included the science of their day but incorporated it into a larger narrative frame, one that would spell out the meaning and purpose of human existence. In addition to supporting the whole enterprise of science, therefore, theology's (sometimes annoying) usefulness to scientists would consist in addressing the question of the purposes of science and technology. Ascertaining that matter is energy—and, according to the formula $E=mc^2$, lots of it—does not tell you what to do with that information. Science does not decide whether you should use it to build a bomb and blow up Hiroshima.

In sum, premodern philosophers, theologians, and their descendants are not asking *what* atoms are about or *how* they function (as science does) but *why* we are here, to what purpose, and if there is any hope for us and the world we dwell in. (Confusingly enough, the concern for purpose would also hold true for Democritus, the ancient atomist.) Theologians, like classical philosophers, reflect on the grounds for a "myth to live by" in Joseph Campbell's sense of the term. This is something modern science, which explicitly excludes final causes (or purpose) from its purview, won't give you.

But if theology doesn't have much to offer the precise content of physics, does physics have anything to offer theology? The inferences scientists draw from the fossil record, DNA research, or the images transmitted by the Hubble Space Telescope do sometimes console and at other times upset the pious faithful. But for most professional theologians the case is otherwise. At least, since the time that Immanuel Kant sharply divided the sphere of inward experience from the "phenomenal" realm that science investigates, the general rule has been that scientific theories, say about atoms and genes, have very little to do with the moral or religious sphere. (I will question the sharpness of this divide as we proceed.) Science and theology are like apples and oranges, not to be confused.

The classic statement here is Augustine's: though he granted that the biblical writers obviously used as backdrop "the form and shape of the heavens" of their time, such things, he argued, are indifferent to their main preoccupation; they "did not wish to teach men things of no relevance to their salvation."[7]

To be concerned with salvation means that you are looking for breaks in a pattern, possibilities of an opening, a change of heart and direction that will make the present different from the past. For theologians, then, time—qualitative time—is of the essence and always urgent. And of course they seek hints and guesses that the world of our experience (which now includes atomic structure and our "selfish genes") supports such qualitative movement. In contrast, physicists—at least physicists in the classic Newtonian mold—are looking for quantifiable symmetries in nature, the signature of which is an invariant, repetitive pattern even amid transformations, something that could be formulated into a law (i.e., a linear equation) for all times and places.[8] To be more exact, their chosen data usually consist of "integral systems," stable, closed systems (found, for the most part, only in a laboratory) whose every instant, like that of an automaton or pendulum, is the integral repetition of the preceding instant. Ideally, then, the time variable is irrelevant (e.g., the film can run backward or forward without affecting Newton's changeless gravitational order). By virtue of its selective attention, therefore, classical physics prescinds from contingency, randomness, and ambiguity. It dismisses irreversible time as of no account. It is purely Apollonian, with eyes only for the changeless.

It follows that scientists who have their professional hats on straight realize that their focus is limited—an abstraction from the whole of human experience—and thus they do not presume to give us a whole worldview extrapolated from their data. Much less do they offer a teaching about the hope of salvation, either pro or con. The impulse to break this rule, however, and to commit what Whitehead called "the fallacy of misplaced concretion"—is clearly irresistible, and scientists like Carl Sagan, Richard Dawkins, and Francis Crick regularly violate it. We call this infraction scientism or reductionism, and it consists of taking the usually deterministic behavior of atoms or genes as the decisive clue to the nature of the whole of things.

A scientific theory, however, does not get you everything—even those theories that name themselves such. Again, consider Mr. Hawking's ambition. He aspires to reconcile two theories, certainly to a physicist the greatest intellectual achievement of the twentieth century. The two theories are currently inconsistent with each other; they cannot both be true. The first is Einstein's general theory of relativity, which describes the force of gravity and the large-scale structure of the universe; the second is quantum mechanics, which deals with small-scale, subatomic phenomena invisible to all but the eye of a supercollider. Before he dies of Lou Gehrig's disease (a motor neuron malady), Hawking wants to devise a set of equations—a mathematical formalism—that would constitute a quantum theory of gravity.[9]

This is something considerably more ambitious than the "grand unified theories" (GUTs), which predict that at very high energy levels three of the four basic forces of nature—namely electromagnetism, the weak nuclear force (responsible for radioactive decay), and the strong nuclear force (holding quarks together within protons and neutrons, and thus binding atoms together)—represent different aspects of a single force. What these unifications omit is gravity. A quantum theory of gravity would amount to what physicists sometimes call a "theory of everything" (TOE) or a unification of all of physics.

But please note: A physicist's theory of everything proposes to explain "everything" only to the extent that everything in the cosmos is composed of subatomic particle-waves.[10] By the nature of its inquiry, then, such a theory will be limited to accounting for fundamental interactions and explaining why subatomic particles have the mass, charge and other characteristics that they do. It will thus predict the behavior of things only at the simplest level; it will not predict the behavior of complex systems like jaguars and human beings, much less the vagaries of the New York Stock Exchange. Physicists abstract from such chancy matters—or until very recently they did.

Physics and theology constitute distinct methods of inquiry. One cannot do what the other does. But this is not to claim that the two inquiries have no bearing on each other. Clearly there are contact points or areas of cross-fertilization between them (more on this later).[11] Faith in the Creator and the consequent orderliness of creation, we already pointed out, supports the scientists' most basic assumption. Conversely, theology must take account of *all* human experience, and that includes any countervailing evidence from physics, chemistry, and biology. Again, Augustine states the classic line: "We must show our Scripture not to be in conflict with whatever [our critics] can demonstrate about the nature of things from reliable sources. . . .")[12]

Augustine's defensive and apologetic stance, however, does not represent the only Christian position on the relationship between science and theology. T. S. Eliot, paraphrasing Aquinas, puts the relationship in bolder, more forceful terms: "A wrong attitude toward nature implies, somewhere, a wrong attitude towards God, and the consequence is an inevitable doom."[13]

In accord with this principle, we must acknowledge that whatever the modern cosmologist discovers about the physical world may very well be relevant to the broader, existential questions the ancients asked. The classic example, I suppose, is the impact of Isaac Newton's inverse square law of gravity upon the seventeenth-century Western mind; it was taken as decisive proof of a mechanical cosmos, changed forever how we understood our relation to nature, and gave us an otiose, clockmaker God. When we moderns ask ourselves the existential questions posed by our ancestors, then, we have to admit the relevance of the narrower concerns of contemporary cosmological theory to them. And whenever we express awe at the latest news about the big bang or sightings of the elusive "dark matter" (which ought to be there in great gobs but which nobody seems able to find in the proper amounts), we do so. Similarly, we acknowledge the ontological import of science when we feel somehow doomed on hearing an astrophysicist predict, say, that our glorious universe may eventually collapse under the force of gravity into a black hole (the so-called "big crunch"). It was just such a sense of impending doom, evoked by the second law of thermodynamics (the law of entropy), that at the beginning of this century drove Henry Adams to turn to the Virgin of Chartres for a way out.[14]

In the presentation to follow, I will deal with the crucial contrast between the attitude toward nature founded on the work of the magisterial Isaac Newton and the different attitude toward nature that finds its ground in the "new physics" of the big bang theory, quantum physics, and chaos theory. The latter, I want to say, is compatible with a sacramental sensibility; the former virtually abolishes it. What I will say here is limited; I mean to offer only some background for the kind of ecological ethic that we all seek.

III. The Premodern Roots of a Sacramental Sense

Our first question really asks whether the cosmology of a premodern manuscript culture—the cultures of Augustine, Aquinas, and Francis of Assisi that still remained in many respects dominated by an oral sensorium—can have any links to a big bang cosmology, which is the product of a visually oriented print and computer culture. On the surface, this is only a little less farfetched than asking if the cosmology of two environmental heroes, the Suquamush Indian Chief Seattle and Black Elk of the Lakota Sioux, is somehow compatible with the cosmology of Stephen Hawking. Not likely, you say. But just wait.

My point is that at least historically, Catholic sacramental theology presupposes at its root an experience of creation that has strong affinities with the experience of nonliterate, traditional primal cultures—whose faith and sense of the world came mainly through hearing, as St. Paul insists that all of ours must (Rom 10:17). Peoples with oral cultures do not find nature at a distance and "in front" of them, as visually oriented people with texts do; rather, they find themselves surrounded, literally enveloped by the sounds of things vibrating in their inner ear. Of an inert, depersonalized nature—the creation of the spectator-literate mind that has detached itself from a primal, oral culture's kinesthetic sense of resonance with its circumambient world—they would know nothing. They dwell in a world that feels like an acoustic womb. The very stones cry out![15]

We can sense this way of understanding the world in "St. Patrick's Breastplate" (also known as "The Deer Cry"), a Celtic Christian prayer whose language indicates a seventh- or eighth-century provenance:

I arise today
Through the strength of heaven:
Light of sun,
Radiance of moon,
Splendor of fire,
Speed of lightning,
Swiftness of wind,
Depth of sea,
Stability of earth,
Firmness of rock.

I arise today
Through God's strength to pilot me:
God's might to uphold me,
God's wisdom to guide me,
God's ear to hear me,
God's word to speak for me,
God's hand to guard me. . . .
From everyone who shall wish me ill,
Afar and near,
Alone and in multitude.[16]

As Thomas Cahill puts it, this is the "first ringing assertion that the universe is the Great Sacrament, magically designed by its loving creator to bless and succor human beings." It is the work, he says, of a "Christian druid."[17] One can feel a similar if less magical spirit in St. Francis of Assisi's litany of praise—through sun, moon and stars, wind and air, water, fire, earth, and death—in "The Canticle of Brother Sun."

Medieval people saw with eyes like ours but did not perceive with the same minds. Those who devised Catholic sacramental theology did not perceive with the same minds either. They had a different figuration of the world—the way of participation or empathy we might call it—than we in a typographic culture commonly do. In particular, Celtic Christianity speaks incessantly of a God who "encompasses," that is, of a God experienced not under the analogy of a visual object (as literate

"And God Saw That It Was Good"

people will) but under the analogy of circumambient sound, as an oral people will.[18] The difference matters: A visual way of synthesizing the world keeps us at a distance, whereas an oral-audial way of synthesizing the world closes distance. Sound wraps us round, penetrates our boundaries without violating them, situates us automatically at the center—and asks for a personal response. In a world dominated by sight, one can readily remain an uninvolved bystander.

A still largely oral people, as the medievals were, will exhibit a sense of connectedness, of the earth's energies being part of them, they of hers. And it is this common-sense awareness of the cosmos, I would say, that underlies Thomas Aquinas's great doctrine of participation in unfathomable Being. It is no wonder that two giants of medieval theology who built on this oral sensorium—Scotus Ereuigena and Meister Eckhart—found themselves within a hair's breadth of pantheism.[19]

The link between the Catholic sacramental outlook and primal cultures is well illustrated, I believe, by Owen Barfield when he places us in the skin of an ordinary medieval man-in-the-street and asks us to imagine ourselves looking at the world through his eyes:

> To begin with, we will look at the sky. We do not see it as empty space, for we know very well that a vacuum is something that nature does not allow. . . . If it is daytime, we see the air filled with light proceeding from a living sun, rather as our own flesh is filled with blood proceeding from a living heart. If it is nighttime, we do not merely see a plain, homogeneous vault pricked with separate points of light, but a regional, qualitative sky, from which first of all the different sections of the great zodiacal belt, and secondly the planets and the moon (each of which is embedded in its own revolving sphere) are raying down their complex influences upon the earth, its metals, its plants, its animals and its men and women, including ourselves. We take it for granted that those invisible spheres are giving forth an inaudible music—the spheres, not the individual stars. . . . As to the planets themselves, without being specially interested in astrology, we know very well that growing things are specially beholden to the moon, that gold and silver draw their virtue from sun and moon respectively, copper from Venus, iron from Mars, lead from Saturn. And that our health and temperament are joined by invisible threads to these heavenly bodies we are looking at. We probably do not think about the extra-sensory links between ourselves and the phenomena. We merely take them for granted.
>
> We turn our eyes on the sea—and at once we are aware that we are looking at one of the four elements, of which all things on earth are composed, including our own bodies. We take it for granted that these elements have invisible constituents, for, as to that part of them that is incorporated in our own

bodies, we experience them inwardly as the four "humours" that go to make up our temperament. (Today we still catch the lingering glimpse of this participation, when Shakespeare makes Mark Antony say to Brutus:

...The elements
So mixed in him, that Nature might stand up
And say to all the world, This was a man.)

Earth, Water, Air, and Fire are part of ourselves, and we of them. And through them also the stars are linked with our inner being, for each constellated Sign of the Zodiac is specially related to one of the four elements, and each element therefore to three Signs.[20]

The medieval person's boundaries were thus permeable. Walls may have been built against the raiding Vikings and Muslims, but like the Native Americans, the medieval man-in-the-street shared in the energies of animals, trees, rivers, sky, and heavenly bodies. He even had a special name for the kind of blood—called "arterial" as opposed to physically nutritive "venous" blood—which circulated between him and nature without and was the channel of "vital spirit."[21] The medieval was, as we might say now, an open system, freely exchanging energy with the environment. This sense of participation in nature, I claim, is the pedestrian source of Aquinas's "analogy of being." The only difference is that the contemplative Aquinas stresses the divine Wisdom or Logos that is mediated through nature. For him, all of nature is a theophany.

Barfield's comment on the above passage is instructive: "The background picture then was of man as a microcosm within the macrocosm. It is clear that he did not feel himself isolated by his skin from the world outside him to quite the same extent as we do. He was integrated or mortised into it, each different part of him being united to a different part of it by some invisible thread. In his relation to his environment, the man of the middle ages was rather less like an island, rather more like an embryo, than we are."[22]

Now contrast this with Western consciousness after Gutenberg's invention of the printing press made sight—the distancing, objectivizing sense—our dominant way of synthesizing the perceptible world. Print enabled a new kind of detachment from nature. We were no longer "mortised" into it; womb-nature vanishes. The metaphors change—we "bestride the world as if on a stage." There is a new sense of mobility and empowerment, with attendant warnings: seventeenth-century poets like John Donne have to remind us we are not "islands." Correlatively, nature loses its "good vibes" and its original sense of being a generative, birth-giving matrix. Nature is neutered. In effect the Western world textualizes nature, reducing it to silence in the image of linear, lead type—so many ingot-letters of an alphabet that we can arrange and recompose at will. Then, through the seventeenth-century scientific revolution that print made possible, we proceeded (as Wordsworth said) to 'disgod' nature."[23]

The payoff was that the new science and the technology it gave rise to enormously increased our leverage on the world, enabled us to stand above and outside it—in a stunning new way, free at last. And we are free to detail it, analyze it, map it, and yes, to dedicate ourselves to it in ways that had never been possible before the existence of modern science. This is all a big piece of the story of the Renaissance—indeed of freedom—in the West and explains why literacy campaigns in the Third World are still vital.[24]

Every advance, however, comes at a price. In this case, we lost our prior sense of being part of nature, her offspring. The price of detachment has certainly been the degradation of nature—our own and that of the physical world around us. Our environmental problems begin here. In the first instance, we have suffered a loss of connection and meaning, that dense surcharge of meaning that is evident in primitive saga, Homeric epic, and biblical poetry. Nature's putative purposelessness invaded our own souls and a great vacuum has been left in Western existence. John Donne captured the sense of disorientation in the lines,

> The Element of fire is quite put out,
> The Sun is lost, and th' earth, and no man's wit
> Can well direct him where to look for it.
> And freely men confess that this world's spent.

> 'Tis all in peeces, all cohearance gone,
> All just supply, and all Relation.
> Prince, Subject, Father, Sonne, are all forgot
> For every man alone thinks he hath got
> To be a Phoenix . . .[25]

Individualism has seized the consciousness of the West.

Second, nature became an adversary—something inert or a potentially devouring mother to be exploited (Francis Bacon's metaphors of making nature a "slave" are decisively revealing in this regard.) As Whitehead once described it, nature as viewed through the lens of classic modern science is a "dull affair, soundless, scentless, colourless; merely the hurrying of material, endlessly, meaninglessly,"[26] which of course means that you can manipulate it at will. Despots and captains of industry have loved this idea.

The loss of meaning would not really sink in until the nineteenth or twentieth centuries. The nature-as-machine that the West has increasingly dominated since the time of Newton mediates no presences; it is alien to us. The responses, of course, have varied. Not feeling that we quite belong—indeed, feeling abandoned—some suffer periodic fits of severe anomie. It is as if one had divorced one's mother, which biologically cannot really be done. Others, like Jean-Paul Sartre, have responded with existential defiance, boasting of their detachment from the deterministic order of nature, celebrating their freedom to "create themselves" from scratch. And still others, usually academics, urge a stony stoicism. The late Jacques Monod, a biologist, put it this way:

> Man must at last finally awake from his millenary dream; and in doing so, awake to his total solitude, his fundamental isolation. Now does he at last realize that, like a gypsy, he lives on the boundary of an alien world. A world that is deaf to his music, just as indifferent to his hopes as it is to his suffering or his crimes. [27]

Our cultural elites make much of this last worldview. They now typically find themselves locked up in a bag of skin, a "ghost in a machine" cut off from the juicy "noumena" of things (as Kant said) and living anomalously on one of those planetary bodies whose timeless laws of motion Isaac Newton had so brilliantly charted. (T. S. Eliot's "Wasteland" diagnoses this condition.) "It is probably no exaggeration to say," writes Nobel chemist Ilya Prigogine,

> that Western civilization is time-centered. Is this perhaps related to a basic characteristic of the point of view taken from the Old and New testaments? It was inevitable that the "timeless" conception of classical physics would clash with the metaphysical conceptions of the Western world. It is not by accident that the entire history of philosophy from Kant through Whitehead was either an attempt to eliminate this difficulty through the introduction of another reality (e.g., the noumenal world of Kant) or a new mode of description in which time and freedom, rather than determinism, would play a fundamental role. [28]

Question: Is there any going back? Is there any way for literate, urbanized people, so distanced now from nature, to retrieve a medieval or primitive sensorium? Or is passage to such a paradise blocked by a fierce angel at the gate? (Of course the Middle Ages were hardly a paradise.) What Walter Ong calls "secondary orality," the product of the new electronic media and their wrap-around sound, may offer an opening—back to the future, as it were. Myself, I see the fierce angel. Indeed, I think that historically the Jews, in campaigning so resolutely against pagan nature religion, had a lot to do with stationing the angel there. In fact, they prefigured Newton & Co. in "disgodding" nature. And one Jew of the first century, namely Jesus of Nazareth, apparently did not find this "desacralization" much of a problem. He simply went around breathing Spirit into the world—in the first instance, in the way modern poets do, by taking dead matter and converting it into symbol and metaphor. Perhaps that's the way out—or back in. And I intend to resort to it. But first we must examine the new cosmology and ask whether it isn't a potential ally of faith.

IV. A Sound of Origins

What does a sacramental tradition have to do with the astronomical world of someone like Stephen Hawking? That is our basic question here. Some would reply that the source of the Catholic sacramental tradition, the story of Jesus Christ, is simply dwarfed by the staggeringly vast universe disclosed by contemporary cosmologists. In comparison, they would claim, the Christ story is altogether too anthropocentric and not capacious enough. "The world of my science classes seemed grander, more marvelously contrived, and infinitely richer than the anthropomorphic and anthropocentric cosmos I studied in Natural Philosophy 101," wrote the Catholic physicist Chet Raymo in a recent issue of *Commonweal.*[29] I would agree this far: Our preaching, especially with regard to the opening chapters of the Book of Genesis and the Prologue to John's Gospel, has to be reconfigured in terms of what we now know about our location in cosmic space-time.

Theologians have their work cut out for them. People will someday wonder, Owen Barfield once wrote, how we could have been so blind to the conjunction between a religion that makes so much of time (as the Greeks did not) and a scientific outlook that stresses the immense journey of evolution. They will ask how it could be that

> a religion which differed from all others in its acceptance of time, and of a particular time, as the cardinal element in its faith; that it had, on the one hand, a picture in its mind of the history of the Earth and man as an evolutionary process; and that it neither saw nor supposed any connection between the two.[30]

One would have expected, Barfield goes on, that anyone who considered Jesus of Nazareth the culminating point in the history of the earth, indeed as its savior, would "feel that we are still very near that turning point, indeed hardly past it; that we hardly know as yet what the Incarnation means. . . ."[31]

The new picture of the cosmos, according to Stephen Hawking, dates back only to 1924, when the American astronomer Edwin Hubble showed that ours was not the only galaxy.[32] (I would claim that things began a century earlier, when Watt's steam engine and Bessemer's steel mills melted all of Newton's stable, sharp-edged objects and geometrical diagrams into fiery clouds—the first sign of nuclear dissemination—and a prophetic British painter by the name of J. M. W. Turner captured it all on his blazing canvases.) However you figure the start-up moment, in 1929 Hubble made the landmark observation that distant galaxies are moving rapidly away from us (the expanding universe) and, by implication, from a big bang "singularity" some 15 billion years ago. (It is called a "singularity" because, according to one theory of the big bang, at 100 billion degrees Centigrade no stable particle could form, and thus none of the laws of physics, as we currently understand them, apply at that point.) Thereafter, the "steady state" theory of the cosmos, until then dominant, was discarded. In 1963 Arno Penzias and Robert Wilson, two Bell Laboratory physicists in Holmdel, N.J., accidentally picked up the very low sound (the 3-degree Kelvin background radiation) of the big bang at the beginning. Their large microwave antenna had detected the still resonating echo of the birth of our universe.

The big bang was not so much like a TNT blast, starting from a definite center and expanding to engulf everything around it. It was more like a bubble ballooning out or, as some physicists have suggested, more like the first fortissimo bars of a great symphony, which occur simultaneously everywhere, filling all space at once. Nanoseconds later, as particles formed, every particle was rushing apart from every other—to eventually form our current curved and expanding galactic space. Dazzling. Nothing has been quite the same since we made this discovery.

The sound that Penzias and Wilson heard undeniably provides an apt image or analogy for another kind of energy effulgence: Aleph, the Great Beginner moving over the void, pouring out, emptying, informing, quickening, breathing into nothingness another frequency, another Sound. But please note, the physical analogue does not "prove" the existence of a Creator, much less an absolute beginning of time or creation *ex nihilo*. No direct inferences can be made in this connection and, besides, the doctrine of creation has very little to do with origins and almost everything to do with dependency on God or why there is something rather than nothing.[33] Penzias and Wilson undoubtedly heard the sound of *our* universe being born, but this does not mean it is *the* big bang. The "hot" theory of the big bang is only one of several competing interpretations of the event.

Equipped with string theory—the mathematics of the tiny, vibrating bits of hyperdimensional space that may turn out to form dimensionless quarks and leptons—today's theoretical physicists speculate like medieval cabalists. (And since no nuclear accelerator ever likely to be built will be able to simulate the energy levels required to test these speculations about our origins, empirical verification is difficult to come by.) Physicist Hugh Everett thinks that an almost infinite number of universes of other dimensions, of which we can know nothing, may exist simultaneously with ours. Or, if the Russian theoretical physicist Andrei Linde is correct, ours may have ballooned out of the space of a prior universe. It could be just one of many more universes, perhaps an infinite number, in a beginningless series and eventually be destined to collapse into an incredibly dense black hole and then explode once more. Hawking has a similar theory—of a finite, self-contained space-time with no singularities to form a boundary or edge—and thus, in his dim understanding of what *creatio ex nihilo* is about, no call for a creator. "So long as the universe had a beginning, we could suppose it had a creator," he writes. "But if the universe is really completely self-contained, having no boundary or edge, it would have neither beginning nor end: it would simply be. What place, then, for a creator?"[34]

When seen in the light of the quantum physics that gave birth to it, though, big bang theory changes everything, not only our picture of nature, but possibly even our image of God. For up until the moment that Einstein unwittingly showed that the order of classical physics was simply a statistical phenomenon—that is, an order built upon an utterly chancy, indeterminate dance of subatomic buzzing—God had suffered from being pushed out of time and space. In the classical Newtonian world, God was all too frequently regarded as an otiose clockmaker, or worse, as some kind of spy satellite "way out there," orbiting earth. As Northrop Frye once observed, thinking of God in the way we now do of atoms and electrons—as forces, fields, and energies rather than "things"—may prove a way of recovering our biblical ancestors' sense that God is linguistically a "word of power," not a noun but a verb.[35]

That "word of power" must match up, or supervene within, a physical cosmos that is much bigger than anyone had previously dreamed. As Hawking writes,

> We now know that our galaxy is only one of some hundred thousand million that can be seen using modern telescopes, each galaxy itself containing some hundred thousand million stars. . . . We live in a galaxy that is about one hundred light years across and is slowly rotating; the stars in its spiral arms orbit around its center about once every hundred million years. Our sun is just an ordinary, average-sized, yellow star, near the inner edge of one of the spiral arms. We have certainly come a long way since Aristotle and Ptolemy, when we thought the earth was the center of the universe.[36]

We are talking about a very big bubble indeed: a hundred billion galaxies across three hundred billion billion light years of expanding space. What would Blaise Pascal have done with this? The spatial distances are equally mind-boggling. To make our position more graphic along the temporal coordinate, Carl Sagan invites us to imagine the entire 15 billion year lifetime of the universe compressed into the span of a single year—as if the primordial big bang were to occur on January 1.[37] The picture would look something like this:

Jan. 1:	Big bang
May 1:	Origin of the Milky Way galaxy
Sept. 9:	Origin of our solar system
Sept. 14:	Formation of earth
Oct. 9:	Date of oldest fossils (bacteria and blue-green algae)
Nov. 15:	Oldest fossil photosynthetic plants
Dec. 1:	Significant oxygen atmosphere develops on earth
Dec. 17:	First invertebrates
Dec. 19:	First vertebrates
Dec. 22:	First amphibians and winged insects
Dec. 24:	First dinosaurs
Dec. 26:	First mammals
Dec. 29:	First cretaceans and primates
Dec. 31:	First humans

By this measure the whole of recorded history would fit into the last ten seconds of New Year's Eve, December 31—and the birth of Christ would have occurred only two seconds later. Indeed, from this perspective the life of Christ has just barely happened. Have we had time to absorb its meaning? What is a mere two thousand years in comparison to billions?

V. The Anthropic Principle

The new cosmological scale of time and space are truly awe-inspiring and can well spin one into vertigo. It raises questions that inevitably have metaphysical overtones. And if theologians are not raising such questions, physicists themselves rush into the breach with "What if's" and "Why's." Consider, for instance, the implications of three sets of phenomena involved in the formation of our universe: (1) the rate at which it is expanding, (2) the formation of elements, and (3) the particle/antiparticle ratio.[38]

As to the first, as Stephen Hawking puts it, "if the rate of expansion one second after the big bang had been smaller by even one part in a hundred thousand million million [the universe] would have recollapsed before it reached its present size."[39] On the other hand, if the expansion rate had been greater by a part in a million, the universe would have ballooned out too rapidly for stars and planets to form, and since the heavier elements required for life are formed in the stars, no life would have happened. As things stand, however, the initial energy, mass, and strength of gravitational forces were precisely balanced so that life could eventually emerge.

Second, the formation of chemical elements. Four force fields hold everything in the expanding universe together and govern its energetic processes: (1) the "strong force" binding atomic nuclei together, (2) the "weak force" responsible for radioactive decay, (3) electromagnetism responsible for light and electrically charged particles, and (4) gravity. If the weak force had been even a trifle stronger, all hydrogen atoms would have dissolved into helium—which would have precluded stable stars, the nuclear reactors that supply energy for life, and water. If, on the other hand, the strong force had deviated from its actual strength by as much as 1 percent, no carbon, the basic building block of DNA, would have been able to form inside stars. In turn, had electromagnetism been even slightly stronger, stars would have been too chill to explode as supernovas, thus depriving the planets of the heavier elements needed to germinate life. Similarly, the ratio between gravity and electromagnetism is critical for stellar and galactic evolution.

Third, the particle/antiparticle ratio: Not only are the force fields precisely calibrated for the development of life in some far-off corner(s) of the galaxies, but so too are particle masses and the charges of neutrons, protons, and electrons. If in the early cosmos every proton had been matched by an antiproton, the result would have been mutual annihilation, a zero-sum game. Our material world would not have emerged. Instead, for every billion antiparticles there were a billion and one particles—and this slight asymmetry provided just enough of an edge to jump-start our world.

What to make of improbable facts like these? Coincidence? Design? It's got to make you wonder. Even Stephen Hawking, no theist, insists that the odds against a universe like ours coming out of something like the big bang are enormous, and he concedes that the extraordinary unlikelihood of the original conditions has to have religious implications. Physicists like John D. Barrow and Frank J. Tipler are more forthright, concluding that from the very outset, our fiery, original universe was somehow exactly primed for the emergence of life, perhaps even for human life. Physicists call it the "anthropic principle."[40] In the weaker version of this principle, which emphasizes the near infinite number of galaxies besides our own Milky Way, the claim is limited to saying only that the conditions necessary for intelligent life are met in certain, limited regions of space-time. It is thus no surprise that we find the conditions for our existence satisfied in our corner of the universe. As Hawking states it, "It is a bit like a rich person living in a wealthy neighborhood not seeing any poverty."[41]

In the stronger version of this principle, however, physicists use Werner Heisenberg's "uncertainty principle"—the fact that at the subatomic level, the observer is always implicated in determining the position or velocity of a particle/wave—to argue that the whole vast construction of the universe exists for our sake. It's as if the knower had been predestined in the very scheme of things from the outset. Long before we ever emerged from the prebiotic soup of mother earth, the cosmos was silently working for us, distilling a sounding board, a voice that might speak for it, tell the big story.

Whatever one thinks of this idea, and physicists are divided, the data upon which it is based should heighten one's awareness of how dependent we are in the most elemental processes of stars and quarks. Whatever else we are, we are nothing if not a fragment, a kind of hologram of the universe itself. Or, as Thomas Berry defines the matter, a human being is "that being in whom the universe comes to itself in a special mode of conscious reflection."[42]

It is no surprise, then, that these days many people find the Tuesday science section of *The New York Times* a quasi-religious experience! On the first page of *A Brief History of Time,* Hawking makes some very big questions explicit: "Where did the universe come from, and where is it going? Did the universe have a beginning, and if so, what happened *before* then? What is the nature of time? Will it ever come to an end?"[43]

The new physics raises such questions—questions that are implicitly ontological and have religious resonances. Thus the "contact points" between St. Augustine and Hawking that I referred to above. (And yes, as Augustine observed in Book 11 of *The Confessions,* God probably is reserving hell for those who ask what happened "before" creation.) Hawking's world is neither Descartes' bifurcated world of *res cogitans* and *res extensa* nor Newton's "dull affair" of billiard-ball atoms mindlessly repeating themselves, running in strict military file within an absolute container-space. So long as that view of nature ruled our mental horizon, physics, the hardest of the natural sciences, was forced to focus attention on the uniform and homogenous aspects of the universe on a large scale and simply abstract itself from all those interesting irregularities we call galaxies, planets, blue-green algae and human beings. In contrast, Hawking takes the arrow of time seriously and is interested in these "irregularities."

The question we must now ask is whether we aren't at this time in the midst of one of those paradigm-shifting "scientific revolutions" to which Thomas S. Kuhn introduced us in the 1960s.[44] Is classical physics—and its image of a mechanical, deterministic universe—giving way, about to be superseded by something different, perhaps a new image of the cosmos that would overcome the division, the wall of separation between nature and the human, that we have lived with since Descartes? If so, something very significant for our culture is afoot. In the classical view that came to dominate Western elites in the nineteenth century, we had to keep subject and object strictly apart. Shakespeare and the periodic table of elements did not belong together. In effect we had to keep two separate accounts, one for the physicist's dynamics of energy and another for all the subtle signs and symbols of our life-world. The great Cartesian divorce—or C. P. Snow's "two cultures" of science and the humanities that divide our universities—ruled our mental horizon. Science brought this division about. Will it now heal it? Does post-Einsteinian physics still require it? I think not.

VI. The Poetics of Matter/Energy

To dramatize the relevance of these questions to our theme of sacramentality, perhaps we could ask this: Does the new physics have a place in its world for the poet? Because, if it does, then *a fortiori* it has a place for the biblical vision, whose language begins with poetry—drawing us in with beauty, as it were—but ends in revelation. So our query here: Does post-Einsteinian physics supply the dream-stuff that poets—that all of us—are made of? To put it another way, do people who see signs everywhere and who have the habit of metaphor, that is, the penchant to assert, in the face of all our culture's disjunctions, the togetherness of things, receive a boost from the folks who named elementary subatomic particles "quarks"? (Caltech physicist Murray Gell-Mann won the 1969 Nobel Prize for his work on these dimensionless components of protons and electrons, taking the name from James Joyce's line, "Three quarks for Master Mark!") The answer, I believe, is yes, and the exposition to follow is meant to nail down that yes.

Contingency, randomness and ambiguity, I said above, are matters that classical physicists refused to attend to, thereby refusing to enter time. (Physics was the one great holdout in this respect, as all the other natural sciences, led by geology in the eighteenth century, plunged into temporal process.) But these are precisely the things that physicists now delve into, especially at the dancing quantum level.[45] And since this started to happen, things get more and more curious.

In the previous section we focused on the very big structures of the universe—where Newton's laws of motion remain applicable. (If you want to shoot a missile to Mars, in fact, they are indispensable.) In this section I want to consider the way in which, if we are scientifically up-to-date, we ought to imagine our relationship to nature. I will examine the implications of three related areas of contemporary physics: (1) quantum physics, (2) information physics, and (3) chaos theory. If I am not mistaken, these areas of Hawking's world begin to show striking affinities to the chancy, interconnected, and semiotic universe of Catholic sacramental theology.

Chance and Interconnection

It was Hegel, as I recall, who remarked that history is a bacchanalian revel in which not a soul is sober. The nineteenth century expected this to be true of the human story and was supremely confident, on Newton's authority, that it was not true of vast, impersonal nature. Nature was supposed to be a machine, sobriety itself. As Einstein put it, against all the evidence he himself had forced his colleagues to examine, "God does not play dice." Well, apparently God does.

What does elemental matter—the microscopic stuff of stars, planets, and DNA molecules—look like in Hawking's universe? The first thing to say, I suppose, is that matter is bound or condensed energy, captured from the torrential, buzzing flow set loose by the big bang. Just as water moves through a whirlpool and simultaneously creates it, so are we and the stars disturbances (or warps) in the free flow of ballooning, random energy sounded with the opening chord of our cosmic symphony (whether it was the first or just one of many). Democritus and the classical atomists (or the Hindus) had it about right: the atoms that compose all object-like entities in the universe are vortices, eddies, or fluctuations within a vast cosmic river. The potency of this bound energy is reflected in Einstein's famous formula, $E=mc^2$; to measure it, one must multiply mass by an enormous constant, the velocity of light squared. At the same time, this contained energy is impossible to pin down; it dances, is fundamentally indeterminate—a mere (but very great) potency waiting to combine and take form. (Einstein didn't like this at all.)[46]

But as Werner Heisenberg showed, if you manage to locate position in a nuclear cloud chamber, the speed of the particle escapes you; and conversely, if you determine the speed, position evaporates (the uncertainty principle). As Stephen Hawking puts it, "In general, quantum mechanics does not predict a single definite result for an observation. Instead it predicts a number of different possible outcomes and tells us how likely each of these is. . . . Quantum mechanics therefore introduces an unavoidable element of unpredictability and randomness into science."[47]

In other words, Newtonian mechanics and the orderly grid of the periodic table of chemical elements are exercises in statistics, a lawfulness at the macroscopic level that rides on a wildly chancy underworld. Hence the whole dream of scientific determinism, that if we knew the complete state of the universe at any one time we could predict everything that would happen in the universe for the rest of time (first envisioned at the beginning of the nineteenth century by the Marquis de Laplace), appears to have been a fool's errand.

Is this elemental stuff particle or wave? Well, it acts like both. On the one hand, Max Planck's quantum hypothesis tells us that it behaves like a particle, coming, like denominations of money, only in certain sized packets or quanta. On the other hand, Heisenberg's uncertainty principle implies that the particles behave like waves; they are not localizable but "smeared out" with a certain probability distribution. This means that at the subatomic level atoms entangle themselves in the fields of everything else in the universe and are thus internally related to everything else. The mutual impact may be slight, but the brilliant Crab Nebula in our starry sky doesn't make a move without affecting you or me, nor do we make a move without affecting it. The truth is that matter/energy is profoundly social.

Rather than imagining subatomic structure as an imprisonment of energy within stable, well-defined boundaries—ideal for pinpointing within hard-edged geometrical diagrams—we do better to imagine these entities as vibrating, oscillating, aleatory clouds. The subatomic underworld, in other words, resembles a Jackson Pollock painting. Hence it is an anachronism (and a sign of cultural lag) that the word "atom" should still serve as metaphor of our insularity and shut-inness. It is precisely the opposite: Due to its field properties, atomic structure means that the whole universe is woven into us and we into it. It may be true, as Aristotle had it, that the soul is potentially all things. The point is that at an invisible (because microscopic) physical level, everything is *actually* implicated in everything else—the one in the many, the many in the one. Or, to put it in a medieval frame, the macrocosm is in the microcosm.

Such interconnection obtains as well at higher levels of organization. Atmospheric chemist James Lovelock theorizes (the Gaia Hypothesis) that the blue-green algae, the first vegetable life on earth, actually manufactured the atmosphere we and all earthly life breathe and that even today it is the green world that regulates the atmosphere's chemical composition and the climate—against the sun's intense radiation, which has steadily increased over the eons.[48] But for the plant world, the sun's intensifying radiation would have turned planet earth into another fiery planet Venus and burnt every living creature to a crisp. Do we breathe or does the green world breath us? The latter seems closer to the truth. Nor is this plant world outside us. For as Lewis Thomas was fond of pointing out, a horde of plant chloroplasts and mitochondria oxidate our cells. Without them, we could not breathe, move a muscle, or think a thought.[49] Planet earth operates like a single cell, or, as St. Paul would have it, like one body of many members, each with its own function, none dispensable.

A Semiotic World

Information physics—the theory underlying transistors and integrated circuits, the components of our televisions and computers—was a spillover of the quantum revolution.[50] Indeed, what energy (and the law of entropy) was to the nineteenth century, information (or signaling in some form) is to the twentieth century. For Einstein, space is inseparable from time; everything from star to proton is a signal system, a warp in space, that takes time to constitute itself. In short, the "things" of this world are not static but fundamentally processes. ("There is no nature," as Whitehead summed it up, "at an instant.") Soon enough Einstein's peers began to link this process-insight to the one great arrow of time that even nineteenth-century physicists had acknowledged: the thermodynamic one, according to which, irreversibly over time, the kinetic energy available for work—be it electrical, chemical or heat—had to be paid for in waste and structural degeneration. Unlike Newton's billiard-ball objects, thermodynamic systems wear down and vary from their initial conditions, and thus their futures differ from their pasts. Time counted, even though this meant (according to the law of entropy) that it ran downhill, in the opposite direction to Darwin's uphill evolutionary arrow, toward heat death or what physicists call thermal "equilibrium." But physicists quickly found a use for the fact that the dice are loaded in favor of entropic flux.

New concepts were introduced—information, redundancy, and noise—and their connection to thermodynamics was easily demonstrated. It was shown, for instance, that information, which is equivalent to organization, is a form of counter-entropy—a warp in space-time that works against the trend toward entropic incoherence or sheer noise. This made it possible to translate a "bit" of information into mathematical terms. Anything—from the message of quasar radiation to that of a DNA molecule—could be measured as the inverse of its entropy. Or, to put it another way, an atom of hydrogen or the Crab Nebula is a time series, a sequence of signals that in the process of constituting itself must vary its signals according to some kind of statistical regularity (or redundancy)—in effect, using a standard code or protoalphabet that is analogous to a set of grammatical rules which generate, within limits, a wide variety of programs or messages. The code of the spiral DNA molecule discovered by Crick and Watson in 1955 is a perfect example: an "alphabet" consisting of four nucleotides forming three-letter "words" for 20 amino acids, which are arranged into "sentences" that can specify one of thousands of proteins necessary for organic life.

After 300 years of Newton's silencing of nature, then, the picture of vibratory, cloud-like matter we spoke of above becomes more interestingly complicated. Even at the most elemental level, we now see, nature gives signs, almost begins to speak again. Nature is, in fact, nothing else than an immensely complicated communication system organizing itself out of all that random noise spewed out from the big bang. All these "irregularities," these eddies or vortices in this great flood of energy that we call galaxies, stars, planets, whooping cranes, and ourselves, are "open systems," wildly exchanging energy with their environment and thus temporarily moving upward against the entropic tide. We and the stars and everything in between are thus highly precarious balancing acts, moment by moment converting chaos into information/organization. Too much random noise on one side (mere chaotic buzz or babble), and you get free, unbound energy that does no work. Or too much redundancy on the other side (mere monotone like the droning of a single note in a stuck telephone signal), and you get just iron-bound rigidity, a stony death that communicates nothing. Signal systems—which physicists study under the label of nonequilibrium thermodynamics—exist between these two extremes.

The implications: If God wanted to construct a universe in which communication and possible communion held the highest importance, God would have had to shoot its redundancies—its repetition compulsions—full of disconcerting chance. (That is, God would have had to write the book of nature as if God were James Joyce rather than a law-and-order Prince Metternich.) And should this God choose to communicate with creation, certainly the circuitry is all there to be used.

There is more: We no longer need to carry the physicist's energy and the humanist's signs and symbols in separate accounts. One balance sheet will do. Information physics has given us back a semiotic universe, a nature that—like the medieval sacramental universe—gives signs. University divisions of the natural sciences and divisions of humanities, while working at different parts of the spectrum, need not figure themselves as concerned with utterly disparate matters. The natural sciences, we may now say, deal with primitive sign systems and their protolanguages and protogrammars, whereas the humanities deal with the more developed sign systems and meanings of the animated star dust we call human cultures. As the French philosopher of science Michel Serres put it:

> It is no longer necessary to maintain the distinction between introspective knowledge, or "deep" knowledge, and objective knowledge. There is only one type of knowledge and it is always linked to an observer, an observer submerged in a system or in its proximity. And this observer is structured exactly like what he observes. . . . There is no more separation between the subject on the one hand, and the object, on the other. . . . Instead, each term of the traditional subject-object dichotomy is itself split by something like a geographical divide: noise, disorder, and chaos on one side; complexity, arrangement, and sitribution on the other. Nothing distinguishes me ontologically from a crystal, a plant, an animal, or the order of the world; we are drifting together toward noise and the black depths of the universe. . . . Knowledge is at most the reversal of drifting. . . .[51]

If I get it right, then, information physics authorizes us to return to the idea, so keenly felt by the ancient Greeks, that the dramas of Aeshylus and Sophocles confront the forces of nature within us: the hurricane, the raging ocean, the wail of the wind, indeed, the vibrations of subatomic particle/waves and the thermonuclear turbulence of the stars. (Given all the unpredictable chanciness we have discovered in post-Einsteinian nature, it is no wonder that psychoanalysis is usually interminable.)

Chaos Theory and Transubstantiation

Nature gives signs. But does it also give birth, as the etymology of the word originally asserted? How is it, we might ask the physicist, that if the overall odds of a thermodynamic universe are stacked in favor of inert heat death do certain systems like the planet earth defy the entropic probabilities? How, that is, does evolution happen? So long as physicists, following Newton, banished all ambiguity and irregularity from their models—and that meant studying "closed systems" that exchanged no energy with their environments—there could be no answer to this question. As I have already indicated, however, post-Einsteinian physics began to pay attention to the erratic side of things, to the breaks in symmetry. And in this regard, nonequilibrium thermodynamics—and the study of so-called open systems far from thermal equilibrium—represents the way in which physicists have been able to get a handle on the evolutionary arrow of time.

Open thermodynamic systems exchange energy with their environment. As such, they include nearly everything of interest to us in nature, from galaxies to organic compounds and embryos. In general, nonequilibrium thermodynamics—or chaos theory, as it has been recently named—focuses on *non*linear systems like inorganic compounds, clouds, the shape of lightning, the microscopic intertwining of blood vessels, or the galactic clustering of stars. Unlike the linear systems examined by classical physics, in nonlinear systems the outcome of a dynamic process is so sensitive to initial conditions that a minimal change in the situation at the beginning of the process results in a large difference at the end.[52] A small change in cholesterol content, for instance, can produce disproportionately large changes in a cell. The flapping of a butterfly's wing in Hawaii may change the ensuing weather over San Francisco. What is important to emphasize here is that such systems are fundamentally unstable; they break symmetry—and it is this flirtation with disorder (or chaos) that facilitates the emergence of an often beautiful and thoroughly unpredictable novelty. In trying to understand such phenomena, physics promises to at last have something relevant to say to evolutionary biology, for example, an insight into how natural selection operating through DNA coding has come to express itself in the particular forms that it does.[53]

The fascinating thing about such unstable, open systems is that they maintain themselves against the eroding tide of entropic decay precisely by metabolizing chaos—in the first instance, the random energy left over from the big bang, out of which, like eddies in its field of force, all the galaxies and their components originally formed. The almost comedic principle here is that what is thrown off as waste or sheer noise at one, simpler level of organization is absorbed down the line and converted (say by a whirlpool that we call a galaxy in formation) into more complex information/structure.[54] The basic two rules for open, recycling energy systems are that (1) they never give back energy in precisely the same form in which it has been taken in; and (2) the more complex the system is, the more it recycles energy. Human beings, having the most porous boundaries of all, are the most recycled beings in the cosmos—and therefore at once both the most unstable and innovative.

Examples of the eating habits of open systems—a kind of chain of free lunches—abound in nature. The interstellar gas left over from the big bang in the course of time manufactured carbon and various organic compounds, and when supernovas exploded, their meteorites very likely bore these vital "waste products" to earth where they proceeded to convert the energy of the sun in entirely new ways. To the sun, of course, the photons it casts off are waste, sheer noise; but to emerging blue-green algae, busy with the alchemy of photosynthesis, such "waste" is nutriment to be converted into information/organization. In turn the plant breaks down carbon dioxide and gives off excess oxygen, again so far as the plant is concerned sheer waste, but the very breath of life for emerging animal organisms. Open systems are converters of random energy (noise) into order, the original, self-organizing, alchemical agents.

The law of large numbers, that is, that the majority always determines the script—or, as a physicist would say, that the inertial pressure of the prior redundant order represses innovation—does not rule open systems with iron force. Determinism (or redundancy) there is, but it is limited. Open systems thrive on breaking symmetries, on departing from the law laid down by a prior order. In some sense (and within limits) turbulence or fluctuation is their life-blood, their way of allowing a "chance variation" into the system. Bolting from the prior order, what looks on the surface like chaos is the germ, physicists now find, that produces a new, more complex level of organization—and possibly, of better adaptation to a changing environment. (In 1977, the Belgian physical chemist Ilya Prigogine was awarded the Nobel Prize for devising an elegant mathematical formalism for such transformative, open systems.)

Thus we can say that anything that develops in our universe, be it a young star in formation, plant life, or the body of an animal, literally eats buzzing, blooming confusion and in the course of doing so, changes the direction (and sign) of the time arrow from negative (degrading, aging, entropic) to positive (upgrading, complexifying, negentropic).[55] Furthermore, the suggestion is that it is precisely this ingestion of chaos that is the catalyst for a potentially new level of complex organization. In thermodynamic terms, complex nature devours noise—and transforms its random nonsense into information that in the case of the star directs thermonuclear operations, in the case of plant life controls photosynthesis, and in animals turns up as DNA code and enzyme production. If I get it right, physics has now decided to write irreversible time—a present and future that really differs from the past—into the fundamental script of nature.

This is a story, nature's story from the bottom up, of continual metamorphosis—or, as I would like to put it, of nature itself as technological transformer. Analogously, without the deliberation that marks human technocrats, the molecules of this world take raw material (random noise and order) and convert it into something else, another story. At a less complex level, that is, they act as we do. In effect, analogously, what we Catholics call transubstantiation has been going on from the very beginning. To put it mildly, there is plenty of time-space in such a story of transformation for the poet-theologian to maneuver and find a home. The world of physics is no longer a humanly alien one. It has its great regularities (thank God, hydrogen atoms do not come apart at the seams like our party politics do!), but the atoms that blindly run in social packs also manifest much of the unstable and creative plasticity of us humans. The analogy of being is back in place.

Organic Life

How do organisms appear within the above perspective? Since I cannot do better, let me defer to Michel Serres once again:

> First, [an organism] is an information and thermodynamic system. Indeed, it receives, stores, exchanges, and gives off both energy and information—in all forms, from the light of the sun to the flow of matter which passes through it (food, oxygen, heat, signals). This system is not at equilibrium, since thermodynamic stability spells death for it, purely and simply. It is in a temporary state of imbalance, and it tends as much as possible to maintain this imbalance. It is hence subject to the irreversible time of the second law [of entropy], since it is dying. But it struggles against this time.... In and by its imbalance, it is relatively stable. But here invariance is unique: neither static nor homeostatic, it is homeorrhetic [the same flowing]. It is a river that flows and yet remains stable in the continual collapse of its banks....
>
> This river ... this basin, poised on its own imbalance in a precarious state of quasi-equilibrium in its flow toward death, ferries energy and information, knowledge of entropy and negentropy, of order and disorder. Both syrrhesis [flow together] (rather than a system) and diarhesis [flow through], the organism is hence defined from a global perspective.... Or, within the context of an even more general circulation which goes from the sun to the black depths of space, the organism is a barrier of braided links that leaks like a wicker basket but can still function as a dam. Better yet, it is the quasi-stable turbulence that a flow produces, the eddy closed in on itself for an instant, which finds its balance in the middle of the current and appears to move upstream.... [56]

Serres goes on to claim that the whole immense journey of evolution is implicated in the flow-through structure of this "leaky wicker basket." That is, it somehow dams up or captures in its eddy the vast script of its origins; it is, among other things, the fallout of the stars, those thermonuclear reactors that manufactured the chemical compounds necessary for life, the product of immemorial genetic variations, and ultimately the upshot of a big bang that plentifully provided it with the energy it binds for work, that is, to move, however briefly, against the tide of collapse and death.

Now, and here is the crux of the matter, all times converge in this temporary knot: the drift of entropy or the irreversible thermal flow, wear and aging, . . . the conservative invariance of genetic nuclei, the permanence of form, the erratic blinking of aleatory mutations, the implacable filtering out of non- viable elements. . . . The living organism is of all times. This does not mean it is eternal, but rather that is an original complex, woven out of all the different times. . . . All the temporal vectors possessing a directional arrow are here, in this place, arranged in the shape of a star. What is an organism? A sheaf of times. What is a living organism? A bouquet of times.[57]

And human organisms, what are we in this perspective? Like the stars or weather formations of our atmosphere, we too are open thermodynamic "wicker baskets" constituted internally by our relationships to the global environment, moving upstream and drifting toward death. "Ah," said Rainer Maria Rilke,

not to be cut off
not through the slightest partition
shut out from the law of the stars.
The inner—what is it?
If not intensified sky, hurled through with birds and deep with
winds of homecoming.[58]

There once was a time, entranced by Newton's "one-eyed sleep," when we were sure that Rilke's identification of inwardness with sky was nothing but a flight of fancy, the raving of a romantic. The poet's habit of saying that I am rock, river, animal, and sky was taken at best as a tolerable exaggeration, but not taken seriously. No more. In light of quantum physics and nonequilibrium thermodynamics, we have to say that such poetry captures the literal truth. The taboo against identifying with nature has been lifted. (For most Westerners, the danger of fusing monistically with nature without distinction is remote; our detachment is secure.) Star time and earth time speak through us; we are their sound, their tongue.

Like the sun and the moon, we are disturbances in the field, vortices in turbulent nature. We are probably the most recycled beings in the universe, even while we live dissolving and re-enfleshing. We regrow our entire physical body as we do our hair and nails. Nothing in our genes was present a year ago. The tissue of our stomach renews itself weekly, the skin is shed monthly, and the liver regenerated every six weeks. Every moment, a portion of the body's 10^{28} atoms is returning to the world outside, and 98 percent of them are replaced annually. Each time we breathe, we take in a quadrillion atoms breathed by the rest of humanity within the last two weeks and more than a million atoms breathed personally by each person on earth.[59]

Ah yes, and like the subatomic particle/waves that compose us, we are both determined and riddled by chance—on one side arrangement, order, and complexity, on the other noise, disorder, and chaos. (Physics would suggest that good and evil lie on both sides, that too much order spells death, that a failure to cherish the chaos in us translates into hopelessness.) And yes, like the rest of the cosmos, we give signs. In fact, within a vast chain of conversions of random energy, we are the final alchemists, the last transformers and interpreters, the ultimate black box of nature. We do not hear its thermal din—its groanings to give birth—because all of that noise has been filtered out by the chain of energy-converters that came before us, in which we are the last link. As Michel Serres says, "We are submerged to our neck, to our eyes, to our hair, in a furiously raging ocean. We are the voice of this hurricane, this thermal howl, and we do not even know it."[60]

VII. Making the Earth a Sacrament

At the outset of this article, I spoke of needing to redeem the valid meaning of the Enlightment, with all its declarations of liberty, its millennial urges and bright democratic hopes for a transformed society that would exclude no one—that would bring everybody into the act. It's now time to deliver on that promise. In the previous section, we have brought a once alien nature back into our act—and us into nature's act. Kinship is reestablished. Still, there is no reason to minimize or deny that over millennia, we have weaned ourselves from nature's breast, detached ourselves from her drives and compulsions. It is just such drivenness that is manifest in Homer's *Iliad* and the early parts of the Old Testament. No one, I suspect, wants to return to that. Indeed, separation from nature was and remains necessary that we might fulfill our role, do our work in this cosmos. But just what is that work? That is our question.

A sacramental consciousness in our first sense, we said earlier, recognizes that nature is good and holy. Why is it holy? Why a sign of the *mysterium tremendum et fascinans*? As the Book of Wisdom has it, it is because "the imperishable spirit" of God dwells in all things:

"And God Saw That It Was Good"

Indeed, before you the whole universe is as a grain from a balance,
or a drop of morning dew come down upon the earth.
But you have mercy on all . . .
For you love all things that are
and loathe nothing that you have made;
for what you hated, you would not have fashioned.
And how could a thing remain, unless you will it;
or be preserved, had it not been called forth by you?
But you spare all things . . .
for your imperishable spirit is in all things! (Wis 11:22–12:1)

The immanence of God in creation, in fact, is the theme that opens the Bible—
"In the beginning . . . the earth was a formless wasteland and darkness covered the
abyss, while a mighty wind swept over the waters" (Gn 1:1–2). And the same motif
recurs in the Prologue to John's Gospel:

In the beginning was the Word, . . .
All things came to be through him,
    and without him nothing came to be.
What came to be through him was life,
    and this life was the light of the human race;
the light shines in the darkness . . . (Jn 1:1, 3–5).

If the Spirit is not experienced as immanent in all creation from the beginning,
Christianity amounts to no more than an especially moralistic form of Platonic idealism. Without the palpable presence of the indwelling Spirit, that is, it would be impossible to take seriously—or to be grasped by—Jesus' preaching that the kingdom
of heaven is not just a futuristic vision but in some sense already earthborn, here and
now. The promise Jesus embodied, the release from fear, the awakening that he elic-
ited—all of this supposes a rampant, fiery Spirit-energy in the world. It blows where it
will. It melts the frozen, warms the chill, guides steps that go astray. Without it, there
would have been no quickening Pentecost, no doing of the truth, no rapid spread of
Christianity around the Mediterranean world. The practice of a sabbath rest and the
whole subsequent Christian contemplative tradition rests upon it, representing, as they
do, ways of tapping into such Energy. Physicists do not, cannot measure it.

Sensitivity to the palpable movements of Spirit in creation lies at the core of a
sacramental attitude in our first sense, but provides the energy and direction for
sacrament in our second sense. The European Enlightenment forgot about this vital
conjunction—and the practice of prayer that underlies it—and consequently much

of its idealism transposed into terror. It is what keeps Catholicism from being a Platonism—and it stands as the proviso for all that I am about to say about sacrament in the second sense of human agency. Awareness of Spirit in the world is the condition of possibly making sacraments sites of promise, of ourselves or of the earth.

A sacramental consciousness of earth survives—just barely and in a somewhat schizophrenic fashion. When we are on holiday in the mountains or by the sea, most of us—whether religious or not—become a little like Wordsworth or Gerard Manley Hopkins. Babbling brooks have tongues, forests whisper, and the "deep down freshness of things" breathes with God's grandeur. But then, back at work, as utilitarian push comes to shove—and jobs are at stake—the beauty and refreshment of nature is not enough. Rainforests and biodiversity are sacrificed; top soil, aquifers, and mineral resources are recklessly depleted, and the atmosphere, its ozone shield rent, heats up with carbon dioxide. When we fail our obligations to the planet, nature falls with us.

We need to see our work and our technology in connection with the poetics of nature we have just sketched. Nature does splendid, beautiful work. Do we? At issue is sacrament in our second sense—which has to do with our role and responsibility in the cosmos. Sacrament here is verb—our doing.

Sacramental activity, I said, does not look backward. Certainly it does not want to return to the social organization and economy of the Middle Ages! It looks forward and asks: What are we making of this world of matter/energy? And what, with God's help, shall we make of it? No religious tradition that asks these questions with such urgency can be antitechnological. The question is how we use technology. Transformation of raw material is our business, as it has been the business, we have seen, of the whole, self-organizing material world for eons. A Judeo-Christian sensibility will not want to forget this; it is not amnesiac. And in this connection, the new physics enables us to vary and expand the usual practice of remembering what God has done for the Israelites and for us personally. It enables us to re-member ourselves within the depths of cosmic space-time. As such, physics belongs in our liturgies. It is testimony to the greatest of God's acts and soundings—nature itself.

Remember, says the Ash Wednesday ritual, thou art dust. And now we may add, with the shock of recognition, that we are star dust, earth stuff, beings who literally have been germinated in far-off parts of the universe and seeded here on this planet. We are thus born in debt, owing the quarks, the stars, and mothering earth an everlasting gratitude. Brother sun and sister moon indeed.

Look into your hand; the whole history of the cosmos is inscribed there, as if in the age-rings of a tree. Imagine you had an electron microscope handy. Increase the magnification and you will see within your hand's cells a mosaic of ribosomes and mitochondria, lysomes and centrioles—the indispensable agents of your respiration, sanitation, and energy-production—whose architecture dates back a billion years. Increase magnification more and you move into the cell nucleus and behold the DNA macromolecule that stores genetic information garnered over some four billion years of evolution. It contains the blueprint that makes you a human being, from internal organs to bones and brain cells. Turn up the magnification once again and see the atoms composing your genes, their nuclei and electron shells bonded in nebula more than five billion years ago. Increase the magnification a hundred thousand times more and you will come upon a single carbon nucleus bound together five to 15 billion years ago. Finally, looking closer still, one can make out trios of quarks that compose each proton and neutron in the nucleus. They were joined together when the cosmos was but seconds old. The whole history of the universe lies in the palm of your hand.[61]

When we speak, laugh, cry, or promise love till death, it is that great chain of nature's energy that speaks, laughs, cries, and loves through us. Each one of us is a distillation, a condensed centrifuge, of cosmic energy. We may leak like a sieve, but we dam up a siderail river. We are "sheafs of time . . . bouquets of time." There are not two destinies here—nature's and ours—but one. Saving our own skins and "saving the appearances" of nature—in a more radical sense than Aristotle ever dreamed—come down to the same project.

Why are we here? Why, asks Rainer Maria Rilke in "The Ninth Duino Elegy," be human when it would be so much easier, indeed serenely so, to spend "this interval of being" as—well, as a laurel bush? We are a tangle of ambivalence, seeking to escape the heavy hand of fate, yet longing for an ennobling destiny. Will sheer curiosity suffice us or the quest for happiness or self-improvement? No, says Rilke, none of these are enough.

But because *truly* being here is so much; because everything here
apparently needs us, this fleeting world, which in some strange way
keeps calling to us. Us the most fleeting of all.
Once for each thing. Just once; no more. And we too,
just once. And never again. But to have been
this once, completely, even if only once:
to have been one with the earth, seems beyond undoing.[62]

We are up to our neck, to our eyes, to our hair in debt. Do we not hear the stars, quarks, rain forests, and whooping cranes "in some strange way calling to us"? Calling for what? We are earth's big chance—plotted, conceived, and hatched over billions of years—to become spirited, to dance, to laugh, to mourn her lost children. Earth groans to be born anew in us, Paul of Tarsus said.

We are here, Rilke tells us, to speak of "things," by our actions to say them in ways they are incapable of.

Oh to say them *more* intensely than the Things themselves
ever dreamt of existing. Isn't that the secret intent
of this taciturn Earth, when it forces two lovers together,
that inside their boundless emotion all things may shudder with joy?[63]

What shall this immense journey of star- and earth-time mean—sound and fury signifying nothing? Physical matter is next to nothingness, a vast potency waiting to happen, said both Aristotle and Aquinas, until it is filtered through the human imagination—in effect, until it is dreamt into being meaningful rather than futile or nightmarish. (Heisenberg's indeterminacy principle seems to endorse such a view.) It is as if all the lively, spinning quarks and leptons in our bellies, all the star-carbon in our bones and the transformed sunlight in our blood stream were urging us to dig the poetry out of them, pour soul into them, make something beautiful out of them. Nature is mute, nameless. If she is to be personified, we are the vehicle. We are her voice—"the voice of this hurricane, this thermal howl."

Once upon a time, nature was universally acknowledged as the medium of the sacred. And at that time, in the early history of the human species, it may have been enough to accept that the giving was mostly one way, from nature to us. But once we detached ourselves from nature and gained our freedom from her, it became obligatory to give back—to return the gift. If nature is to be sacred in our day, it will be by our fiat, by what we make of material things. Thus do we honor nature's immense labor in giving birth to us. We are last in the line of nature's transformers and interpreters—the ultimate black box. Nature's meaning—or meaninglessness—hinges on us.

Jesus breathed spirit into confined and dark places, straightened the bent, delivered the sick and the demonized. He violated all the prescribed eating habits of his culture, ate with sinners and publicans, the reprobate and the pious, rich and poor, women, slaves and children, the clean and the unclean. According to some scholars, nothing he did offended more.[64] All are invited to his table—Gentile and Jew, slave and free, male and female—it makes no difference. He took bread and wine and identified himself with these elements that were originally manufactured in exploding supernovas. Even before human hands had intervened to change grain and grape into bread and wine, these materials incorporated billions of years of evolution. "This bread," he said, "is my body. . . . This wine my blood." By fiat, he takes the simplest elements of earth—once the ash of a dying star—and turns them into a sign of lavish divine hospitality, revealing that God wills that not a solitary thing shall be lost.

We are bid to do likewise—to deliver this unfinished earth from futility by freely claiming some part of it as our body and blood. The idea is to make soul-food and feast of that part, some particular work of our hands, heart, and mind that will be

"And God Saw That It Was Good"

worthy to delight another human being—that would be worthy of offering to God. What is this but craft and city-planning for the New Jerusalem in which, "behold, all things are new"?

So I ask: What sign are we giving? What are we making of earth, of our region of the starry Milky Way? Inevitably, we leave our graffiti scrawl, our stamp and mark upon the planet. How will our collective signature read? What are we making of fossil fuel, silicon, mineral deposits, rain forests, soil, the air, and the seas? Do we make really fine beer? Engines and water systems? Or books? Or public parks? Legal systems or livable cities? What kind of story have we been telling thus far? As Thomas Berry reminds us,

> we have changed the very chemistry of the planet, we have altered the biosystem, we have changed the topography and even the geological structure of the planet, structures and functions that have taken hundreds of millions and even billions of years to bring into existence. Such an order of change in its nature and its order of magnitude has never before entered either into Earth history or into human consciousness.[65]

What story shall we choose to tell for the future? Will it be one of promise? Or the reverse of promise? Of life, or of death? Such questions are those of sacrament as verb. But what I am suggesting here is a wider sense of sacramental action than the canonical seven of the Council of Trent. A home can be a sacrament (we have little trouble seeing that), but can we also understand that what goes on inside a farm, a factory, a subway system, a concert hall, a parliament, or a whole city may be a sacrament as well? Do Los Angeles and New York City still welcome the immigrant? Is the United States still the land of promise? It is time that we took sacraments, signs that give grace, out of the churches and into the open air and public spaces.

It is as if the Master of the Universe, the Holy One, had gone out onto the byways and invited us to a glorious feast, the only condition being that in return for the superb food and drink we have and shall receive so abundantly (i.e., all the transformed energy of the sun), we have to tell a wonderful story for our host, the Poet-Maker of the cosmos. According to Rilke, our task is to tell the "Unsayable One"—or an angel—of "things," things of this earth that we have known, handled, transformed, and loved. These things "want us to change them, utterly, in our invisible heart,/within—oh endlessly—within us! . . . Earth, isn't this what you want: to arise within us/invisible? . . . What, if not transformation, is your urgent command?" Our shared project, I might say, is to move mountains, to make metaphor of this taciturn earth. It is poet's work, the poet-maker in each one of us. We are in this together.

Notes

1. Walter J. Ong, *Faith and Contexts: Selected Essays and Studies 1952-1991,* vol. I, Thomas J. Farrell and Paul A. Soukup, eds. (Atlanta, Ga.: Scholars Press, 1991), 2.

2. Alfred North Whitehead, *Adventures of Ideas* (New York: Macmillan, 1933), 216.

3. See Toulmin, "Cosmology as Science and as Religion" in Leroy S. Rouner, ed., *On Nature* (Notre Dame, Ind.: University of Notre Dame, 1984), 27-41, esp. 28. Also Toulmin's *The Return to Cosmology: Postmodern Science and the Theology of Nature* (Chicago: University of Chicago, 1982), 21-85.

4. Cf. Bernard Lovell, *Emerging Cosmology* (New York: Columbia University, 1981), passim.

5. See Alfred North Whitehead, *Science and the Modern World* (New York: Macmillan, 1926), 1-28, esp. 18-24 where Whitehead argues that without the medieval world's "inexpungnable belief that every detailed occurrence can be correlated with its antecedents in a perfectly definite manner . . . the incredible labours of scientists would be without hope. . . . The faith in the possibility of science . . . is an unconscious derivative from medieval theology."

6. *A Brief History of Time: From the Big Bang to Black Holes* (New York: Bantam Books, 1988), 9. On the crucial test of falsifiability, see Karl Popper, *Conjectures and Refutations,* 2nd ed. (London/New York: Routledge and Kegan Paul, 1965), 33-39.

7. *De Generis ad Litteram,* II.9. For an explication of Augustine's position and an overview of the relation of theology to science, see Ernan McMullin, "How Should Cosmology Relate to Theology?" in Arthur R. Peacocke, ed., *The Sciences and Theology in the Twentieth Century* (Notre Dame, Ind.: University of Notre Dame, 1981), 17-57.

8. See Timothy Ferris, *Coming of Age in the Milky Way* (New York: Doubleday Anchor Books, 1988), 301-334.

9. *A Brief History of Time,* 10-13.

10. See Timothy Ferris, "On the Edge of Chaos," in *The New York Review of Books* (Sept. 21, 1995), 40.

11. For a clear exposition of the "contact" and "consonance" between theology and science, see John Haught, *Science and Religion: From Conflict to Conversation* (New York/Mahwah, N.J.: Paulist Press, 1995), 17-21 et passim. Also Ernan McMullin, Ted Peters, and Robert Russell inter alia in Ted Peters, ed., *Cosmos as Creation: Theology and Science in Consonance* (Nashville, Tenn.: Abingdon, 1989).

    For a counter-argument, that science and religion will always remain at odds, see Brian Appleyard, *Understanding the Present: Science and the Soul of Modern Man* (New York: Doubleday, 1992), esp. 187-235.

12. *De Generis ad Litteram,* II.9.

13. T. S. Eliot, *The Ideal of a Christian Society* (New York: Harcourt Brace, 1940), 62. The reference to Aquinas will be found in *Summa Contra Gentiles* II.3.

14. See Henry Adams, *Mont-Saint-Michel and Chartres* (Boston/New York: Houghton Mifflin, 1913).

15. See Walter J. Ong, *The Presence of the Word: Some Prolegomena for Cultural and Religious History* (Minneapolis: University of Minnesota, 1981 [Yale, 1967]), passim. Also his *Orality and Literacy: The Technologizing of the Word* (London/New York: Metheun, 1982), 5-138. See also Eric A. Havelock, *The Literate Revolution in Greece and Its Cultural Consequences* (Princeton: Princeton University, 1982), passim, and Julian Jaynes, *The Origins of Consciousness in the Breakdown of the Bicameral Mind* (Boston: Houghton Mifflin, 1976).

16. Cited in Thomas Cahill, *How the Irish Saved Civilization: The Untold Story of Ireland's Heroic Role from the Fall of Rome to the Rise of Medieval Europe* (New York: Doubleday, 1995), 116-119.

17. Ibid., 116.

18. See Esther De Waal, ed., *The Celtic Vision: Prayers and Blessings from the Outer Hebrides* (Petersham, Mass.: St. Bede's, 1988), esp. 160-170. See also James Charles Roy, *Islands of Storm* (Chester Springs, Penn.: Dufour Editions, 1991).

19. When Gary Zukav *(The Dancing Wu Li Masters,* 1979) and Fritjof Capra *(The Tao of Physics,* 1975) interpret the "new physics" in an Eastern, monistic direction, Protestants tend to object. See Chapter 9, "The Environmental Movement: Searching for a New Religion" in Loren Wilkinson, ed., *Earthkeeping in the Nineties: Stewardship of Creation* (Grand Rapids, Mich.: William B. Eerdmans, 1991), 181-199. Catholics seem more at ease with the mystical language of oneness.

20. Owen Barfield, *Saving the Appearances: A Study in Idolatry,* 2nd ed. (Middletown, Conn.: Wesleyan University, 1988 [1965]), 76-77.

21. Ibid., 79-80.

22. Ibid., 78.

23. See Walter J. Ong, *Orality and Literacy,* 78-135. Also Michel Serres, "Lucretius: Science & Religion," in *Hermes: Literature, Science, Philosophy,* Josue V. Harari and David F. Bell, eds. (Baltimore: The Johns Hopkins University, 1982), 98-124, esp. 100.

24. I am far from wanting to romanticize the psychology of an oral culture; it is inclined to impulsivity and going beserk—as illustrated in contemporary Rwanda and Sudan. See Walter J. Ong, *Fighting for Life: Contest, Sexuality, and Consciousness* (Ithaca/New York: Cornell University, 1981), 51-96. Also Owen Barfield, *History, Guilt, and Habit* (Middletown, Conn.: Wesleyan University, 1979), passim. Also his *Saving the Appearances,* 92-95, 116-132.

25. John Donne, "An Anatomie of the World."

26. *Science and the Modern World,* 80.

27. Jacques Monod, *Chance and Necessity* (New York: Vintage Books, 1972), 172-173.

28. From *Being to Becoming: Time and Complexity in the Physical Sciences* (San Francisco: W. H. Freeman, 1980), xvii.

29. *Commonweal* (Sept. 23, 1994), 11; see also Raymo's *Honey from a Stone: A Naturalist's Search for God* (New York: Dodd Mead, 1987), x.

30. *Saving the Appearances,* 167

31. Ibid., 168.

32. *A Brief History of Time,* 36–39.

33. See Ian G. Barbour, *Religion in an Age of Science* (San Francisco: Harper & Row, 1990), 128–135. See also Ernan McMullin, "How Should Cosmology Relate to Theology?" op. cit., 28–40.

34. *A Brief History of Time,* 141. Cf. 132–140.

35. Northrop Frye, *The Great Code: The Bible and Literature* (New York: Harcourt Brace Jovanovich, 1982), 17–18.

36. *A Brief History of Time,* 37.

37. Carl Sagan, *The Dragons of Eden: Speculations on the Evolution of Human Intelligence* (New York: Random House, 1977), 14–16.

38. See John D. Barrow and Frank J. Tipler, *The Anthropic Cosmological Principle* (New York: Oxford University, 1986).

39. *A Brief History of Time,* 12.

40. See Barbour, op. cit., 135–136, 144–146.

41. *A Brief History of Time,* 124.

42. Thomas Berry, *A Dream of the Earth* (San Francisco: Sierra Club, 1988), 16.

43. *A Brief History of Time,* 1.

44. Thomas S. Kuhn, *The Structure of Scientific Revolutions* (Chicago: University of Chicago, 1962). For the argument that we are in the midst of just such a paradigm shift, see Erich Jantsch, *The Self-Organizing Universe: Scientific and Human Implications of the Emerging Paradigm of Evolution* (New York: Pergamon, 1980).

45. On the reluctance of physics to deal with time, see Lancelot Law Whyte, *The Unconscious Before Freud* (New York: St. Martin's, 1978), 53–57. Also Ilya Prigogine and Isabelle Stengers, *Order Out of Chaos: Man's New Dialogue with Nature* (New York: Bantam Books, 1984), 27–77.

46. See Heinz R. Pagels, *The Cosmic Code: Quantum Physics as the Language of Nature* (New York: Simon and Schuster, 1982). Also Nick Herbert, *Quantum Reality: Beyond the New Physics* (Garden City, N.Y.: Anchor/Doubleday, 1985). Cf. also Timothy Ferris, *Coming of Age in the Milky Way,* 285–299, and Stephen Hawking, *A Brief History of Time,* 63–79.

47. *A Brief History of Time,* 55.

48. James Lovelock, *Gaia: A New Look at Life on Earth* (New York: Oxford University, 1979, revised 1987).

49. Lewis Thomas, *The Lives of a Cell: Notes of a Biology Watcher* (New York: Bantam, 1975), 2ff.

50. For a lucid account of this material, see Jeremy Campbell, *Grammatical Man: Information, Entropy, Language and Life* (New York: Simon and Schuster, 1982).

51. Michel Serres, "The Origin of Language: Biology, Information Theory, & Thermodynamics" in *Hermes,* 1982, 83.

52. For an intelligible account, see James Gleick, *Chaos: Making a New Science* (New York: Viking, 1987). Also Roger Lewin, *Complexity: Life at the Edge of Chaos* (New York: Macmillan, 1992) and Murray Gell-Mann, *The Quark and the Jaguar: Adventures in the Simple and Complex* (San Francisco: W. H. Freeman, 1995).

   For a visual image of the beauty of "chaotic" patterns, see John Briggs, *Fractals: The Patterns of Chaos, A New Aesthetic of Art, Science and Nature* (New York: Simon and Schuster, 1992).

53. Cf. Timothy Ferris, "On the Edge of Chaos," in *The New York Review of Books* (Sept. 21, 1995), 40.

54. See Ilya Prigogine and Isabelle Stengers, *Order Out of Chaos: Man's New Dialogue with Nature* (New York: Bantam, 1984), 131-209. Their chapters on "Rediscovering Time" (213-232) and "From Earth to Heaven—The Reenchantment of Nature" (291-313) in this volume also address this.

55. Cf. Serres, op. cit., 73-76.

56. Ibid., 74-75.

57. Ibid., 75.

58. Rainer Maria Rilke, *The Enlightened Heart: An Anthology of Sacred Poetry*, Stephen Mitchell, ed. (New York: Harper & Row, 1989), 144.

59. See Larry Dossey, *Space, Time & Medicine* (Boulder, Colo.: Shambala, 1982), 72-81.

60. Serres, Ibid., 77.

61. The basic idea of this paragraph comes from Timothy Ferris, *Coming of Age in the Milky Way*, 138-401.

62. Rilke, "Ninth Duino Elegy," in Mitchell, ed., op. cit., 140.

63. Ibid., 141.

64. See John Dominic Crossan, *The Historical Jesus: The Life of a Mediterranean Jewish Peasant* (San Francisco: Harper San Francisco, 1991), 303-353.

65. Thomas Berry, *Dream of the Earth*, xiii.

THE SACRAMENTALITY OF CREATION AND THE ROLE OF CREATION IN LITURGY AND SACRAMENTS

Kevin W. Irwin

MY PURPOSE IN THIS ESSAY IS TO ARTICULATE SOME OF THE THEOLOGICAL issues that lie at the heart of liturgical and sacramental celebration regarding the sacramentality of creation and the use of creation in worship. I will deal with (1) liturgical theology in general; (2) the interrelatedness of liturgy, sacraments, creation, and human life; (3) how creation is used in the liturgy since Vatican II; (4) the contemporary convergence between liturgical and creation theology; and (5) some critique of the liturgy regarding creation. The argument throughout is, in the main, from within the Roman Catholic tradition.

Liturgical Theology

The phrase *legem credendi lex statuat supplicandi*[1] (dated between 435–442 and generally ascribed to Prosper of Aquitaine)[2] has become something of a theme statement for many contemporary liturgists and sacramental theologians engaged in developing a method to articulate the theological meaning of the liturgy and the theology that can be derived from liturgical enactment.[3]

While there is no agreed-upon meaning for "liturgical theology," two general meanings are operative in much contemporary writing.[4] First, liturgical theology is considered to be a reflection on the Church's act of worship that draws out and explores in catechesis and systematic theology (particularly sacramental theology) the theological meaning of the liturgy: the actualization of the paschal mystery for the believing Church through an act of proclaiming and hearing the word and celebrating sacramental rituals. Second, liturgical theology means using the liturgy as a source for systematic theology in the sense that the theological meaning of terms and concepts operate theologically in liturgy; for example, God, Christ, Spirit, redemption, salvation, and sanctification can be probed for their theological meaning as derived from their use in liturgy.

The uniqueness of liturgy as fundamentally a *ritual action* is clearly understood and respected here with the result that the texts of the liturgy are not regarded as equivalent to other sources of positive theology (e.g., scripture, magisterium). Liturgical texts accompany symbolic actions and ritual gestures, and it is only through these elements together that theological and spiritual meanings are disclosed. The fact that the Church celebrates liturgy in order to experience the paschal mystery in a ritual event suggests both how important liturgy is as a source for theology and also the difficulty in delineating an acceptable method for engaging in liturgical theology.

More recently, many liturgists and sacramental theologians[5] have argued in favor of expanding the *lex orandi, lex credendi* equation to include *lex agendi* so that the method of liturgical theology would include a critique of the present revised liturgy in light of liturgical tradition and contemporary needs. At present at least two meanings of *agendi* are commonly emphasized.

Actual Celebrations as a Theological Source

A number of contemporary proposals for liturgical method address the phenomenon of liturgy as *enacted* rites. These proposals point to the importance of using enacted liturgical rites as sources, *orandi*, from which to determine the Church's belief, *credendi*. Thus, contemporary emphasis on *liturgy as event* sets the framework for developing a method in liturgical theology that deals with more than texts and with the texts themselves in the context of the liturgical action.[6] Such an investigation would consider how effectively the scriptures are proclaimed, prayed over, and preached, and how effectively they lead to the rest of the ritual, including the sacramental action that occurs through using elements from creation and euchological texts. This investigation would also consider to what extent symbolic interaction has been realized in the liturgy and to what extent the maximizing of symbolic engagement, as expressed in the general instructions (*praenotandae*) that accompany the rites as presently revise does in fact occur.[7] For example, this investigation would call for asking whether baptism by immersion rather than infusion occurs commonly.

Another factor adding to the rationale of why a new method for engaging in liturgical theology is necessary is the nature of the present reform of the liturgy in Roman Catholicism and in other Christian Churches which include the variety and flexibility of rites and texts within a ritual structure and the necessity of adapting, accommodating, and inculturating even this reformed liturgy.[8] On one level the variety possible in the reformed liturgy concerns *how* the liturgy is prepared and actually celebrated. The next level (of particular interest here) concerns how the celebration of the reformed liturgy is used as the source for liturgical theology developed from such varied rites. Attention moves beyond the texts found in ceremonial books to the shape and components of actual liturgical celebration where celebration provides the requisite context within which to interpret liturgical texts, symbolic actions, ritual gestures.[9]

In addition to asking the question of "what is experienced" in actual liturgical rites, most liturgists who study the contemporary rites also inquire whether what is offered in the revised liturgy reflects the faith vision enunciated at Vatican II. The question pertains also to subsequent church documents calling for and shaping the reform of the liturgy, as well as to the general instructions that accompany the revised rituals.[10] Thus the corollary of using actual celebrations as a theological source is evaluating the adequacy of liturgical celebrations in terms of what is said and enacted liturgically. This aspect of contemporary liturgical study is often termed the "critical function" of liturgical theology.[11]

Liturgy and Ethics

This second meaning of *lex agendi* concerns living out in life the implications of liturgical participation, a relationship that has traditionally been understood to constitute the act of worship. It recalls the work of pioneers in the liturgical movement who argued for an appreciation of liturgy that concerned the renewal of the Church's whole life and the spiritual lives of those who participate.[12]

In this understanding, liturgical theology also addresses how what occurs in liturgy is reflected in the lives of its participants. The *lex orandi, lex credendi* axiom also gives attention to the *lex agendi* beyond actual celebration to what is sometimes called the *lex vivendi*[13]—how what is celebrated and believed is reflected in how the Church lives its faith. Hence the two foci of *lex orandi* and *lex credendi* yield a third element to the equation: *lex vivendi*, the life relation of the liturgy.[14]

Our argument deriving theological meanings from *enacted* rites means paying attention to creation as cited in liturgical texts, to how creation itself offers motives for praising God, to how creation itself is a demonstration of the divine in human life. It means attending to how the present reformed liturgy reflects a positive regard for the things of this earth simply because they are used in worship. The *vivendi* aspect of contemporary liturgical method can locate our inquiry into ecological awareness and concern as germane to liturgical theology and concomitant with celebrating liturgy.

Liturgy, Sacraments, Creation, and Human Life

Among the underlying philosophical presuppositions and theological principles for considering liturgy as a privileged source for creation theology is the anthropological aptness[15] of liturgical and sacramental acts in terms of their constitutive elements. The use in worship of speech, gesture, elements of nature, and symbols that are the result of human manufacture is most fitting because these constitutive aspects of worship draw on commonly accepted aspects of human life, things from creation used in daily experience or actions regularly performed in life. For example, the use of water in baptism builds on the act of bathing, the use of bread and wine in the eucharist presumes the act of dining, the use of oil in the anointing of the sick presumes the human act of salving one's skin. In other words, these "daily and domestic things" in human life, to use David Power's term, are the anthropological substratum for the liturgical/sacramental event.[16]

Some distinctions need to be made concerning the constitutive elements of liturgy and sacraments, for example, between words and symbols. On one level one may cautiously distinguish words from symbols because words are the means of verbal communication and symbols are the means of nonverbal interaction; yet, on another level as we will soon see, words themselves are symbols. A further distinction can be made between symbols that are derived from nature (e.g., water) and symbols that are the result of human productivity (e.g., bread and wine). That liturgy uses words and symbols together in a repertoire of ritual activity is to acknowledge the anthropological rootedness of worship in human life and particularly in human behavior. The joint use of words and symbols in worship is respectful of the human person and the means humans use for communication and interaction.

In this connection, Louis Marie Chauvet argues for a symbolic understanding of both word and creation as used in worship.[17] If the literal meaning of the Greek term *symballein* is "to throw together" and the noun form is "that which is thrown together," then the liturgy of the word at its most profound level is "symbolic." The liturgy of the word is a "symbolic rehearsal of salvation" in the sense that the repeated hearing and appropriation of the word implies the requisite response of the faith assembly. The literal meaning of the Greek verb implies that symbols require a response from one already in a relationship of shared meaning; in liturgy this means shared faith. The purpose of the scriptural word is to place in relationship, to encounter the other, to reunite that which ought to be understood together. One can argue that the notion of "symbolic language" is redundant in the sense that the word as a medium for communication implies a speaking to and a response by those addressed. What is offered in the symbolic word requires a response of acceptance, encounter, and appropriation. Similarly, symbols from material creation are themselves elements that by their nature require a response by the believing community.

What is central here is the *use* of symbols taken from creation and the *symbolic engagement* in worship made possible by the use of creation. Such engagement is opposed to *objectification* of symbols or their reduction to being *signs* since both objectification and signs most usually convey *one* meaning and have a one-to-one correspondence with what they signify. On the other hand, the polyvalent meanings intrinsically attached to symbolic engagement are all unleashed in liturgy by the very fact that elements from creation and symbolic actions are used. These meanings can be either positive or negative.[18] In sacramental celebration, some of these meanings are articulated verbally in the blessing prayers that accompany symbolic usage. Hence the theological value of euchology (i.e., blessing prayers, especially the eucharistic prayer and other presidential prayers). Generally these significations are derived from salvation history wherein these events are paradigmatic and applicable in the present through the experience of liturgy. These meanings from salvation history most often articulate obvious positive meanings; sometimes they give a positive dimension to what would otherwise be understood as negative.[19] The variety of meanings present in such texts, when appropriated into a liturgical theology of what is celebrated, gives direction to the polyvalent meanings inherent in the use of symbols.

In addition, the use of symbols from creation has the effect of expressing what is really inexpressible—that liturgy draws us into an ever deepening relationship with God in the manifold ways that salvation can be understood and reflected in liturgical prayer texts. Thus, the use of water in initiation is meant to evoke its pluriform meanings through the act of washing; the act draws those bathed in water into a relationship with God, through Christ's paschal mystery in the power of the Spirit enacted in the Church.

Furthermore, the use of symbols that result from human productivity, for example, bread and wine, point to the theological meaning of the use of elements from creation that require human ingenuity for their manufacture. The classical argument that bread and wine are constitutive of the eucharist suggests (at least on one level) that human intelligence and ingenuity also form part of the reality of the liturgy. This example implies and underscores the importance of the agrarian cycle of planting and harvesting and the acts of refining wheat into grains, mixing ingredients for the dough (including "destroying" the grains to make the dough and the dough rising, usually twice before baking) and baking that signify that human work is necessary for the eucharist to take place. This prizing of human productivity also conveys the theological value of such work. "No work, no worship." In the current debate, however, bread and wine are not regarded as necessarily constitutive. Arguments in favor of "staple food" and "festive drink" replace the convenient "bread and wine" couplet in such discussions. Such an adjustment to alternate foods should not, however, diminish the value of our argument about human ingenuity and productivity, in particular the cycles of nature and agrarian "dying and rising."[20]

The fact that liturgy rests on symbolic words and a symbolic use of created elements from human life articulates for Christians that God is discoverable in human life and that the encounter with God in liturgy derives from and returns to human life. One of the purposes of the graced events of liturgy and sacraments is to experience Christ's mediation of salvation to the believing Church. This mediation occurs through the power of the Spirit in ritual actions that derive from the incarnational principle that the Christian God is experienced in all life through the eyes of faith (for example, in seven sacraments, in praying the liturgy of the hours, in rites of profession and burial).

One of the purposes of liturgy and sacraments is to articulate how God is experienced as savior in and through the liturgy and how this same God is discoverable and discovered in the rest of life. The patristic maxim *caro salutis est cardo* (the flesh is the instrument of salvation) grounds the act of liturgy as based on human means of communication and self-expression.[21] Put in more explicitly theological language, the principles of incarnation and mediation are articulated in the act of liturgy and the act of liturgy continues the mediation of salvation in explicit ways (again in seven sacraments, in praying the liturgy of the hours, in rites of profession and burial).

In our argument, priority is always given to symbolic engagement and liturgical participation through symbol as means used to draw the community to share more fully in the mystery of God, a communion that can be imaged in a number of ways and experienced through the use of symbol. The objectification of given symbolic elements used in liturgy, for example, bread and wine for the eucharist, can paradoxically diminish the *reality* of the symbols on which sacramental liturgy and liturgical theology are based for at least two reasons.

First, because symbolic elements complement the symbolic word as essentially dialogic realities, to emphasize symbols as objects reduces, for example, the essentially dialogic character of consecrated bread and wine as a specification of having shared in the proclaimed word, which itself is inherently dialogical, and of Christ's paschal mystery as presented in the texts of the preface and eucharistic prayer. The act of communion signifies the ratification on the human's part of the offer of Christ through these symbolic means. Bread and wine are consecrated to be eaten and drunk by those who participate. This traditional tenet of Roman Catholic theology and practice is in the canons of the Council of Trent which note that the eucharist, by its nature, is "to be received" (*ut sumatur* [cf. Mt 26:26] *insitiutum*, DS 1643). "To put it another way: the first truth of the eucharistic doctrine is, 'this is my body,' not 'here I am present.' "[22]

Second, because the presumed ecclesial community for whom symbols function in liturgy is often left out of a theology based on objectified symbols, such as real presence, there is a diminished ecclesiological aspect to eucharistic theology that is all the more jarring since the eucharistic prayers that have been added to the Roman rite in the present reform all contain explicit epicleses about drawing the church community into deeper unity. These prayers are legitimately used to illustrate the traditional (often termed "Augustinian") emphasis placed on church unity as deepened through eucharistic sharing and as specified in other euchological texts, the prayers over the gifts, and prayers after communion.[23] That the text of 1 Corinthians 11:23-32 about the one bread signifying church unity is based on the image of one loaf being shared by all is a significant illustration of the range of meanings that can be derived from the use of creation and symbol in worship. Most fitting is the way the prayer in the *Didache* 9:4 elaborates on the symbolic meaning of broken bread when it refers to the process of human ingenuity involved in how bread is manufactured: "As this broken bread was scattered over the mountains, and when brought together became one, so let your Church be brought together from the ends of the earth into your kingdom."[24]

Thus, in our understanding the operative notion of symbol in the liturgy is dynamic; it involves and ultimately transforms the community. Consequently, the liturgical theology derived from symbols used in the context of the liturgy simply cannot concern "objects" alone. Nor can it refer to symbols, especially those from creation, simply as a means to an experience of God. To use creation in liturgy is to show reverence for creation through, with, and in which the incarnate God is disclosed and discovered. The use of material creation in the liturgy has traditionally been understood to reflect back to the creator and to imply an understanding that rests on the sound foundation of theological anthropology.[25] The use of creation in the liturgy overcomes the problem of the spiritual/material dualism sometimes found in theology.[26]

In the case of the theological anthropology of liturgy and sacraments, representative Roman Catholic thought in a similar vein asserts:

A sacrament is not a stand-in for something else, a visible sign for some other invisible reality. The essence of a sacrament is the capacity to reveal grace, the agapic self-gift of God, by being what it is. By being thoroughly itself, a sacrament bodies forth the absolute self-donative love of God that undergirds both it and the entirety of creation. By its nature a sacrament requires that it be appreciated for what it is and not as a tool to an end; in Buber's terms, a sacrament is always "thou."[27]

Thus part of the fundamental anthropological and theological foundation upon which the act of liturgy is based is the use of creation and symbolic interaction through which means the divine is disclosed and faith in the divine is shaped and renewed in the Church. If one of the purposes of liturgy and sacraments is to give voice and expression to the inarticulate but nonetheless real praise of God in creation by the very use of creation in worship, it is the purpose of the next two sections of this paper to articulate some of the ways in which the present revised liturgy does this. *Lex orandi* will be used to indicate directions for a *lex credendi*, wherein the role of creation in liturgy and sacraments is emphasized, and of *lex vivendi* about living out in all of life what was celebrated in the liturgy.

Contemporary Lex Orandi: How Creation Is Used

Times for Celebration

The determination of times for celebration[28] of the daily liturgy of the hours, the seasons of the church year, and some feast days derive from the rhythm of the cosmos. The determination of dawn for morning prayer and dusk for evening prayer is underscored in the General Instruction on the Hours, which states that morning prayer is "celebrated . . . as the light of a new day is dawning" (no. 38). It is appropriate that Zechariah's canticle is always used at this hour:

The dawn from on high shall break upon us,
to shine on those who dwell in darkness
    and the shadow of death. . . . (Lk 1:79)

It is not a coincidence that this same text is used as the communion antiphon for the Solemnity of the Birth of John the Baptist since the date of this feast, June 24, was deliberately chosen in accord with the length of the sun's rays as experienced in the northern hemisphere.[29] Just as the daylight begins to diminish after June 21 (often called "the longest day of the year"), the Church commemorates the birth of the Baptist whose saying "Jesus must increase, but I must decrease" (Jn 3:30) determined the date for this commemoration. The sign of diminishing daylight in the cosmos has determined the feast of the one whose self-effacement ("decrease") led to people's putting their faith in Christ ("the dawn from on high"). That this feast has a rich tradition of liturgical importance is attested to by the fact that the only other births commemorated in the calendar are those of Jesus and the Blessed Virgin Mary. Its significance is further emphasized by the number of Mass formulas honoring the Baptist in the (very early) Verona collection of euchology.[30] In the present Sacramentary, moreover, the only saints who have their own preface besides John the Baptist are the Blessed Virgin Mary, St. Joseph (March 19), and Saints Peter and Paul (June 29).

With regard to evening prayer the same instruction states that "when evening approaches and the day is already far spent, evening prayer is celebrated . . . [when] we join the Churches of the East in calling upon the 'joy-giving light of holy glory'. . . [and we sing in praise] now that we have come to the setting of the sun and seen the evening star. . ." (no. 39). The Jewish tradition of the *lucernarium*, the lighting of the lamps in the Temple at evening prayer, is also part of the liturgical ritual traditionally attached to this hour.[31]

The phases of the moon and its location determine the date for our celebration of Easter.[32] The diminishing of the intensity of the sun in the northern hemisphere is reflected in the lectionary and euchology of Advent and Christmas, which texts become the more compelling when this natural phenomenon is recalled and experienced. Part of the Johannine Prologue, the traditional Gospel on Christmas morning, states:

> The light shines on in darkness
> a darkness that did not overcome it. (Jn 1:5)[33]

The following euchological texts now used at Christmas and Epiphany are the more notable when their cosmic context is recalled.

> Father,
> you make this holy night radiant
> with the splendor of Jesus Christ
> our light.
> (Opening Prayer, Mass at Midnight)[34]

> Father,
> we are filled with new light
> by the coming of your Word among us.
> (Opening Prayer, Mass at Dawn)[35]

> In the wonder of the incarnation
> your eternal Word has brought to the eyes of faith

a new and radiant vision of your glory.
(Christmas Preface I)[36]

Today in him a new light has dawned upon the world.
(Christmas Preface III)[37]

Today you revealed in Christ your eternal plan of salvation
and showed him as the light of all peoples.
(Epiphany Preface)[38]

The addition of the Isaiah 9:1-6 ("A people who walked in darkness have seen a great light") to the traditional scripture readings for Midnight Mass (Ti 2:11-14 and Lk 2:10-11) also underscores the light symbolism of Christmas.

It is commonly asserted that a preexisting (pagan) feast of ingathering the first fruits of the fall harvest influenced Judaism's practice of celebrating *sukkoth* ("tabernacles" or "booths") as a fall festival of covenant renewal.[39] This same idea is congenial in Christianity with celebrations commemorating the "first fruits of creation" in the apocalyptic and eschatological themes reflected in the Lectionary for Mass prior to and on the First Sunday of Advent. The second reading on the Last Sunday of the Year "B" cycle (the Solemnity of Christ the King) contains the text "Jesus Christ is the faithful witness, the first-born from the dead and ruler of the kings of earth" (Rv 1:5).[40]

That the Johannine prologue (read on Christmas day) uses a variation on the word "booths" or "tabernacles" is also significant; it acclaims that "the Word . . . made his dwelling among us" (Jn 1:14). The verb form in Greek is literally "he set up his tent" or "he tabernacled" among us. (Though it is not part of the historical rationale that led to the commemoration of All Saints and All Souls at this time of year, our present celebration of All Saints and All Souls is connected with the theme of "first fruits of creation.")

Motivation for Celebration

Praise to God the creator[41] is constitutive of the theology of the liturgy of the hours. For example, a hymn of praise for the days of creation was assigned to ferial vespers for each day (except First Vespers of Sunday) in the former breviary.[42] This usage is retained in the *editio typica* of the present revision. These texts, probably from the same author (some would say Gregory the Great), devote four stanzas to the work of each day of creation. Sunday's vesper hymn, *Lucis creator optime*, which reflects the light and darkness motif of evening prayer, begins with the following verses:

O blest Creator of the light,
Who mak'st the day with radiance bright,
And o'er the forming world didst call
The light from chaos first of all;
Whose wisdom joined in meet array
The more and eve, and named them Day:
Night comes with all its darkling fears;
Regard thy people's prayers and tears.[43]

The rest of the vesper hymns reflecting praise for the days of creation are *Immense coeli Conditor*, "O great Creator of the sky" (Monday);[44] *Telluris alme Conditor*, "Earth's mighty maker, whose command/ Raised from the sea the solid land" (Tuesday); *Caeli Deus sanctissime*, "O God whose hand hath spread the sky, And all its shining hosts on high" (Wednesday); *Magnae Deus potentiae*, "O Sovereign Lord of nature's might, Who bad'st the water's birth divide; Part in the heaens to take their flight, And part in ocean's deep to hide" (Thursday); and *Hominis supernae Conditor*, "Maker of man, who from Thy throne,/Dost order all things, God alone" (Friday). The hymn for First Vespers of Sunday, *Iam sol recedit igneus*, by a different author (perhaps St. Ambrose), moves from the days of creation to praising the Trinity[45] in the morning and evening.[46]

What makes the retention of these hymns in the *editio typica* of the revised breviary of particular note is that in the present structure for evening prayer the third "psalm" is actually a christological hymn from the New Testament, two of which deal specifically with praise for creation. One could make a case for the appropriate juxtaposition at this hour of praise for the days of creation and for our re-creation in Christ. Because these hymns specify Christ in connection with praise for creation, any "generic deism" associating the Christian God with creation is avoided. (More will be said below about these christological hymns.)

At Sunday morning prayer the use of the canticle from Daniel 3 (vv. 57-88, 56 are used Sunday week I and vv. 52-57 are used Sunday weeks II and IV) is significant in this connection. The opening verse: "Bless the Lord, all you works of the Lord/praise and exalt him above all forever" (v. 57) is followed by a series of acclamations citing various facets of creation and redemption as motives for praising God. These include verses about praise for creation[47] and praise for redemption,[48] with praise for redemption ending the canticle.[49] These same motives for praising God are found in much of the psalter, and in the present arrangement of the hours "praise psalms" are used as the third psalm at morning prayer, many of which contain explicit praise of God for creation (e.g., Ps 19, 29, 65, 147, 148, 150).[50]

That the liturgy of the hours classically begins with Psalm 94, parallelling the combined themes of praising God for creation and redemption, is an additional illustration of acclaiming the God of creation.[51] Two phrases from the *Te Deum* (used at the conclusion of the office of readings on most Sundays and solemnities) capture and summarize this theology:

> All creation worships you. . . .
> Holy, holy, holy, Lord, God of power and might,
> heaven and earth are full of your glory.

Fittingly, these last two lines are repeated in the preface acclamation (*Sanctus*) in the present eucharistic prayers. These prayers praise God for the *mirabilia Dei*,[52] especially in creation and redemption; they are derived from the "blessing" (*berakah*) and "thanksgiving" (*todah*) traditions of Jewish prayer.[53]

> Appropriately, our song is a quotation from the seraphim who surround God's throne with fiery praise. While in the Jerusalem temple, Isaiah sees a vision of God's transcendent holiness, and the angels are singing "Holy, Holy, Holy Lord, God" (Isa 6:3). Again in the Apocalypse the creatures around the heavenly throne join the angels in chanting: "Holy, Holy, Holy is the Lord God Almighty"(Rev 4:8). Both visions attest God's majesty. In Isaiah, all space, heaven and earth, is filled with God; in Revelation, all time—past, present, and future—is filled with the Lord.[54]

This acclamation combines praise for creation with praise for redemption and specifies the obedient life, death, and resurrection of Jesus. This combination of themes is part of the "classical" shape of eucharistic anaphoras,[55] even though this motif is all too briefly expressed.[56]

The theology operative in the fourth eucharistic prayer in the present Sacramentary concerns praising God who has made all things and who is the source of all life.[57] It brings out the universal need for the paschal mystery and the universal effects that flow from it.[58] The preface to this prayer refers to the entire creation and to the Father as the ultimate source of creation and the one who is manifested in creation. Human beings fulfill the purpose of creation in giving voice to creation's praise of God by joining in the praise that is voiced in liturgy,[59] in particular the eucharist. This prayer is a worldview in a capsule form.

> Because of the goodness of the Father, the Church joins in the hymn of the angels. All other creatures on earth are enabled to express their praise through

the voices of those in the Church who speak for the mute creatures. Thus the praise takes on cosmic proportions.[60]

An important example of how praising God for creation functions as a motive for giving thanks, recounting the fall, and establishing why humankind needed a savior is found in the *Apostolic Constitutions,* Book VIII.[61] Significantly, this prayer concerns praising God for creation, for sustaining in life all that God has created, for the history of salvation, and for sending Jesus as redeemer. Its christological section capitalizes on a number of paradoxes, notably the statement that he who was present at creation is now "the firstborn of all creation."

In the liturgy, the value of creation, as reflecting the power of God and as the arena in which divine salvation overturns universal estrangement from God, is exemplified by the selection of the first creation account, Genesis 1:1–2:2, as the first reading at the Easter Vigil.[62] The recounting of this text, which is allied with other such texts called "cosmogonic myths,"[63] praises God the creator, redeemer, and sustainer of all life.[64] It has special poignancy because it accompanies the annual recreation of the earth in the spring. Its repetition reflects the belief that the act of creation is not simply what happened once in history but something eternally accomplished by God's creative word.[65] In fact, one could argue that this text really recounts what God intended in creation, not what really resulted, and that its annual proclamation at Easter facilitates an interpretation that creation happens still among us through Christ even as we yearn for the "new heavens and a new earth." The texts of the prayers that follow this reading at the Easter vigil are significant:

Almighty and eternal God,
you created all things in wonderful beauty and order.
Help us now to perceive
how still more wonderful is the new creation
by which in the fullness of time
you redeemed your people
through the sacrifice of our passover, Jesus Christ. . . .[66]

Lord, God,
the creation of man was a wonderful work,
his redemption still more wonderful.
May we persevere in right reason
against all that entices to sin
and so attain to everlasting joy.[67]

At the very beginning of the (preface to the) Roman canon, the Roman liturgy has traditionally used the title *Domine, sancte Pater, omnipotens et aeternae Deus,*[68] containing the three dominant names for God found in most contemporary prayers.[69] Fittingly, the last phrase of the preface contains the phrase (from Is 6:3) and leads to naming God in the following way: *Sanctus, sanctus, sanctus Dominus Deus Sabaoth. Pleni sunt caeli et terra gloria tua* (discussed above).

The mediating function of creation is exemplified in its specific *christological* sense in the liturgical use of such scripture texts as the Johannine prologue (Jn 1:1-14) used on Christmas day and the christological hymn in the letter to the Colossians (1:15-20, specifically vv. 15-18) used as one of the New Testament hymns at evening prayer. According to the Johannine prologue, God's creative idea is the Logos, the second divine person. The "high" christology of the preexistent Logos in the prologue and the introductory words of the prologue "in the beginning" (recalling the first words of Genesis as used at the Easter vigil) combine to underscore how Christ was present and active at the creation of the world. Verse 3 summarizes this by stating, "Through him all things came into being, and apart from him nothing came to be." The recreation of the world was accomplished through the same Christ, cited at the prologue's end as "the Word [who] became flesh, and made his dwelling among us, and we have seen his glory, filled with enduring love" (v. 14).

Similarly, the Colossians hymn (1:12-20) emphasizes how Christ is preexistent. The purpose of all creation consists in our union with Christ and through him with the Father, the origin and fulfillment of all creation, including humanity. Of particular note is verse 16: "In him everything in heaven and on earth was created, things visible and invisible . . . all things were created through him." Thus we can assert that the stated motivation for (praise in) liturgy is from creation and redemption and that the dynamic of Christian liturgy is to offer back creation to the Creator through Christ, the co-creator.[70]

This emphasis on the christological axis of liturgy, specifically the paschal mystery, has recently been appropriately supplemented by a pneumatologically rich emphasis on liturgy and sacraments as experiences through and in which the Church is drawn into the life of the triune God. All liturgy is triune. It is the triune God who makes it occur. Just as Jürgen Moltmann can rightly argue that creation is the result of the power and life of the Spirit, thus ending what perhaps can be regarded as too christological an approach to how God creates, so we can emphasize how the liturgy is dependent on the dynamism of the Trinity (particularly when understood both immanently and economically[71]). The renewed emphasis on the theological meaning of the epiclesis in the eucharistic anaphoras added to the Roman rite in the present reform and in all other blessing prayers (e.g., to bless water at initiation, etc.) gives added stimulus to the theological elaboration of the role of the Trinity, and particularly of the Spirit, in all liturgy. It is the triune God who gathers the assembly into the praying Church ("the family you have gathered here before you"[72]). In addition to the use of the indicative mood in verbs in the anaphora, the use of the subjunctive characterizes the epiclesis. When the text of the second eucharistic prayer reads:

> Let your Spirit come upon these gifts to make them holy,
> so that they may become for us
> the body and blood of our Lord, Jesus Christ. . . .
> May all of us who share in the body and blood of Christ
> be brought together in the unity of the Holy Spirit.[73]

The *lex orandi* of the Roman rite overcomes the weakness of the lack of an explicit epiclesis in the Roman canon and draws on a wider euchological tradition to substantiate the addition of such texts which explicitly invoke the Spirit with the deferential verb form the subjunctive.[74] Such usages illustrate the central importance of understanding liturgy as initiated by, sustained in, and reaching its perfection in the Trinity.

Explicit faith in the Trinity is also illustrated in the creed:[75]

> Credo in unum Deum,
> Patrem omnipotentem, factorem caeli et terrae
> visibilium omnium et invisibilium
> Et in unum Dominum Iesum Christum . . .
> per quem omnia facta sunt . . .
> Et in Spiritum Sanctum, Dominum et vivificantem

Thus, the act of creation is not limited to the Father; it is equally christological and pneumatological.[76]

That the Christian Church has traditionally used the doxology to end the psalms at the hours and now also uses it to end the New Testament hymns at evening prayer[77] is another explicit attestation of the role of the Trinity in the liturgy. When the doxology is added to Psalm 94, a happy coincidence of praising the triune God for creation occurs. The text of the original doxology: "Glory to the Father, through the Son in the (unity of the) Holy Spirit . . ." is especially applicable because of its connotation of the Church being drawn into and abiding in the Trinity.

Water: The Use of Symbols

The methodological concern in this section is merely to illustrate the importance of the use of symbols in liturgy as derived from the general instruction of a given rite and from the liturgical ritual itself. The specific example chosen is water as described and used in the present Rite of the Christian Initiation of Adults (hereafter RCIA).[78]

Symbolic Use: The general instruction on Christian initiation states that "the water used in baptism should be true water and, both for the sake of authentic sacramental symbolism and for hygienic reasons, [it] should be pure and clean" (no. 8).[79] "The baptismal font . . . should be spotlessly clean and of pleasing design" (no. 9). These texts overturn centuries of usage (from Trent on) when the baptismal water blessed at the Easter vigil was stored in baptisteries to be used for a whole year. Water's freshness and life-giving properties are underscored in this rubrical change. Now, the water blessed at Easter is used only during the Easter season in which case a "thanksgiving" prayer for water already blessed is used. The instruction goes on to explain how the water will be used in the act of water baptism: "either immersion, which is more suitable as a symbol of participation in the death and resurrection of Christ, or pouring may lawfully be used" (no. 22). Thus, the water blessing leads to water being used in the baptismal bathing with water.

The rite for adult initiation offers three texts for blessing the water and two for offering thanksgiving for the blessed water. The rubrics for the first of these prayers state that toward the end of the prayer (after recounting a host of images about the use of water in salvation history), the celebrant "touches the water with his right hand." This simple rubric suggests that the freshness and life-giving properties of water are to be emphasized by hearing and seeing the water move, thus becoming "living" water. The text that accompanies this gesture derives from Romans 6:3-11, a correlation that is particularly important when this passage and blessing are used together at the Easter vigil:

> We ask you, Father, with your Son
> to send the Holy Spirit upon the waters of this font.
> May all who are buried with Christ in the death of baptism
> rise also with him to newness of life.
> We ask this. . . . (222 A)

The rite for adult initiation also states that the celebration of baptism takes place at "the baptismal font, if this is in view of the faithful; otherwise in the sanctuary, where a vessel of water for the rite should be prepared beforehand" (218). These explicit directions indicate the value of communal participation in the use of water in the liturgy of baptism. That pluriform meanings belong to the liturgical use of symbol is exemplified in the following discussion of water as used in the rite of adult initiation.

Theological Meanings

The rubrics to the RCIA state that "water is God's creation," and immediately describe the "sacramental use of water" as important for the "unfolding of the paschal

"And God Saw That It Was Good"

mystery" in water baptism and in remembering "God's wonderful works in the history of salvation" (210). Then the RCIA invokes "the Holy Trinity at the very outset of the celebration of baptism" calling to "mind the mystery of God's love from the beginning of the world and the creation of the human race."

> By invoking the Holy Spirit and proclaiming Christ's death and resurrection, [the use of water] impresses on the mind the newness of Christian baptism, by which we share in his own death and resurrection and receive the holiness of God. (210)

The importance of water is cited in the introduction to the Litany of the Saints: "May [God] give them the new life of the Holy Spirit, whom we are about to call down on this water" (220). In both thanksgiving prayers the term "consecrated water" is used to designate the effects to be derived from it:

> By the mystery of this consecrated water
> lead them to a new and spiritual birth." (222 D, E)

The act of baptizing in water is described in no fewer than five places as *washing*. The rite states clearly:

> The celebration of baptism has as its center and high point the baptismal washing and the invocation of the Holy Trinity. Beforehand there are rites that have an inherent relationship to the baptismal washing. (209)

At the conclusion of the preparatory rites on Holy Saturday the final blessing of the elect draws on the example of the "holy prophets" who proclaimed to all who draw near to God "wash and be cleansed." The result of this act is "rebirth in the Spirit," being "reborn as [God's] children" and entering "the community of [God's] Church" (203). During the rite, immediately after the profession of faith, the elect receive Christ's paschal mystery "as expressed in the washing with water" (212). The rubrics state:

> The washing with water should take on its full importance as the sign of that mystical sharing in Christ's death and resurrection through which those who believe in his name die to sin and rise to eternal life. (212)

It then places immersion before infusion as the way to administer the baptismal washing (as stated also in 226), which usages are to be understood not as a mere "purification rite but the sacrament of being joined to Christ" (213).[80]

The allied usage of baptismal *cleansing* also finds a prominent place in four of the blessing prayers. In one, God is praised for having "created water to cleanse and give life" (222 B). Three others end with the same phrase:

You have called your children . . .
to this cleansing water and new birth. (222 C, D, E)

In addition, both options for the exorcism to be prayed over the elect at the first scrutiny capitalize on the gospel story of the Samaritan woman (Jn 4:5-42) proclaimed that day,[81] and the prayer over the elect at the presentation of the Lord's Prayer adapts the "living water."[82]

The scriptural allusion to Jesus' crucifixion in John 19:34, "and immediately blood and water poured out" (and at least indirectly, 1 Jn 5:8, "there are three witnesses, the Spirit, the water, and the blood"[83]) is incorporated in two of the three blessing prayers for water and in one of the two thanksgiving prayers for water already blessed.[84] It is also used in the prayer accompanying the anointing after baptism when confirmation is separated from baptism.[85]

The description of the effects of the water used at baptism[86] is stated in the general instruction on Christian initiation: "This first sacrament pardons all our sins, rescues us from the power of darkness, and brings us to the dignity of adopted children, a new creation through water and the Holy Spirit" (no. 2).[87] The rite itself cites "life," "new life," "new birth," and "rebirth" resulting from baptism.[88]

It is clear from this methodological example about one aspect of the *lex orandi* for adult initiation that the revised rites offer a wealth of material from which to develop a liturgical theology of baptism. The value placed on creation is implicit throughout the rite, and the theological meaning of sharing in the paschal mystery is reiterated throughout and is particularly clear when water baptism is done by immersion. Thus we have exemplified the crucial role that symbolic usage plays in the doing of sacraments and in theological reflection about the Church's *lex orandi*.

Bread and Wine

Manufactured Symbol: In addition to symbols from creation the liturgy uses symbols that result from the "work of human hands," among which are bread and wine, though I do not mean to ignore in my argument the indigenization issue concerning whether bread and wine ought not be replaced by other foods—making "substantial food and festive drink" a more suitable phrase in this discussion.

Philippe Rouillard has argued that the institution of the eucharist during the course of a meal "is deeply rooted in a human action indispensable to life and . . . rich in human and sacred symbolism: eating and drinking and having a meal."[89] In so treating the "symbolism of bread and wine," Rouillard asserts that these "fundamental elements of the nourishment of people in the Mediterranean basin ... are rich in symbolism"[90] and that their manufacture relies on the cycle of dying and rising in nature, which most fittingly symbolizes the dying and rising of Jesus.

That these elements rely on the agrarian cycle (and the cosmic symbolism) of planting seeds, which then "die" in the earth and "rise" to become mature stalks of wheat and bunches of grapes is most significant. At their harvesting the plants "die" once again by being picked and are then crushed to produce the raw material of wheat flour and grape juice. Other ingredients are then added to the flour, especially yeast, to make a dough that rises (at least once) and which, after baking, becomes bread. The liquid derived from crushing the grapes is preserved in casks to age, to mature, and thus to become wine. These "produced" elements are then taken as the most apt symbols to commemorate the death and resurrection of Jesus in the eucharistic meal (at least as classically understood in Western Christianity). These elements of nourishment are then consecrated as the eucharistic food to nourish the Church.

The aptness of the use of bread and wine points to the central, christological axis of the liturgy. A harmony between creation theology and the paschal mystery is disclosed here by the fact that the symbolism of using manufactured symbols at the eucharist sustains both creation and redemption. The key to interpreting these elements is human ingenuity and productivity. In other words, the cycle of dying and rising and the employing of the "work" of human labor are factors intrinsic to the eucharist and for the liturgical theology of the eucharist.[91]

Our interest in symbolic usage is borne out in the eucharistic species in two ways. First, the context for the celebration of the eucharist requires that cycles of nature and human manufacture together form the source for the eucharistic symbols. Second, the consecrated bread and wine are designated for symbolic use in the liturgy in such a way that the breaking and sharing one bread and sharing one cup in the church assembly (as found in 1 Cor 11 and frequently repeated in patristic and subsequent descriptions of the eucharist)[92] is the focal point toward which consecration and transformation leads.

Pluriform Meanings: The use of the eucharist in varying settings draws out different theological emphases. For example, the celebration of the eucharist as part of the Easter vigil is the clearest symbolic usage of the "first fruits" of the new creation. The rubrics state that the eucharist is only given as viaticum on Holy Saturday and that the bread and wine to be used at the vigil are "brought forward by the newly baptized." Behind these rubrical guidelines is an understanding of the end of the "old leaven" (signifying our former way of life) and the beginning of the new leaven with new eucharistic breads (signifying new life in the risen Christ). This symbolism is sustained in one of the options for the second reading on Easter Sunday from 1 Corinthians 5:6-8 (part of which is the communion antiphon for the vigil, 1 Cor 5:7-8).

Other contexts for the celebration of the eucharist draw out other theological meanings. These include the motif of the renewal of the covenant of baptism since the cup-word at the institution narrative speaks about "the new and everlasting covenant." Sunday eucharist is particularly noteworthy in this regard when the rite of blessing and sprinkling with holy water is used. The eucharist as a rite of passage is clearly specified when the eucharist is given outside of Mass to the dying. The special prayers for the rite of administering viaticum are most helpful to draw out this somewhat neglected aspect of eucharistic theology.[93] The following instances are of special interest: the rubric that "the priest explains [in the homily] the meaning and importance of viaticum" (no. 189); an alternative to the customary invitation to communion, "Jesus Christ is the food for our journey; he calls us to the heavenly table"; and two prayers after communion that refer to the eucharist as a rite of passage, specifically of being led "safely into the kingdom of light" and of entering "your kingdom in peace" (no. 209).[94]

This explication of the Church's *lex orandi* reflects our contention that liturgical rites taken as a whole (i.e., symbols, scripture, and euchological texts) disclose how the Church's prayer both reveres and uses creation in its liturgical prayer.

Convergence: Liturgical and Creation Theology

This particular moment in history affords a unique opportunity to articulate important strands of convergence between liturgical studies and creation theology, the combination of which articulates theological depth and argues for the preservation of creation for the integrity and quality of liturgical and sacramental engagement. The present reform of the liturgy builds on the Roman rite's use and reverence for symbol and symbolic engagement and maximizes such engagement because it is precisely through these means that God is revealed and encountered.

The rubrical directives for greater use of elements from creation in worship[95] are faithful to the tradition of the Roman rite. They also transcend the minimalist approach to symbolic interaction in liturgy and sacraments that resulted from the rubrical precision and fixity of the Roman rite after Trent. This kind of theological statement substantiates the contemporary concern for the environment because the very act of liturgy is imperiled when creation is threatened. The foundations for reviving a theology of symbol for liturgy and sacrament are similarly imperiled because of the diminished quality of the earth's resources. Simultaneously, however, the rootedness of Christian liturgy in creation needs to be articulated all the more today so that liturgical and sacramental theology may be faithful to their anthropological roots and articulate a theology in harmony with the revised rites.

A creation-centered theology of liturgy would ground the liturgical act as anthropologically apt. A creation focus for liturgical theology would ground and express the trinitarian theology of worship by emphasizing how the Trinity was operative in creation and is operative in sustaining creation as an expression of God's nature and goodness. A creation focus for liturgical theology would offer the most appropriate category within which the value of aesthetics would be argued. Such an argument would emphasize how that which is aesthetically pleasing reflects the glory of God and that aesthetically pleasing arts and artifacts are intrinsic to the experience of liturgy and theology. As the categories of the good, the true, and the beautiful are being revived as crucial for contemporary ethics, so the theology developed from the reformed liturgy necessarily includes them and gives them shape.[96] The various arts that collaborate with the celebration of liturgy include architecture, painting, sculpture, music, choreography. Everything that participants see: lights and colors, the harmony of the space; everything they hear (presuming that the acoustics are suitable and functioning properly): voice, song, playing instruments; everything they smell: incense, perfumed oils like chrism; everything they taste: bread and wine; everything they touch: offering the sign of peace, kissing the gospel book, contact with the various objects in worship; and every movement they are engaged in: stational masses, processions on Palm Sunday, Candlemas, and Rogation days[97]— everything about the liturgy presumes a creation focus.

A creation focus for liturgical theology will insist upon the significance of symbolic engagement in worship as the chief means that liturgy has of experiencing (not just conceptualizing) God. This experience will naturally ground the ethical imperative of worship to revere and preserve creation. Further, a creation focus for the theology of liturgy and sacraments will ground the global relatedness of every act of worship, the paradigm for which at present is the annual spring feast of Easter when the location of the moon and the rebirth of the earth provide the requisite cosmic context for the sacred rites of being reincorporated annually in the deepest sense possible in Christ's paschal mystery. Understandably this paradigm is much discussed in the context of liturgical inculturation since it presumes the locus of such a festival in the northern hemisphere. Although our concern here is to illustrate a classical association and coincidence, creation focus for liturgical theology is less grounded in the spring/Easter combination than in emphasizing liturgy as an experience of God's "power and might" in continuing the salvific deeds of creation and redemption.

A creation focus for liturgical theology would ground the appropriateness of symbolic integrity and the fullness of symbolic interaction in the celebration of liturgy because it is through creation and symbolic elements that God is discovered, revealed, and encountered.[98] A creation focus for liturgical theology also necessarily implies and argues for the value of quality construction and the use of quality materials in church construction. Just as some liturgical symbols are the result of human ingenuity and productivity, so the construction of church buildings and liturgical spaces articulates the creative spirit and human manufacture intrinsic to the liturgy.[99]

A creation focus for the theology of liturgy can be used as one way to describe what occurs theologically in the liturgy of the word. Each time the word is proclaimed in the liturgical assembly the chaos and confusion that can dominate even an assembly of believers is overcome in the act of creation that is the liturgy of the word. And a creation focus for the theology of worship gives specificity to the *lex vivendi* because responding in life to what one celebrates would necessarily include environmental concerns.

A creation focus to liturgical theology may broaden categories of salvation that focus too intensely on an (individual or collective) experience of forgiveness to wider notions that include cosmic regeneration and renewal. The liturgy could be interpreted properly as the closest we can come here and now to what will only be perfected in the kingdom—the renewal of all things in heaven and earth and their recapitulation in Christ.[100] More particularly the Easter triduum would be a perfect setting for understanding liturgy as the way the human race overcomes paradise lost and experiences paradise regained. It could also appropriately image salvation as freedom for life in God on earth until the Church enjoys eternal salvation in a "new heavens and new earth." This primal celebration of earth, air, fire, and water that accompanies scripture readings such as the Genesis creation account (with its accompanying prayer), the Pauline exhortation to dying and rising with Christ in Romans 6:3-11, and the resurrection Gospels— that begin "as the first day of the week was dawning" (Mt 28:1) and "on the first day of the week at dawn" (Lk 24:1)—are important indications of the cosmic centeredness of this celebration and the appropriateness of drawing more fully on cosmic images for salvation.

Two particular examples from the Catholic tradition, Benedictine and Franciscan, are helpful indicators of the way an integral view of revering creation and of showing reverence for others in faith is intrinsically connected to liturgy. In a particularly compelling section of chapter 31:9-11 of his *Rule*, St. Benedict asserts that the monastery cellarer shall show reverence for persons and things.

> He must show every care and concern for the sick, children, guests, and the poor, knowing for certain that he will be held accountable for all of them on the day of judgment (9). He will regard all utensils and goods of the monastery as sacred vessels of the altar (10), aware that nothing is to be neglected (11).

This short statement, which reflects the thorough incarnationalism of the *Rule*, articulates the heart of the Benedictine life in terms of seeing and revering all aspects of creation and human life. It also expresses the harmony between work and prayer that is proper to Benedictine monasticism. The striking role that showing reverence for the brethren and for the tools of the monastery has in the *Rule* is particularly noteworthy since cenobite monasticism places such a priority on liturgical prayer. A central idea and value in monasticism is thus the harmonious integration of all aspects of life seen from a particularly christological and incarnational perspective. In Benedictine monasticism,

Human life is a whole, and everything in creation is good. There is no aspect of life in this world that cannot, if rightly understood and used, contribute to leading us to our final end. Temporal reality and human endeavor are reflections of the perfections of God. Material things are *sacramenta*, symbols that reveal the goodness and beauty of the Creator. Consequently, Benedict can say that ordinary tools for work should be treated like the sacred vessels intended for liturgical use (31:10). It is only sin that has disfigured the beauty of creation and diverted things from their purpose. The monastic life is an effort to restore the lost paradise, to regain the image of God in man that has been distorted. Therefore, the temporal order cannot be despised or neglected. In the monk's life there is no area that can be exempted from subjection to the divine precepts and the regime of grace. This is no disincarnate spirituality; conversion embraces the whole of life.[101]

The mendicant tradition of St. Francis of Assisi stands alongside the monastic as a helpful example of an integral view of the Christian life predicated on a wide notion of sacramentality and of incarnationalism.[102] Pope John Paul II asserts as much:

In 1979, I proclaimed St. Francis of Assisi as the heavenly Patron of those who promote ecology.[103] He offers an example of genuine and deep respect for the integrity of creation. As a friend of the poor who was loved by God's creatures, St. Francis invited all of creation—animal, plants, natural forces, even Brother Sun and Sister Moon—to give honor and praise to the Lord. The poor man of Assisi gives us striking witness that when we are at peace with God we are better able to devote ourselves to building up that peace with all creation which is inseparable from peace among all peoples. It is my hope that the inspiration of St. Francis will help us to keep ever alive a sense of "fraternity" with all those good and beautiful things which almighty God has created. And may he remind us of our serious obligation to respect and watch over them with care, in light of that greater and higher fraternity that exists within the human family. (no. 16)[104]

The Franciscan tradition's prizing of conventual liturgy (both the eucharist and hours), preaching, and their particular kind of communal life (among other things) stands as another significant example of how the principle of the sacramentality of human life functions in the Christian life as well as how the sacramentality of creation functions in this specific context.[105]

There are, at present, timely and significant convergences between creation theology and liturgical theology, which are particularly noted by (and also probably challenging) the Benedectine and Franciscan traditions.

Critique

In accord with the method I proposed in the beginning of this text, I now make some observations on the "critical function of liturgical theology" with regard to the way creation is described and used in the present reformed liturgy.

The first critique concerns texts. The eucharistic prayer, particularly its introductory section, is a classic locus for explicit reference to praise and thanks for creation.[106] Theologically, it leads to praising God for redemption, a section that is highly christological. In the present euchology, only the preface to the fourth eucharistic prayer contains any notable reference to praise for creation. While it can be granted that a highly christological emphasis has classically marked the Roman prefaces, it is certainly regrettable that the inroads in this direction signaled by the fourth eucharistic prayer were not more deeply made in the rest of the euchology.

Allied with this criticism is the debate often engaged in by liturgical theologians about what ought to be in a eucharistic prayer text and whether or not the anaphora should reflect general themes or a particular need. Some liturgists argued against the publication of eucharistic prayers for reconciliation and a preface for Masses when the anointing of the sick takes place because such prayers focus too directly on a single theme. A possible loss to the structure and contents of the eucharistic prayer may be this praise motif when prefaces and eucharistic prayers for particular needs are developed.

A second critique concerns symbolic engagement in the revised rites and how the revised liturgy is celebrated. The issue concerns whether the contemporary Roman liturgy is sufficiently primal, explicitly related to creation and evocative of the produce and productivity of the earth. Roman Catholic eucharistic liturgy is all too frequently celebrated in a way that its more didactic than evocative, more educational than attitudinal, more informational than formational, more oriented toward learning than encounter, and more concerned with greater understanding than a

"AND GOD SAW THAT IT WAS GOOD"

progressively complete experience of assimilation into the mystery of God. A chief symptom here is the paradoxical situation in which the Roman Mass, previously noted for its "other-worldly" liturgy in terms of language, ritual, and gestural movement, and in particular the rites surrounding consecration, now finds itself with a comparatively overlong liturgy of the word. At the same time, the liturgy of the eucharist is flat and often seems to be a description of God, rather than a sensual and compelling evocation of God's mystery and otherness.

The issue is at least twofold: disproportionate liturgy of the word and relatively minimal involvement of the assembly in symbolic (inter)action. Could it be that the theology of liturgy operative at present is too *christ*ological and *theo*logical in the sense that the primal and earthy aspects of liturgy are submerged in consciousness and not experienced sufficiently in the liturgical act? The celebration of the Easter vigil is the most striking example we have at present of a symbolically rich liturgy. However, if the overriding focus that night is on the incorporation of catechumens into the Church by means of the Easter sacraments, certainly an important aspect of the revived rites of adult initiation, then what happens to the environmental context of this celebration in terms of the Spring renewal of the earth, the light of the moon, and the reading of the Genesis creation account (among others) on which adult initiation is predicated? There is a clear danger here of ignoring the polyvalent meanings of this celebration and making them too catechumenal.

In point of fact, however, not all celebrations of the Easter vigil are concerned with the initiation of new adults. Such celebrations can contribute to acknowledging and broadening the theological appreciation of the vigil. For example, when the vigil is celebrated in a monastic community, it is obvious that the initiation of new members is less compelling than a theology of Easter that concerns renewing baptismal and monastic vows. In addition, if the monastic community happens to rely on farming for its livelihood, the celebration of the vigil there might well be more adequately and obviously based on the renewal of the cosmos taking place in nature at that time. The very real yet symbolically imaged combat between God and Satan, redemption and condemnation, life and death, grace and sin, and virtue and temptation have a fuller meaning and take on a richer connotation when set within the cosmic struggle at this time of year when spring strains to renew the earth and winter hangs on to breathe its last. The cosmic battle between warmth and cold and between light and darkness provides the requisite and theologically rich context within which to consider the christologically and pneumatically rich theology of the Easter victory.

A final point to be made regarding symbolic engagement in the reformed liturgy concerns the absence as yet of any attention to the rogation days that traditionally served as concrete demonstrations of the bond between altar and earth. The General

Norms for the Liturgical Year and the Calendar state that rogation and ember days are days of particular intercession "for the needs of [all], especially for the productivity of the earth and [human] labor," (no. 45) and that the time and manner of these observations "should be determined by the episcopal conference" (no. 46). Especially at a time of rising ecological awareness and of concern to fill the gap that all too often exists between liturgy and real life, it is regrettable that no action has yet been taken in these matters in the United States. Since the norms state that "the competent authority should set up norms for the extent of these celebrations" (no. 46), much latitude could be exercised to allow authentic and indigenous observances to mark these days when the Church's prayer is explicitly concerned with creation and the things of the earth.

A third critique of the present Roman liturgy is the common overuse of hymns during the eucharist that are concerned with praising God. There is something repetitive, not to say redundant, in using hymns of praise, especially at the entrance and presentation of the gifts, because this motif is classically constitutive of the eucharistic prayer. "It is right to give him thanks and praise." A cause of this common error may be that we have yet to develop suitable musical theory and practice for the revised liturgy. In addition, the absence of hymns in the present *Missale Romanum* and *Antiphonale* for Mass (except for the Glory to God, and Holy, holy, holy) indicates the problematic nature of any use of hymns at the eucharist. That praise themes dominate the hymns makes this phenomenon all the more regrettable.

A fourth critique concerns the sphere of aesthetics, a topic that deserves particular care in the selection of terms and categories. To agree that liturgy ought to be aesthetically pleasing and that its component elements should be qualitatively beautiful would not be difficult. A challenge to this statement could rightly be mounted when aesthetics is equated with ostentation and beauty merely with expense. Nuance and precision of argument is clearly necessary. It is also difficult to determine how aesthetics and beauty should be intrinsic parts of the liturgical experience. But the lack of these qualities in the conduct of worship (despite the money spent) and in the construction of houses for worship requires that these matters be raised.

Too often the contemporary liturgy is criticized for a lack of beauty that can raise the human heart to God and a lack of artistic depth and integrity in church buildings, art, music, artifacts, vesture, and decorum in enactment. That these qualities may be prized for their own sake and be used derogatorily in worship are obvious dangers. However, it would be equally dangerous to relegate the category of aesthetics or the category of beauty to relative nonimportance in planning and constructing churches or in the planning and celebration of liturgy. Theologically, liturgy presumes the contribution of the "work of human hands." Aesthetics requires that these works reflect high artistic standards in continuity with the premises on which the theology of liturgy is based and reflects the breadth of the Catholic tradition in terms of the use of art and architecture for worship.

A fifth critique draws on the observations made above that the present euchology and calendar reflect the northern hemisphere and ignore the experience of liturgical praying and feasting in the southern hemisphere. The argument in favor of composing a new euchology for the major seasons of Advent-Christmas-Epiphany and Lent-Easter-Pentecost rests on viewing the many traditional and time-honored euchological texts used at this time of year as *paradigmatic* of the theology of these feasts and seasons, not as literal norms. In fact, because this euchology would not be predicated on the passing of the longest nights of the year (Christmas) or the renewal of the earth in Spring (Easter), it could break ground in articulating the kind of hope believers have in viewing redemption as still to be completed. Eschatological yearning and hope from such euchology could serve the renewal of the Church's euchology for the Church in both hemispheres.

A final critique concerns the contribution that concern for creation and the environment can make to the theology of the presentation of the gifts at the eucharist. Several recent studies in English have summarized the debate about the theological adequacy of these rites in the present reform and avenues for their further refinement in the Roman rite.[107] Most authors agree that the simplification of these rites from the Tridentine Missal was long overdue and that the present reform at least eliminates any kind of proleptic eucharistic prayer that had, unfortunately, burdened the former rite. The reform calls these rites the "preparation of the gifts" or the "preparation of the altar and the gifts"—not the "offertory." The simplified rites are a distinct improvement. The parallel texts "blessed are you, Lord God of all creation" are unfortunately problematic; like praise hymns at the eucharist, they reiterate what is explicitly and traditionally a central theological theme of the eucharistic prayer: to praise, bless, and thank God for the *mirabilia Dei*, especially as these continue to be experienced here and now through the eucharist.

An examination of the present rites of the preparation of the gifts reveal a too exclusive focus on the particular gifts of bread and wine, whereas reference to God's providence in providing all the goods of earth for nourishment and sustenance would be helpful. In addition, and more theologically pertinent, explicit reference to the contribution of human ingenuity, industry, and productivity in the manufacture of the elements of bread and wine is also missing. Not that I am arguing for a Pelagian-like theology of earning the gifts of salvation by work but for some clear statement that the gifts presented represent a wealth of human productivity, including planting, harvesting, refining, making flour, pressing grapes, baking loaves of bread, and aging the fruit of the vine to become wine. Put somewhat differently, the theol-

ogy reflected in this rite should take some cognizance of the fact that these polyvalent symbols, bread and wine, reflect the contribution of human productivity to
the liturgy, as opposed to the use of symbols taken from nature such as water. In this
connection, it is significant that the recently revised *Lutheran Book of Worship* [108] offers
the following as one "offertory" hymn to be sung while "the offering is received as
the Lord's table is prepared" (no. 24).

> Let the vineyards be fruitful, Lord,
> and fill to the brim our cup of blessing.
> Gather a harvest from the seeds that were sown,
> that we may be fed with the bread of life.
> Gather the hopes and dreams of all;
> unite them with the prayers we offer now.
> Grace our table with your presence,
> and give us a foretaste of the feast to come.

In these days of ecumenical convergence and mutual enrichment, it is significant
that this text says more theologically than do our double "blessed are you" prayers,
and it is far more expansive in terms of evoking images of harvest and of human productivity. It also offers an explicitly eschatological reference without which the focus
of the rite can be limited to the presentation of this particular bread and wine. While
the adoption of this text in the Roman rite would have its own set of problems, this
example of Lutheran *lex orandi* affords a significant example of how ecumenical cooperation can offer insight and guidance for continuing liturgical revision and for
developing the theological implications of revision.

This last example of a contemporary critique of liturgical reform is an appropriate note on which to end and with which to indicate that what is argued here is for
the wider Christian world. It is hoped that the particular contribution of the Roman
Catholic tradition to these matters will help a wider Christian community validate
the doctrine of the sacramentality of creation in worship. At the same time, it is
hoped that the ecumenical convergence in liturgical and sacramental rites now
emerging will lead to deepening convergence among the Churches, enabling the
gap in the *lex credendi* between and among Christian Churches to decrease.

Notes

1. Not everyone who uses the original phrase understands it in the same way. An example is the debate on the weight that ought to be given to *statuat* in this formula: whether the Church's prayer grounds belief, or belief grounds the formulas for liturgical prayer, or a mutual influence is operative between prayer and belief. This debate is reflected in Geoffrey Wainwright's review of Kavanagh's *On Liturgical Theology* in *Worship* 61(2): 183–86. (Some contemporary authors prefer to use the shortened phrase *lex orandi, lex credendi*.)

2. The authorship of this phrase, found in the so-called *Capitula Coelestini* (statements added to a letter of Pope Celestine I dated in the early fifth century [P.L. 51:205-12] also called the *Capitula* or *Auctoritates de gratia*) is now generally ascribed to Prosper of Aquitaine. See M. Cappuyns, "L'origine des Capitula Pseudo-Célestiniens Contre le Semi-pélagianisme" *Revue Bénédictine* 41(2): 156-70; Paul De Clerck, "*Lex orandi, lex credendi*: Sens Originel et Avatars Historiques d'un Adage Équivoque" *Questions Liturgiques* 59(3): 193-212, and "La Prière Universelle dans les Liturgiques Latines Anciennes. Témoinages Patristiques et Textes Liturgiques" *Liturgiewissenschaftliche Quellen und Forschungen* 62 (Munster: Aschendorff, 1977), 88-89. See also what is generally regarded as a "classic" commentary and analysis, Karl Federer, *Liturgie und Glaube, Eine Theologiegeschichtliche Untersuchung*, Paradosis IV, "Legem Credendi Lex Statuat Supplicandi" (Fribourg: Paulusverlag, 1950), 19-41. On the original text and a standard interpretation of its usefulness for liturgical theology, see Mario Righetti, *Manuale di Storia Liturgica*, 4 volumes, 2d. edition (Milano: Ancora, 1950), 1:25-27.

3. See Mark Searle, "Renewing the Liturgy—Again," *Commonweal* 140(2): 617-22. In this same connection see the introduction and collected essays in *Liturgie—Ein Vergessenes Thema der Theologie?* ed. Klemens Richter (Freiburg: Basel, 1987). Undoubtedly the statement of the Liturgy Constitution has influenced some of this work:

   > The study of liturgy is to be ranked among the compulsory and major courses in seminaries and religious houses of studies; in theological faculties it is to rank among the principal subjects. It is to be taught under its theological, historical, pastoral, and juridical aspects. (no. 16)

   For an overview of the historical evolution of this aspect of liturgical study, see Kevin W. Irwin, *Liturgical Theology: A Primer* (Collegeville, Minn.: The Liturgical Press, 1990), 11-17; "Sacrament," in *New Dictionary of Theology*, ed. Joseph A. Komonchak, et. al. (Wilmington, Del.: Glazier, 1987), 910-22; and *Context and Text* (Collegeville, Minn.: Liturgical Press, 1993).

4. See among others the writings of Alexander Schmemann, Cipriano Vagaggini, Irénée H. Dalmais, and Salvatore Marsili. For an overview see my *Liturgical Theology*, 19-29, 40-44, and bibliography, 74-77.

5. Among these, the work of Albert Houssiau and Gerard Lukken is particularly important. See *Liturgical Theology*, 29-34, and the bibliography, 75-76.

6. See among others, Pedro Fernandez, "Liturgia y Teología. Una Cuestion Metodologica," *Ecclesia Orans* 6(3): 261-83.

7. A comparison of the former Roman ritual for baptism with the post-Vatican II revised rites yields important insight on this matter. For example, the introduction to the former rite describes valid administration "by pouring the water, or by immersion or by sprinkling" (Philip T. Weller, ed., *The Roman Ritual* [Milwaukee: Bruce Publishing Co., 1964],

34, no. 10). The rite itself presents the formula and the rubrics together: "N., I baptize you in the name of the Father (here he pours the first time), and of the Son, (pouring a second time), and of the Holy Spirit (pouring a third time" [nos. 19, 58]). The present General Instruction on Christian Initiation states that "as the rite for baptizing, either immersion, which is more suitable as a symbol of participation in the death and resurrection of Christ, or pouring may lawfully be used" (no. 11). The rite itself separates the two forms, placing immersion first (no. 226).

8. The terms "adaptation," "accommodation," and "inculturation" are variously defined and understood. The descriptions offered by Anscar J. Chupungco have been rather influential. See *Cultural Adaptation of the Liturgy* (New York: Paulist, 1988); *Liturgies of the Future* (New York: Paulist, 1990); "Toward a Definition of Inculturation," *Ecclesia Orans* 5(1): 11-29; and "Popular Religiosity and Liturgical Inculturation," *Ecclesia Orans* 8(1): 97-115. Another author whose work has been very influential in this area is D. S. Amalorpavadass. See "Theological Thoughts on Inculturation," *Studia Liturgica* 20(1): 36-54, 116-36.

9. A particularly useful statement of the need for a new method in liturgical theology based on ritual studies as a relatively new discipline and one that is germane to our argument is Theodore W. Jennings, "Ritual Studies and Liturgical Theology: An Invitation to Dialogue," *Journal of Ritual Studies* 1(1): 35-56. Important examples of this methodological approach include the past and ongoing work of two study groups in the North American Academy of Liturgy, the "Liturgy and Social Sciences" and "Liturgy and Ritual Studies." On the European side, an important example is the method developed and exemplified in the Pastoral Liturgy Institute of Santa Giustina in Padua, Italy. See the important publications from this Institute, especially R. Cecolin, A. N. Terrin, and P. Visentin, eds., *Una Liturgia per L'uomo*. La Liturgia Pastorale e I Suoi Compiti "Caro Salutis Cardo," Studi 5. Padova: Edizioni Messagero, 1986; the monograph on method by Giorgio Bonaccorso, *Introduzione allo Studio della Liturgia*, "Caro Salutis Cardo," Sussidi 1. Padova: Edizioni Messagero, 1990; and the two-volume summary of the work of Pelagio Visentin, ed. R. Cecolin and F. Trolese, *Culmen et Fons, Raccolta di Studi di Liturgia e Spiritualità*, "Caro Salutis Cardo," Studi 3 and 4. Padova: Edizioni Messagero, 1987.

10. See Mary Collins, "Critical Questions for Liturgical Theology," *Worship* 53(4): 302-17; "Liturgical Methodology and the Cultural Evolution of Worship in the United States," *Worship* 49(2): 85-102; and "The Public Language of Ministry," *Official Ministry in a New Age*, in Permanent Seminar Studies. No. 3, ed. James H. Provost (Washington: Canon Law Society of America, 1981), 7-40.

11. On this comparatively new and underexplored aspect of liturgical method, see among others, Angelus Haussling, "Die Kritische Funktion der Liturgiewissenschaft," in Hans B. Meyer, ed., *Liturgie und Gesellschaft* (Innsbruck: Tyrolia Verlag, 1970), 103-30; David N. Power, "Cult to Culture: The Liturgical Foundation of Theology," *Worship* 54(16): 482-95; "People at Liturgy," *Twenty Years of Concilium—Retrospect and Prospect*, Concilium 170 (Edinburgh: T. and T. Clark, 1983), 8-14; and Mary Collins, "The Public Language of Ministry."

12. For an overview of the important contributions made in this area in the present century, see Franco Brovelli, "Movimento Liturgico e Spiritualita Liturgica," *Rivista Liturgica* 73(4): 469-90. Particularly notable are the works of Cipriano Vagaggini, Lambert Beauduin, and Romano Guardini.

13. See Matias Auge, "Le Messe 'pro Sancta Ecclesia': Un' Espressione della 'Lex Orandi' in Sintonia con la 'Lex Credendi' e la 'Lex Vivendi.'" *Notitiae* 26(8): 566-84.

14. This life-relation of liturgy has been given added stimulus in contemporary discourse by liberation theologians who theologize about the ethical demands of the Christian faith in situations that hinder or actually inhibit the development of the Christian life as taught by Jesus and experienced in liturgy. The challenge to live as we celebrate may mean critiquing and revitalizing oppressive social structures. It can also mean emphasizing individual commitments to reform oneself as well as structures of society.

15. See Bernard J. Leeming, *Principles of Sacramental Theology* (London/New York: Longmans Green, 1956), 601, fn. 41. Leeming states, "The *Catechism of the Council of Trent* gives seven reasons to show the fitness of sacraments to man's present condition [the first of which is] (1) visible signs fit man's dual nature of body and soul."

16. David N. Power, *Unsearchable Riches: The Symbolic Nature of the Liturgy* (New York: Pueblo Publishing Co., 1984). See Bernard J. Leeming, *Principles of Sacramental Theology,* 600:

    ... in simple things God is to be found: in the authority of human beings, in words spoken by men, in water, bread, oil, wine, and human gesture. Man is reminded that he is not pure spirit, and that his holiness must consist, as it is found, in the sanctity of both body and soul, in both the spiritual and the material.

17. See Louis-Marie Chauvet, *Symbole et Sacrement: Une Relecture Sacramentelle de L'existence Chrétienne* (Paris: Cerf, 1987), 195-232.

18. See Gordon Lathrop, "Holy Things: Foundations for Liturgical Theology," *Institute of Liturgical Studies,* no. 7 (Valparaiso: Valparaiso Institute, 1991). He makes this helpful comment about the eucharist: "The meal is both the thanksgiving and the eating and drinking. The thanksgiving prayer gives words to what happens in communion. The eating and drinking is always more than the prayer can say" (35).

19. For example, regarding the use of water in baptism, the section of the blessing prayer referring to the Genesis account of Noah's ark regards it most positively and as a victory ("The waters of the great flood you made a sign of the waters of baptism that make an end to sin and a new beginning of goodness"), whereas the event itself can be interpreted on many other levels, some of which reflect a negative judgment against sinful humanity.

20. In what follows, "the bread and wine" terminology is used for convenience, not to settle the argument about appropriate elements for the eucharist.

21. *De Carnis Resurrectione,* Corpus Scriptorum Ecclesiasticorum Latinorum 47(9): 25-125. See Cipriano Vagaggini, *Caro Salutis est Cardo—Corporetá, Eucaristia e Liturgia* (Rome: Desclee, 1966). It is also noteworthy that this phrase of Tertullian is the title of the series from the Santa Giustina Liturgical Institute of Padua (see note 9).

22. See Karl Rahner, "The Presence of Christ in the Sacrament of the Lord's Supper," *Theological Investigations* 4, trans. Kevin Smyth (Baltimore: Helicon Press, 1966), 309.

23. For a helpful summary of the importance of the epiclesis in the contemporary Roman Catholic and other Churches' eucharistic prayers, see John H. McKenna, "The Epiclesis Revisited," *New Eucharistic Prayers: An Ecumenical Study of their Development and Structure,* ed. Frank C. Senn (New York: Paulist Press, 1987), 169-94.

24. Translation from R. C. D. Jasper and G. J. Cuming, *Prayers of the Eucharist: Early and Reformed*, 3d. revised ed. (New York: Pueblo Publishing Co., 1987), 24.

25. A generally helpful summary of Karl Rahner's thought in this regard occurs in Michael Skelley, *The Liturgy of the World* (Collegeville, Minn.: Liturgical Press/A Pueblo Book, 1991), 85–158.

26. See the Ecumenical Forum, "Creation and Culture: An Ecumenical Challenge," *The Ecumenical Review* 37(4): 506–11, quoting the Orthodox theologian Emilie Dierking Lisenko who

> pointed to the spiritual/material dualism, and to a certain arrogance against nature. In the Eastern Christian vision God did not create the world for the sake of human welfare per se and thus for exploitation, but as an element for human communication with God, the human person being a priest for eucharistic celebration of the world. Liturgy comprehends the whole of creation and shows definitely a communal orientation! The fall expresses human love for the world as an end in itself, separating it from God and thus from its very source of life. Nature is not evil, salvation is for all of creation (507).

And citing Harold Ditmanson:

> Everything exists because God existed first. Therefore, grace is prior to creation. The world has only a relative independence, and is—in its goodness—God's self-expression. Nothing in creation is essentially unclean. Sin is a secondary concept, and redemption means restoration. Some idea of a continuous creation is necessary. Nature must be seen as a single coherent event (510).

27. Michael J. Himes and Kenneth R. Himes, "The Sacrament of Creation," *Commonweal* 142(2): 44–45.

28. See Jürgen Moltmann's interesting thesis, "The Sabbath: The Feast of Creation," in *God in Creation: A New Theology of Creation and the Spirit of God* (San Francisco: Harper and Row, 1985), 276–95, and the Appendix: "Symbols of the World," 297–328.

29. The presumption in this section is the experience of light/darkness and the seasons in the northern hemisphere. In the final ("critique") section of this paper much more will be said about possibilities for varied euchology based on other ways daylight and the seasons are experienced.

30. There are five Mass formulas for "VII Kalens Iulias Natale Sancti Iohannis Baptistae" in the Verona Collection. See *Sacramentarium Veronense, Rerum Ecclesiasticarum Documenta 1*, L. Cunibert Mohlberg, et. al., eds. (Rome: Herder, 1978), nos. 232–56.

31. Insightful descriptions of the *lucernarium* and its influence on Christian vespers are found in Paul Bradshaw, *Daily Prayer in the Early Church* (New York: Oxford University Press, 1982), 22, 51, 57, 75–77, 80, 116, 119, 135; George Guiver, *Company of Voices: Daily Prayer and the People of God* (New York: Pueblo, 1988), 62–66, 202; and Robert Taft, *The Liturgy of the Hours in East and West* (Collegeville, Minn.: The Liturgical Press, 1986), 26–28, 36–38, 55–56, 211–12, 355–56.

32. One of the disadvantages to the proposal to establish a "fixed date" for Easter (largely for ecumenical purposes) is the fact that this would mitigate the sense of relying on cosmic rhythms to establish its dating.

33. See Bernhard W. Anderson, "Creation in the Bible," in Philip N. Joranson ed. *Cry of the Environment* (Santa Fe: Bear and Co., 1984):

> The doctrine of creation, then, underlines and validates the truth that history, from beginning to end, is under the sovereign purpose of God as revealed in Jesus Christ. The Fourth Gospel begins by echoing the opening words of Genesis: "In the beginning" and speaks about the light shining in darkness (cf. 2 Corinthians 4:6). And even as Christ was in the beginning, so he will triumph at the end (1 Corinthians 15:24-28; Revelation [40]).

34. All the English translations of texts presented here are from the International Committee on English in the Liturgy (hereafter ICEL) texts now in use. That these translations will be adjusted in the new edition of the Sacramentary is almost certain. The Latin original of this prayer is from the former Roman missal. See Pierre Bruylants, *Les Oraisons du Missel Romain* (Louvain: Abbeye de Mont César, 1952), no. 347.

35. From former Roman usage, P. Bruylants, *Les Oraisons*, no. 176.

36. From former Roman usage, originally from the Hadrianum. See Jean Deshusses, *Le Sacramentaire Grégorien* (Fribourg: Editions Universitaires, 1979), no. 51.

37. From the Leonine sacramentary, *Sacramentarium Veronense,* no. 1260.

38. From former Roman usage, from a combination of two sacramentary texts: *Sacramentarium Veronense,* no. 1247, and the old Gelasian sacramentary, *Liber Sacramentorum Romanae Ecclesiae Ordinis Anni Circuli,* ed. L. C. Mohlberg, Rerum Ecclesiasticarum Documenta IV, (Rome: Herder, 1960), no. 59.

39. See among others Gerhard von Rad, *Old Testament Theology,* trans. D. M. G. Stalker (New York: Harper and Row, 1962), 15-35; and John Bright, *A History of Israel* (Philadelphia: Westminster, 1959). Bright states:

> Unleavened Bread (and Passover), Weeks, and Ingathering . . . were far older than Israel and, save for Passover, were agricultural in origin. Israel borrowed them [and] gave them a new rationale by imparting to them a historical content. They ceased to be mere nature festivals and became occasions when the mighty acts of Yahweh toward Israel were celebrated. Presumably these feasts were for practical reasons celebrated at local shrines as well as at Shiloh. But there is evidence of a great annual feast at Shiloh to which godly Israelites repaired (Judges 21:19; 1 Samuel 1:3, 21). Though we are not told, this was probably the autumn feast of Ingathering and the turn of the year. It is exceedingly probable, too, and very likely in connection with this annual feast, that there was a regular ceremony of covenant renewal (Deuteronomy 31:9-13) . . . (148).

40. It is not coincidental that the continuous reading from Revelation occurs in the Office of Readings in the Liturgy of the Hours from Monday of the Second Week of Easter through Saturday of the Fifth Week of Easter and as the second reading at Mass during the Easter season "C" cycle, indicating that Easter is a season of rebirth and sharing of the first fruits of the resurrection.

41. That creation can serve the mediating function of coming to know God is also explicitly confirmed through the New Testament. A classic text used to support the notion that creation can lead to knowledge of God is Romans 1:19-20:

> In fact whatever can be known about God is clear to them; he himself made it so. Since the creation of the world, invisible realities, God's eternal power and divinity, have become visible, recognizable through the things he has made. Romans 1:25 ("the Creator . . . is blessed forever") is printed in the present text of the liturgy of the hours as the phrase that can be meditated on when praying the canticle of Dan 3:52-57 at Sunday morning prayer.

42. Besides these hymns for ferial evening prayer, a number of other texts, prescribed for use in the former breviary, are similarly inspired by or refer to creation. Among them: *Creator Alme Siderum*, vespers Sundays and weekdays of Advent; *Audi Benigne Conditor*, vespers Sundays and weekdays of Lent; *Quem Terra, Pontus, Sidera*, matins of the Blessed Virgin Mary without a proper matins hymn; *Rerum Creator Optime*, Wednesday matins; *Rerum Deus Tenax Vigor*, none throughout the year; *Salutis Humanae Sator*, vespers Ascension to Pentecost; *Aeterne Rerum Conditor*, Sunday lauds; *Ecce Jam Noctis*, Sunday lauds; *Splendor Paternae Gloriae*, Monday lauds; *Primo Die, quo Trinitas*, Sunday matins; *O Sol Salutis, Intimis*, Lent lauds; *Rex Sempiterne Coelitum*, matins Eastertide; *Veni Creator Spiritus*, vespers and terce on Pentecost and through octave. See *The Hymnal for the Hours* (Chicago: Gregorian Institute of America, 1989), nos. 148-57; and *The Summit Choirbook* (Summit: Dominican Nuns, 1983), nos. 179-86, for vesper hymns translated into English and set to various metrical settings.

43. All English translations are from Matthew Britt, *The Hymns of the Breviary and Missal* (New York: Benziger Brothers, 1922), 74.

44. Each of these hymns is discussed in succession in Britt, *The Hymns*, 73-85, with Latin and English texts, notes on authorship, and a theological commentary.

45. Martien E. Binkman, "A Creation Theology for Canberra?" *The Ecumenical Review* 42(2):150-56. Binkman asserts that creation no longer preeminently bound to the first person of the Trinity but to the third person, and that here the bond between Christ and the Spirit is emphasized. Therefore we cannot, for example, casually substitute the Son (christology) in creation theology with the Spirit (pneumatology).

46. The text (from Britt, *The Hymns*) is

> As fades the glowing orb of day,
> To Thee, great source of light, we pray;
> Blest Three in One, to every heart
> Thy beams of life and love impart.
> At early dawn, at close of day,
> To Thee our vows we humbly pay;
> May we, mid joys that never end,
> With Thy bright Saints in homage bend (84).

47. Sun and moon, bless the Lord;
> stars of heaven, bless the Lord.
> Every shower and dew, bless the Lord;
> all you winds, bless the Lord (62-64).

48. Blessed are you, and praiseworthy,
    O Lord, the God of our Fathers,
    and glorious forever is your name.
    For you are just in all you have done;
    all your deeds are faultless,
    all your ways right (26-27).

49. Hannaniah, Azariah, Mishael,
    bless the Lord praise and exalt him above all forever.
    For he has delivered us from the nether world,
    and saved us from the power of death;
    he has freed us from the raging flame
    and delivered us from the fire.
    Give thanks to the Lord, for he is good,
    for his mercy endures forever.
    Bless the God of gods,
    all you who fear the Lord;
    praise him and give him thanks,
    because his mercy endures forever (88-90).

50. The General Instruction on the Liturgy of the Hours states: "The psalmody of morning prayer consists of one morning psalm, then a canticle from the Old Testament, and finally a second psalm of praise, following the tradition of the Church (no. 43)."

51. Come, let us sing to the Lord
    and shout with joy to the Rock who saves us.
    Let us approach him with praise and thanksgiving
    and sing joyful songs to the Lord.
    The Lord is God, the mighty God,
    the great king over all the gods.
    He holds in his hands the depths of the earth
    and the highest mountains as well.
    He made the sea; it belongs to him,
    the dry land too, for it was formed by his hands
    Come, then, let us bow down and worship,
    bending the knee before the Lord, our maker
    For he is our God and we are his people.

    See B. Anderson, "Creation":

    Creation is the foundation of the covenant; it provides the setting within which Yahweh's saving work takes place. But it is equally true that creation is embraced within the theological meaning of covenant. Therefore, psalmists may regard creation as the first of God's saving deeds (Psalm 74:12-17) and in the recitation of the *Heilgeschichte* may move without a break from the deeds of creation to historical deeds of liberation (Psalm 136[26]).

52. See B. Anderson, "Creation":

    It seems, then, that Israel's earliest traditions did not refer to Yahweh as creator in a cosmic sense but concentrated, rather, on Yahweh's "mighty deeds" of liberation, through which the Holy God became known and formed Israel as a people out of the chaos of historical oblivion and oppression (23f).

53. A significant example of how contemporary liturgical scholarship has rediscovered and appropriated the Jewish cultic terms *berakah* and *todah* as central to understanding the eucharistic prayer are in Cesare Giraudo, *La Struttura Letteraria della Preghiera Eucaristica. Saggio Sullagenesi Letteraria di una Forma. Tòda Veterotestamentaria Berakah Giudaica, Anafora Cristiana* (Rome: Biblical Institute Press, 1981); and *Eucaristia per la Chiesa*, Prospettive Teologiche sulla l'Eucaristia a Partire della "Lex Orandi" (Rome: Gregorian University Press, 1989). A much earlier use of the *berakah* to explain the theology of the eucharistic prayer is in Louis Bouyer, *Eucharist* (Notre Dame, Ind.: University of Notre Dame, 1968), 15-135. Boyer relies on earlier scholars such as J. P. Audet.

54. Gail Ramshaw-Schmidt, *Christ in Sacred Speech* (Philadelphia: Fortress Press, 1986), 77-78.

55. The use of "classic" indicates those elements that are most generally found in eucharistic prayers in the tradition. It is not meant to suggest that there is but one model for eucharistic praying. In fact a review of these prayers discloses much variation within the commonly agreed-upon anaphoral structure. See, for example, the useful overview of these ritual and theological differences in Hans Bernhard Meyer, *Eucharistie, Geschichte, Theologie, Pastoral: Handbuch der Liturgiewissenschaft* 4 (Regensburg: Friedrich Pustet, 1989), esp. Chapter 3, "Vom Herrenmahl zur Eucharistiefeier," and Chapter 4, "Die Ritusfamilien des Ostens und des Westens," 87-164. A helpful comparison summary of the Antiochean and Alexandrian anaphoral structure is on p. 133. For a collection of such texts and appropriate comparisons within and among liturgical families, see Anton Hanggi and Irmgard Pahl, *Prex Eucharistica: Textus e Variis Liturgiis Antiquioribus Selecti* (Fribourg: Editions Universitaires, 1968), and the translations in R. C. D. Jasper and G. J. Cuming, *Prayers of the Eucharist*.

56. That this motif is underexplored in the present reformed liturgy will be explained in section five.

57. Louis Bouyer argues that the sources for this prayer are Eastern and include the *Apostolic Constitutions*, the Liturgy of St. James and of St. Basil. See *Eucharist,* 448.

58. Joseph Keenan, "The Importance of the Creation Motif in the Eucharistic Prayer," *Worship* 53(4): 341-56.

59. B. Anderson, "Creation":

> Although all God's creatures are summoned to praise their Creator, human beings are the only earthlings in whom praise can become articulate. They are made for conversation with God, for a dialogue in an I-and-thou relation.... Israel's calling is to vocalize the praise that wells up from all peoples and nations (34).

60. J. Keenan, "The Importance of the Creation Motif," 349.

61. The full text is found in A. Hanggi and I. Pahl, *Prex Eucharistica.* 82-95; see also Jasper-Cuming, *Prayers of the Eucharist*, 104-13.

62. See B. Anderson, "Creation":

> Apparently Canaanite mythology does not deal with creation in the cosmic sense but with the maintenance of the created order in the face of the periodic threats of chaos.... The OT contains reminiscences of these ancient myths of creation against chaos (44).

He then cites Herman Gunkel, "The Influence of Babylonian Mythology Upon the Biblical Creation Story," Charles A. Muenchow, trans., in B. W. Anderson, ed. *Creation in the*

Old Testament (Philadelphia: Fortress Press, 1984), 25-52; and Anderson, *Creation Versus Chaos: The Reinterpretation of Mythical Symbolism in the Bible* (New York: Association Press, 1967), chapter one.

63. On this term in the history of religions and why is was repeated annually, most usually in the spring, see Mircea Eliade, *Cosmos and Myth*, trans. Willard Trask (New York: Harper Torchbooks, 1959).

64. On the intrinsic connection among these things, see Susan Power Bratton, "Christian Ecotheology and the Old Testament," *Environmental Ethics* 6(2): 195-209.

65. B. Anderson, "Creation," 29-30: "Creation by the Word came to be the normative expression of the mode of God's creative work. . . . God's word is an act, an event, a sovereign command, which accomplishes a result. The creation story affirms that God's Word, mighty in history, is also the very power which brought the creation into being. Since the creative Word establishes a personal relationship between the creator and the creation, the Christian faith affirms with theological consistency that the Logos (Word) became flesh in a person (John 1:1-18)."

66. Here is the Latin original (of the first prayer after the creation account):

> Omnipotens sempiterne Deus,
> qui es in omnium operum tuorum dispensations mirabilis,
> intelligant redempti tui, non fuisse excellentius,
> quod initio factus est mundus,
> quam quod in fine saeculorum
> Pascha nostrum immolatus est Christus.

The source for this prayer is the previous Roman Missal, see P. Bruylants, *Les Oraisons*, no. 385.

67. A review of the Latin text of this second (i.e., alternative) prayer yields something of the balance customarily found in Latin collects, which text is from the former Roman Missal. See P. Bruylants, *Les Oraisons*:

> Deus, qui mirabiliter creasti hominem
> et mirabilius redemisti,
> da nobis, quaesumus,
> contrea oblectamenta peccati mentis ratione presistere,
> ut mereamur ad aeterna gaudia prevenire.
> Per Christum Dominum nostrum. (no. 786)

68. A comparison of the titles for God in the present Latin *Missale Romanum* reveals that among the most frequently used terms, *omnipotens* is used 277 times, whereas *creator* is used 5 times. See Thaddaus A. Schnitker and Wolfgang A. Slaby, *Concordantia Verbalia Missalis Romani* (Westfalen: Aschendorff Munster, 1983), col. 398-99, 1704-16.

69. In *Christ in Sacred Speech*, p. 30, Gail Ramshaw-Schmidt states:

> Thus at the beginning of the Great Thanksgiving, we pray along with Abraham who obeyed the call (Genesis 12:4), with Moses, who received the Torah (Exodus 19:20), and with Jesus, who was the Word (John 1:1). As we eat bread and wine, we recall Abraham, who shared his food with three mysterious visitors (Genesis 18:8), Moses, who ate and drank with God on Sinai and did not die (Exodus 24:11), and

Jesus, who breaking bread on Sunday evening, showed forth his wounds (Luke 24:31).

70. See among others Jürgen Moltmann, *The Future of Creation: Collected Essays*, trans. Margaret Kohl (Philadelphia: Fortress Press, 1979), 119-30.

71. See Edward J. Kilmartin, *Christian Liturgy* (Kansas City: Sheed and Ward, 1988), especially 100-99; and Jean Corbon, *The Wellspring of Worship*, trans. Matthew O'Connell (New York: Paulist Press, 1988).

72. Because of the weaknesses in the present ICEL translation, the Latin text is particularly illustrative:

> Vere sanctus es, Domine,
> et merito te laudat omnis a te condita creatura,
> quia per Filium tuum,
> Dominum nostrum Iesum Christum,
> Spiritus Sancti operante virtute,
> vivificas et sanctificas universa,
> et populum tibi congregare non desinis,
> ut a solis ortu usque ad occasum
> oblatio munda offeratur nomini tuo.

73. The Latin reads:

> Haec ergo dona, quaesumus,
> Spiritus tui ruore sanctifica,
> ut nobis Corpus et Sanguinis fiant
> Domine nostri Iesu Christi.
>
> Et supplices deprecamur
> ut Corporis et Sanguinis Christi participes
> a Spiritu Sancto congregemur in unum.

74. This assertion is not to ignore the difficulty some liturgists have with the present "split epiclesis," that is the now separate invocations for the transformation of the gifts and the intercession for the Church.

75. See Cinette Ferriere, "A Propos de *Dieu-potier* Images de la Création et Foi Chrétienne en Dieu Créateur," *Paroisse et Liturgie* 48(6): 533-48.

76. See J. Moltmann, *God in Creation*, 9-13; and Lukas Vischer, "Giver of Life—Sustain Your Creation!" *The Ecumenical Review* 42(2): 143-49.

77. For example, Phillipians 2:6-11, Colossians 1:15-20, 1 Timothy 3:16. See B. Anderson, "Creation," 41-42: Jesus Christ is the "likeness of God" (2 Cor 4:4) and the "image of the invisible God, the first-born of all creation" (Col 1:15). This language recalls the "image of God" in Genesis 1:26 just as Hebrews 2:5-9 interprets the "man" who is "crowned with glory and honor" (Ps 8:4-6) christologically.

78. See Jordi Gilbert Tarruell, "Los Formularios de la Benedicion del Agua en el 'Ordo Baptismi Parvolorum' y en el 'Ordo Initiationis Christianae Adultorum,'" *Ephemerides Liturgicae* 88(4): 275-309; and the recent studies in English by Mark Searle, "*Fons Vitae*: A Case Study in the Use of Liturgy as a Theological Source," in *Fountain of Life*, ed. Gerard Austin (Washington: Pastoral Press, 1991), 217-42, an important essay in the methodology of

liturgical theology; and Dominic E. Serra, "The Blessing of Baptismal Water at the Paschal Vigil in the Post-Vatican II Rite," *Ecclesia Orans* 7(3): 343-68.

79. The General Instructions and Rites of Christian Initiation for Adults and for Children are introduced by another document called the General Instruction [on] Christian Initiation (hereafter GICI). All quotations from General Instruction on Christian Initiation and from the adult rite of initiation (RCIA) are from the ICEL translation of 1988. The numbering cited is that used in the *Study Edition* (Chicago: Liturgy Training Publications, 1988).

80. The second form of the blessing prayer also capitalizes on the notion of washing by asking God to

> Make holy this water which you have created,
> so that all who are baptized in it may be washed clean of sin
> and born again to live as your children. (222 B)

81.
> Grant that these catechumens,
> who, like the woman of Samaria,
> thirst for living water. (154 A)
> Now, by your power,
> free these elect from the cunning of Satan,
> as they draw near to the fountain of living water. (154 B)

82.
> Deepen the faith and understanding
> of these elect, chosen for baptism.
> Give them new birth in your living waters,
> so that they may be numbered among your adopted children. (182)

83. Sebastian P. Brock has investigated these rites and forwarded interesting theses. See "The Consecration of Water in the Oldest Manuscripts of the Syrian Orthodox Baptismal Liturgy," *Orientalia Christiana Periodica* 37(2): 317-32.

84. Your Son willed that water and blood should flow from his side as he hung upon the cross (222 A).

> Praise to you, Lord Jesus Christ, the Father's only Son,
> for you offered yourself on the cross,
> that in the blood and water flowing from your side
> and through your death and resurrection
> the Church might be born. (222 B; repeated in 222 D)

85.
> The God of power and Father of Our Lord Jesus Christ
> has freed you from sin
> and brought you to new life
> through water and the Holy Spirit.
> He now anoints you with the chrism of salvation,
> so that, united with his people,
> you may remain for ever a member of Christ
> who is Priest, Prophet and King. (228)

This prayer refers to the important notions of remaining "a member of Christ who is Priest, Prophet and King" which remain left out of the celebration if confirmation follows immediately. In our judgment the inclusion of this statement into the sequence of water—baptism-confirmation-first eucharist at the Easter Vigil would be a helpful adjustment to this rite.

86. The reference here is specific in that our concern is with what occurs because of the use of water, not what occurs through the use of any other symbolic gestures or elements, such as tracing the cross, imposing hands, kiss of peace, or the use of the oil of catechumens, chrism, and bread and wine.

87. The footnote to this text cites Romans 8:15, Galations 4:5, Trent Denziger, 1524.796. Our concern here is not to describe in full all the results of baptism as, for example, those listed in GICI 5, but merely to indicate the results of using the symbol of water or in tests that refer to the use of water.

88. As seen in the texts, thus:

> May he give them the new life of the Holy Spirit
> whom we are about to call down upon this water. (220)

> Praise to you, almighty God and Father,
> for you have created water to cleanse and give life. (222 D)

> By water and the Holy Spirit
> you freed your sons and daughters from sin
> and gave them new life. (234)

> By the power of the Holy Spirit
> give to this water the grace of your Son,
> so that in the sacrament of baptism
> all those whom you have created in your likeness
> may be cleansed from sin
> and rise to a new birth of innocence. . . . (222 A)

> You have called your children, N. and N.,
> to this cleansing water and new birth . . . . (222 C,D,E)
> We pray for these your servants,
> who eagerly approach the waters of new birth
> and hunger for the banquet of life. (175 B)

> Let us pray for these elect, that God in his mercy may make them responsive to his love, so that through the waters of rebirth they may receive pardon for their sins and have life in Christ Jesus our Lord. (182)

> Give them new birth in your living waters,
> so that they may be numbered among your adopted children. (182)

> As proclaimed in the prayers for the blessing of the water, baptism is a cleansing water of rebirth that makes us God's children born from on high. (GICI, 5)

89. Philippe Rouillard, "From Human Meal to Christian Eucharist," in *Living Bread, Saving Cup: Readings on the Eucharist*, ed. R. Kevin Seasoltz (Collegeville, Minn.: The Liturgical Press, 1982), 126. This article appeared originally in *Notitiae* (1977), nos. 131-32.

90. See Philippe Rouillard, "From Human Meal to Christian Eucharist."

91. The general instruction on the Roman Missal states that "following the example of Christ, the Church has always used bread and wine with water to celebrate the Lord's Supper" (no. 281). It then states:

> The nature of the sign demands that the material for the eucharistic celebration truly have [sic] the appearance of food. Even though unleavened and baked in the traditional shape, the eucharistic bread should be made in such a way that . . . the priest is able actually to break the host into parts and distribute them to at least some of the faithful. . . . The action of the breaking of the bread, the simple term for the eucharist in apostolic times, will more clearly bring out the force and meaning of the sign of the unity of all in the one bread and of their charity, since the one bread is being distributed among the members of one family. (no. 283)

92. See Jerome Murphy O'Connor, "Eucharist and Community in 1 Corinthians," in *Living Bread*, 1-30. For some important patristic sources, see Willy Rordorf, et. al., *The Eucharist of the Early Christians*, trans. Matthew O'Connell (New York: Pueblo, 1978). This work contains descriptions of the eucharist from the *Didache* through the *Apostolic Constitutions* and helpful commentaries.

93. See the 1983 edition of *Pastoral Care of the Sick: Rites of Anointing and Viaticum*, noting in particular the distinction between rites for the sick and those for the dying as well as the new Mass formula in the Sacramentary if either the rite of anointing, viaticum, or both, take place during Mass.

94. The rite presumes the distribution of communion under the forms of bread and wine even when viaticum is given outside of Mass (nos. 193, 207).

95. See, for example, *General Instruction of the Roman Missal* (nos. 281-85) about bread and wine for the eucharist.

96. See Don Saliers, "Liturgical Aesthetics," in *New Dictionary of Sacramental Worship*, ed. Peter E. Fink (Collegeville, Minn.: The Liturgical Press, 1990), 80-89.

97. See Pelagio Visentin, "Creazione—Storia della salvezza—Liturgia," *Rivista Liturgica* 77(3): 267.

98. One of the premises of the document from the (United States) Bishops' Committee on the Liturgy, *Environment and Art in Catholic Worship*, is this authenticity in sign and symbolic interaction in liturgy; see nos. 12-26 for some theoretical grounding for the document.

99. John Paul II addresses this point in "Peace With God the Creator, Peace With All of Creation: Message of His Holiness Pope John Paul II for the Celebration of the World Day of Peace, 1 January, 1990," *Origins* 19(28): nos. 14-16:

> Finally, the aesthetic value of creation cannot be overlooked. Our very contact with nature has a deep restorative power; contemplation of its magnificence imparts peace and serenity. The Bible speaks again and again of the goodness and beauty of creation, which is called to glorify God (cf. Genesis 1:4ff.; Psalm 8:2; 104:1ff.; Wisdom 13:3-5; Sirach 39:16, 33; 43:1, 9). More difficult perhaps, but no less profound, is the contemplation of the works of human ingenuity. Even cities can have a beauty all their own, one that ought to motivate people to care for their surroundings. Good urban planning is an important part of environmental protection, and respect for the natural contours of the land is an indispensable prerequisite for ecologically

sound development. The relationship between a good aesthetic education and the maintenance of a healthy environment cannot be overlooked.

100. See Denis Carroll, "Creation," in *New Dictionary of Theology*, 249. Carroll states that "the Eastern conception of Christ's universal rule—Christ the Pantocrator or Cosmocrator—has much to offer this reconstruction."

101. Taken from the commentary on the *Rule* entitled "The Abbot," in *RB80: The Rule of St. Benedict in Latin and English with Notes*, ed. Timothy Fry, et. al. (Collegeville, Minn.: The Liturgical Press, 1981), 370. A contemporary perspective on how the Catholic approach to the sacramentality of life can influence both sacramental and liturgical theology is offered by Philip J. Murnion, "A Sacramental Church in the Modern World," *Origins* 14(6). Particularly notable is Murnion's call for "Benedictine-like" communities that can reflect a new order for the world based on the principle of the sacramentality in all of life. He states: Central to any notion of sacramentality is the fact of and a belief in the incarnation. We believe that in and through Christ there is a permanent union of God and this world, the divine and the human condition. We cannot look at the special actions we call the sacraments or the particular challenges faced by the Church as sacrament without considering the present state of our world and our human condition, which are the flesh of God's presence among us.

> . . . The new order is one that recognizes explicitly, not begrudgingly, the community of all life, the interdependence of all persons, the symbiosis of human life and the environment. It also rewards relationships rather than acquisitions as the measure of success.

102. See Paul Weigand, "Escape from the Birdbath: A Reinterpretation of St. Francis as a Model for the Ecological Movement," in P. N. Joranson, ed., *Cry of the Environment*, 148-57.

103. Apostolic Letter *Inter sanctos*: Acta Apostolicae Sedis 71(16): 1509f.

104. John Paul II, "Peace With God the Creator."

105. Some indications of the similarities and differences between these two traditions as they bear on reverence for creation are found in René Dubois, "Franciscan Conservation Verses Benedictine Stewardship," in *Ecology and Religion in History*, ed. David and Eileen Spring (New York: Harper and Row, 1975), 114-36.

106. For a critique that in the reformed liturgy, liturgical scholars did not concern themselves with creation despite the fact that it was present so strongly in patristic writings about Sunday and also in oriental liturgies, see Yves M. Congar, "Le Thème de Dieu-Créateur et les Explications de l'Hexamèrons dans la Tradition Chrétienne," *L'Homme devant Dieu* 1 (Lyons: Editions Montaigne Aubiere, 1963), 189-215.

107. See Annibale Bugnini, *The Reform of the Liturgy, 1948-1975*, trans. Matthew J. O'Connell (Collegeville, Minn.: The Liturgical Press, 1990), 337-92; Frederick R. McManus, "The Roman Order of Mass from 1964-1969: The Preparation of the Gifts," *Shaping English Liturgy*, ed. Peter Finn and James Schellmam (Washington: Pastoral Press, 1990), 107-38; Thomas A. Krosnicki, "Preparing the Gifts: Clarifying the Rite," *Worship* 65(2): 149-59; and Edward Foley, Kathleen Hughes, and Gilbert Ostdiek, "The Preparatory Rites: A Case Study in Liturgical Ecology," *Worship* 67(1): 17-38.

108. In a publication prepared by the Churches participating in the Inter-Lutheran Commission on Worship, *Lutheran Book of Worship* (Minneapolis: Augsburg Publishing House, 1978), 66.

WATCH THE CROWS: ENVIRONMENTAL RESPONSIBILITY AND THE BENEDICTINE TRADITION

Hugh Feiss, OSB

EVERY ADULT ACT OF BELIEVING IS A *PARTICULAR* PERSPECTIVE ON THE world—*particular*, because hardly unique or totally original, but *particular* also because never simply an exact replication of a previous believer's faith. Analogously, every saint is both a unique instance of holiness and "the founder of a new, fruitful way of life in God within the community. . . ." A few saints become paradigms for thousands of other saints. In them the Spirit initiates a way of imitating Christ, which becomes a living mirror for others. Among these exemplary saints we may count the founders of religious orders: for example, Basil, Augustine, Benedict, Dominic, Francis and Clare, Ignatius, Teresa of Avila, and John of the Cross.[1] The writings, biographies, and traditions stemming from these founders of religious orders have guided the lives of thousands of people in fruitful ways.

In this chapter, I would like to examine the form of sanctity inaugurated by St. Benedict, embodied in his Rule, and lived by hundreds of thousands of Benedictines during the last fifteen centuries. In *Renewing the Earth*, the American bishops state: "Our Christian way of life, as saints like Benedict, Hildegard, and St. Francis showed us, is a road to community with all creation."[2] It is Benedict and Hildegard and the tradition they lived and represented on which I will concentrate in this chapter to discover how their way of Christian life is a road to community with all creation. One could also speak of Francis, Clare, Bonaventure, and Anthony, or of Dominic, Thomas Aquinas, and Suso. I use the Benedictine tradition as a test case only because it is the tradition in which I am most expert.

I. Benedict's Rule

The Rule of Benedict (RB) is a sober, practical document that distills, or better, holds in suspension many of the ideas of earlier writers.[3] It is one of the ironies of modern historical research that this Rule, long praised for its moderation and sobriety, is now thought to derive in large part from a bizarre document called *The Rule of the Master*.[4]

Benedict gives few hints about his attitude toward the natural world. Apart from legislation about not eating meat, Benedict doesn't mention animals anywhere in the Rule. Nowhere does he say that monasteries should be situated in idyllic spots. Benedict's own monastery, Monte Cassino, was located on the top of what is today a rocky and rather uninviting hill overlooking a main highway traversed by Huns in his time and by the Axis and Allied armies in World War II. Nevertheless, his followers through the ages have tended to choose their sites carefully and to husband their surroundings with care.

Stability and a Sense of Place

An important reason for the care Benedictine men and women have shown for their surroundings is their vow of stability. For better or worse, Benedictines join a particular community located in a particular set of buildings in a particular geographic location. Monks live their entire lives either at that particular spot or in association with it. Monastics have no particular inclination to foul their own nest. They do have every opportunity to know their place well, even if they don't work directly on the land. Benedictines become aware even of slow changes. For example, when I first came to the monastery of which I am a member, older members told me of nighthawks, bluebirds, and meadow larks that once lived on or near our monastery property, but which have now disappeared. I myself have seen the demise of the acorn woodpecker and the expansion of crows and feral cats around the monastery. Because of the vow of stability, one thinks in terms of long periods of time, of an inheritance of land and buildings, and of values conveyed from generation to generation, and one is aware of subtle changes in the place that is one's own.

Creatures in the Presence of Their God

Because Benedictines are tied to a single place, it is in that place that they must find God. The Rule of Benedict is suffused with the idea of the presence of God.[5] God is everywhere; God sees everything that happens. Although, as Terrence Kardong says, Benedict is too hierarchical in his outlook to think of humanity and other species as companions, Benedict does think of all created species on this side of the infinite qualitative distance that separates creation from God. The monastery is fundamentally God's house, just as the world is God's world. We are pilgrims, guests, and workers in his world, not owners. Hence, however much human beings may differ from other species by the measures proper to a finite world, from the standpoint of the infinite God they are like all other species, creatures made to praise and glorify God. If humans give this praise and glory by their prayer, work, and reading, they do so in the name of all creation.

To this ontological situation of creaturehood corresponds the particular virtues that Benedict emphasizes. Of all human attitudes and vices, he is most suspicious of overweening pride. The only proper attitude of a human being in the presence of God is humility, a frank acknowledgment that one's being and happiness are God's gift. "Humility" derives from "humus," "soil"; human beings were made by God from the dust of the earth. This is an honorable enough pedigree; to be ashamed of one's origins or to pretend that one is self-created is a bitter mistake.[6] Hence, a craftsman who takes undue pride in his work is to be given a different job until he comes to his senses. A priest is not to think he deserves special consideration (RB 62). The abbot is not to disdain the counsel of the newest and youngest member of the community (RB 3.3). All are to obey superiors (RB 5), and all are to obey each other (RB 71). The first word of the Rule is "listen"[7]: listening befits the learner, the healer, the person of prayer and devout reading, those who serve, and the humble of the earth.

Hence, the Rule is penetrated by a doctrine of universal reverence: for God in the liturgy, for all human beings, for their bodily and behavioral weaknesses (RB 72), for God-given offices (RB 3, RB 60), and for physical things. Reverence is at once an admiration for the being of the other and an action aimed at the other's well-being. Monks, Benedict says, quoting Romans 12:10, should vie with one another in showing respect to the other (RB 72).[8]

Service, Not Control

Benedict's emphasis on humility involves something else—a preference for people over procedures, for service over managerial control. Benedict makes this clear in his masterful description of the task of the cellarer, who, while completely subject to the abbot, looks after the temporal needs of the community:

> As cellarer of the monastery, there should be chosen from the community someone who is wise, mature in conduct, temperate, not an excessive eater, not proud, excitable, offensive, dilatory, or wasteful, God-fearing, and like a father to the whole community. . . . He should not annoy the brothers. . . . He must show every care and concern for the sick, children, guests, and the poor. . . . He should do everything with moderation. . . . Above all, let him be humble. He will provide the brothers their allotted amount of food without any pride or delay. . . .[9]

Thus, one by one Benedict denies to the cellarer those little delays and words and gestures that he might use to trumpet the fact that he is in control. The cellarer is in charge, under the abbot, but God is in control.[10]

Need, Moderation, and Work

Although Benedict required no vow of poverty, he did want the vice of private ownership to be eliminated within the community (RB 33). Each was to work at what was commanded; each was to receive what was needed (RB 34). What was to be avoided above all was superfluity, satiety, or overindulgence.[11] Even at the corporate level, greed was to be avoided. Abbey products were to be sold at slightly less than the going rate.

Benedict's Rule is credited with having done much to raise esteem for physical labor in Western society. He doesn't advance any explicit theory about physical work, but he did inherit and endorse the idea that manual labor was part of monastic life. He was certainly not a man ashamed that he had a body. The physical world was there as a part of creation; human beings had to find a way to live in this world. Ordinarily, this implied some physical work.

Communities of monastics, working hard (though perhaps for shorter hours than those around them) and living frugally, often accumulated wealth. Moreover, monastic establishments often attracted donations (sometimes they competed for them by developing pilgrimage centers). The net result was extra wealth. Monastics used this surplus for church-building, for charity toward the needy, and for hospitality. But, as critics have alleged, the economic surplus has sometimes served to support a monastic lifestyle that has not been limited to necessities but has included superfluities.[12]

Benedict, though, urged frugality and moderation, as well as adaptation to the local situation. He legislated for a moderate use of wine, but observed: "where local circumstances dictate an amount much less than what is stipulated above, or even none at all, those who live there should bless God and not grumble" (RB 40.8).

"AND GOD SAW THAT IT WAS GOOD"

Clothing should suit the climate; "monks should wear what is available in the vicinity at a reasonable cost" (RB 55.7). This is a far cry from golf courses in the desert, strawberries in December, and grocery stores where the average product is transported over 1,300 miles before reaching the shelves of the store.

The Sacredness of the Ordinary

In the chapter on the cellarer quoted above, Benedict writes: "He will regard all utensils and goods of the monastery as sacred vessels of the altar, aware that nothing is to be neglected" (RB 31.10-11). There are several ways to interpret this sentence. (1) Benedict is drawing an analogy: just as the vessels belonging to the altar should be carefully cared for, so should the tools belonging to the monastery. (2) Benedict thinks that tools as such are sacred. Perhaps he meant both. If so, Benedict may see the use of tools as a way to participate in God's ongoing creative care for humanity, to fulfill one's God-given vocation as *homo faber*. Viewed this way, as means by which human necessities are provided, tools are instruments of the kingdom of God.[13] This service of physical tools parallels the spiritual tools of good works (RB 4), which are also instruments of the kingdom of God.[14]

If tools are sacred, then people are all the more so. In the statement about the cellarer quoted above, Benedict observed: "He must show every care and concern for the sick, children, guests, and the poor." St. Benedict's christology was typical of its time. In reaction to Arianism he emphasized the full divinity of Christ. His own particular concerns showed up in his concern for Christ in his little ones: the poor and the sick, the elderly and the young, and guests and pilgrims.[15] Christ is really present in these needy people; in fact the monks are told to bow to the guests, so that the Christ who is welcomed in them may be adored (RB 53.7). No effort should be spared in taking care of their needs. For their sake prohibitions against bathing and eating meat are lifted, and for them rules of fasting are mitigated (RB 36.1-2, 8-9). Although it is not a long step from venerating the Christ in guests and the poor to venerating the cosmic Christ, the Christ in the helpless species and ecosystems that depend totally on human restraint and care for their survival, this is a step the Rule of Benedict does not take.

Conclusion

In the end, the Rule of Benedict is concerned with guiding beginners in the monastic life (RB 73.9), with inculcating those virtues that will enable monastics to climb to the heights of perfection (RB 73.2). Benedict says little about what attitudes a monk should have toward nature. But he says a great deal about what sort of person the monk should be—frugal; reverent toward God, the abbot, other monks, guests, and the tools of the monastery; humble and hard-working; kind and compassionate

(RB 72.5); and quiet and thoughtful (RB 6). Benedict expected that such a person's way of acting would make him alien to the ways of the "world" (RB 4.20), that is, the ways of those who live for worldly power and gratification. Benedict's monk would certainly be out of place in a culture whose measures of success are power and money, which employs maximum technological force to squeeze as much as possible out of the natural world as quickly as possible. On the contrary, Benedict's monks are told to live in a way that will make them "friends of the planet and not its enemies."[16] Benedict's monk should be looking for the Christ, where others may be looking for a customer or contributor.[17] Benedict's monk should be striving for genuine humility by viewing himself in the presence of almighty God, where others may be seeking humanly bestowed status and power. Benedict's monk should work to support a frugal and healthy life devoted primarily to prayer and reading, where others may be working in order to consume. "Whoever needs more should feel humble because of his weakness, not self-important because of the kindness shown him" (RB 34.4).

II. Exemplary Lives

The Life of St. Benedict

St. Benedict's life is known only through the second book of the *Dialogues* of Pope St. Gregory the Great. Gregory was an effective and dedicated leader of the Church, as well as a brilliant theologian. He was not a historian in the modern sense, but he did have a talent for storytelling. The Rule of Benedict may be the fount of the Benedictine tradition, but the stories Gregory told in his *Dialogues* are the first great tributary to that diverse and meandering Benedictine stream.

After being a hermit at Subiaco and attracting a group of followers, Benedict went on to accept the position of abbot. A local priest named Florentius became jealous. He sent a poisoned loaf of bread to Benedict. The holy abbot accepted the gift graciously, though he knew it was poisoned. A crow used to come from the nearby woods at meal-times and take bread from the saint's hand. Benedict gave him the poisoned bread and told him to take it somewhere where no one could find it. The crow was reluctant, but eventually did what the saint asked. It returned after three hours and received its usual meal from the man of God. Benedict decided not long afterwards to move to Monte Cassino.[18]

Such stories are almost required elements in the lives of the early desert monks and medieval hermits. At this point, Benedict was in transition from being a hermit to being a full-fledged cenobite or member of an organized community of monastics. Of cenobites and animals there are fewer such stories. I believe the reason is twofold: hermits have deliberately abandoned human company, so they are more likely to seek out companions in the animal world. Secondly, hermits are not doing anything—not building anything and not even there to help anybody. With apologies to Barry Lopez, we might say hermits are there not to impose, not even to propose,[19] but at most to suppose and repose. They are there to listen, and what they hear is not just God speaking to their souls, but the God-given natural world speaking to their senses. The message is the same: "Be still, fear not, I am your God."

Bede's Life of Cuthbert

Cuthbert of Lindisfarne was not a Benedictine, but his life was written by St. Bede, a model Benedictine monk and scholar. Cuthbert joined the abbey of Melrose in 651 and later became prior. He did a good deal of missionary preaching in the north of England, and like St. Benedict, he was only a part-time hermit. Cuthbert eventually became bishop of Lindisfarne, but would often live alone at Inner Farne, a rocky, wind-swept island seven miles away, where he died in 687.[20]

Once, Cuthbert and a servant were on a preaching expedition and ran out of food. Cuthbert said God would provide for them through the ministry of an eagle. An eagle—no doubt the white-tailed sea eagle hunted to extinction in the British Isles, but now being reintroduced—caught a fish. The servant took the fish from the eagle. Cuthbert made the servant give half the fish back to the eagle, then shared the other half with the family of a woman who cooked it for him.

In the Celtic manner, Cuthbert would sometimes pray standing up to his neck in the ocean. At dawn he would come to the shore, kneel down, and pray some more. Sea otters could come and warm his feet with their breath and dry him with their fur. Cuthbert gave them a blessing, and back they went to the sea.

Another time, he performed a miracle which, Bede notes, recalls that of Father Benedict. Some ravens were tearing thatch out of a guest-house the brothers had built. Cuthbert ordered them to leave immediately. Three days later, one raven came back and indicated by its demeanor that it was sorry. Cuthbert said it could stay. The raven brought its mate, and she brought Cuthbert some hog's fat. Afterward, when he loaned this fat to the brothers to grease their boots, he pointed out what a fine example of penitence the ravens were.

Here is one last story about Cuthbert. One Friday he was traveling and fasting. He couldn't reach his destination, so he stopped at some deserted shepherds' huts. He collected some hay from the roof of one hut for his horse, then started singing psalms. The horse then pulled some hay off the roof, and they found a cloth containing bread and meat. Cuthbert gave half of the bread to the horse. He and the horse literally became companions, those who break bread together.

If we combine these Cuthbert stories we find a pattern: the animals help Cuthbert, Cuthbert helps them. Cuthbert shares what he receives from nature with his fellow human beings, with whom he shares a frugal way of life, and with his animal companions. Thus, human beings are at peace with their environment and with each other. This is the heart of the eremetical tradition, the central moral of the hundreds of stories in the lives of the hermit saints. Something very similar is the heart of the bishops' document, *Renewing the Earth,* the second paragraph of which sums up the signs of our times: "At the core of the environmental crisis is a moral challenge. It calls us to examine how we use and share the goods of the earth, what we pass on to future generations and how we live in harmony with God's creation" (425).

St. Wulstan of Worcester

As a boy, Wulstan of Worcester was educated at Benedictine monasteries, and, purposely spurning more lucrative possibilities, eventually entered the Benedictine Cathedral Priory at Worcester. In 1062 he became bishop of Worcester. An excellent bishop, he was able to retain his post after the Norman conquest and died in 1095.

Wulstan wore cheap clothes "and preferred to keep out the cold with the fleeces of sheep rather than with other kinds of skins." Some people suggested that he should at least wear cat skin. He responded that he had heard people singing "*Agnus Dei,*" but never "*Cattus Dei.*" Of this episode his biographer remarked, "What others would turn into ostentation, Wulstan turned into the stuff of compunction."[21]

Conclusion

These saints are in harmony with animals and all of nature. They recall the Garden of Eden. They anticipate the end-time when "The wolf shall be a guest of the lamb, and the leopard shall lie down with the kid; The calf and the young lion shall browse together, with a little child to guide them" (Is 11:6). Thus could claustrals and the cloister constitute a figurative paradise.

However, all this took place not *in illo tempore,* but in the space and time which we inhabit, within the terms of the widest of all the covenants save that of Christ: the covenant with Noah. The story of Noah's covenant with God has a message similar to these saint stories and the U.S. bishops' reading of the signs of the times. After Noah had disembarked from his long boat ride with the animals, "God said to Noah and to his sons with him: 'See, I am now establishing my covenant with you and your descendants after you and with every living creature that was with you: all the birds, and the various tame and wild animals that were with you and came out of the ark'" (Gn 9.8-10). This single covenant embraces Noah and his sons (communally, not individually), their descendants, and all the animals wild and tame.

III. Theology

Hildegard of Bingen (1098-1179) is not the typical theologian of Benedictine monasticism. She was in fact a very unique woman and visionary. Nevertheless, if I interpret her correctly, much of what she wrote was intended to provide a model of sound theology and to nudge prelates and pastors to show more zeal in teaching.[22] She teaches the theology developed during what Cardinal Newman called "the Benedictine Centuries."

Explanation of Benedict's Rule

Hildegard very seldom refers to Benedict or his Rule apart from a small work in which she offers some explanations of the Rule in response to some questions posed to her. There she says Benedict was remarkable for his discretion. His doctrine was like a hole punched in the middle of a barrel, at a height accommodating the majority of thirsty people. He didn't legislate just for those who could reach exceptionally high. She goes on to declare:

> Blessed Benedict drank his doctrine most mildly in the fear of God; he taught the commandments of God in piety; he constructed the wall of the Rule's holiness in charity; and in chastity he was a stranger to the pomps and delights of this world.[23]

Creation

Hildegard's doctrinal synthesis, the *Scivias*, is divided into three books. Like most of her works, the *Scivias* begins with a sketch of the theology of creation. We are concerned here with the first four visions in book one of the *Scivias*, which she devotes to creation, and the first vision of book three, which recapitulates some of the same material. These sections of the *Scivias* can be supplemented with the first four visions of the *De operatione Dei* (Do)[24] and the beginning of *Causae et Curae* (Ho), her medical treatise.[25]

The first vision of the *Scivias* places God on a great mountain the color of iron, which symbolizes the strength and stability of God's eternal kingdom (Sc 1.1.1; CC 8:52-54).[26] In the Godhead all visible and invisible things exist eternally in an incorporeal way (Do 1.7; 746A). God is the supreme Maker, who brings everything else into being (Ho 1).

Hildegard's third vision in the *Scivias* is of a great cosmic egg.[27] The fundamental truth about the cosmos is that "the visible and temporal is a manifestation of the invisible and eternal." The Triune God "created all things by His will, created them so that His Name would be known and glorified, showing in them not just the things that are visible and temporal, but also the things that are invisible and eternal" (Sc 1.3.1; CC 41:106-111).

The eternal God "marvelously by His will created every creature and marvelously by His will set it in its place" (Sc 1.6.1; CC 101:61-63). Each divine work is complete for the function proper to it (Do 1.7; 746B). Humanity is the most profound of all the works of God's mighty creation, made in a wondrous way with great glory from the dust of the earth and so entangled with the other parts of creation that it can never be separated from them. Human nature is a microcosm that contains the entire creation within itself (Ho 30, 41) Because they are so closely interconnected, the natural elements and humanity affect each other (Ho 17, 39, 44-45). The elements of the earth wait on humanity, which presides over them (Sc 1.3.16; CC 48:296-300).

Sin and Virtue

In the second vision of *Scivias* (book one), after a long excursus on marriage, Hildegard speaks of the doctrine of original sin. She maintains that creation, which had been made for the service of humanity, turned against humans and now opposes them (Sc 1.2.27; CC 32:660-671). Human beings, made in God's image and likeness, are tested by every creature (Sc 1.2.29; CC 33:684-685, 690-691).[28] Through sin some human beings desert the humanity of their nature (Sc 3.1.5; CC 333:235-236); others learn to live according to the dignity human nature has taught them (Do 1.9; 747B). Christ's coming has restored many virtues to humanity. Hildegard commends humility explicitly (Sc 1.2.31; CC 34:733-734, 729). Christ, who came into the world out of humility and charity, conquered the arrogant power of the devil through humility. By charity and humility human beings can vanquish the devil (Sc 1.2.33; CC 37:815-845).

The fourth vision of *Scivias* (book one), entitled "soul and body," speaks at length of the soul's experience of moral conflicts between virtue and vice. Reason struggles against carnal desire, depression, anger, hatred, and pride. The soul conquers these vices by finding in God's sublimity "the sweetest good, which is humility" (Sc 1.4.7; 71:365-366). It is useless to oppose God, who "never established anything unjust, but in the equity of His goodness He ordained all that is right" (Sc 1.4.10; CC 74:462-463). Using metaphors that are prominent in the Rule of Benedict, Hildegard compares the lot of humanity to that of a workman earning wages, or a sick person in need of a physician to prescribe the medicine of repentance (Sc 1.4.3; CC 90:972-979).

God knows the aims of all human acts (Sc 1.1.5; CC 10:108-110). Hence, fear of the Lord stands humbly in God's presence and gazes on his kingdom (Sc 3.1.1; CC 330:130-136). "God is to be dreaded by every creature with single-mindeness, so that they know He is the one true God, since there is no one apart from him and no one like him" (Sc 3.1.1; Hart 311; CC 331:140-143). Still it is "hard for human minds to fear God; for this is a heavy burden for soft and fragile dust, and human nature rebels against it" (Sc 3.1.1; Hart 311; CC 331:148-150).[29] Fear of the Lord is followed by poverty of spirit, which loves simplicity and sobriety of mind and attributes its good works to God (Sc 1.1.3; CC 9:80-85). On those who have these virtues,

God bestows many others (Sc 1.1.4; CC 10:100-103).

In summary, Hildegard sees the universe as a wondrous artifact of God. Creation reveals God and elicits praise. Every creature has its place, and all that God created is just. Humanity is the greatest of God's earthly creatures, but is inextricably bound with all others. Other creatures serve humanity; humanity presides over them. Humanity is one with creation, yet other than the rest of creation by reason of its presiding role.

Hildegard's moral view derives from her theology of creation. Her explanation of her first vision is a faithful echo of the basic teachings of the Rule of Benedict. Recognizing that God is God and that all else is "ashes of ashes" (Sc. Prol. CC 1:9), Benedict's twelfth-century disciple urges her readers to stand reverently in God's praise, to contemplate his realm, to love simplicity and sobriety, and to recognize that all that one is and has is God's gift.

A Lyrical Echo

In addition to writing theological treatises, Hildegard also composed poetry and music, a number of which are devoted to creation. God is the creator, and all that he made is orderly:

> O eternal strength
> You ordered all things within your heart.
> All things were created through your Word,
> Just as you wished.[30]

The first human being was a microcosm of the entire universe:

> When God looked upon
> The face of the human being which he had formed,
> He saw all his works whole
> In that human form.[31]

IV. History

Travelers to Benedictine monasteries in Europe are invariably impressed by the beauty of the sites and the upkeep of these institutions. I believe the reasons for the careful upkeep of monasteries lie in the virtues that Benedict's Rule inculcates: stability, moderation, and humble awareness of the presence of God in every aspect of life. The beautiful sites are another matter.

Pre-Benedictine monks had gone out to the desert to avoid temptation and to fight with the devil. They certainly didn't experience the desert the way a member of the Desert Trail Association experiences the deserts of the Great Basin. For the latter, and for many Americans, the desert and the mountains of western North America are the quintessential wildernesses—places of unspoiled natural beauty and freedom from societal constraints.[32] The early monastics were in search of freedom, not beauty. In the twelfth century, when the Cistercians made a point of going into deserted or wilderness areas, they, too, were drawn not by beauty, but by isolation, though they usually found or created both.

That monasteries today occupy beautiful sites is partially because of choice and partially because of accidents of history. Early monasteries, deriving their layout and ethos at least partially from the rural estates of the later Roman Empire, aimed at being self-sufficient, as Benedict had urged (RB 66.6-7). This required rather specific, naturally endowed locations. However, urban and suburban monasticism also prospered during the Benedictine centuries. It was the romanticism-tinged revival of the nineteenth century that established the mental association between monasteries and idyllic rural spots. This association was aided by the fact that the ruins of the hundreds of monasteries destroyed at the Reformation or the French Revolution had a much better chance of surviving in an isolated rural spot than in an urban environment.

Today's wilderness, and perhaps the place where tomorrow's monastics will decide is the best place to avoid the seductions of wealth and power, may well be the desolation of the inner city. Certainly, the urban landscape could use a few settlers committed to stability and moderation. Whether that will happen only those endowed with foreknowledge know—God and perhaps the crows.

V. A Concluding Message from the *Corvidae*

The pioneer Benedictine monastics who came to the United States in the second half of the nineteenth century were influenced by the romantic view of monasticism. For the most part, they settled in beautiful rural sites where they farmed large areas of land. They recruited their new candidates largely from among German immigrant populations with close ties to the land. But all of that is changed now. Most American monasteries have sold or leased their farms to others. There are so few farmers left in America that the odds are that a monastery will not have any members who are knowledgeable and enthusiastic farmers. In any case, the primary lessons which Benedictine tradition brings to theological reflection on ecology have to do not with farming technique, but with human attitudes.

Earlier, we learned how a crow saved Benedict from being poisoned. We learned also that Cuthbert pointed out to the brethren of Farne what a good example of penitence two ravens were. This use of animals as moral exemplars has precedents in the earliest days of the Church. These moral examples at least show a sense of relatedness and comradeship with the natural world.

The *Physiologus*, a collection of natural history lore and moral applications, said of the crow:

> Let human beings learn to love their children from the example and from the sense of duty of crows. They diligently follow their offspring as an escort when they fly, and, fearing that the babies might possibly pine away, food is laid in, then they do not neglect their chore of feeding for a long time.[33]

Moreover, crows rightly divided their inheritance among all their sons, rather than favoring only the first born.

The honorable place crows have in the vitae of the Benedictine saints and the exemplary account of crows given in the *Physiologus* are reminiscent of the place they had among the native peoples of North America. Crows were associated with the new world anticipated by the Ghost Dancers of the late 1800s:

> Stand ready, stand ready,
> So that when the crow calls you,
> So that when the crow calls you,
> You will see him,
> You will see him.

The crow has finished a road: "His children,/He has brought them together." Hence, one may hope the time is coming when his children may sing: "He has renewed our life. He has taken pity on us."[34]

When I was a boy in the monastery school, the monks of the monastery logged the north side of the hill on which the monastery was built: an idyllic site overlooking the Willamette Valley with a view of a number of volcanic peaks in the Cascade Range. Eventually, Douglas fir were planted on the logged-over hillside. When the trees there had grown to about twenty feet in height, a large flock of crows began to roost in them. For a decade or so these crows never came to the top of the hill. Then, about twenty years ago they began looking for food on the hilltop lawn. Finally, over the last ten years, these crows began nesting on the top of the hill. As I wrote the first draft of this paper, they were feeding their young in their nests around the top of hill. They were feeding them a combination of garbage from the dumpster and baby birds from the nests of robins and other birds. The lure of discarded table scraps in the dumpster is probably the main factor for the spread of the crows to the hilltop. The dumpster itself was installed as part of a large-scale, well-meaning recycling and refuse disposal plan.

In this there is a lesson. The abiding ecological relevance of the Benedictine tradition lies in its emphasis on stability of place, moderation, and a humble awareness of

God's presence in every place and act and person. If Benedictine monastics today are true to their tradition, they will know their place well, they will treat it respectfully, and, like Noah who sent out a corvid to explore the newly verdant earth, they will observe the crows. Benedictines, if true to their tradition, will love the next generation enough not to squander its patrimony in indulgent living today. They will neither overproduce nor overconsume. They will cooperate together to make sure that all landscaping and land use are for the benefit of all the interdependent species of their particular place. They will try to protect the weak and threatened. For, as Hildegard taught us, God has made all things in order, and each thing has its place both in the world of God's green creation and in the chorus of praise, which is the highest fulfillment of every creature on earth.

We may end by following this advice and once more observing the crows:

Infant in a pinewood
Lying in a basket
Not owning anything . . .
I listened to the shiny
Crows outside my window . . .
And even now
When I wake up early
And overhear the crows . . .
My heart grows light
As light as if the world
Had never fallen.[35]

Notes

1. Hans Urs von Balthasar, *Die Grossen Ordensregeln* (Einsiedeln: Benziger, 1961), 7-8.

2. "Renewing the Earth: An Invitation to Reflection and Action on the Environment in Light of Catholic Social Teaching," *Origins* 21 (December 12, 1991), 428. Also published as a booklet by the United States Catholic Conference, Washington, D.C.

3. It has been my good fortune to spend many hours in conversation with the foremost American scholar of the Rule of Benedict, Fr. Terrence Kardong, OSB. I have also been an eager student of his writings. There is little that I know about the Rule of Benedict that I did not learn or relearn from him. In particular, the following section owes a great deal to his article "Ecological Resources in the Benedictine Rule," *Assumption Abbey Newsletter* vol. 23, no. 1 (January 1955), 1-8, which also appeared in *Embracing the Earth: Catholic Approaches to Ecology*, ed. Albert J. LaChance and John E. Carroll (Maryknoll, N.Y.: Orbis, 1994), 163-173. Fr. Terrence will be relieved to hear that nevertheless he is not responsible for the ideas set forth here.

4. *The Rule of the Master*, trans. Luke Eberle (Kalamazoo, Mich.: Cistercian Publications, 1977).

"AND GOD SAW THAT IT WAS GOOD"

5. See the thematic index to *RB 80: The Rule of Benedict*, ed. Timothy Fry (Collegeville, Minn.: Liturgical Press, 1981), 565.

6. RB 7, "Humility." It is extremely difficult to interpret Benedict's idea of humility in a way that makes complete sense to a late twentieth-century monastic, much less a late-twentieth-century psychologist. The reasons for this are many. My interpretation of the essential core of what Benedict meant should be clear enough.

7. "*Obsculta*" (or "*ausculta*"). The root of the Latin word "to obey" (*ob-edire*) is "to hear" (*audire*).

8. Charles Cummings, "Benedictine Reverence Revisited," *American Benedictine Review* 41 (1990), 325-334.

9. *RB 80*, ch. 31, 226-229.

10. See Hugh Feiss, "The Spirituality of St. Bernard for Managers," *Cistercian Studies* 25 (1990), 267-276.

11. RB 55:11: "*superfluum est, amputari debet.*"

12. There are several ways in which medieval Benedictines did not manifest the ecological sensitivity present in the Rule. As agriculturists, they shared the attitudes of their time regarding draining wet lands and cutting forests. Of course, to know the significance of wetlands in the year 1100 would have required almost preternatural wisdom. Secondly, as centers of literacy and culture, the monasteries and their inhabitants tended to gravitate toward the wealthier classes and "clerical" work. Probably, monks were more often farm managers than farm laborers. Even the Rule of Benedict seems to assume that usually monks would not be engaged in heavy farm work (RB 48.7). Thirdly, as Brendan Bradshaw argued regarding Ireland, *The Dissolution of the Monasteries in Ireland* (New York: Cambridge, 1974) and John Davies says of Wales in the *History of Wales* New York: Penguin, 1994, 227-229), by the time of the Reformation the underpopulated monasteries were essentially leasers of land, not farmers and not even managers. Those who leased that land from them were the squires, not the peasants who actually worked the land. Unfortunately, this can be the case today again in America, where some monasteries, unable to operate their own farms, lease them to corporate farmers. There are certainly other, more creative possibilities. Some monasteries have a policy of selling off any land they are not actively cultivating. Also, monastery lands could be leased on a long-term basis to young people who would like to establish family farms that follow practices to promote the health both of the land and the food consumers. In any case, there is still much to be learned about the agricultural practices of medieval monastics, especially women. Whatever their practice, the validity of the teaching in the Rule remains the same.

13. I owe the kernel of this idea to Fr. Terrence Kardong's forthcoming commentary on Benedict's Rule (Liturgical Press). The parts of Benedict's chapter on the cellarer that I emphasize here are for the most part Benedict's own and not derived from *The Rule of the Master*.

14. Judith Sutera, "Stewardship and the Kingdom in RB 31-33," *American Benedictine Review* 41 (1990), 353-355.

15. Benedict mentions Christ explicitly in connection with guests (RB 53.1, 7, 15) and the sick (RB 36.1-3), but he would no doubt affirm the same identification with Christ for children and the elderly (RB 37) for whom he urges special consideration (cf. Mt 25). See also RB 4.14-19.

16. Kardong, "Ecological Resources," 2.

17. David Noble, *A World Without Women: The Christian Clerical Culture of Western Science* (New York: Knopf, 1992), 83-107, suggests a counter example. He argues that the Carolingian monarchs and Benedictine monks collaborated in a mutually beneficial interaction, which worked against local aristocracy and the involvement of women in learning and public life. He argues further that monasteries, by being called upon to supply money and troops to the imperial armies and by being expected to pray for the rulers, became militarized. Noble's arguments, which draw in part on Workman's rather dated work, are so all-embracing that it is difficult to respond. One could certainly cite counter-evidence showing that double monasteries and strong-willed and energetic abbesses flourished long after Carolingian legislation about cloister for nuns and edicts forbidding the foundation of double monasteries. The notion of monastics as intercessors, which was one of the engines leading to an expansion of the liturgical side of monastic life at the expense of work and reading, was not limited to prayer for rulers and armies, nor was it limited to males. For one Carolingian monk, see footnote 21, below. I will make much of crows in what follows. In world mythology, crows are regarded both positively and negatively. They are Benedictine-like in their polyvalent goodness and wickedness, as well as in their color. See A. Coormaraswamy, "The Dove and the Crow," *Studies in Comparative Religion* (1984), 141-147. My point is not to glorify Benedictines unduly but to find in their rich tradition guidance for human beings who want to live as part of the seamless garment of nature.

18. Gregory the Great, *Liber Dialogorum* 2.8.1-3, ed. A. de Vogüé (Paris: Cerf, 1979), 160-163. In Gregory the Great, *The Life of Saint Benedict* (Petersham, Mass.: St. Bede's, 1993), Adalbert de Vogüé comments in detail on book two of the *Dialogues*. The incident of the crow is discussed on 53-63.

19. Barry Lopez, *The Rediscovery of America* (Lexington, Ky.: University Press of Kentucky, 1990).

20. The examples that follow are taken from David Bell, *Wholly Animals: A Book of Beastly Tales* (Kalamazoo, Mich.: Cistercian Publications, 1992), 48-54, 122-123.

21. This story is in William of Malmesbury's *De Gestis Pontificum Anglorum* (book 4, section 141). In a forthcoming study of the *Vita* of St. Othmar (Jean Leclercq Festschrift, Cistercian Publications), the founder of the great Swiss monastery of St. Gall, I have shown how the authors of this *Vita* take pains to show that Othmar, the man of God ("vir Dei," Gregory's term for Benedict), in spite of royal favor and great material resources, never ceased to devote himself to the poor. Othmar used to leave the monastery at night to minister to the sick. He worked many miracles, but never for anyone who was rich. Thus, the material wealth that accrued to the great Carolingian monastery was returned to the service of God and his poor, so that the monks were spared the temptations of luxury.

22. See, for example, *Scivias*, Declaration, trans. Columba Hart and Jane Bishop (New York: Paulist Press, 1990), 59: "Explain these things in such a way that the hearer, receiving the words of his instructor, may expound them in those words. . . ." The critical edition, *Hildegardis Scivias*, ed. Adelgundis Führkötter and Angela Carlevaris, CCCM 43 (Turnhout: Brepols, 1978), 3, lines 15-18: "*sic edisserendo proferens, quemadmodum et auditor verba*

praeceptoris sui percipiens, ea secundum tenorem locutionis illius, ipso volente, ostendente et praecipiente propalat."

23. Hildegard of Bingen, *Explanation of the Rule of Benedict*, 2-3, trans. Hugh Feiss (Toronto: Peregina, 1990), 19.

24. I will give references to Mansi's edition in Migne's *Patrologia Latina*, vol. 197, cc. 739-1038, indicating column and segment, for example, 746A. For an English version, see *Book of Divine Works*, ed. Matthew Fox (Santa Fe: Bear, 1987).

25. Hildegard of Bingen, *Holistic Healing* (Collegeville, Minn.: Liturgical Press, 1994), 1. I do not have the Latin edition of this work available, so I must rely on this English translation.

26. Henceforth, in parentheses in the text I will give the reference to the *Scivias* themselves by book, vision, and chapter, then if necessary a reference to Hart's translation, and finally a reference by page and line to the critical edition cited above [=CC]. The translations are Hart's, but sometimes I have modified them.

27. Hildegard explicitly returns to this image in DO 1.2.8. There she says she had seen it in her third vision twenty-eight years ago.

28. Here Hildegard echoes Genesis. Human beings, who need to find or cultivate food and clothing in the natural world, find that nature is not always amenable to their needs and wants. Hildegard's experience as the abbess of a feudal monastery no doubt reinforced the teaching of the author of Genesis. It seems to me that this sense of competition or warfare with nature would arise or increase greatly at a time when society was passing from a food-gathering to a farming economy. Agriculturalists (herdsmen and farmers) are prone to see nature as hostile. The struggle to keep weeds out of the fields and predators away from the herds became a struggle to the death when technology provided humanity with suitable weapons. For example, in the Faroe Islands humans and raptors competed for puffins and eggs. A *nevtollur* or bill-tax was in place for centuries. Every person with a boat had to bring a certain number of bills of eagles, ravens, hooded-crows, and greater black-backed gulls to Tórshavn each year. Reimposed in sharper terms in 1741 on a citizenry who could then make use of improved weapons, the tax led to a great reduction in the number of hooded-crows and other proscribed species. The white-tailed sea eagle, which we met above in connection with St. Cuthbert, was probably already extinct in the Faroes by 1741. See Kenneth Williamson, The Atlantic Islands (London: Collins, 1948), 66-67, 122. Faroese folklore at least paid the hooded-crow the compliment of attributing a capacity for prescience and judicial assembly (*krákuting*) to the wily birds.

29. See also *Scivias* 3.2.2; Hart 326; CC 351-352:139-142: ". . . fear is the beginning of a just intention, and when that flowers into sanctity by good works, it joins with blessed faith and reaches God in full perfection."

30. "*O vis eternitatis*," ed. Barbara Newman, Saint Hildegard of Bingen, Symphonia (Ithaca, N.Y.: Cornell University Press, 1988), 98-99, translation mine. On the idea of creation through the Word see also "*O eterne Deus*," 106-107; on foreknowledge in the Word, "*O Verbum Patris*," 258-259.

31. "*O quam mirabilis*," in Newman, 100-101.

32. Simon Schama, *Landscape and Memory* (New York: Knopf, 1995) studies the interaction of natural settings and human perfection. He quotes Thoreau: "It is in vain to dream of a wildness distant from ourselves. There is none such. It is the bog in our brain and bowels, the primitive vigor of Nature in us, that inspires that dream."

33. T. H. White, *The Bestiary* (New York: Putnam, 1960), 142-143.

34. Catherine Feher Elston, *Ravensong: A Natural and Fabulous History of Ravens and Crows* (Flagstaff, Ariz.: Northland, 1991), 80-95.

35. Anne Porter, *An Altogether Different Language: Poems 1934-1994* (Cambridge, Mass.: Zoland, 1994), 95.

"AND GOD SAW THAT IT WAS GOOD"

CATHOLIC
SOCIAL TEACHING
AND
ECOLOGICAL ETHICS

Christine Firer Hinze

Introduction

"Modern Catholic social teaching" usually refers to a body of papal and episcopal pronouncements on society, economy, and politics that spans the past century, beginning with the 1891 encyclical of Pope Leo XIII, *Rerum Novarum*, "On the Condition of Labor." Motivating Leo was the desire to address what was then called "the social question," a summary term for the complex of problems and issues that had accompanied industrialization and urbanization of the West. In the years since 1891, the scope of official Catholic social teaching has expanded, but the plight of those whom modern industrial society shortchanges, marginalizes, or harms has remained one of its focal concerns.

This recent body of official teaching is anchored in traditions of Christian reflection and practice traceable back through the centuries. For Catholic social teaching more broadly understood encompasses the beliefs and practices of Christians in relation to their social milieu from scriptural times forward. This stream of Christian social reflection and wisdom is carried in theology, liturgy, mysticism, the lives of saints, and the whole gamut of the living beliefs and practices of everyday Christians.[1] Official teaching of the past century is most properly understood as a subset of this multifaceted, dynamic heritage.[2]

Situating recent Catholic social teaching in its larger context reminds us that Christian social thought and practice is diverse, culturally and historically shaped and limited, and vulnerable to the effects of sin and finitude. When educed or extrapolated from these sources, Catholic beliefs and practices with respect to the environment, including official teachings, bear these same marks. Thus, Christians' historical disregard for the environment as a religio-moral issue has been congruent with the unconcern of society at large.

The past twenty-five years, however, have witnessed the rise of a new ecological consciousness. Catholics experiencing this cultural shift have been led to inquire about the relationship between their modern social teachings, which focus on humans' communal well-being, and concern for the well-being of the ecosphere. The pope and U.S. bishops have promulgated a strong claim that modern Catholic social teaching is, in fact, fundamentally compatible with religio-moral attention to ecology.[3] This essay will explore some prominent aspects of that general claim and seek to contribute to the more specific claim that the mutual and interpenetrating influence of social and ecological concern must undergird an adequate Catholic ethics for the new century.

I will begin by noting thematic links that have been made in recent official pronouncements between Catholic social thought and environmental questions. Second, I will turn to critiques concerning anthropocentrism leveled by some environmentalists at Christianity in general and recent Catholic social thought in particular.[4] Focusing on the much-emphasized theme of "human dignity" in contemporary Catholic social thought, I will argue that this moral ideal necessarily includes interdependent responsibility within the physical environment, beginning with the environment bordered by one's skin. While a Christian theocentric perspective warrants our belief and hope that humankind, as *imago Dei*, has a special role within the ecosphere, Catholic social teaching also calls for humility and respect in the face of nature in its own right, and not only because it is the material prerequisite for human survival and thriving.[5]

The third part of the essay will draw attention to an important dimension of the ecology-Catholic social teaching nexus: its relationship to questions of work and economy.[6] Economic matters have had a central place in modern Catholic social teaching. But the economic sphere stands squarely at the intersection of—and thus crucially mediates between—ecological realities on the one hand and humanly constructed communities on the other. Christian economic ethics thus presupposes and requires an ecological-ethical counterpart. As a way of suggesting how Catholic ethicists might mine traditional sources to elaborate this claim, I will make only the briefest remarks about the legacy of St. Thomas Aquinas and then look in a bit more depth at the way this country's most influential twentieth-century Catholic economic ethicist, Monsignor John A. Ryan, articulated—in Thomistic, natural law idiom—the connections between personal virtue, social justice, and temperate enjoyment of economic and material resources.

I. Recent Catholic Social Teaching and Ecology

Inspired by openings into the subject by Pope John Paul II, especially in his 1989 World Day of Peace Message, and galvanized by the heightened sense of ecological crisis that marks the "signs of the times," the U.S. bishops' 1991 statement *Renewing the Earth* inaugurates official U.S. Catholic reflection on environmental issues in light of basic themes of Catholic theology and social teaching. The bishops are convinced that to attend to ecology is not to set aside concerns for human flourishing, but instead to join them at a deeper and more appropriately inclusive level. "Above all," they stress, "we seek to explore the links between concern for the person and for the earth, between natural ecology and social ecology."[7] They concur with scientists like Thomas Malone who regard the key problems facing humanity today—environment, energy, economics, equity, and ethics—as interrelated. The bishops especially highlight connections between ecological degradation and harm to working people and poor persons, and links between ecological responsibility and the attainment of a just, sustainable global economy and polity.[8]

The bishops ground their reflections in the scriptural vision of God's earth as good, and the gospel message of Jesus as one whose teaching and practice bespoke a love for nature and the earth. They further note, "Our Christian way of life, as saints like Benedict, Hildegaard, and Francis showed us, is a road to community with all creation."[9] The document goes on to identify eight themes of Catholic social teaching which, the bishops believe, also express integral dimensions of ecological responsibility. These are *a God-centered and sacramental view of the universe*, which underpins human accountability for the fate of the earth; a consistent *respect for human life*, which extends to respect for all creation; a worldview affirming the ethical significance of *global interdependence and the common good; an ethics of solidarity* promoting cooperation and a just structure of sharing in the world community; an understanding of *the universal purpose of created things* which requires equitable use of the earth's resources; *an option for the poor* which gives passion to the quest for an equitable and sustainable world; and a conception of *authentic development*,[10] which offers a direction for progress that respects human dignity and the limits to material growth.[11] The bishops elaborate briefly on each of these themes, but make clear the need for persons in every ecclesial and social setting to reflect, pray, and act in order to discover for themselves the implications of social teaching for ecological matters. As they recognize, this is a moment for development of doctrine as Catholic Christians encounter a new and urgent set of circumstances and problems.

II. Recent Catholic Teaching's Emphasis on "Human Dignity": Stumbling Block or Fruitful Norm?

Ethicist Daniel M. Cowdin has recently considered the problematic relationship between contemporary Catholic moral theology's stress on human dignity and the project of creating a sound ecological ethics.[12] Cowdin contends that today, a *kairotic* moment in human ecological consciousness has made an explicit Catholic ecological ethic not only appropriate, but required. In making this claim he appeals both to the complex fact of humankind's relationship to nature and to the traditional attention to nature found in Catholic moral theology.

> Nature exists. Nature is real. It exists beyond human being and is not merely subsumable or tributary to it, in fact or in value. We are dependent on nature not only for our survival but for the richness of our life. It is part of who we are as human beings, not only of our origins but of our present identity and who we will and should become. Nature is good in itself though not in an unqualified way. And, . . . we hope it is part of what our life will be as ultimately transformed by God. We should thus pursue an environmental ethic, joining our Catholic voice to the worldwide attempt to stem the current direction of nature-exploitation before the earth is damaged beyond repair.[13]

Cowdin believes that a Catholic treatment which seriously engages ecological realities will reconfigure, not simply supplement, previous understandings of human dignity. He is especially critical of some Catholic moralists' tendencies to define personhood as a nonmanipulable end in itself, in sharp contrast to manipulable and instrumental "things."[14] An ecologically sensitive approach to human dignity will actually alter our understanding of what that dignity entails by placing its relationship to the natural world in clearer, more precise, relief. If we acknowledge that "we exist within a continuum of life, sharing degrees of consciousness, mobility, and vitality, . . . much of nonhuman nature can [then] be valued intrinsically and thus treated as an end in some sense . . . ."[15] Once this is acknowledged, however, exactly how people's treatment of each other ought to be distinguished from their treatment of nonhumans will require discriminating analysis.

"And God Saw That It Was Good"

Although he agrees that Catholics must relinquish an inaccurate and harmful anthropocentrism, Cowdin rejects interpretations that completely renounce any special role for humanity amid nature as descriptively unsound and theologically faulty. In the first place, scripture and tradition prompt Catholics to respect nature as God's creation, to care for it, even to love it in a certain analogous sense. But ecological ethicists who seek to replace overly authoritarian notions of dominion with models of interdependence or cooperation must avoid misunderstandings in the other direction. The fact is that humans are far more dependent on nature than nature is upon us. What is more, uncritical use of terms like interdependence and mutuality threatens to cloak another, equally important feature of humanity's relation with nature: its irreducibly conflictual aspects. Cowdin urges Catholics to keep in mind that in order to appreciate or care for nature, humans must survive. Historically, that quest for survival has pitted us against viruses, preying animals, the elements, and scarcity of resources. Anyone who has ever been caught out in a small boat during a sudden storm, lost in the woods, or seriously ill knows this truth from the gut. Our mysterious and real rootedness in, and companionship with, nature is simultaneously intertwined with the potential for conflict and danger.[16] Catholic ecological ethics, while rightly challenging alienation from the earth in its various historical guises, must remain realistic about this deeply cutting ambiguity in the human-nature relation.

A Catholic ecological viewpoint will acknowledge, then, that nature has its own existence and flourishing apart from, and sometimes over and against, those of the human species alone. At the same time, human interaction with nature is ubiquitous, and human action or inaction will inevitably have an impact on the future of nonhuman nature. The "is" of our entanglement with and unavoidable impact on nature leads to a moral "ought": humans, because of who we are within nature, have particular responsibilities in relation to nature. This view does lend support to a certain primacy of humans in the scheme of nature. But, a Christian perspective confirms that humans are obliged to enact their solidarity with nature with humility and service. In light of these insights, Cowdin concludes, Christian ethicists must challenge any environmental perspective that makes humans purely instrumental to the good of the biosphere, that depicts the role of humans as purely on a par with any other biota, or that draws hasty or overblown comparisons between the intentions, needs, and rights of humans and those of nonhumans.[17]

Scripture and tradition (along with evidence of common experience) confirm the judgment that humanity is distinct from other aspects of nature, perhaps especially in its capacity to care for nature at all. Some ethicists call for a theocentric perspective whereby humans are led neither to dominate the natural or subordinate the human species, and where human responsibility within nature is made practically operative.[18] But again Cowdin warns Catholics not to overdraw images of co-creation and stewardship. We are not creators in the same way as God; we do not have the same relationship with nature as God does. Drew Christiansen agrees, and suggests that, for making appropriate comparisons and contrasts between humans and other earth-forms, retrieving classic categories of analogy may prove useful.[19]

In summary, Cowdin and Christiansen affirm from a Catholic perspective the general lines of the position taken by Protestant scholars like James A. Nash and James M. Gustafson. Theologically, nature, as God's good creation shot through with *vestigia Dei*, is the occasion for profound, contemplative encounters that are both strange and familiar and evoke both fear and reverence.[20] Regarded through an ecologically attentive lens, theological anthropology, pertaining as it does to religious understanding of our human creaturehood, confirms the profundity of the commerce of humans with nature, whose impact reaches down into our very embodiedness.

In light of these religious insights, a Catholic social and ecological ethics will affirm human dignity. But that dignity will be reinterpreted in light of humanity's complex relationships and responsibilities within the ecosphere. An ecological ethics appropriate to Catholic theology will champion the good of the earth and all its constituent parts. Simultaneously, as an ethics for human beings, it will seek to discern how humans' peculiarly self-conscious and potent impact on the planet ought to be directed for the common good.[21]

Striving to articulate this view of human dignity in the context of ecological responsibility has led ethicists to propose normative imperatives such as Cowdin's multifaceted "Respect everything for what it most fully is and treat it as far as possible in accordance with that perception." Acknowledging human dignity is one instance of this overarching imperative. Integral to human dignity is treating others and being treated as human and not as something else. We ought also to treat nonhuman individuals or systems as what they are and not as something else. "The special status of human being is therefore maintained while the real status of other life around us is not blocked from view or reduced. We can simultaneously insist on the unique demands of the human moral community without making such demands the beginning or end of all morality."[22] Gustafson concurs, stating, "We are in a situation that calls for respect for nature, but not a Schweitzerian reverence"; he offers an analogous general imperative: "Act so that you consider all things never *only* as a means to your ends, or even to collective ends."[23]

These restrained formulations are not immune from corruption or regression into damaging anthropocentric forms, whether dichotomous, dominating, or indifferent. In light of this threat, more prophetic voices, including those of liberation and feminist theologians, are indispensable to the evolving Catholic ecological conversation.[24] For prophets and ethicists alike, resisting the slide into sinful anthropocentrism demands that this point be repeatedly underscored: human dignity can be realized only in the midst of ecological respect and responsibility, never apart from it. Conversely, an ecological ethics that fails to give particular attention to the welfare of human beings, especially those who are poor, marginalized, or powerless, will not suffice.[25]

III. Resources for a Catholic Ecological–Economic Ethics

The U.S. bishops, we have seen, argue that the central themes of modern Catholic social teaching have important, if heretofore underdeveloped, ecological dimensions and implications. We have also considered ways that the focus of that teaching on human dignity, reflective of the modern "turn to the subject" will be modified, but not discarded, by a Catholic "turn to the environment." In this section, I will point out some important connections between ecology and economy in Christian theology and modern Catholic social thought and explore in more detail one of them.

A. Oikonomia *and Its Mediating Role*

Modern economics focuses on production, consumption, labor, capital, and profit-making in the context of competition for scarce resources. But economics in its fuller, classical sense is the science whose subject is the gathering, cultivating, and distributing of the earth's material resources, with a view to the survival and thriving of human communities. Thus understood, economy, *oikonomia*, mediates between ecology on the one hand and the *oikoumene* (from which the English word "ecumenical" is derived) of human interconnected community on the other.[26]

When these terms are situated within a theological understanding of *oikonomia* as God's own creative, redeeming, and reconciling work and the *oikos* that work sustains, their deeper relatedness is further revealed. From the perspective of biblical traditions, Methodist theologian M. Douglas Meeks tells us, *oikos* may be understood as, first, the household in which God wants to give people access to life: this is the deeper theological meaning of "economy," whose traditional concern has been livelihood. Second, *oikos* may refer to the household of creation in which God wants God's creatures to live together in interdependence: here is the religious ground for "ecology," whose concern is mutual and beneficial relatedness with nature. In a third usage, *oikos* refers to the world that God wants to make into a home by establishing divine justice and peace among the peoples and nations. Meeks connects this usage to the root meaning of *oikoumene*, "ecumenics"—the inhabited world drawn close together, whose concern is "mutually recognized and supportive habitat in peace." "The integrity of God's righteousness and of human justice holds these three concerns together as mutually interdependent. Economic justice includes the question of justice for the land and justice for the peoples on the land. [Hence,] every economic question is also an ecological and ecumenic question and vice versa."[27]

Meeks's creative reappropriation draws attention to the classical meaning of economy as the communal household whose purpose is access to livelihood for all its members. Besides its power to conceptually integrate the various dimensions of the economic, this approach invites Christian ethicists to think about economics and ecology within a richly textured descriptive and theological context. Within this divinely embraced *oikonomia*, it becomes clear that ecology, economy, and ecumenics all play constitutive and interdependent roles.

What happens when we bring this insight about the connection between economy and ecology into dialogue with Catholic social thought? Catholic economic teaching's theology of the dignity of persons and the rights and obligations flowing therefrom, its persistent advocacy of the right of workers and their families to a decent livelihood in return for reasonable amounts of labor, and its stress on the duties of employers and capitalists to behave justly with regard to their privileged access to natural resources and the means of livelihood for workers—all of these teachings are receptive to, and call for, ecological contextualization. Also germane to this task is the perennial focus in Catholic teaching upon protecting and empowering the most vulnerable and weak, and growing evidence that environmental degradation afflicts the poor disproportionately.

B. The Integrating Legacy of St. Thomas Aquinas

In discerning the lineaments of a distinctly Roman Catholic ecological-economic ethics, it is fitting that we consider the potential contribution of the thought of St. Thomas Aquinas and later traditions of Thomistic thought. Jamie Ehegartner Schaefer's recent study of Aquinas in relation to contemporary ecological questions thoughtfully advances the claim that between Thomism and ecologism, there exist multiple points for fruitful contact and mutual enrichment.[28] Schaefer analyzes, on the one hand, Thomas's humanly centered, but theologically undergirded, ethics of ownership and the proper human use of material goods with an eye for the common good. Simultaneously, she demonstrates the importance of Thomas's understanding of the intrinsic value and interrelatedness of all the parts of creation in terms of their source, meaning, and finality. Bringing these two aspects of Thomas's thought together, she makes a persuasive case for a profound receptivity within Thomistic theological ethics to the ecological awareness that characterizes our own era.

Schaefer considers Thomas's treatment of the proper use of material things; of the virtues; and of the rightly graduated love for God, self, others, and the created order. She also lifts up the connections Aquinas draws between personal virtue, societal relations, and the common good, connections illustrated in his treatment of general justice. Encompassing all these facets of Aquinas's theological ethics is a worldview which envisages the parts of creation as interrelated and places the meaning and telos

"AND GOD SAW THAT IT WAS GOOD"

of all within the pseudo-Dionysian schema of *exitus-reditus*, origination from and return to the divine source. There is no doubt that Thomas puts the human being at the center of his natural law-oriented moral theology; to this extent his ethics is anthropocentric. However, Schaefer suggests that properly understood, Thomas affirms precisely that distinctiveness-yet-relation between humanity and cosmos that contemporary writers like Cowdin and Nash are striving to promote.

Schaefer's case for the pertinence of Thomas's legacy to contemporary Catholic ecological reflection is convincing. Her work suggests one important avenue by which nascent Catholic teaching on ecology may strengthen and enrich its theological and traditional rootage. As Catholic social thinkers consider the intriguing possibilities of an "eco-Thomism" for a new century, they will also benefit from a reconsideration of twentieth-century neo-Thomist social reflection from an ecologically attuned vantagepoint.

C. A Twentieth-Century Thomistic Illustration:
John A. Ryan on Authentic Human Welfare

Precise ways that Catholic social ethics might fuse with Catholic ecological ethics by way of creative reappropriations of scripture and tradition can only be hinted at here. In closing, I will attempt to shed light on one possibility by elaborating the above-mentioned suggestion concerning twentieth-century Thomist social thought. Many potential points of contact between Catholic economic teaching and ecological ethics can be uncovered in the work of the premier U.S. Catholic economic ethicist of the first half of this century, Monsignor John A. Ryan (1869-1945).[29] Ryan's work self-consciously interpreted for an American economic context the Catholic social teachings of Leo XIII and Pius XI. The centerpiece of his economic ethics was an understanding of human dignity and welfare, grounded in a neoscholastic anthropology that reflected the teleological, natural law focus of the Thomism of his day.[30] The economic questions treated by Ryan ranged from macro issues like the relative merits of capitalism versus socialism to the minutia of individual families' income and spending; and from sophisticated matters of public policy to the details of everyday civic and economic comportment. Ryan's comprehensive scope matches that demanded by a contemporary ecological ethics. Further, many facets of Ryan's Thomistic argumentation are receptive to development along ecological lines. This can be shown by a glance at his writings concerning true and false human and economic welfare.

Ryan frequently warned that modern Western culture's temptation to seek happiness through unlimited material acquisition augurs profoundly deleterious outcomes, both spiritual and moral.[31] These negative consequences included, first, the surrender of a reasonable human life (one that values "thinking, knowing, communing, loving, serving, and giving") in favor of an impoverished ideal of human life (consisting of "having and enjoying").[32] Morals and character are damaged in the pursuit of "high-society" activities such as entertaining, whose chief goal is to outdo or keep up with others' sumptuousness of dress, food, and equipage. Excessive pursuit of material satisfactions easily leads to gluttony and drunkenness, as well as lust, as persons lower themselves to the servile control of their animal instincts. Another evil effect is the weakening of the religious sense and the altruistic sense. Ryan adduces evidence that indicates that when people rise above a certain level of affluence, their contributions to the common welfare tend to decrease.

Ryan goes a step further to claim that even habitual and prolonged use of modern conveniences that are not immoral in themselves (he lists street cars and electric bells—we might list microwaves and personal computers!) can injure our character. We become dependent on such conveniences, and

> less capable of that measure of self-denial and of endurance which is indispensable to the highest achievement. These and many other contrivances of modern life are undoubtedly an obstacle to the development of the invaluable ingredient of character which consists in the *power to do without.* They contribute insensibly, yet effectively, to a certain softness of mind, will, and body which is no advantage in life's many-sided struggle. It does not follow that these conveniences ought not to be utilized at all; it follows that they are not the unmixed blessing which they are commonly assumed to be.[33]

Furthermore, "The indefinite pursuit of material satisfaction is, in considerable measure, injurious to health." Rich foods, sexual unchastity, intemperance all take their toll. "Even the claim that a larger volume of happiness will result from the development and satisfaction of a larger volume of wants is unfounded." For the greater number of wants that are activated, the greater the suffering and disappointment when these wants are unsatisfied. We are, in a sense, all slaves to the wants we habitually satisfy.[34]

Ryan advanced his case against excessive acquisition and consumption on philosophical, common sense, and explicitly religious grounds. For Christians, he found ample warrants within the New Testament, the teachings of the Fathers, and the continuous teaching of the Church for "a certain asceticism," and a suspicion of wealth. In choosing housing, clothes, food, and recreation, the tests of simplicity, moderation, and comparative inexpensiveness should be applied, with an upper limit being set on the amount any family may legitimately spend for comforts.[35]

Ryan saw a direct relationship between the personal degradation wrought by selfish materialistic habits and social and economic injustice. Along with attacking the idol of unlimited material satisfaction, Ryan launches out against the intransigence that causes so many "good Christians" to spurn the moral conversion required for economic justice. Far too many Catholics, he contends, give only lip service to the serious moral obligations surrounding their economic lifestyles. Members of all classes allow themselves to fall prey to the cultural illusion that "to be worthwhile life must include a continuous and indefinite increase in the number and variety of wants, and a corresponding growth and variation in the means of satisfying them," and they are seduced into placing desires for purely physical gratification on the same level with the demands of the spiritual, moral, and intellectual faculties. Since these satisfactions are susceptible to indefinite increase, variety, and cost, it is easy to assume that there can be no practical limit set to the amount of goods or income needed to keep life worth living. The category of "surplus" or of "superfluous goods" which one is obliged to distribute to the needy neighbor effectively drops out. People in all classes who accept this "working creed of materialism" embrace propositions not only against right reason, but against scriptural revelation and centuries of church teaching.[36] For Ryan, the person, family, or society that fails to heed these sorts of limitations is seriously jeopardizing both their earthly and their eternal happiness. For what forms or deforms good human character simultaneously does so for spiritual character; the two are wholly intertwined.

Besides combining the personal and communal in his argument for material moderation, Ryan yokes together individual and social effort in his schemes for social betterment. He consistently refuses to designate either individual charity or social policy as the sole path to a decent economic livelihood for all.[37] One of Ryan's major contributions to U.S. Catholic social ethics is his insistence that moral and religious conversion are crucial but not sufficient to produce justice; "social effort" through political, economic, and cultural associations and structures is also needed.

Ryan's humane and Christian vision of moderate, decent economic conditions universally distributed, and of the means for attaining them, resonates strongly in Catholic social teaching today. The struggle to find ways of converting both hearts and social structures and policies also continues, in even more difficult and complex circumstances. Contemporary Christian ecological ethicists share Ryan's conviction about the need for both personal and social effort and transformation. Given the scope of ecological problems, as Nash points out, fidelity to the principle of subsidiarity leads us to recognize that in many cases, the smallest possible unit for effective decisionmaking and action is the international community.[38] On this count, as well as in his ruminations on human material welfare, Ryan's economic ethics provides scaffolding for the further advances that official and theological reflection on the ecology are now attempting.

Ryan, relying on his neoscholastic Thomist training and his study of economic "facts," perceived strong ties between virtues of economic moderation, personal flourishing, and social justice. Contemporary Christian ecologists like Nash and Schaefer, also appealing to classical theological sources and to empirical data, highlight the further conjunction between personal and social habits of producing and consuming and ecological well-being.[39] When we also compare Ryan's creative reliance on the Catholic social teaching of his day (mainly the writings of Leo XIII and Pius XI) with contemporary Catholic ecologists' appeals to more recent official teachings of Pope John Paul II and the U.S. bishops, the threads of continuity, as well as the potential for further dialogue, are clear.

Conclusion

Significantly, the compatibility we have been proposing between Catholic social teaching and ecological ethics, and the Thomistic illustrations we have offered, pivot on a theological anthropology in which human dignity, properly understood, is a central motif. Human personhood comprises intimate and complex links between the self and a physical environment that begins with one's own body. This embodiment-ecology connection, while perhaps receiving the most extensive treatment by feminist thinkers, invites further, nuanced reflection within Catholic ethics. If my ecological location includes my body, and my survival as an embodied, spiritual being depends on certain positive relations to my physical environment, then it is not possible to speak morally about human dignity apart from ecological concern. Bodily and personal ecology, social and economic ecology, and cosmological ecology are interactive and mutually influential. An earlier point is reconfirmed: Catholic social thought need not jettison a commitment to personal dignity in order to focus on ecosystemic responsibility; the two, in fact, entail one another.

This is not to say that ecological responsibility will never clash with human well-being. As with Catholic teaching on the common good, there are times when the individual member or group may be asked to sacrifice for the sake of the whole. However, Catholics embracing a Thomistic understanding of the common good will also insist that, due to their shared finality in the ultimate common good of God, proper care for humanity and proper care for the environment can never finally conflict. When operative ecological norms demand inconvenience or sacrifice for humans, two key questions must be addressed. First, are persons' dignity or rights actually being contravened? Second, if this is the case, how can the negative consequences be minimized or offset to the extent possible? Both Ryan and contemporary liberation thinkers would insist that these questions may only be legitimately posed in communities wherein the right of all members to minimum degrees of human dignity and the material conditions for such is effectively acknowledged.

Once that crucial reorientation occurs, many purported violations to the rights of some (for instance, loss of surplus revenue or of unlimited opportunities for material acquisition or possession) are unmasked for what they truly are: the curtailment of privileges or the imposition of relative inconveniences.[40]

This discomfiting realization should prod us in the rich, consumerist West to ponder the countercultural attitudes and actions that ecological responsibility may imply, especially when set in the context of a religio-moral obligation to seek social justice for all societal members. During a historical period when large numbers of U.S. Roman Catholics are "making it" into the ranks of the upper middle class and higher, the severity of this challenge should not be underestimated. Honest deliberation on our Catholic social tradition, ancient and recent, and on the facts at hand leads inescapably to this conclusion: Every Catholic really is called to participate in the virtues of economic temperance and frugality for the sake of our fragile physical environment, for the sake of our obligation to rightly use and justly distribute economic and ecological wealth, and for the sake of our personal and communal flourishing. There really are, as Ryan saw and ecologists today insist, maximum levels of material welfare beyond which Catholics and other righteousness-loving persons cease to be right-living.[41] More than that: excessive and thoughtless living, at the extreme, threatens the future possibility of any kind of living at all. What might this imply concretely, for ourselves personally and for the ecclesial, civic, and economic institutions in which we participate, and on which our own jobs may depend? This daunting question calls for clear-eyed, courageous reflection. As part of that reflection, it is essential to continue to clarify the fully ecological-economic theological ethics adumbrated in Catholic social teaching.

Notes

1. Just such wide-ranging exploration is under way among Catholics and other Christian scholars in response to the ecological challenge. Provocative and worthwhile treatments include the following: from the perspective of liturgy, see Albert J. Fritsch, SJ, "Appropriate Technology and Healing the Earth," in Albert J. LaChance and John E. Carroll, eds., *Embracing the Earth: Catholic Approaches to Ecology* (Maryknoll, N.Y.: Orbis Books, 1994), 96–114; and Kevin W. Irwin's article in this volume, "Sacramentality and the Role of Creation in Liturgy and Sacraments." For articles focusing on the saints, including Francis, see H. Paul Santmire, *The Travail of Nature: The Ambiguous Ecological Promise of Christian Theology* (Philadelphia: Fortress Press, 1985); James A. Nash, *Loving Nature: Ecological Integrity and Christian Responsibility* (Nashville, Tenn.: Abingdon, 1991), 79–87; and Roger Sorrell, *St. Francis of Assisi and Nature; Tradition and Innovation in Western Christian Attitudes Toward the Environment* (New York: Oxford University Press, 1988). For articles focusing on scripture and its use, see Richard J. Clifford, "The Bible and the Environment," in Kevin W. Irwin

and Edmund Pellegrino, eds., *Preserving the Creation: Environmental Theology and Ethics* (Washington, D.C.: Georgetown University Press, 1994), 1-26; and Norman K. Gottwald, "The Biblical Mandate for Eco-Justice Action," in Dieter T. Hessel, ed., *For Creation's Sake: Preaching, Ecology and Justice* (Philadelphia: Geneva, 1985).

2. On historical context and antecedents to Leo XIII's social teaching see Michael J. Schuck, in "Modern Catholic Social Thought," Judith Dwyer, ed., *The New Dictionary of Catholic Social Thought* (Collegeville, Minn.: The Liturgical Press, 1994), 611-20; Stephen J. Pope, "*Rerum Novarum,*" ibid., 828-30. See also Paul Misner, *Social Catholicism in Europe: From the Onset of Industrialization to the First World War* (New York: Crossroad, 1991).

3. See Pope John Paul II, "The Ecological Crisis: A Common Responsibility." Message, December 8, 1989 (Washington, D.C.: United States Catholic Conference); U.S. Catholic bishops, *Renewing the Earth: An Invitation to Reflection and Action on Environment in Light of Catholic Social Teaching*, November 14, 1991 (Washington, D.C.: United States Catholic Conference, 1992).

4. The pivotal article, which has prompted, in James Nash's words, a virtual tradition of Christian ethical responses is Lynn White, "The Historical Roots of Our Ecologic Crisis," *Science* 155 (March 10, 1967): 1203-07.

5. The essay thus seeks to respond to the bishops' call to "theologians, scriptures scholars and ethicists to help explore, deepen, and advance the insights of our Catholic tradition and its relation to the environment," and in particular to "explore the relationship between this tradition's emphasis upon the dignity of the human person and our responsibility to care for all of God's creation." U.S. bishops, *Renewing the Earth*, 13.

6. Elsewhere I have sought to illumine ways that dynamics of gender and power play into economic and ecological matters, a theme that is not treated here. See Christine Firer Hinze, "Bridge Discourse on Wage Justice: Roman Catholic and Feminist Reflections on the Family Living Wage," *The Annual of the Society of Christian Ethics* (1991): 108-132; "Women, Work, and the Environmental Common Good," paper presented for the USCC consultation on Labor, the Environment, and Catholic Social Teaching, Washington, D.C., June 27, 1994. Catholic social ethics has yet to satisfactorily engage or respond to feminist theologians' arguments tracing both sexism and environmental denigration to a pernicious, "hierarchical dualistic" approach to reality in the West. For a clear articulation of these critiques see Elizabeth A. Johnson, *Women, Earth, and Creator Spirit* (Mahwah, N.J.: Paulist, 1993), esp. 10-40. See also the concise overview by Lois K. Daly, "Ecofeminisms and Ethics," *The Annual of the Society of Christian Ethics* (1994): 285-90.

7. U. S. Catholic bishops, *Renewing the Earth*, 2.

8. Ibid., 1. Cf. Pope John Paul II, "The Ecological Crisis," nos. 7, 10.

9. U.S. bishops, *Renewing the Earth*, 4-5.

10. Authentic social development is most explicitly treated in Pope Paul VI's 1967 encyclical *Populorum Progressio* and in the 1987 encyclical by Pope John Paul II commemorating the twentieth anniversary of Paul's document, *Sollicitudo Rei Socialis.* The latter text was threatened with early obsolescence in the wake of changes in the world scene that occurred in 1989. However, *Sollicitudo* remains a key document for those, like myself, who approach ecological matters from the vantage point of social ethics. Not only does the pope for the first time advert to ecological issues in a major encyclical (nos. 29, 34), raise up the concept of economic, social, and cultural "structures of sin" (no. 36), and propose "solidarity"

as a new Christian virtue for our day (nos. 38-40), but he also offers rich reflections on the connections between environmental degradation and misuses of technology; poverty and exploitative international trade policies; and underdevelopment in the southern hemisphere and a "harmful superdevelopment" fed by consumerism, economism, and materialism in the north. All of this is undergirded by an appeal to a theological anthropology that centers on being rather than having, and a true understanding of development that supersedes economic improvement. See the fine analysis of *Sollicitudo* in Drew Christiansen, SJ, "Morality, Ecology, Justice, and Development," in Carol S. Robb and Carl J. Casebolt, eds., *Covenant for a New Creation: Ethics, Religion, and Public Policy* (Maryknoll, N.Y.: Orbis, 1991), 251-72, esp. 254-57.

11. U.S. bishops, *Renewing the Earth*, 5-6.

12. Daniel M. Cowdin, "Toward an Environmental Ethic," in Irwin and Pellegrino, eds., *Preserving the Creation*, 112-47.

13. Cowdin, "Toward an Environmental Ethic," 129.

14. While acknowledging legitimate historical reasons for the stress on human subjectivity in recent Christian ethics, Cowdin nonetheless castigates such prominent authors as David Hollenbach, Timothy O'Connell, and Richard Gula for the anti-ecological import of their formulations of humanity as over and against the non-human, thingified world. Ibid., 128-29.

15. Ibid., 130. Cowdin goes on to note Kenneth Goodpaster's argument that something need not be accorded the status of moral agent to be regarded as "morally considerable." Cf. Kenneth Goodpaster, "On Being Morally Considerable," in Donald Scherer and Thomas Attig, eds., *Ethics and the Environment* (Englewood Cliffs, N.J.: Prentice Hall, 1983).

16. James M. Gustafson makes this point well in *A Sense of the Divine: The Natural Environment from a Theocentric Perspective* (Cleveland, Ohio: The Pilgrim Press, 1994), chs. 1, 2.

17. Cowdin identifies as examples of these three erroneous approaches a "strong holist" or radical biocentric view; an "organismic egalitarianism"; and views that too readily attribute human agency and moral valuation to nonhuman aspects of nature. On this last, Cowdin finds objectionable statements such as that of Patricia Mische, who proposes that "love, cooperation, communion is . . . what makes the universe work." That statement "is plainly false. The way in which nonhuman nature holds together and achieves order out of chaos is qualitatively different from the way in which human beings achieve order with each other and God. The attribution . . . is either a fideistic leap in spite of everything we know about the universe scientifically or a poetic projection (*in which case it cannot really do the ethical work it purports to do*)." Ibid., 140-41. The feminist ecological theologies of Elizabeth Johnson and Rosemary Ruether, it appears, would be vulnerable to such a critique in Cowdin's eyes. Catholic ecological ethics needs to more explicitly follow out this line of debate.

18. The contemporary "theocentric perspective" discussion in relation to Christian ethics and more recently, to humans' responsibility in the biosphere has centered on the influential work of James M. Gustafson and his commentators. See, e.g., James M. Gustafson, *Ethics from a Theocentric Perspective*, 2 vols. (Chicago: University of Chicago Press, 1981, 1984); *A Sense of the Divine: The Natural Environment from a Theocentric Perspective* (Cleveland, Ohio: The Pilgrim Press, 1994); William C. French, "Ecological Concerns and the Anti-Foundationalist Debates: James Gustafson on Biospheric Constraints" *The Annual of the Society of*

Christian Ethics (1989): 113-130. Also advocating a theocentric perspective are Herman E. Daly and John B. Cobb, Jr., *For the Common Good: Redirecting the Economy Toward Community, the Environment, and a Sustainable Future* (Boston: Beacon Press, 1989), esp. 395-98. Aside from the writings of William French, I am not aware, however, of specifically Roman Catholic interpretations of theocentrism in relation to ecological ethics. How, for example, might Jacques Maritain's critique of anthropocentrism and defense of a "theocentric humanism" (a term employed in the social encyclicals of Pope Paul VI) play into a Catholic contribution to this discussion? See Jacques Maritain, *Integral Humanism*, Joseph Evans, trans. (Notre Dame, Ind.: University of Notre Dame Press, [1936] 1967).

19. See Drew Christiansen, SJ, "Response to Daniel Cowdin: Nature's God and the God of Love," in Irwin and Pellegrino, eds., *Preserving the Creation*, 148-153.

20. Themes of "homelessness" and being "at home on the earth," which run through the ecological literature, reflect a similar bipolar relation to nature.

21. Christiansen states the point strongly: "On this planet . . . there is no longer any nature apart from humanity. If the future of the earth itself is so entwined with conscious human decision, then one cannot avoid granting a special place to human beings in the cosmos. Respect for nature must be, therefore, as much an act of intelligence and reason as an act of contemplative awareness." "Moral Theology, Ecology, Development," 260.

22. Cowdin, "Toward an Environmental Ethic," 131-32.

23. Gustafson, *A Sense of the Divine*, 106. He summarizes his stance on 103-104.

24. Feminist and other liberation theologians seek to wed the prophetic and the analytical in their treatments of social justice and ecological matters. See, e.g., Elizabeth Johnson's feminist theological affirmation of "kinship" with creation in *Women, Earth, and Creator Spirit*, 27-31, 37-40.

25. A gift of environmentalism to the Church has been to alert us to the fact that no future Catholic social ethic may legitimately ignore the ecosphere. The credibility and adequacy of a Catholic social ethics that does not take ecological questions into account is seriously undermined. A similarly important gift to the Church from liberation theology has been its treatment of the dynamics of class, gender, race, and ethnicity as fundaments of our *social* ecology, which, like the realities and crises of our physical environment, we ignore to our common peril. This means that Catholic ecological reflection, too, will be flawed to the degree that it proceeds in isolation from, or fails to seriously engage, these social-ecological realities.

26. Methodist theologian M. Douglas Meeks has recently explored the links between economy, scriptural sources, and the doctrine of God in his work, *God the Economist: The Doctrine of God and Political Economy* (Minneapolis: Fortress Press, 1989). Jewish and Christian faith has consistently rendered God in relation to *oikos*, most especially for Christians within the *oikonomia tou theou*—the economy of God, by which is understood the creative, judging, and redeeming relations of God to humankind in history. Meeks's work suggests that attention to *oikonomia* among Catholic social ethicists may disclose similarly illuminating links between theology and economic life. For a concise synopsis of his larger argument, see M. Douglas Meeks, "The Holy Spirit and Human Needs: Toward a Trinitarian View of Economics," in Kenneth Aman, ed., *Border Regions of Faith* (Maryknoll, N.Y.: Orbis Books, 1987), 474-86.

27. Meeks, *God the Economist*, 34-35. Modern economics, Meeks argues, has harmfully narrowed the meaning of *oikonomia* to the arena of market exchange, whose goal is profit. "The friction between biblical religion and any prevailing economics comes at the point of defining the household, at defining economy. The modern history of economics has changed the meaning of economy. This is what theology should question today." Ibid., 37.

28. See Jame Ehegartner Schaefer, "Ethical Implications of Applying Aquinas's Notions of the Unity and Diversity of Creation to Human Functioning in Ecosystems," unpublished Ph.D. dissertation (Marquette University, 1994). Schaefer acknowledges but finds inadequate other recent treatments of Thomas's potential legacy for contemporary ecological ethics, including James M. Gustafson, William C. French, and H. Paul Santmire. See Schaefer, *Ethical Implications*, 6-14.

29. Ryan is probably most well known for his two major economic treatises, *A Living Wage* (London: Macmillan, 1906) and *Distributive Justice* (New York: Macmillan [1916, 1927] 3rd edition, 1942). In these volumes and many other writings Ryan articulated a comprehensive theory of the good economic order and of the rights and duties of its various members, with particular attention to the right of workers and their families to attain a decent livelihood, understood as the basic material conditions for reasonable degrees of human development.

30. Two excellent, historically illuminating expositions of Ryan's theological-ethical approach are Charles E. Curran, *American Catholic Social Ethics* (South Bend, Ind.: University of Notre Dame Press, 1982), 26-92, and Harlan Beckley, *Passion for Justice: Retrieving the Legacies of Walter Rauschenbusch, John A. Ryan, and Reinhold Niebuhr* (Louisville, Ky: Westminster/John Knox Press, 1993), 110-188.

31. See, for example, John A. Ryan, "The Fallacy of Bettering One's Position," *Catholic World*, 1907; *Distributive Justice: The Right and Wrong of Our Present Economic System* (New York: Macmillan [1916, 1927] 1942), esp. 1942 edition, Chapter 18, "The Duty of Distributing Superfluous Wealth; "Minimum and Maximum Standards of Living," in *Declining Liberty and Other Papers* (New York: Macmillan, 1927), 315-329.

32. John A. Ryan, "False and True Welfare," in *The Church and Socialism and Other Essays* (Washington, D.C.: The University Press, 1919), 184-94.

33. Ibid., 186-87. To Ryan, a lifestyle too dependent on creature comforts and conveniences led, it seemed inevitably, to the diminution of "mental powers and activities." Ibid., 188-89. As proof, Ryan points to the increasing proportion of college and university students who choose those courses of study that have a "practical" rather than a theoretical or academic aim and outcome. "Those who select this will almost all devote their energies later to the business of money-getting. This means the exercise of the lower powers of the brain and intellect." Ibid., 188.

34. Ibid., 190-91. Ryan goes on to rebut the claim that the pursuit of beauty and refinement requires higher and higher standards of living, arguing that upward mobility may actually attenuate refinement by making for gaudy display and weak accession to fashion fads, appealing to the writings of Thorsten Veblen and Charlotte Perkins Gilman.

35. For an insightful and succinct summation of Ryan's economic thought, with emphasis on his views on the moral limits of income and wealth, see John A. Coleman, *An American Strategic Theology* (New York: Paulist Press, 1982), 85-97.

36. Ryan cites a proposition condemned as "scandalous and pernicious" by Pope Innocent XI in 1679 to the effect that "It is scarcely possible to find among people engaged in worldly pursuits, even among kings, goods that are superfluous to social position. Therefore, hardly any one is bound to give alms from this source." Ryan, *Distributive Justice*, 1942, 243; citing Denzinger, Enchiridion, prop. 12, p. 259. For a recent discussion on the elusive quality of the category of "sufficiency" in a consumer capitalist economy, see Prentis J. Pemberton and Daniel Rush Finn, *Toward a Christian Economic Ethic* (Minneapolis: Winston, 1986).

37. Generous giving by individuals "is obviously no substitute for justice and the deeds of justice." Yet given the fact that complete justice is a long way from realization, "benevolent giving deserves a place in any complete statement of proposals for a better distribution of wealth. Moreover, we are not likely to make greater advances on the road of strict justice until we acquire saner conceptions of welfare and a more effective notion of brotherly love. So long as men put senses above the soul, they will be unable to see clearly what is justice and unwilling to practice the little that they are able to see. Those who exaggerate the value of sense gratifications cannot be truly charitable, and those who are not truly charitable cannot perform adequate justice. The achievement of social justice requires not merely changes in the social mechanism, but a change in the social spirit, a reformation in men's hearts. To this end nothing could be more immediately helpful than a comprehensive recognition of the stewardship of wealth and the duty of distributing superfluous goods." Ryan, *Distributive Justice*, 245.

38. Nash, *Loving Nature*, 66.

39. Writing from within the Wesleyan tradition, James Nash has drawn upon classic Thomistic treatments of the virtues and extended them explicitly to a Christian ecological ethic. Among the list of nine "ecological virtues" propounded in his important book, *Loving Nature* (1991), he has since extended his treatment of one, "frugality." See James A. Nash, *Loving Nature*; "Toward the Revival and Reform of the Subversive Virtue: Frugality," *Annual of the Society of Christian Ethics* (1995): 137-160. Besides frugality, Nash names as ecological virtues sustainability, adaptability, relationality, equity, solidarity, biodiversity, sufficiency, and humility. *Loving Nature*, 63-66.

40. Daniel C. Maguire details a similar line of argument concerning the need to distinguish genuine infringements of rights from the imposition of legitimate sacrifices and inconveniences for the sake of the common good in *A Case for Affirmative Action* (Dubuque, Iowa: Shepherd Press, [1980] 1992).

41. See the thought-provoking and creative presentation of this point in Herman E. Daly, "The Biblical Economic Principle and the Steady-State Economy," in Robb and Casebolt, eds., *Covenant for a New Creation*, 47-60.

ECOLOGY AND THE COMMON GOOD

CATHOLIC SOCIAL TEACHING AND ENVIRONMENTAL RESPONSIBILITY

Drew Christiansen, SJ

THE *COMMON GOOD* IS ONE OF THE OLDEST PRINCIPLES OF WESTERN political philosophy. It has its roots in the politics of the city states of ancient Greece and especially the democratic politics of Athens. It was revived and developed in the republican politics of the Italian communes of the high Middle Ages. From there it continued to develop and be debated by canonists and theologians, ultimately coming to play a central part in modern Catholic social teaching. Until recently appeals to the common good had a foreign ring in American political discourse. The liberal political tradition born of the British Enlightenment, on which Anglo-American democracy was built, rested on a notion of competing interests and occasionally viewed "the common good," like Rousseau's "general will," to be a fanciful idea at best and at worst a mask for totalitarian control. Only since the liberal political tradition has come under criticism for neglecting the social and moral fabric underlying democratic life has the common good become a familiar, noncontroversial term.[1]

Through 2,500 years, the principle of the common good has served as a standard of social integrity demanding that all sectors of society have a stake in the welfare and the well-being of the polity. Aquinas argued that tyranny and faction violated the unity of society and its common good because they placed the good of an individual or group ahead of the good of the whole society.[2] Thus, even in the thirteenth century, it was clear government should be for the benefit of all people.

In modern Catholic social teaching, the common good has been discussed in political, economic, social, and even human rights terms. Accordingly, in the narrow technical sense, ecology is relatively new as an explicit component of the common good. But the social and ecclesiastical history of the West shows that, in their time and in their own way, our ancestors also dealt with environmental problems and found institutional solutions to those problems that promoted the good not only of society but of creation.[3]

In the pages that follow, I will (1) explore the resources that the concept of the common good, as it is found in contemporary Catholic social teaching, brings to our concern for the earth, (2) explicate the ecological dimensions of the global or planetary common good, as that term is currently used in the Church's teaching and social ministry, and (3) highlight the culture-transforming capacity of environmental ideals in gradually expanding our understanding of the common good.

1. The Common Good: The Concept and Its Uses

In an earlier effort to translate the meaning of "common good" to the language of American political philosophy, I suggested that the common good consisted in "sharing in a common [and improving] quality of life."[4] The two standard papal definitions, derived from Pope John XXIII—namely, "conditions of social living" and the "promotion, safeguarding and defense of human rights"—amount to catch-all phrases.[5] They are what philosopher Nicholas Rescher calls "convoy concepts," embracing a number of loosely related goods. In a short-hand way, we might say the common good refers to the good to be enjoyed by all. Such usage was most evident in the encyclicals of Pope John XXIII and in the Second Vatican Council pastoral constitution *Gaudium et Spes*. In *Mater et Magistra,* Pope John, for example, called for government to correct imbalances in social conditions between management and labor, between urbanites and rural dwellers, between industry and agriculture.[6] Vatican II's *Pastoral Constitution on the Church in the Modern World* likewise made the rectification of social and economic inequities a major concern.[7] Pope Paul VI's apostolic letter *Octagesima Adveniens* likewise addressed the "flagrant inequalities [that] exist in the economic, cultural and political development of nations."[8] In an ecological context, the community in question is not just the human community but an ecological or biotic community—in theological language, "all creation" (Wesley's and Herriot's *All Creatures Great and Small*)—sharing according to their capacity in conditions that allow for the survival and flourishing of a complex variety of members. In general, however, the common good serves as a kind of ultimate arbiter of whether one particular good has become imbalanced with the overall good of a community. In that sense, it remains an elastic, or better, an analogous term, which can apply to different goods depending on the social, economic, and political context.

It is not surprising that as people have become more aware of the earth's ecology and the risks of unrestrained economic growth, Catholic social teaching has come to think of ecology as an essential component of the common good. As Pope John Paul II says in his 1990 World Day of Peace Message, "In our day, there is a growing awareness that world peace is threatened not only by the arms race, regional conflicts and continued injustices among peoples and nations, but also by a lack of *due respect for nature*."[9] Indeed, ecology, whether global, regional or local, is by definition a good or a complex set of goods we share and, therefore, one to which we bear a common moral responsibility.

2. Ecological Dimensions of the Common Good

Authentic Development

Before we look at explicitly environmental concerns, we should consider one aspect of contemporary Catholic social teaching on the common good: the notion of "authentic development" (sometimes called "integral development").[10] Environmentalists frequently regard development as the enemy of ecological integrity.[11] But the concept of "authentic development," while it affirms the right of all persons to conditions of social living that permit their full development, also contains within it a critique of a purely economic conception of development and assumptions about the ends of human life that hold considerable potential for Christian environmentalism. "Authentic development," unlike reductionist concepts of economic growth, contains built-in restraints and limits that help it readily cohere with an ecological reading of the common good.

Ecology and Balance in Life. In the first place, authentic development views human well-being as consisting of a balance of a variety of goods.[12] A purely economic measure of well-being, such as the gross national product (GNP), fails to capture the variety of goods that contribute to human happiness and indeed produces a great deal of confusion and dissatisfaction in our pursuit of happiness.[13] St. Benedict understood such a need for balance. The Benedictine motto, *Orare et laborare,* actually represents a three-part division of monastic life into prayer *(orare),* physical work *(laborare),* and study *(legere)*.[14] In contrast to the post-modern work ethic, the genius of the monastic life, when it is lived well, is that it creates a harmonious balance of these elements, which enriches not only the lives of the monks but of guests and the local people to whom the monks minister. Adaptation of the composite and balanced understanding of human well-being found in Catholic social teaching could not only assist in cultivating what I have called "the ecology of the soul," but it could also contribute to a more balanced and sustainable way of life for us as a people.[15]

In any case, in the Catholic tradition, the good life consists of a variety of goods and even more of finding a balance among the goods we pursue and enjoy. The risk of what Pope John Paul II called "economism" is that it reduces everything to its economic value, so that, in a pursuit of profit, we lose our appreciation of the goods that make us whole.[16] In this respect, I pose a simple example: the ecology of time. How many of us experience the loss of family time, time for friends, genuine leisure time, time for prayer and contemplation, as a result of overcommitment to work? Even if we do not measure our success in dollars earned, work, following the culturally dominant model of economism, often drives other vital human activities out of our lives. The standard of authentic development reminds us that our lives are distorted unless we can give time to pursuing a variety of goods and attain a balance among the various goods that make us whole.

Contemplation of Creation. Not the least of these goods, it seems to me, is the enjoyment and contemplation of nature. Some psychologists and others now talk about "ecophilia," the human tendency to find solace and renewal in nature. Moreover, the peace and solitude provided by wilderness and countryside provide favorable conditions for prayer and contemplation. Whether it is Buddhist monasteries high on mountainsides or Cistercian abbeys nestled in beautiful valleys, monks and contemplative nuns through the centuries have chosen beautiful landscapes as the place to seek the divine.[17] In the western spiritual tradition, the enjoyment of nature resulted in exercises that led the mind to God through contemplation of the natural world and in a rich literature built around the six days of creation, the hexamera.[18] Ecophilia is really a matter of common sense. Most people find themselves revived and freed of stress in the outdoors. What makes contemplatives special is that they have learned how to savor the outdoors and to balance their lives by immersing themselves in it through prayer, study, and labor.

Our relation to the natural world, of course, is different today than in earlier centuries. We are not often threatened directly by nature, except in storm and earthquake, and many rockclimbers and whitewater canoeists seek in the wild a kind of challenge that their daily routine denies them. Still, whether it is to find another sort of challenge or to rest in nature's beauty, our connection with nature is an important part of human happiness. It is quite reasonable to conclude, then, that one of the goods that make for authentic human development is the enjoyment of nature. In that respect, we should be grateful to the founders of our national park system for anticipating the need of future generations to enjoy the treasures of the American landscape. They understood that enjoying these lands was an important component of the common good of the United States.

Moderation. Connected with the notion of authentic development in Catholic social teaching is the virtue of moderation. The teaching on authentic development repeatedly warns developing nations not to follow the excesses of the industrial nations.[19] In particular, it urges moderation in the use of material resources.[20] This reticence about material accumulation, though not an evident theme in the Hebrew scriptures, is very much a theme in the New Testament—especially Luke and Luke Acts—and among the fathers of the Church.[21] Recent Catholic social teaching on property has drawn on patristic thinking to emphasize a double use of material resources: sufficiency (*autarchia*) and community (*koinonia*).[22] The principle of community refers to the issue of distributive justice that I will address below. The principle of sufficiency, however, ensures, on the one hand, that people (households) have sufficient resources to live with dignity, and, on the other, that they seek no more than they need for a dignified living. (The surplus then belongs to the community, i.e., to those who lack the means to live decently.) The notion of sufficiency leads to a distinction in the writings of Pope John Paul II among "development," "underdevelopment," and "superdevelopment," with "development" being a mean between degrading poverty and the self-indulgent consumerism of the industrial nations.

In some contexts, to possess the conditions for living with dignity is what Catholic social teaching designates as "the common purpose of created things," namely, that God intends the goods of the earth, insofar as they may be used for the benefit of human beings, to ensure the flourishing of the entire human community. This is the classic meaning of the psalmist's declaration, "The earth is the Lord's and all it holds" (Ps 24:1). Human beings are stewards of creation, in the interest not just of other creatures but of the whole creation, human and non-human, and the test of stewardship is establishing conditions of flourishing for the whole human community together with other species.

The patristic principle of sufficiency, rooted in the biblical tradition and adapted by Catholic social teaching to modern economic conditions, is eminently consistent with the restraints in consumption demanded by ecological responsibility.[23] This principle instills the virtue of moderation in lifestyle, avoidance of excessive consumption, and suspicion of growth for growth's sake. The economic self-restraint inherent in authentic development serves especially as an incentive to lifestyle and social changes. The virtue of moderation tests our unexamined notions of the good life and of the good society as measured by material accumulation. In the end, it should also lead to exploration of structural economic change in the interest of human well-being as well as of planetary survival.[24]

Pope John Paul II's teaching ministry has been especially firm in warning against the materialism and the consumerism of western culture. In his 1979 homily at Yankee stadium, Pope John Paul II strongly urged that "Christians will want to be in the vanguard in favoring ways of life that decisively break with the frenzy of consumerism, exhausting and joyless."[25] The pope has steadily pointed out the risks of "superdevelopment."[26] He has noted its debilitating effects on our appreciation of our human potential, on justice for the worlds of underdevelopment and future generations, and on the biosphere.[27] The pope's critique of western materialism and "superdevelopment" is a sober reminder of how destructive economics can be in the absence of human and ecological considerations. "Sufficiency," while a difficult concept to square with today's hypercapitalism, should serve as a guide as we seek to find a new and much-needed balance in our way of life.

Sacrifice. Finally, authentic development admits of sacrifice. Theologically, sacrifice is a requirement of humanity as one family under God. The goods of the earth, insofar as they are for human use, are according to Catholic social teaching given by God for the good of all.[28] Accordingly, sacrifice is warranted to bring about greater equity, to see that no one is excluded from the banquet of the Lord.[29] Sacrifice is the converse of the notion of sufficiency. After we use what we need to live with dignity, the surplus belongs, after God, to people in need. In *Populorum Progressio* Pope Paul VI went even further in the name of solidarity, requesting sacrifice from the substance of well-advantaged nations and not just from their surplus, in the interest of sharing within the greater human family.[30]

Sacrifice may also serve as a response to the worry of some environmentalists that still greater distribution of resources among the world's poor would exceed the earth's carrying capacity. Distributive justice does not demand that all people be able to lead the consumerist American dream. Rather, it demands sacrifices in present material standards of living for the sake of an improved and sustainable standard of life for the future of humanity and of creation. In the interest of sustainable development, balances can and ought to be found between the levels of development enjoyed by the global North and the global South.[31] In the long-term, this will demand readjustment and sacrifice on the part of the North, so that the global majority can enjoy a degree of development consistent with their human dignity and the sustainability of the ecosphere. In Catholic social teaching, this sacrifice is social as well as personal. Groups and nations, not just individuals, are expected to sacrifice for the sake of the universal common good.[32]

Distributive Justice, Equality, and the Common Good

The justification of sacrifice for the sake of the common good brings us back to the principle of community or distributive justice, the patristic notion that material goods beyond what is needed for living with dignity (sufficiency) are owed to the community so that all may live in dignity. Questions of distributive justice are always with us, but the ecological crisis raises them in an especially acute way. In the first instance, an ecologically sustainable economy must eventually face the limits of growth. Much can and ought to be done in terms of technological improvement and shifts in the composition of the economy—for example, the move from an industrial to an information-based economy to reduce stresses on the environment—but eventually we must meet the limits of growth, especially in the area of fossil fuel consumption. For too long, western political systems have relied on the engine of growth to provide greater equity. Faced with physical limits to growth, the industrial economies, in particular, will face the classic political dilemma of either finding some fair pattern for the distribution of wealth or facing social conflict and political disorder.

Secondly, the need for distribution is intensified by the globalization of the economy and the aspiration and moral claims of the world's poor to share in the material well-being of affluent societies. Finally, the concern to bequeath a sustainable future to successor generations will impose costs in terms of environmental restoration and the sacrifice of opportunity which will, in turn, narrow the base of resources available for distribution among our near contemporaries.

To the question of distribution in a sustainable economy, Catholic social teaching offers only general guidance. As we have seen, it insists on a basic stake for all people, and it requires redistribution from the affluent to the needy, in some form, to ensure that everyone has that stake. In recent Catholic social teaching, moreover, there is also a preference for keeping the differences between classes and sectors of society relatively narrow in the interest of preventing an acceleration of inequality and with it growth in degrading poverty.[33] For the Catholic tradition, then, there is no separating questions of sustainability from those of justice. The Catholic form of the problematic of planetary sustainability will always be one of environmental justice.

3. Ecology and the Common Good: The State of the Question

Up to this point, I have been making a case that the notion of authentic development found in contemporary Catholic social teaching provides many moral resources in support of environmental responsibility: a sense of the variety and balance of goods that make up a good life, moderation as both a personal and a public virtue, a place for sacrifice in pursuit of the global common good, and a concern for justice in the transition to sustainability. While authentic development by no means provides a complete ecological ethic, it does correct many of the defects in a culture based on growth-oriented development. Even more, it fosters many of the moral dispositions and virtues necessary for establishing and sustaining an ethos of global responsibility.

The Universal Common Good

Recent Catholic social teaching also provides other important resources for dealing with global environmental problems, chief among which is "the universal common good."

Historically, the common good was understood in the context of a limited political setting, a city-state or nation. In his 1963 encyclical letter *Pacem in Terris,* Pope John XXIII specified for the first time the notion of a universal or global common good, that is, interests of the human family that were not or in principle could not be provided by individual nations or groups of nations under treaty.[34] Pope John had in mind problems like nuclear disarmament, development, even refugee flows.

Ecology, in major respects, represents a global problem for which global solutions are needed. So, planetary ecology must be regarded as a key facet of the universal common good. In *Renewing the Earth,* the bishops of the United States termed this "the planetary common good" to indicate the close connection between the global environment and the universal common good.[35] In *Sollicitudo Rei Socialis,* Pope John Paul wrote:

> Nor can the moral character of development exclude respect for the beings which constitute the natural world. . . . One must take into account *the nature of each being and of its mutual connection* in an ordered system, which is precisely the "cosmos."[36]

Thus, Catholic social teaching has come to formally recognize the ecological nature of the common good.

Concretely, what does the planetary common good comprise? Here there is no avoiding some of the cataloguing Pope John XXIII provided in *Mater et Magistra* (no. 77) for the conditions of social living. A primary component, of course, would be the global commons: the air, water, and soil resources together with migratory stocks of fish and birds, which use vast ranges in their yearly life pattern or over an entire life-cycle. Likewise, the safe disposal of products, such as nuclear and toxic waste, which take collective action to secure, would be part of the common good.

Here, I should note in passing that the principle of the common good should transmute our adversarial interest-group approach toward greater burden-sharing

"AND GOD SAW THAT IT WAS GOOD"

overall. As I shall point out later, this transition depends even more on changes in attitude and disposition than on clarity of principle. Still, common good is a principled response to burden-shifting and to what has been called the NIMBY ("not in my backyard") syndrome.

Sustainable Development

From the point of view of Catholic social teaching, sustainable development is also a requirement of the planetary common good. There are moral imperatives both to preserve the environment for future generations (and for creation's sake) and to ensure that our contemporaries have the wherewithal to live with dignity. In continuing to champion distributive justice on a global scale, Catholic environmentalism will diverge from movements like Deep Ecology and even some religious environmentalists. Nonetheless, the requirement here favors sustainable development with redistribution and with all the limits on unwarranted growth specified by "authentic development" discussed above. The pressures that expanding growth place on the planetary environment demand more than a North-South pact, as proposed by the Brundtland Commission in its report *Our Common Future.*[37] They will require both intensive economic transformation and technological innovation.

Weighted Principles

Global commons and sustainable development would be two norms of a stronger sort. For the norm of global commons, under the principle of the universal common good, it is quite clear that institutions, programs, and policies to preserve shared resources, such as air, water, or the ozone layer, and to dispose safely of hazardous waste are warranted. They are shared goods and shared burdens that cannot be enjoyed or shouldered without common action. They are needed for the welfare of the human community as well as for sustaining life on earth.

Sustainable development is a slightly different issue, although the tradition of Catholic teaching on the priority of development for all gives exceptionally strong backing to this goal. Once again, since sustainable development entails global collaboration, both for the good of the planet and the good of humanity, sustainable development could be considered a component of the universal common good. Moreover, sustainable development, because it looks to the future of the planet and of future generations, participates in the universal common good in a temporal as well as contemporaneous sense. The notion of a planetary common good appears to be most perplexing because it aspires to a threefold good: (1) the welfare of the planet as a web of natural systems, (2) justice for the living, an aspiration still far beyond our political reach, and (3) a just sharing in the earth's bounty for future generations.

Not everything all environmentalists may find desirable can be preserved or enhanced, at least initially, under the principle of the planetary common good. For example, take locales once regarded as barren waste, such as deserts and wetlands, and now regarded as fragile ecologies requiring public protection: it may not be possible, on balance, to preserve every parcel for which someone wants protection. Conversely, it may not be possible to exclude a waste disposal site from every neighborhood that would prefer not to receive one in its backyard. The common good may still require the sacrifice of some desirable open space or the acceptance of some unwanted environmental burden. In such cases, the common good will continue to have its customary role balancing claims in conflict.

Still other environmental goals will be, ethically speaking, more contestable, for example, returning the Great Plains to the buffalo, preserving wilderness on a large scale, or protecting certain small species against extinction. Some such proposals may be highly desirable and they may even be required under law, but they may also not be morally required. The environmental movement needs to learn the difference.

Different moral weights attach to different policy goals. The preservation of our national park system may be by consensus and as part of our cultural heritage a component of our domestic common good. The preservation of further parkland whether here or elsewhere may not be so, until other components of the common good, for example, hazardous waste treatment or sustainable development for the poor, are achieved.

4. The Common Good as an Ideal and Social Change

Now, the differential weighting of moral goods may not be comforting to many environmental activists. They seek the support of moral sanction equally for every cause they embrace. The diminished valence of a claim does not mean they are without moral tools. Many goals may increase in value with time. Changing society's values takes persuasion and the honoring, in word and action, of competing values that are part of the common good.

I spoke earlier of the common good as an ideal, an unrealized pattern that is a guide to balancing the moral claims of competing parties.[38] Now, ideals function in several ways. One way is to provide a pattern toward which people actually aspire in their actions. In this sense, the good of all sectors of a society is the aim, in Catholic teaching, of all public authorities.

Another way to conceive of the ideal is as a moral norm that calls for a perfection of conduct not attainable by most human beings. In this sense, it is legitimate for some people to pursue such a goal, but inappropriate for them to expect that others also share in such moral perfectionism. In liberal societies, like the United

States, where the underlying politics is professedly realist, people may pursue the ideal by way of personal commitment or through shared commitment in a lifestyle enclave, but may be expected not to impose their ideal commitments on others. This distinction between duties and perfectionist ideals, however, is not restricted to liberal polities. It has been a standard part of Catholic tradition through the centuries. Thus, for example, poverty, nonviolence, or virginity are "counsels of perfection," which are options for those who choose to follow the Gospel more closely but are not obligatory for ordinary Christians. So, in the environmental movement, some goals, like those of Deep Ecology, will also be perfectionist.

Moral ideals have a significant role in changing what people desire. Work for the protection of endangered species or for preservation of the wilderness can lead, as it has in the United States, to changed perceptions and evaluations. In the end, those evaluations may result in once-contested goods becoming part of the global common good, such as the immunity of civilians in wartime or the prevention of cruelty to animals.

These changes will come about only if other basic goods are protected. In the case of global ecology, this means working to secure authentic development for the poor or employment for workers. So there is a double task, changing perceptions and reducing value conflict through what some policy makers now call "common-sense solutions," that is, win-win strategies that serve social as well as environmental goals.

The search for common-sense solutions will itself go far toward changing public attitudes on controversial issues. But education is also needed to change public sensitivities toward the more refined goods that belong neither to the class of core goods, such as clean air and water, comprising the planetary common good, nor to the middle-level goods where common-sense solutions become feasible. With time and proper respect for the balance of goods that constitute the common good of the human community, environmental ideals can change attitudes so that goods like biodiversity are widely shared and the common good of the human community will coincide with the planetary common good of creation.

Notes

1. Drew Christiansen, SJ, "The Common Good and the Politics of Self-Interest" in Donald Gelpi, SJ, ed. *Beyond Individualism: Toward a Retrieval of Moral Discourse in America.* Notre Dame, Ind.: University of Notre Dame Press, 1989, 54–86.

2. *Summa Theologica* 2-2, q. 42, 2nd article.

3. For examples of attitudes toward nature, free of the historical prejudice that respect for nature began with the first Earth Day, see Clarence Glacken, *Traces on a Rhodian Shore.*

Berkeley, Calif.: University of California Press, 1967.

4. Drew Christiansen, SJ, "On Relative Equality: Catholic Egalitarianism After Vatican II." *Theological Studies* 45 (1984): 651-675.

5. On conditions of social living, cf. *Mater et Magistra*, no. 77, and on human rights, cf. Pope John XXIII, *Pacem in Terris*, April 11, 1963, nos. 53-66, 139. Also, cf. Christiansen, "The Common Good and the Politics of Self-Interest," especially 62-72.

6. Pope John XXIII, *Mater et Magistra*, May 15, 1961, no. 77; Second Vatican Council, *Gaudium et Spes*, December 7, 1965, nos. 26 and 76.

7. *Gaudium et Spes*, no. 66.

8. Pope Paul VI, *Octogesima Adveniens*, May 14, 1971, no. 2. Also, cf. Christiansen, "On Relative Equality."

9. Pope John Paul II, *The Ecological Crisis: A Common Responsibility*, December 8, 1989, no. 1.

10. The key texts for understanding authentic development are Pope Paul VI's *Populorum Progressio*, March 26, 1967, and Pope John Paul II, *Sollicitudo Rei Socialis*, December 30, 1987.

11. On the tension between development and environment, cf. Christiansen, "Learn a Lesson from the Flowers: Catholic Social Teaching and Global Stewardship," a paper delivered for a conference on Catholic Theology and Global Stewardship, University of Notre Dame, April 1995.

12. For a more extended treatment of the balance of goods as one dimension of authentic development, cf. Pope Paul VI's *Populorum Progressio*.

13. Christiansen, "Learn a Lesson from the Flowers."

14. Dom Jean Leclerq, *The Love of Learning and the Desire for God: A Study of Monastic Culture*. New York: Fordham, 1985.

15. On "the ecology of the soul," cf. Christiansen, "Learn a Lesson from the Flowers."

16. Pope John Paul II, *Laborem Exercens*, September 14, 1981, no. 13.

17. On siting of Cistercian monasteries, cf. Glacken, *Traces on a Rhodian Shore*.

18. Charles Avila, *Ownership: Early Christian Teaching*. New York: Orbis Books, Maryknoll Press, 1983.

19. For warnings against inauthentic development, cf. *Sollicitudo Rei Socialis*, nos. 27-29.

20. Ibid.

21. Avila, *Ownership*.

22. Cf. *Gaudium et Spes* and *Populorum Progressio* as well as Avila for commentary on the twin principles of sufficiency and community relative to ownership.

23. Ibid.

24. National Conference of Catholic Bishops, *Renewing the Earth*. Washington, D.C.: United States Catholic Conference, 1991.

25. Pope John Paul II, Address at Yankee Stadium, *Origins* Vol. 9, No. 19 (October 25, 1979),

311-312.

26. *Sollicitudo Rei Socialis*, no. 31.

27. Ibid., no. 34.

28. *Gaudium et Spes*, no. 69.

29. *Populorum Progressio*, no. 47.

30. Ibid., nos. 48-49.

31. On equity as a component of development, cf. World Commission on Environment and Development, "Our Common Future: the Bruntland Commission Report." Oxford: Oxford University Press, 1987.

32. On social sacrifice, cf. Pope Paul VI, *Populorum Progressio*, nos. 48-49; also, cf. Pope John Paul II, *Sollicitudo Rei Socialis*.

33. Christiansen, "On Relative Equality." Some commentators have seen Pope John Paul II's treatment of the market in *Centessimus Annus* as a refutation of this tendency. Subsequent papal teaching warns against exaggerating this commentary and limiting it to the post-Communist situation to which it was addressed in Eastern Europe. *Sollictudo Rei Socialis*, released only three years earlier, represents a continuation and intensification of this teaching.

34. Pope John Paul XXIII, *Pacem in Terris*, nos. 80-85.

35. National Conference of Catholic Bishops, *Renewing the Earth*.

36. *Sollicitudo Rei Socialis*, no. 34.

37. World Commission on Environment and Development, "Our Common Future."

38. On the place of ideals in political discourse, see Christiansen, "The Common Good and the Politics of Self-Interest," 70-72.

Toward a
Sustainable Ethic:
Virtue
and the
Environment

&

Deborah D. Blake

&

In the midst of a global ecological crisis, claimed to be the result of human negligence, narrow self-interest, and greed, it seems paradoxical to explore virtue as a constructive response. In the face of so much human moral failure and omission, such a negative experience of human nature, it seems contradictory to accept the positive moral anthropology suggested by a theory of virtue, particularly a theory from the Roman Catholic tradition. Yet paradox often provides a point of new insight, a creative opportunity to re-envision and to respond anew, to formulate an environmental ethic that is adequate and sustainable.

Virtue has returned to our public discourse, from the front page of *Time* magazine and William Bennett's *The Book of Virtues* to more respected scholarship represented by the work of Jean Porter, *The Recovery of Virtue*; Robert Bellah, et al., *Habits of the Heart*; Alasdair MacIntyre, *After Virtue*; and Stanley Hauerwas, *A Community of*

Character. These appeals to virtue are presented to a North American audience in response to a perceived moral impasse. Yet, while there is now little reluctance to discuss "virtue," there is no conformity and consistency in the meaning of virtue and the underlying assumptions of the varied theoretical frameworks. There are, according to Yves Simon, "many modern substitutes for virtue."[1]

Working within the Roman Catholic tradition, this chapter will return to Thomas Aquinas's theory of virtue. This provides an opportunity both to stand within the tradition and to re-envision the current moral discourse within the Church. "Moral teaching," wrote Romano Guardini, "has become too negative; [reflections on the virtues] seek to do justice to the living majesty, nobility, and beauty of the good."[2] A recovery of virtue ethics can provide for a more adequate and sustainable ethic within the Church.

The pursuit of the question of "Ecology and Catholic Theology: Contribution and Challenge," leaves open to interpretation the source of contribution and the recipient of challenge. I intend to sustain that imprecision as a means of maintaining a dialectic, a tension that allows for both the recovery and the development of the richness of the traditional teaching on virtue in response to the ecological crisis that we face together.

Virtue ethics will be considered as a logical development of the Church's response to the environmental crisis from the tradition of social teaching in this century. The appeal to the principle of justice opened the door to the virtue of justice and a fuller consideration of a unified theory of virtue. Thomas Aquinas's theology has a central place in the Church's tradition and provides a starting point for discussion. Jean Porter's work on Aquinas, *The Recovery of Virtue: The Relevance of Aquinas for Christian Ethics*, will be relied upon heavily but not exclusively. Narrative will then provide a context for the practical discussion of possible ecological virtues.

Roman Catholic Response

When human life and human flourishing were threatened by assaults upon the environment, the Roman Catholic Church responded to the environmental crisis. This response was an outgrowth of the concern for peace and justice. In his message for the World Day of Peace (January 1, 1990), John Paul II wrote:

World peace is threatened not only by the arms race, regional conflict and continued injustices among peoples and nations, but also by lack of due *respect for nature*, by the plundering of natural resources and by the progressive decline in the quality of life.[3]

Rerum Novarum (1891) began this "environmental trend," according to Sophi Jakowska, with the claim that the goods of the earth are to be shared by all.

Quadragesimo Anno (1931) sustained the theme of the shared use of natural resources and suggested limits on private property to ensure equitable use. These early documents were concerned with the material and spiritual well-being of human persons, a well-being that was threatened by the social and economic consequences of the industrial revolution.

The documents of Vatican II reaffirmed these claims. In *Pacem in Terris* (1963), John XXIII maintained that sharing natural resources was essential for attaining peace and justice. In *Gaudium et Spes* (1965), Paul VI reaffirmed the human responsibility to care for the earth (no. 67), the necessity of just and equitable sharing of the earth's resources so that human persons can live in dignity and develop physically and spiritually (no. 69). The environmental impact of industrial nations and consumer culture was challenged in *Octogesima Adveniens* (1971); "because of irrational exploitation of nature, man is now in danger of destroying the earth and becoming a victim of degradation."[4] John Paul II continued the themes of responsible use of environmental resources for all people and the criticism of consumer culture (e.g., *Redemptor Hominis* [1979]; *Laborem Exercens* [1981]).

Environmental justice is the logical complement to the Church's social teaching on justice and peace. The Church takes a self-consciously human-centered view. "The earth is important because it sustains human life."[5] At the same time there is no suggestion that human persons should "dominate" the earth; human practices are to support the availability of resources in this generation and in generations to come. Issues of peace, justice, and the environment point to a holistic perspective; all action and all of creation are interconnected.[6]

Environmental Crisis

The environmental problems we face can be described at three levels: (1) the technological or scientific aspects of specific environmental problems and solutions—technocratic approach, (2) the social and political factors, and (3) foundational issues of basic character, both social and individual. These levels of description correspond to several different approaches in Roman Catholic ethics. The first level focuses on specific situations, much like an ethic that focuses on the morality of specific acts. The second level parallels the Church's teaching on social justice in its emphasis on institutional, or systemic, injustice. The third level has similarities with the Church's ethic of virtue in its attention to a fuller discussion of the good and with the development of good habits, or virtues, that incline the person to act in a consistent and characteristic fashion. The development of alternative energy sources, the destruction of rain forests, and the practice of community ownership of a commons illustrate these three methods of ethics in relation to the environmental crisis while demonstrating the need for a complex environmental ethic that includes an ethic of virtue.

Technological and scientific definitions of the environmental crisis reflect efforts to manage the immediate effects of specific problems. Polluted air and waters, deforestation, endangered species and ecosystems, toxic waste (chemical, nuclear, pesticide), and ozone layer depletion are examples of these problems. They suggest that the environmental crisis is a "war between the technosphere and the ecosphere."[7] The solution is the transformation of production technologies into ecologically sound applications.[8]

The development of alternative energy sources reflects this first level of analysis and response—technological and scientific. Consider the development and use of alternatives to petrochemical products as a means of reducing air pollution from sulfur dioxide. Environmental improvement can begin with the substitution of natural gas for oil and coal; its sulphur dioxide emissions are less than those of coal and oil. Yet, all three are nonrenewable resources. Relying on technology, the next step is to develop a solar methane, a renewable resource, as a substitute for natural gas.[9] This "act-specific" methodology attempts to resolve environmental problems by a kind of crisis management that is reactive rather than proactive.

The destruction of the rain forests provides an example that extends beyond the first level of analysis to the second—political and economic. It is difficult to imagine technologically sound practices for the rain forests. The destruction of rain forests is caused by logging, slash-and-burn farming, cattle ranching, human population growth, and worldwide demand for forest products.[10] Consequences of deforestation include "biological diversity and species loss, impact on indigenous cultures, effects on soils and global climate, loss of products, and social and economic considerations."[11] Current logging technology reduces whole trees to chips in a matter of seconds; "the dragging away of the logs leaves a trail of colossal devastation."[12] "Many acres of forest are felled because this action provides instant benefits, . . . trees mean wealth."[13] The economic factor is complex. It is tied to the debts of developing nations to first-world nations for large-scale development projects, promoted in the 1970s by the policies of the World Bank.[14]

The economic and political factors of the environmental crisis increase the complexity of analysis and response. The disparity of environmental burden carried by the southern hemisphere reflects the disparity in economic and political power between the North and South. "Marginal people and marginal environments are chained together and become the agents of each other's destruction."[15] Palmer suggests that there is a kind of environmental neocolonialism operating.[16] Other environmentalists tie this inequity to the features of a capitalist, market economy.[17] "The environment is threatened by human practices that are organized institutionally. Environmental problems are social problems."[18] Their resolution is tied to reform of social institutions.

"AND GOD SAW THAT IT WAS GOOD"

Beyond specific social institutions there is a persistent "culture" that threatens the environment, our third level of analysis. Attitudes, motivations, and perceptions of reality are tied to culture.[19] Domination of people in economic and political systems is tied to domination of the environment. The practice of common ownership of commons provides an example. In "The Tragedy of the Commons," Garrett Hardin makes this claim:

> Each man is locked into a system that compels him to increase his herd without limit—in a world that is limited. Ruin is the destination toward which all men rush, each pursuing his own best interest in a society that believes in the freedom of the commons. Freedom in a commons brings ruin to all.[20]

The ruin that Hardin fears is the result of "human habits" informed by a social construction of the good that disvalues ecological responsibility and the needs of future generations. It is the "culture" of domination, hierarchy, and inequity in a market economy that is problematic.

A different view of the commons is found in the historical practice and traditional Hispanic culture of the San Luis Valley in Southern Colorado. In this community the ethos of communal ownership and personal responsibility for the good of the community is a matter of tradition and practice. In Northern New Mexico and Southern Colorado, land grants, *mercedes,* were made by the Spanish government and held in trust by communities; the common land was used to benefit the entire community.[21] There were common uses of water, grazing land, and town squares; there was also common responsibility for the care of the land. "Ownership" and responsibility were communal. Decisions were not based upon private, individual interests but on consideration of the common good of all members of the community. This sense of the commons is still practiced by the community in San Luis, Colorado.

Habits shaped by the "responsibility to the commons" differ radically from habits shaped by an ethos of the "freedom in the commons." The view of how the world should be and the motivations for action differ. In addition to reforming social institutions it is necessary to reform the dominant culture, to infuse our daily lives with a new social and environmental vision of the good that will provide sustained action.

A sustainable environmental ethics requires more than an act-specific ethic, more than technological attention to specific problems. It also requires more than attention to social, political, and economic systems and the reform of social institutions. A sustainable ethics requires a larger cultural framework that will provide a living context for environmentally responsible communities and persons. We need a new cultural context for the development of environmental virtues that can sustain an ongoing course of action.

"The Recovery of Virtue"

In the Roman Catholic tradition the discussion of culture and habit in relation to the environmental crisis leads us to consider the Thomistic theory of virtue as a traditional source for the development of a more comprehensive environmental ethic. This is not to suggest that a theory of virtue can stand alone or that Thomistic theology is without its problems, but rather that in conjunction with present social teaching virtue ethics can provide a fuller moral theory.[22] A theory of virtue moves us from a focus on specific acts, something of a short-term response, to a morality directed toward a unified life, both personal and communal. The strength of virtue theory is that it provides the basis for a sustained course of activity even when one is not thinking explicitly about each discrete action.[23] A person's "spontaneous desires" are directed by the virtues one acquires. Virtues reflect and shape our vision of the world.

Virtue and the Good

Virtue is an integrated quality of character that embodies our conception of the good. A virtuous person does not always think about doing the good; she is "a desiring creature in such a way that she spontaneously desires and seeks what is in accordance with the truly good life she is trying to lead.[24] "Virtue is a good quality of the mind, by which we live righteously, of which no one can make bad use."[25]

Aquinas's understanding of the good is dependent upon his understanding of the nature of being.

> We have said that the good is everything which is desirable.[26] And so, since every nature desires its being and its own perfection, it is necessary to say that the being and perfection of any nature has the character of goodness.[27]

Human good is attained by rational activity, "by sustaining a lifelong course of activity that is determined by our rational grasp of that in which the truly human good consists."[28] The ultimate human good, or desire, is union with God, yet there are innumerable intermediate or particular goods that must be properly ordered in accord with the ultimate goal. This is a key to understanding the role of Aquinas's theory of virtue in relation to the environmental crisis. Through choices that lead to environmental degradation, choices that threaten physical and spiritual development, the person is forced from his or her path of perfection. The good of the individual, the community, and the created universe are interdependent.

In Aquinas's theory, there are a clear theocentrism and the possibility of human transcendence that can move us beyond a narrow salvific individualism and anthropocentric ordering of the world. According to Aquinas,

Every creature exists for its own proper act and perfection. . . . Furthermore, each and every creature exists for the perfection of the entire universe. Further still, the entire universe, with all its parts, is ordained towards God as its end, inasmuch as it imitates, as it were, and shows forth the divine goodness which is the glory of God.[29]

Moreover, according to Robert Ayers,

It appears that the Augustinian-Thomistic view of man's relation to nature reflects the biblical perspective, namely, that there is a dialectical tension between humanity's transcendence of and radical oneness with the rest of creation.[30]

The Thomistic worldview requires self-transcendence and the proper ordering of choices in light of relationality and interdependence.

Virtues

Virtues enable a person to act well. "The moral virtues are enduring traits of character that persons must possess if they are to be able to sustain a course of activity;"[31] they are voluntarily acquired. Aquinas identifies four cardinal or moral virtues: fortitude, temperance, prudence, and justice; and three theological virtues: faith, hope, and charity.

[According to Aquinas] the four cardinal virtues are the primary moral virtues because they represent the four fundamental modes, so to speak, by which the individual appropriates the human good as discerned by reason: *Prudence* appropriates the good directly by the action of the intellect, which determines how best to actualize one's specific good; *justice* directs external actions in such a way as to conform with reason—it does this by conforming the will to a wider good than the individual's own; and *fortitude* and *temperance* moderate the irascible and desiring passions in such a way that the individual spontaneously desires what is true in accordance with the specific good of the human person and avoids what is not in accord with the human good.[32]

Our discussion will focus on the moral virtues.

The virtues are "open ended" in that there are many particular ways in which they can be realized. Temperance and fortitude rectify subrational passions and contribute to the well-being of the person. Justice transcends the individual and contributes to the good of others. Prudence completes and unifies the virtues by directing human actions towards the good in specific situations.

Virtues are context bound. Discussions of the environmental crisis have resulted in the suggestion of several "qualities of character" as candidates for ecological virtues that may be viewed as particular virtues or as subvirtues, falling under the broad categories of Aquinas's moral virtues. A representative list includes (1) tolerance ("unity-in-diversity"), mutuality, sustainability, communitarian vision, and egalitarian cooperation[33]; (2) love, friendship, mercy, humility, forgiveness[34];(3) relationality and responsibility[35]; and (4) "cooperation, respect, far-sightedness, tolerance, and trust."[36]

The suggestion of specific environmental virtues requires a rubric for discerning the adequacy of suggested "virtues." Jean Porter suggests "four elements that go to make up a concept of a particular virtue":

(1) A notion of a particular kind of action that is characteristic of the virtue (although not necessarily linked with it in every instance), which will include some idea of the kind of context in which the sort of action would be appropriate; (2) some idea of kinds of actions that are characteristically failures to act well, in the contexts that provide the setting for the virtue in question; (3) some idea of what it would mean, concretely, for a person to display this virtue through his actions and reactions over a substantial period of time; and finally, (4) some guidelines for distinguishing true from false exemplifications of the virtue in question, guidelines derived from a higher principle that will enable us to say whether in a particular instance this putative virtue is truly being exercised in such a way as to promote the true good of the human person.[37]

These criteria will be used to evaluate and further refine the candidates for ecological virtues.

Narrative

Narratives provide a context in which the meaning of particular virtues is made clear and exemplified by concrete actions.[38] "Ideal narratives of typical kinds of human lives are nothing other than schemata for inclusive life plans; they indicate how certain of the goods of human life are to be achieved in an orderly way."[39] The narrative of the Globeville/ASARCO case in Colorado will provide a context for our consideration of possible ecological virtues. The narrative is based upon interviews and background information reported in the *Rocky Mountain News*, a Denver newspaper. Narrative also demonstrates the foundational importance of an ethic of virtue for sustained action.

Globeville is a low-income, Hispanic community in North Denver. It is a neighborhood of immigrants—German, Russian, Slavic, and now Mexicano and Latino. It is also a community that is disvalued by the larger Denver metropolitan community. According to the local paper,

"AND GOD SAW THAT IT WAS GOOD"

Interstates knocked down homes; industrial development wiped out others; city planners figured that one day the entire neighborhood would be leveled for factories, so they long ignored its future; the unemployment rate is three times higher than that of Denver as a whole.[40]

Yet, according to Josephine Duran, Globeville goes on and that's because of the kind of people who call the area home. "There's a real sense of family here," Duran said. "It's a good place to buy a first home. . . . My life is in Globeville," Duran said. "This is my neighborhood. I care about this place. This is my hometown. That's what all of this is about."[41]

In 1989 the Globeville community filed a class-action suit against a high-grade metals refinery, ASARCO. The residents claimed that ASARCO, Inc. had released "dangerously high levels of cadmium and other heavy metals" into the air, soil, and ground water for more than fifty years.[42] Two studies showed that people living near the smelter face higher than normal risks for cancer and other illnesses because cadmium, lead, and arsenic contaminate the soil, air, and groundwater.[43] One article reported as follows:

Margaret Escamilla washed away dirt that was 10-30 ppm of cadmium from Angelina Gallegos after she played outside. At her day care center Escamilla allows the children to play outside only one hour in the morning and one hour in the afternoon. She has two of every toy, one for the outside, one for the inside. . . . The Escamillas moved to Globeville in 1981 when they bought a HUD house that cost $38,000. They added a three-car garage, finished the basement, carpeted the bedrooms, and tiled a room for their children. The tile stops at the door to the kitchen, and there has been a strip of unfinished floor for three years. It marks the date that the Escamillas found out about the contamination from ASARCO. . . . "We wanted to make this our home but all of a sudden we didn't know if we should stay and make this the home we always wanted. Then," says Margaret Escamilla, "we went to a neighborhood meeting and found out what ASARCO was doing. We realized we had to stay and fight."[44]

Early in the community action against ASARCO, Emma Flores commented,

"The concern I really have is, if they throw us out, where will we go? We're poor. We don't have money."[45]

According to Patrick Bustos, an EPA State Liaison Officer for Denver, "We have to come up with an environmental justice plan to determine whether we are treating people of color and low-income people differently. . . . [Do] low-income peoples . . . get less stringent cleanups?" Yet following the court decision, Al Montoya proclaimed, "Look at the people here—we're the little people. And we just showed the big company you can't pollute."[46]

Four years after the suit was filed the Federal District Court awarded residents $28 million for cleanup costs in residential areas and $12 million in compensation for lost property values. An earlier settlement with the Colorado Department of Health had committed $31 to $38 million in cleanup costs for nonresidential areas. Commenting on the case:

Josephine Duran reflected, "I was really naive. I didn't think the government would let a business do that kind of thing."[47]

Jurors were appalled by ASARCO's blatant polluting. "It was disgusting to me that they were that negligent for that long," said juror Susan Poulos. Jurors also criticized the State Health Department for failing to require ASARCO in the cleanup plan to reduce cadmium levels to those in other Denver neighborhoods.[48]

Because jurors did not think that a previous settlement with the state guaranteed cadmium levels would be reduced to safe levels in residents' yards they awarded a separate settlement property owners could control.[49]

Lorraine Granados [a Globeville resident and organizer] and others are trying to mobilize American Indians, African Americans and Hispanics to join the environmental movement, which some have perceived as the elitist domain of white backpackers.[50]

The key to a successful network, [Maria] Valdez believes, is one that emerges from local people and connects them. . . . These networks have to be groups of individuals that really come from the grass roots.[51]

These people are survivors, but that is not enough. They don't want to just survive—they want to thrive.[52]

This narrative provides some clarity and insight into several of the suggested ecological virtues and traditional moral virtues. It also provides evidence for the "four elements that go to make up a concept of a particular virtue":[53] context for action, characteristic failures, action over time, and guidelines for true and false examples of virtue. Calling upon the suggested ecological virtues, equity, communitarian vision/relationality, cooperation, and farsightedness come to mind. Fortitude and prudence come to mind from the list of traditional moral virtues.

The virtue of equity is most noticeable by its absence. The city government long ignored the community. Early court settlements did not require cleanup standards equal to those in other Denver neighborhoods. Al Montoya characterized the inequity by describing ASARCO as the "big company" and his community as the "little people."

The ecological virtues of communitarian vision/relationality and cooperation are woven throughout the narrative. The action of the community arose from a sense of family and neighborhood. The activism of the Globeville citizens was directed towards the improvement of the environmental quality of life for the whole community, not merely a series of individual settlements.

Farsightedness is exemplified in two prominent ways: cleanup and political organization. The adults of the community clearly recognized the importance of an environmentally safe community for the future of their children. The court settlement also set a precedent for future litigation in other communities. Globeville residents continue to organize beyond their own community, forming alliances with other peoples of color. Perhaps in their farsightedness they understood that "environmental racism" would not end with the cleanup of their neighborhood. Farsightedness may be an example of prudence, both in these particular illustrations and in a more contemporary rendering of language.

The most striking virtue, in my mind, is that of fortitude. This community demonstrated perseverance in the face of seemingly insurmountable odds. There was a self-respect and confidence that accompanied their determination. "Fortitude" does not quite convey the meaning of their character. In the Globeville community one might more appropriately speak of *ganas*, a kind of self-respect and determination that leads to success, success which is returned to the community.

The community of Globeville did not meet ASARCO head-on based upon their discussion of abstract ideals of justice. They responded out of moral outrage and a vision of what was right. Perhaps being a marginalized community and a Hispanic community was to their "moral advantage"; they embodied the values and virtues of their cultural tradition in their "everyday lives." These values include family (*la familia*), relationships based upon respect and politeness (*simpatia*), trust (*confianza*), and respect—especially towards the elderly (*respeto*).[54] And, it was these virtues, embodied in the life of the community, that initiated and sustained action.

Conclusion

The strength of using virtue ethics to address the environmental crisis is that it provides for a sustained course of activity. The weakness is that the moral teaching of our communities and our Church does not focus on the unity and development of the virtues in everyday life. Habits are acquired in our society but too often we are not self-critical and we embody the values and worldview that have contributed to the current crisis: individualism, self-interest, market-modeled competition. Our values and habits are not always virtuous. On the other hand, the Church, and especially living communities within the Church, have maintained a tradition of values that can contribute constructively to the crisis: common good, dignity of all persons, stewardship, common use of resources, respect, trust, and community life. However, the Church's traditional language of virtue is in need of interpretation and rearticulation if it is to be meaningful in distinct, contemporary communities. The means by which the Church teaches about moral matters would be well served, in terms of attention to virtue theory, by using narrative discourse, the experience of local communities, and critical analysis. Finally, the Church must model, in its daily life, the virtues necessary for a sustainable future.

Notes

1. Yves Simon, *The Definition of Moral Virtue* (New York: Fordham Press, 1986), 2.

2. Romano Guardini, *The Virtues: On Forms of Moral Life* (Chicago: Henry Regenery Company, 1963), vi.

3. John Paul II, "Peace with God the Creator: Peace with All of Creation," Message for the World Day of Peace (January 1, 1990), no. 1.

4. Sophie Jakowska, "Roman Catholic Teaching and Environmental Ethics in Latin America," in *Religion and Environmental Crisis*, ed. Eugene C. Hargrove (Athens, Ga.: The University of Georgia Press, 1986), 134.

5. James Roth and Debra Starkey, ed. *Earth Abuse: A Sociological Reader on Environmental Issues* (Denver: Regis University, 1994), photocopied course reader, 1.

6. Peter Beyer, "The Global Environment as a Religious Issue: A Sociological Analysis," *Religion*, 22:10.

7. Barry Commoner, "Ending the War Against the Earth," *The Nation* (April 30, 1990), 589.

8. Ibid., 590.

9. Ibid. See also Paul Harrison, *The Third Revolution: Environment, Population, and a Sustainable World* (New York: I. B. Tauris & Co. Ltd., 1992), 195-220.

10. Joy A. Palmer, "Destruction of the Rain Forests: Principles or Practices" in *The Environment in Question: Ethics and Global Issues,* ed. David E. Cooper and Joy A. Palmer (New York: Routledge, 1992), 88-89.

11. Ibid., 90.

12. Ibid., 89.

13. Ibid., 88, 89.

14. Ibid., 88.

15. Harrison, *The Third Revolution*, 127.

16. Joy A. Palmer, "Destruction of the Rain Forests: Principles or Practices."

17. Cf. John Bellamy Foster, "'Let Them Eat Pollution': Capitalism and the World Environment," *Monthly Review* 44, 8 (1993):10-20; Roth and Starkey, eds, *Earth Abuse;* and Howard Hawkins, "Ecology," *Z Papers* 1, 1 (1992):31-42.

18. Roth and Starky, *Earth Abuse*, 2.

19. Clifford Geertz, *The Interpretation of Cultures* (New York: Basic Books, 1973), 90.

20. Garret Hardin, "The Tragedy of the Commons," *Science*, 162 (1968).

21. Unlike Spanish land grants in California and other parts of New Spain, the operation of land grants in Southern Colorado did not involve the enslavement and exploitation of indigenous peoples and immigrant laborers. In 1863 Carlos Beaubien issued a deed to all the settlers on the Sangre de Cristo land grant conveying rights to pastures, water rights and the use of wood and lumber in order to protect the community's interests in the event of future sales of the land. In 1916 the U.S. District Court denied much of the original intent of the deed and sided with the claims of the Costillo Estates Land Development Company. The San Luis community is still fighting for the restoration of the communal use of the land (Randall Teeuwan, ed, *La Cultura Constante de San Luis* [San Luis, Colo.: The San Luis Museum Cultural and Commercial Center, 1985]).

22. Jean Porter, *The Recovery of Virtue: The Relevance of Thomas Aquinas for Christian Ethics* (Louisville, Ky.: Westminster Press, 1990), 103.

23. Ibid., 103; *Summa Theologia* (ST) I-II.6 ad 3.

24. ST I-II.55.4.

25. Ibid.

26. Ibid., I.5.1.

27. Ibid., I.48.1.

28. Porter, *The Recovery of Virtue,* 67.

29. ST I.65.2.

30. Robert H. Ayers, "Christian Realism and Environmental Ethics," in *Religion and Environmental Crisis*, ed. Eugene C. Hargrove (Athens, Ga.: The University of Georgia Press, 1986), 158.

31. Porter, *The Recovery of Virtue,* 70.

32. Ibid., 166; ST I–II.61.2,3.

33. Howard Hawkins, "Ecology," *Z Papers*, 1 (1) (1992), 33.

34. Larry Rasmussen, "Planetary Environment," *General Theology and Public Policy* Vol. 2 (Summer 1990), 12.

35. Donal O'Mahoney, OFM.Cap, "International Debt and Ecological Connections," Sedos Seminar, 1992, 325–339.

36. Palmer, *The Environment in Question*.

37. Porter, *The Recovery of Virtue*, 109.

38. Porter, *The Recovery of Virtue;* Alasdair MacIntyre, *After Virtue,* 2d ed. (Notre Dame, Ind.: University of Notre Dame Press, 1984); Stanley Hauerwas, *A Community of Character* (Notre Dame, Ind.: University of Notre Dame Press, 1981); and John Crossin, OSFS, *What Are They Saying About Virtue* (New York: Paulist Press, 1985).

39. Porter, *The Recovery of Virtue,* 80.

40. *Rocky Mountain News* (March 10, 1993), 8.

41. Ibid.

42. *Rocky Mountain News* (June 3, 1993), 4a.

43. *Rocky Mountain News* (June 14, 1990), 6.

44. "Toxicologist Calls Smelter's Poisons Eternal," *Rocky Mountain News* (February 18, 1993), 18.

45. *Rocky Mountain News* (June 14, 1990), 61.

46. "Globeville Takes Victory in Stride," *Rocky Mountain News* (March 13, 1993): 22.

47. *Rocky Mountain News* (March 1, 1993).

48. *Rocky Mountain News* (March 13, 1993), 6.

49. "ASARCO Settlement Set at $28 Million," *Rocky Mountain News* (April 24, 1993), 4a.

50. "Pollution Mixes With Racism," *Rocky Mountain News* (May 29, 1994), 72a.

51. Ibid.

52. "Globeville Survivors Hope to Win," *Rocky Mountain News* (March 11, 1993), 6.

53. Porter, *The Recovery of Virtue,* 109.

54. Josephine A. Hibeln, MSN, RN, "Minority Health Issues: Hispanic Americans," *Ohio Nurses Review* (1992), 11.

APPENDICES

INTRODUCTION TO THE APPENDICES

THE UNITED STATES CATHOLIC CONFERENCE OFTEN RECEIVES REQUESTS for Pope John Paul II's 1990 World Day of Peace Message and the U.S. bishops' 1991 pastoral statement, *Renewing the Face of the Earth*. We also receive numerous requests for copies of ecological and environmental statements by other bishops' conferences. We reprint here Pope John Paul II's message, the U.S. bishops' pastoral statement, and several selections of statements from other bishops' conferences that are available to the USCC in English. We hope that they are helpful to students and others who seek to understand the Church's growing conern for this issue. (See note 4 of the introduction for a more complete listing of statements by other bishops' conferences.)

THE
ECOLOGICAL CRISIS:
A COMMON
RESPONSIBILITY

Message of His Holiness Pope John Paul II
for the Celebration of the World Day of Peace

January 1, 1990, Vatican City

Peace with God the Creator,
Peace with All of Creation

Introduction

1. In our day, there is a growing awareness that world peace is threatened not only by the arms race, regional conflicts and continued injustices among peoples and nations, but also by a lack of *due respect for nature*, by the plundering of natural resources and by a progressive decline in the quality of life. The sense of precariousness and insecurity that such a situation engenders is a seedbed for collective selfishness, disregard for others and dishonesty.

Faced with the widespread destruction of the environment, people everywhere are coming to understand that we cannot continue to use the goods of the earth as we have in the past. The public in general as well as political leaders are concerned about this problem, and experts from a wide range of disciplines are studying its causes. Moreover, a new *ecological awareness* is beginning to emerge which, rather than being downplayed, ought to be encouraged to develop into concrete programmes and initiatives.

2. Many ethical values, fundamental to the development of a *peaceful society*, are particularly relevant to the ecological question. The fact that many challenges facing the world today are interdependent confirms the need for carefully coordinated solutions based on a morally coherent world view.

For Christians, such a world view is grounded in religious convictions drawn from Revelation. That is why I should like to begin this Message with a reflection on the biblical account of creation. I would hope that even those who do not share these same beliefs will find in these pages a common ground for reflection and action.

I. "And God Saw That It Was Good"

3. In the Book of Genesis, where we find God's first self-revelation to humanity (Gen 1-3), there is a recurring refrain: "And God saw that it was good." After creating the heavens, the sea, the earth and all it contains, God created man and woman. At this point the refrain changes markedly: "And God saw everything that he had made, and behold, *it was very good*" (Gen 1:31). God entrusted the whole of creation to the man and woman, and only then—as we read—could he rest "from all his work" (Gen 2:3).

Adam and Eve's call to share in the unfolding of God's plan of creation brought into play those abilities and gifts which distinguish the human being from all other creatures. At the same time, their call established a fixed relationship between mankind and the rest of creation. Made in the image and likeness of God, Adam and Eve were to have exercised their dominion over the earth (Gen 1:28) with wisdom and love. Instead, they destroyed the existing harmony *by deliberately going against the Creator's plan*, that is, by choosing to sin. This resulted not only in man's alienation from himself, in death and fratricide, but also in the earth's "rebellion" against him (cf. Gen 3:17-19; 4:12). All of creation became subject to futility, waiting in a mysterious way to be set free and to obtain a glorious liberty together with all the children of God (cf. Rom 8:20-21).

4. Christians believe that the Death and Resurrection of Christ accomplished the work of reconciling humanity to the Father, who "was pleased . . . through (Christ) to reconcile to himself all things, whether on earth or in heaven, making peace by the blood of his cross" (Col 1:19-20). Creation was thus made new (cf. Rev 21:5). Once subjected to the bondage of sin and decay (cf. Rom 8:21), it has now received new life while "we wait for new heavens and a new earth in which righteousness dwells" (2 Pt 3:13). Thus, the Father "has made known to us in all wisdom and in-

sight the mystery . . . which he set forth in Christ as a plan for the fulness of time, to unite *all things* in him, all things in heaven and things on earth" (Eph 1:9-10).

5. These biblical considerations help us to understand better *the relationship between human activity and the whole of creation.* When man turns his back on the Creator's plan, he provokes a disorder which has inevitable repercussions on the rest of the created order. If man is not at peace with God, then earth itself cannot be at peace: "Therefore the land mourns and all who dwell in it languish, and also the beasts of the field and the birds of the air and even the fish of the sea are taken away" (Hos 4:3).

The profound sense that the earth is "suffering" is also shared by those who do not profess our faith in God. Indeed, the increasing devastation of the world of nature is apparent to all. It results from the behaviour of people who show a callous disregard for the hidden, yet perceivable requirements of the order and harmony which govern nature itself.

People are asking anxiously if it is still possible to remedy the damage which has been done. Clearly, an adequate solution cannot be found merely in a better management or a more rational use of the earth's resources, as important as these may be. Rather, we must go to the source of the problem and face in its entirety that profound moral crisis *of which the destruction of the environment is only one troubling aspect.*

II. The Ecological Crisis: A Moral Problem

6. Certain elements of today's ecological crisis reveal its moral character. First among these is the *indiscriminate application* of advances in science and technology. Many recent discoveries have brought undeniable benefits to humanity. Indeed, they demonstrate the nobility of the human vocation to participate *responsibly* in God's creative action in the world. Unfortunately, it is now clear that the application of these discoveries in the fields of industry and agriculture have produced harmful long-term effects. This has led to the painful realization that *we cannot interfere in one area of the ecosystem without paying due attention both to the consequences of such interference in other areas and to the well-being of future generations.*

The gradual depletion of the ozone layer and the related "greenhouse effect" has now reached crisis proportions as a consequence of industrial growth, massive urban concentrations and vastly increased energy needs. Industrial waste, the burning of fossil fuels, unrestricted deforestation, the use of certain types of herbicides, coolants and propellants: all of these are known to harm the atmosphere and environment. The resulting meteorological and atmospheric changes range from damage to health to the possible future submersion of low-lying lands.

While in some cases the damage already done may well be irreversible, in many other cases it can still be halted. It is necessary, however, that the entire human community—individuals, States and international bodies—take seriously the responsibility that is theirs.

7. The most profound and serious indication of the moral implications underlying the ecological problem is the lack of *respect for life* evident in many of the patterns of environmental pollution. Often, the interests of production prevail over concern for the dignity of workers, while economic interests take priority over the good of individuals and even entire peoples. In these cases, pollution or environmental destruction is the result of an unnatural and reductionist vision which at times leads to a genuine contempt for man.

On another level, delicate ecological balances are upset by the uncontrolled destruction of animal and plant life or by a reckless exploitation of natural resources. It should be pointed out that all of this, even if carried out in the name of progress and well-being, is ultimately to mankind's disadvantage.

Finally, we can only look with deep concern at the enormous possibilities of biological research. We are not yet in a position to assess the biological disturbance that could result from indiscriminate genetic manipulation and from the unscrupulous development of new forms of plant and animal life, to say nothing of unacceptable experimentation regarding the origins of human life itself. It is evident to all that in any area as delicate as this, indifference to fundamental ethical norms, or their rejection, would lead mankind to the very threshold of self-destruction.

Respect for life, and above all for the dignity of the human person, is the ultimate guiding norm for any sound economic, industrial or scientific progress.

The complexity of the ecological question is evident to all. There are, however, certain underlying principles, which, while respecting the legitimate autonomy and the specific competence of those involved, can direct research towards adequate and lasting solutions. These principles are essential to the building of a peaceful society; *no peaceful society can afford to neglect either respect for life or the fact that there is an integrity to creation.*

III. In Search of a Solution

8. Theology, philosophy and science all speak of a harmonious universe, of a "cosmos" endowed with its own integrity, its own internal, dynamic balance. *This order must be respected.* The human race is called to explore this order, to examine it with due care and to make use of it while safeguarding its integrity.

On the other hand, the earth is ultimately *a common heritage, the fruits of which are for the benefit of all.* In the words of the Second Vatican Council, "God destined the earth and all it contains for the use of every individual and all peoples" (*Gaudium et Spes*, 69). This has direct consequences for the problem at hand. It is manifestly unjust that a privileged few should continue to accumulate excess goods, squandering available resources, while masses of people are living in conditions of misery at the very lowest level of subsistence. Today, the dramatic threat of ecological breakdown is teaching us the extent to which greed and selfishness—both individual and collective—are contrary to the order of creation, an order which is characterized by mutual interdependence.

9. The concepts of an ordered universe and a common heritage both point to the necessity of a *more internationally coordinated approach to the management of the earth's goods*. In many cases the effects of ecological problems transcend the borders of individual States; hence their solution cannot be found solely on the national level. Recently there have been some promising steps towards such international action, yet the existing mechanisms and bodies are clearly not adequate for the development of a comprehensive plan of action. Political obstacles, forms of exaggerated nationalism and economic interests—to mention only a few factors—impede international cooperation and long-term effective action.

The need for joint action on the international level *does not lessen the responsibility of each individual State*. Not only should each State join with others in implementing internationally accepted standards, but it should also make or facilitate necessary socio-economic adjustments within its own borders, giving special attention to the most vulnerable sectors of society. The State should also actively endeavour within its own territory to prevent destruction of the atmosphere and biosphere, by carefully monitoring, among other things, the impact of new technological or scientific advances. The State also has the responsibility of ensuring that its citizens are not exposed to dangerous pollutants or toxic wastes. *The right to a safe environment* is ever more insistently presented today as a right that must be included in an updated Charter of Human Rights.

IV. The Urgent Need for a New Solidarity

10. The ecological crisis reveals the *urgent moral need for a new solidarity*, especially in relations between the developing nations and those that are highly industrialized. States must increasingly share responsibility, in complementary ways, for the promotion of a natural and social environment that is both peaceful and healthy. The newly industrialized States cannot, for example, be asked to apply restrictive environmental standards to their emerging industries unless the industrialized States first apply them within their own boundaries. At the same time, countries in the process of industrialization are not morally free to repeat the errors made in the past by others, and recklessly continue to damage the environment through industrial pollutants, radical deforestation or unlimited exploitation of non-renewable resources. In this context, there is urgent need to find a solution to the treatment and disposal of toxic wastes.

No plan or organization, however, will be able to effect the necessary changes unless world leaders are truly convinced of the absolute need for this new solidarity, which is demanded of them by the ecological crisis and which is essential for peace. *This need presents new opportunities for strengthening cooperative and peaceful relations among States.*

11. It must also be said that the proper ecological balance will not be found without *directly addressing the structural forms of poverty* that exist throughout the world. Rural poverty and unjust land distribution in many countries, for example, have led to subsistence farming and to the exhaustion of the soil. Once their land yields no more, many farmers move on to clear new land, thus accelerating uncontrolled deforestation, or they settle in urban centres which lack the infrastructure to receive them. Likewise, some heavily indebted countries are destroying their natural heritage, at the price of irreparable ecological imbalances, in order to develop new products for export. In the face of such situations it would be wrong to assign responsibility to the poor alone for the negative environmental consequences of their actions. Rather, the poor, to whom the earth is entrusted no less than to others, must be enabled to find a way out of their poverty. This will require a courageous reform of structures, as well as new ways of relating among peoples and States.

12. But there is another dangerous menace which threatens us, namely *war*. Unfortunately, modern science already has the capacity to change the environment for hostile purposes. Alterations of this kind over the long term could have unforeseeable and still more serious consequences. Despite the international agreements which prohibit chemical, bacteriological and biological warfare, the fact is that laboratory research continues to develop new offensive weapons capable of altering the balance of nature.

Today, any form of war on a global scale would lead to incalculable ecological damage. But even local or regional wars, however limited, not only destroy human life and social structures, but also damage the land, ruining crops and vegetation as well as poisoning the soil and water. The survivors of war are forced to begin a new life in very difficult environmental conditions, which in turn create situations of extreme social unrest, with further negative consequences for the environment.

13. Modern society will find no solution to the ecological problem unless it *takes a serious look at its life style*. In many parts of the world society is given to instant gratification and consumerism while remaining indifferent to the damage which these cause. As I have already stated, the seriousness of the ecological issue lays bare the depth of man's moral crisis. If an appreciation of the value of the human person and

of human life is lacking, we will also lose interest in others and in the earth itself. Simplicity, moderation and discipline, as well as a spirit of sacrifice, must become a part of everyday life, lest all suffer the negative consequences of the careless habits of a few.

An education in ecological responsibility is urgent: responsibility for oneself, for others, and for the earth. This education cannot be rooted in mere sentiment or empty wishes. Its purpose cannot be ideological or political. It must not be based on a rejection of the modern world or a vague desire to return to some "paradise lost." Instead, a true education in responsibility entails a genuine conversion in ways of thought and behaviour. Churches and religious bodies, non-governmental and governmental organizations, indeed all members of society, have a precise role to play in such education. The first educator, however, is the family, where the child learns to respect his neighbour and to love nature.

14. *Finally, the aesthetic value of creation cannot be overlooked.* Our very contact with nature has a deep restorative power; contemplation of its magnificence imparts peace and serenity. The Bible speaks again and again of the goodness and beauty of creation, which is called to glorify God (cf. Gen 1:4ff; Ps 8:2; 104:1ff; Wis 13:3-5; Sir 39:16, 33; 43:1, 9). More difficult, perhaps, but no less profound, is the contemplation of the works of human ingenuity. Even cities can have a beauty all their own, one that ought to motivate people to care for their surroundings. Good urban planning is an important part of environmental protection, and respect for the natural contours of the land is an indispensable prerequisite for ecologically sound development. The relationship between a good aesthetic education and the maintenance of a healthy environment cannot be overlooked.

V. The Ecological Crisis: A Common Responsibility

15. Today, the ecological crisis has assumed such proportions as to be the responsibility of everyone. As I have pointed out, its various aspects demonstrate the need for concerted efforts aimed at establishing the duties and obligations that belong to individuals, peoples, States and the international community. This not only goes hand in hand with efforts to build true peace, but also confirms and reinforces those efforts in a concrete way. When the ecological crisis is set within the broader context of the search for peace within society, we can understand better the importance of giving attention to what the earth and its atmosphere are telling us: namely, that there is an order in the universe which must be respected, and that the human person, endowed with the capability of choosing freely, has a grave responsibility to preserve this order for the well-being of future generations. I wish to repeat that the ecological crisis is a moral issue.

Even men and women without any particular religious conviction, but with an acute sense of their responsibilities for the common good, recognize their obligation to contribute to the restoration of a healthy environment. All the more should men and women who believe in God the Creator, and who are thus convinced that there is a well-defined unity and order in the world, feel called to address the problem. Christians, in particular, realize that their responsibility within creation and their duty towards nature and the Creator are an essential part of their faith. As a result, they are conscious of a vast field of ecumenical and interreligious cooperation opening up before them.

16. At the conclusion of this Message, I should like to address directly my brothers and sisters in the Catholic Church, in order to remind them of their serious obligation to care for all of creation. The commitment of believers to a healthy environment for everyone stems directly from their belief in God the Creator, from their recognition of the effects of original and personal sin, and from the certainty of having been redeemed by Christ. Respect for life and for the dignity of the human person extends also to the rest of creation, which is called to join man in praising God (cf. Ps 148:96).

In 1979, I proclaimed Saint Francis of Assisi as the heavenly Patron of those who promote ecology (cf. Apostolic Letter *Inter Sanctos*: AAS 71 [1979], 1509f.). He offers Christians an example of genuine and deep respect for the integrity of creation. As a friend of the poor who was loved by God's creatures, Saint Francis invited all of creation—animals, plants, natural forces, even Brother Sun and Sister Moon—to give honour and praise to the Lord. The poor man of Assisi gives us striking witness that when we are at peace with God we are better able to devote ourselves to building up that peace with all creation which is inseparable from peace among all peoples.

It is my hope that the inspiration of Saint Francis will help us to keep ever alive a sense of "fraternity" with all those good and beautiful things which Almighty God has created. And may he remind us of our serious obligation to respect and watch over them with care, in light of that greater and higher fraternity that exists within the human family.

Renewing the Earth

*An Invitation to Reflection and Action on
Environment in Light of Catholic Social Teaching*

A Pastoral Statement of the
United States Catholic Conference,
November 14, 1991

Faced with the widespread destruction of the environment,
people everywhere are coming to understand that we cannot continue to
use the goods of the earth as we have in the past. . . . [A] new *ecological
awareness* is beginning to emerge. . . . The ecological crisis is a moral issue.
(Pope John Paul II, *The Ecological Crisis: A Common Responsibility*,
nos. 1, 15, December 8, 1989)

I. Signs of the Times

At its core, the environmental crisis is a moral challenge. It calls us to examine how
we use and share the goods of the earth, what we pass on to future generations, and
how we live in harmony with God's creation.

The effects of environmental degradation surround us: the smog in our cities;
chemicals in our water and on our food; eroded topsoil blowing in the wind; the loss of
valuable wetlands; radioactive and toxic waste lacking adequate disposal sites; threats to
the health of industrial and farm workers. The problems, however, reach far beyond our
own neighborhoods and workplaces. Our problems are the world's problems and burdens for generations to come. Poisoned water crosses borders freely. Acid rain pours on
countries that do not create it. Greenhouse gases and chlorofluorocarbons affect the
earth's atmosphere for many decades, regardless of where they are produced or used.

Opinions vary about the causes and the seriousness of environmental problems. Still, we can experience their effects in polluted air and water; in oil and wastes on our beaches; in the loss of farmland, wetlands, and forests; and in the decline of rivers and lakes. Scientists identify several other less visible but particularly urgent problems currently being debated by the scientific community, including depletion of the ozone layer, deforestation, the extinction of species, the generation and disposal of toxic and nuclear waste, and global warming. These important issues are being explored by scientists, and they require urgent attention and action. We are not scientists, but as pastors we call on experts, citizens, and policymakers to continue to explore the serious environmental, ethical, and human dimensions of these ecological challenges.

Environmental issues are also linked to other basic problems. As eminent scientist Dr. Thomas F. Malone reported, humanity faces problems in five interrelated fields: environment, energy, economics, equity, and ethics. To ensure the survival of a healthy planet, then, we must not only establish a sustainable economy but must also labor for justice both within and among nations. We must seek a society where economic life and environmental commitment work together to protect and to enhance life on this planet.

A. Aims of This Statement

With these pastoral reflections, we hope to add a distinctive and constructive voice to the ecological dialogue already under way in our nation and in our Church. These are beginning reflections for us, not final conclusions. We want to stimulate dialogue, particularly with the scientific community. We know these are not simple matters. We speak as pastors, offering our thoughts on a global problem that many people also recognize as a moral and religious crisis as well. In speaking out at this time, we have six goals:

1. To highlight the ethical dimensions of the environmental crisis;
2. To link questions of ecology and poverty, environment and development;
3. To stand with working men and women and poor and disadvantaged persons, whose lives are often impacted by ecological abuse and tradeoffs between environment and development;
4. To promote a vision of a just and sustainable world community;
5. To invite the Catholic community and men and women of good will to reflect more deeply on the religious dimensions of this topic; and
6. To begin a broader conversation on the potential contribution of the Church to environmental questions.

Above all, we seek to explore the links between concern for the person and for the earth, between natural ecology and social ecology. The web of life is one. Our mistreatment of the natural world diminishes our own dignity and sacredness, not only because we are destroying resources that future generations of humans need, but because we are engaging in actions that contradict what it means to be human. Our tradition calls us to protect the life and dignity of the human person, and it is increasingly clear that this task cannot be separated from the care and defense of all of creation.

B. Justice and the Environment

The whole human race suffers as a result of environmental blight, and generations yet unborn will bear the cost for our failure to act today. But in most countries today, including our own, it is the poor and the powerless who most directly bear the burden of current environmental carelessness. Their lands and neighborhoods are more likely to be polluted or to host toxic waste dumps, their water to be undrinkable, their children to be harmed. Too often, the structure of sacrifice involved in environmental remedies seems to exact a high price from the poor and from workers. Small farmers, industrial workers, lumberjacks, watermen, rubber-tappers, for example, shoulder much of the weight of economic adjustment. Caught in a spiral of poverty and environmental degradation, poor people suffer acutely from the loss of soil fertility, pollution of rivers and urban streets, and the destruction of forest resources. Overcrowding and unequal land distribution often force them to overwork the soil, clear the forests, or migrate to marginal land. Their efforts to eke out a bare existence adds in its own way to environmental degradation and not infrequently to disaster for themselves and others who are equally poor.

Sustainable economic policies, that is, practices that reduce current stresses on natural systems and are consistent with sound environmental policy in the long term, must be put into effect. At the same time, the world economy must come to include hundreds of millions of poor families who live at the edge of survival.

C. Catholic Responses

In the face of these challenges, a new spirit of responsibility for the earth has begun to grow. Essential laws are being passed; vital anti-pollution efforts are underway; public concern is growing.

American Catholics are an integral part of this new awareness and action. In many small ways, we are learning more, caring more, and doing more about the environment and the threats to it. As a community of faith, we are also seeking to understand more clearly the ethical and religious dimensions of this challenge. This pastoral message, building on the previous statements and actions of individual bishops, dioceses, state conferences, and the episcopal conferences of other nations, as well as on the reflections and research of theologians, scientists, and environmentalists, is an effort to help that understanding. A distinctively Catholic contribution to contemporary environmental awareness arises from our understanding of human beings as part of nature, although not limited to it. Catholics look to nature, in natural theology, for indications of God's existence and purpose. In elaborating a natural moral law, we look to natural processes themselves for norms for human behavior. With such limits in mind, Pope John Paul II in *Centesimus Annus* urged that in addition to protecting natural systems and other species, we *"safeguard the moral conditions for an authentic 'human ecology'"* in urban planning, work environments, and family life (*Centesimus Annus* [=CA], no. 38). Nature is not, in Catholic teaching, merely a field to exploit at will or a museum piece to be preserved at all costs. We are not gods, but stewards of the earth.

We recognize with appreciation the efforts of other Christian churches and people of other faiths on behalf of the planet. We accept our common religious responsibility to shape an ethic of care for the earth.

Our own Campaign for Human Development supports a wide variety of local environmental efforts. Among them are the following projects:

- In Washington state, a farm worker organization tries to reduce pesticides in the apple industry.
- In rural Mississippi, a community coalition seeks to secure greater access to drinkable water.
- In Jersey City, forty local parishes and congregations seek the removal of chromium wastes from the building site for 600 affordable homes they have sponsored.
- In Oakland, California, immigrant Asian women try to monitor the exposure of electronics workers to hazardous chemicals.
- In our nation's capital, victims of radiation released from government nuclear programs lobby for medical treatment of their injuries.

Across our nation, the National Catholic Rural Life Conference continues to urge greater respect for the land; to advocate sustainable agricultural practices; to combat soil loss and water pollution; to promote a fair living for those who work the land; and to assist religious communities and local churches in the management of the farms, forests, and wetlands they hold.

In addition, Catholic Relief Services (CRS) furthers the Church's commitment to proper use of technology in its rural development projects, which aim at sustainable agriculture and community-based development in other countries. To help reverse the cycle of poverty and environmental decline in the Third World, CRS assists projects such as these.

- In the highlands of Peru, fifty-four communities have been able to increase agricultural production by readopting sustainable farming methods used by their pre-Inca ancestors that help crops resist drought and frost damage.
- In Bangladesh, a local organization has developed a program to process the toxins from waste water using an aquatic surface plant, duckweed, so that river-dwellers are protected from water-borne diseases.
- In Madagascar, where overcrowding has caused serious deforestation, the government and local groups are training transient farmers to grow crops in productive but environmentally safe ways.
- In Egypt, two communities have established a waste water collection and disposal system, benefiting 3,500 families.

D. A Call to Reflection and Action

Grateful for the gift of creation and contrite in the face of the deteriorating condition of the natural world, we invite Catholics and men and women of good will in every walk of life to consider with us the moral issues raised by the environmental crisis.

We ask the Catholic community: How are we called to care for God's creation? How may we apply our social teaching, with its emphasis on the life and dignity of the human person, to the challenge of protecting the earth, our common home? What can we in the Catholic community offer to the environmental movement, and what can we learn from it? How can we encourage a serious dialogue in the Catholic community—in our parishes, schools, colleges, universities, and other settings—on the significant ethical dimensions of the environmental crisis?

To other people of good will across this country, we say: How do we proceed to frame a common and workable environmental ethic? What steps can we take to devise a sustainable and just economy? What can we do to link more firmly in the public mind both the commitment to justice and duties to the environment? How can we recognize and confront the possible conflicts between environment and jobs, and work for the common good and solutions that value both people and the earth? How do we secure protection for all God's creatures, including the poor and the unborn? How can the United States, as a nation, act responsibly about this ever more global problem? And how, in working for a sustainable global economy, do we fulfill our obligations in justice to the poor of the Third World?

These are matters of powerful urgency and major consequence. They constitute an exceptional call to conversion. As individuals, as institutions, as a people, we need a change of heart to preserve and protect the planet for our children and for generations yet unborn.

II. The Biblical Vision of God's Good Earth

Biblical studies are deepening our understanding of the creation story and its meaning for our developing views of the natural world.

A. The Witness of the Hebrew Scriptures

Christian responsibility for the environment begins with appreciation of the goodness of all God's creation. In the beginning, "God looked at everything he had made, and he found it very good" (Gn 1:31). The heavens and the earth, the sun and the moon, the earth and the sea, fish and birds, animals and humans—all are good. God's wisdom and power were present in every aspect of the unfolding of creation (see Prv 8:22-31).

It is no wonder that when God's people were filled with the spirit of prayer, they invited all creation to join their praise of God's goodness.

> Let the earth bless the Lord;
> > praise and exalt him above all forever.
> Mountains and hills, bless the Lord;
> > praise and exalt him above all forever.
> Everything growing from the earth, bless the Lord;
> > praise and exalt him above all forever.
> You springs, bless the Lord;
> > praise and exalt him above all forever.
> Seas and rivers, bless the Lord;
> > praise and exalt him above all forever.
> You dolphins and all water creatures, bless the Lord;
> > praise and exalt him above all forever.
> All you birds of the air, bless the Lord;
> > praise and exalt him above all forever.
> All you beasts, wild and tame, bless the Lord;
> > praise and exalt him above all forever (Dn 3:74-81).

The earth, the Bible reminds us, is a gift to all creatures, to "all living beings—all mortal creatures that are on earth" (Gn 9:16-17).

People share the earth with other creatures. But humans, made in the image and likeness of God, are called in a special way to "cultivate and care for it" (Gn 2:15). Men and women, therefore, bear a unique responsibility under God: to safeguard the created world and by their creative labor even to enhance it. Safeguarding creation requires us to live responsibly within it, rather than manage creation as though we are outside it. The human family is charged with preserving the beauty, diversity, and integrity of nature, as well as with fostering its productivity. Yet, God alone is sovereign over the whole earth. "The Lord's are the earth and its fullness; the world and those who dwell in it" (Ps 24:1). Like the patriarch Noah, humanity stands responsible for ensuring that all nature can continue to thrive as God intended. After the flood, God made a lasting covenant with Noah, his descendants, and "every living creature." We are not free, therefore, to use created things capriciously.

Humanity's arrogance and acquisitiveness, however, led time and again to our growing alienation from nature (see Gn 3-4, 6-9, 11ff). In the Bible's account of Noah, the world's new beginning was marked by the estrangement of humans from nature. The sins of humankind laid waste the land. Hosea, for example, cries out:

> There is no fidelity, no mercy,
>> no knowledge of God in the land.
> False swearing, lying, murder, stealing and adultery!
>> in their lawlessness, bloodshed follows bloodshed.
> Therefore, the land mourns,
>> and everything that dwells in it languishes:
> The beasts of the field,
>> the birds of the air,
>> and even the fish of the sea perish (Hos 4:1b-3).

In the biblical vision, therefore, injustice results in suffering for all creation.

To curb the abuse of the land and of fellow humans, ancient Israel set out legal protections aimed at restoring the original balance between land and people (see Lv 25). Every seventh year, the land and people were to rest; nature would be restored by human restraint. And every seventh day, the Sabbath rest gave relief from unremitting toil to workers and beasts alike. It invited the whole community to taste the goodness of God in creation. In worship, moreover, the Sabbath continues to remind us of our dependence on God as his creatures, and so of our kinship with all that God has made. But people did not honor the law. A few went on accumulating land, many were dispossessed, and the land itself became exhausted. God then sent his prophets to call the people back to their responsibility. Again the people hardened their hearts; they had compassion for neither the land nor its people. The prophets promised judgment for the evil done the people of the land, but they also foresaw a day of restoration, when the harmony between humanity and the natural world would be renewed (see Is 32:15b-20).

B. The Gospel Message

Jesus came proclaiming a jubilee (see Lk 4:16-22) in which humanity, and with us all creation, was to be liberated (see Rom 8:18-25). He taught about salvation, however, with a countryman's knowledge of the land. God's grace was like wheat growing in the night (see Mk 4:26-29); divine love like a shepherd seeking a lost sheep (see Lk 15:4-7). In the birds of the air and the lilies of the field, Jesus found reason for his disciples to give up the ceaseless quest for material security and advantage and to trust in God (see Mt 6:25-33). Jesus himself is the Good Shepherd, who gives his life for his flock (see Jn 10). His Father is a vineyard worker, who trims vines so that they may bear more abundant fruit (see Jn 15:1-8). These familiar images, though they speak directly to humanity's encounter with God, at the same time reveal that the fundamental relation between humanity and nature is one of caring for creation.

The new covenant made in Jesus' blood overcomes all hostility and restores the order of love. Just as in his person Christ has destroyed the hostility that divided people from one another, so he has overcome the opposition between humanity and nature. For he is the firstborn of a new creation and gives his Spirit to renew the whole earth (see Col 2:18; Ps 104:30). The fruits of that Spirit—joy, peace, patience, kindness, goodness, trustfulness, gentleness, and self-control (see Gal 5:22)—mark us as Christ's own people. As they incline us to "serve one another through love" (Gal 5:13), they may also dispose us to live carefully on the earth, with respect for all God's creatures. Our Christian way of life, as saints like Benedict, Hildegard, and Francis showed us, is a road to community with all creation.

III. Catholic Social Teaching and Environmental Ethics

The tradition of Catholic social teaching offers a developing and distinctive perspective on environmental issues. We believe that the following themes drawn from this tradition are integral dimensions of ecological responsibility:

- *A God-centered and sacramental view of the universe*, which grounds human accountability for the fate of the earth;
- A consistent *respect for human life*, which extends to respect for all creation;
- A worldview affirming the ethical significance of *global interdependence and the common good*;
- *An ethics of solidarity* promoting cooperation and a just structure of sharing in the world community;
- An understanding of *the universal purpose of created things*, which requires equitable use of the earth's resources;
- *An option for the poor*, which gives passion to the quest for an equitable and sustainable world;
- A conception of *authentic development*, which offers a direction for progress that respects human dignity and the limits of material growth.

Although Catholic social teaching does not offer a complete environmental ethic, we are confident that this developing tradition can serve as the basis for Catholic engagement and dialogue with science, the environmental movement, and other communities of faith and good will.

A. A Sacramental Universe

The whole universe is God's dwelling. Earth, a very small, uniquely blessed corner of that universe, gifted with unique natural blessings, is humanity's home, and humans are never so much at home as when God dwells with them. In the beginning, the first man and woman walked with God in the cool of the day. Throughout history, people have continued to meet the Creator on mountaintops, in vast deserts, and alongside waterfalls and gently flowing springs. In storms and earthquakes, they found expressions of divine power. In the cycle of the seasons and the courses of the stars, they have discerned signs of God's fidelity and wisdom. We still share, though dimly, in that sense of God's presence in nature. But as heirs and victims of the industrial revolution, students of science and the beneficiaries of technology, urban-dwellers and jet-commuters, twentieth-century Americans have also grown estranged from the natural scale and rhythms of life on earth.

For many people, the environmental movement has reawakened appreciation of the truth that, through the created gifts of nature, men and women encounter their Creator. The Christian vision of a sacramental universe—a world that discloses the Creator's presence by visible and tangible signs—can contribute to making the earth a home for the human family once again. Pope John Paul II has called for Christians to respect and protect the environment, so that through nature people can "contemplate the mystery of the greatness and love of God."

Reverence for the Creator present and active in nature, moreover, may serve as ground for environmental responsibility. For the very plants and animals, mountains and oceans, which in their loveliness and sublimity lift our minds to God, by their fragility and perishing likewise cry out, "We have not made ourselves." God brings them into being and sustains them in existence. It is to the Creator of the universe, then, that we are accountable for what we do or fail to do to preserve and care for the earth and all its creatures. For "the LORD'S are the earth and its fullness; the world and those who dwell in it" (Ps 24:1). Dwelling in the presence of God, we begin to experience ourselves as part of creation, as stewards within it, not separate from it. As faithful stewards, fullness of life comes from living responsibly within God's creation.

Stewardship implies that we must both care for creation according to standards that are not of our own making and at the same time be resourceful in finding ways to make the earth flourish. It is a difficult balance, requiring both a sense of limits and a spirit of experimentation. Even as we rejoice in earth's goodness and in the beauty of nature, stewardship places upon us responsibility for the well-being of all God's creatures.

B. Respect for Life

Respect for nature and respect for human life are inextricably related. "Respect for life, and above all for the dignity of the human person," Pope John Paul II has written, extends also to the rest of creation (*The Ecological Crisis: A Common Responsibility* [=EC], no. 7). Other species, ecosystems, and even distinctive landscapes give glory to God. The covenant given to Noah was a promise to all the earth.

> See, I am establishing my covenant with you and your descendants after you and with every living creature that was with you: all the birds, and the various tame and wild animals that were with you and came out of the ark (Gn 9:9-10).

The diversity of life manifests God's glory. Every creature shares a bit of the divine beauty. Because the divine goodness could not be represented by one creature alone, Aquinas tells us, God "produced many and diverse creatures, so that what was wanting to one in representation of the divine goodness might be supplied by another . . . hence the whole universe together participates in the divine goodness more perfectly, and represents it better than any single creature whatever" (*Summa Theologica*, Prima Pars, question 48, ad 2). The wonderful variety of the natural world is, therefore, part of the divine plan and, as such, invites our respect. Accordingly, it is appropriate that we treat other creatures and the natural world not just as means to human fulfillment but also as God's creatures, possessing an independent value, worthy of our respect and care.

By preserving natural environments, by protecting endangered species, by laboring to make human environments compatible with local ecology, by employing appropriate technology, and by carefully evaluating technological innovations as we adopt them, we exhibit respect for creation and reverence for the Creator.

C. The Planetary Common Good

In 1963, Pope John XXIII, in the letter *Pacem in Terris*, emphasized the world's growing interdependence. He saw problems emerging, which the traditional political mechanisms could no longer address, and he extended the traditional principle of the common good from the nation-state to the world community. Ecological concern has now heightened our awareness of just how interdependent our world is. Some of the gravest environmental problems are clearly global. In this shrinking world, everyone is affected and everyone is responsible, although those most responsible are often the least affected. The universal common good can serve as a foundation for a global environmental ethic.

In many of his statements, Pope John Paul II has recognized the need for such an ethic. For example, in *The Ecological Crisis: A Common Responsibility*, his 1990 World Day of Peace Message, he wrote,

> Today the ecological crisis has assumed such proportions as to be the responsibility of everyone. . . . Its various aspects demonstrate the need for concerted efforts aimed at establishing the duties and obligations that belong to individuals, peoples, States and the international community (no. 15).

Governments have particular responsibility in this area. In *Centesimus Annus*, the pope insists that the state has the task of providing "for the defense and preservation of common good such as the natural and human environments, which cannot be safeguarded simply by market forces" (no. 40).

D. A New Solidarity

In the Catholic tradition, the universal common good is specified by the duty of solidarity, "*a firm and persevering determination* to commit oneself to the *common good*," a willingness "to 'lose oneself' for the sake of the other[s] instead of exploiting [them]" (Pope John Paul II, *Sollicitudo Rei Socialis* [=SRS], no. 38). In the face of "the structures of sin," moreover, solidarity requires sacrifices of our own self-interest for the good of others and of the earth we share. Solidarity places special obligations upon the industrial democracies, including the United States. "The ecological crisis," Pope John Paul II has written, "reveals the *urgent moral need for a new solidarity*, especially in relations between the developing nations and those that are highly industrialized" (EC, no. 10). Only with equitable and sustainable development can poor nations curb continuing environmental degradation and avoid the destructive effects of the kind of overdevelopment that has used natural resources irresponsibly.

E. Universal Purpose of Created Things

God has given the fruit of the earth to sustain the entire human family "without excluding or favouring anyone." Human work has enhanced the productive capacity of the earth and in our time is as Pope John Paul II has said, "increasingly important as the productive factor both of non-material and of material wealth" (CA, no. 31). But a great many people, in the Third World as well as in our own inner cities and rural areas, are still deprived of the means of livelihood. In moving toward an environmentally sustainable economy, we are obligated to work for a just economic system which equitably shares the bounty of the earth and of human enterprise with all peoples. Created things belong not to the few, but to the entire human family.

F. Option for the Poor

The ecological problem is intimately connected to justice for the poor. "The goods of the earth, which in the divine plan should be a common patrimony," Pope John Paul II has reminded us, "often risk becoming the monopoly of a few who often spoil it and, sometimes, destroy it, thereby creating a loss for all humanity" (October 25, 1991 address at conference marking the presentation of the Second Edition of the St. Francis "Canticle of the Creatures" International Award for the Environment).

The poor of the earth offer a special test of our solidarity. The painful adjustments we have to undertake in our own economies for the sake of the environment must not diminish our sensitivity to the needs of the poor at home and abroad. The option for the poor embedded in the Gospel and the Church's teaching makes us aware that the poor suffer most directly from environmental decline and have the least access to relief from their suffering. Indigenous peoples die with their forests and grasslands. In Bhopal and Chernobyl, it was the urban poor and working people who suffered the most immediate and intense contamination. Nature will truly enjoy its second spring only when humanity has compassion for its own weakest members.

A related and vital concern is the Church's constant commitment to the dignity of work and the rights of workers. Environmental progress cannot come at the expense of workers and their rights. Solutions must be found that do not force us to choose between a decent environment and a decent life for workers.

We recognize the potential conflicts in this area and will work for greater understanding, communication, and common ground between workers and environmentalists. Clearly, workers cannot be asked to make sacrifices to improve the environment without concrete support from the broader community. Where jobs are lost, society must help in the process of economic conversion, so that not only the earth but also workers and their families are protected.

G. Authentic Development

Unrestrained economic development is not the answer to improving the lives of the poor. Catholic social teaching has never accepted material growth as a model of development. A "*mere accumulation* of goods and services, even for the benefit of the majority," as Pope John Paul II has said, "is not enough for the realization of human happiness" (SRS, no. 28). He has also warned that in a desire "to have and to enjoy rather than to be and to grow," humanity "consumes the resources of the earth, subjecting it without restraint . . . as if it did not have its own requisites and God-given purposes."

Authentic development supports moderation and even austerity in the use of material resources. It also encourages a balanced view of human progress consistent with respect for nature. Furthermore, it invites the development of alternative visions of the good society and the use of economic models with richer standards of well-being than material productivity alone. Authentic development also requires affluent nations to seek ways to reduce and restructure their overconsumption of natural resources. Finally, authentic development also entails encouraging the proper use of both agricultural and industrial technologies, so that development does not merely mean technological advancement for its own sake but rather that technology benefits people and enhances the land.

H. Consumption and Population

In public discussions, two areas are particularly cited as requiring greater care and judgment on the part of human beings. The first is *consumption of resources*. The second is *growth in world population*. Regrettably, advantaged groups often seem more intent on curbing Third World births than on restraining the even more voracious consumerism of the developed world. We believe this compounds injustice and increases disrespect for the life of the weakest among us. For example, it is not so much population growth, but the desperate efforts of debtor countries to pay their foreign debt by exporting products to affluent industrial countries that drives poor peasants off their land and up eroding hillsides, where in the effort to survive, they also destroy the environment.

Consumption in developed nations remains the single greatest source of global environmental destruction. A child born in the United States, for example, puts a far heavier burden on the world's resources than one born in a poor developing country. By one estimate, each American uses twenty-eight times the energy of a person living in a developing country. Advanced societies, and our own in particular, have barely begun to make efforts at reducing their consumption of resources and the enormous waste and pollution that result from it. We in the developed world, therefore, are obligated to address our own wasteful and destructive use of resources as a matter of top priority.

The key factor, though not the only one, in dealing with population problems is sustainable social and economic development. Technological fixes do not really work. Only when an economy distributes resources so as to allow the poor an equitable stake in society and some hope for the future do couples see responsible parenthood as good for their families. In particular, prenatal care; education; good nutrition; and health care for women, children, and families promise to improve family welfare and contribute to stabilizing population. Supporting such equitable social development, moreover, may well be the best contribution affluent societies, like the United States, can make to relieving ecological pressures in less developed nations.

At the same time, it must be acknowledged that rapid population growth presents special problems and challenges that must be addressed in order to avoid damage done to the environment and to social development. In the words of Pope Paul VI, "It is not to be denied that accelerated demographic increases too frequently add difficulties to plans for development because the population is increased more rapidly than available resources . . ." (*Populorum Progressio*, no. 37). In *Sollicitudo Rei Socialis*, Pope John Paul II has likewise noted, "One cannot deny the existence, especially in the southern hemisphere, of a demographic problem which creates difficulties for development" (no. 25). He has gone on to make connections among population size, development, and the environment. There is "a greater realization of the limits of available resources," he commented, "and of the need to respect the integrity and the cycles of nature and to take them into account when planning for development . . ." (no. 26). Even though it is possible to feed a growing population, the ecological costs of doing so ought to be taken into account. To eliminate hunger from the planet, the world community needs to reform the institutional and political structures that restrict the access of people to food.

Thus, the Church addresses population issues in the context of its teaching on human life, of just development, of care for the environment, and of respect for the freedom of married couples to decide voluntarily on the number and spacing of births. In keeping with these values, and out of respect for cultural norms, it continues to oppose coercive methods of population control and programs that bias decisions through incentives or disincentives. Respect for nature ought to encourage policies that promote natural family planning and true responsible parenthood rather than coercive population control programs or incentives for birth control that violate cultural and religious norms and Catholic teaching.

Finally, we are charged with restoring the integrity of all creation. We must care for all God's creatures, especially the most vulnerable. How, then, can we protect endangered species and at the same time be callous to the unborn, the elderly, or disabled persons? Is not abortion also a sin against creation? If we turn our backs on our own unborn children, can we truly expect that nature will receive respectful treatment at our hands? The care of the earth will not be advanced by the destruction of human life at any stage of development. As Pope John Paul II has said, "protecting the environment is first of all the right to live and the protection of life" (October 16, 1991 homily at Quiaba, Mato Grosso, Brazil).

I. A Web of Life

These themes drawn from Catholic social teaching are linked to our efforts to share this teaching in other contexts, especially in our pastoral letters on peace and economic justice and in our statements on food and agriculture. Clearly, war represents a serious threat to the environment, as the darkened skies and oil soaked beaches of Kuwait clearly remind us. The pursuit of peace—lasting peace based on justice—ought to be an environmental priority because the earth itself bears the wounds and scars of war. Likewise, our efforts to defend the dignity and rights of the poor and of workers, to use the strength of our market economy to meet basic human needs, and to press for greater national and global economic justice are clearly linked to efforts to preserve and sustain the earth. These are not distinct and separate issues but complementary challenges. We need to help build bridges among the peace, justice, and environmental agendas and constituencies.

IV. Theological and Pastoral Concerns

Today's crises in global ecology demand concerted and creative thought and effort on the part of all of us: scientists, political leaders, business people, workers, lawyers, farmers, communicators, and citizens generally. As moral teachers, we intend to lift up the moral and ethical dimensions of these issues. We find much to affirm in and learn from the environmental movement: its devotion to nature, its recognition of limits and connections, its urgent appeal for sustainable and ecologically sound policies. We share considerable common ground in the concern for the earth, and we have much work to do together. But there may also be some areas of potential confusion and conflict with some who share this common concern for the earth. We offer some brief comments on three of these concerns in the hope that they will contribute to a constructive dialogue on how we can best work together.

A. The Creator and Creation

Nature shares in God's goodness, and contemplation of its beauty and richness raises our hearts and minds to God. St. Paul hinted at a theology of creation when he proclaimed to the Athenians, the Creator who "made from one the whole human race to dwell on the entire surface of the earth, and he fixed and ordered the seasons and the boundaries of their regions, so that people might seek God, even perhaps grope for him, though indeed he is not far from any of us" (Acts 17:26-27). Through the centuries, Catholic theologians and philosophers, like St. Paul before them, continue to search for God in reasoning about the created world.

Our Catholic faith continues to affirm the goodness of the natural world. The sacramental life of the Church depends on created goods: water, oil, bread, and wine. Likewise, the Western mystical tradition has taught Christians how to find God dwelling in created things and laboring and loving through them.

Nonetheless, Christian theology also affirms the limits of all God's creatures. God, the Source of all that is, is actively present in all creation, but God also surpasses all created things. We profess the ancient faith of God's people.

Hear O Israel! The LORD our God is LORD alone!
You shall love the LORD your God with all your
heart, with all your soul, with all your mind, and
with all your strength (Dt 6:4-5; Mk 12:29-30).

An ordered love for creation, therefore, is ecological without being ecocentric. We can and must care for the earth without mistaking it for the ultimate object of our devotion. A Christian love of the natural world, as St. Francis showed us, can restrain grasping and wanton human behavior and help mightily to preserve and nurture all that God has made. We believe that faith in a good and loving God is a compelling source of passionate and enduring care for all creation.

B. Human Reason and Invention

Guided by the Spirit of God, the future of the earth lies in human hands. To maintain landscapes in integrity, to safeguard endangered species, to preserve remaining wilderness, to ensure the feeding of a hungry world will require much human decision, social cooperation, experimentation, and invention. To restore the purity of air and water, to halt the loss of farmland, to sustain ecological diversity in plant and animal life, concerted human action will be needed over many decades. To avert further depletion of the ozone layer, to check the production of greenhouse gases, and to redress the effects of global warming will require unprecedented collaboration and commitment among the nations of the earth. Even as humanity's mistakes are at the root of earth's travail today, human talents and invention can and must assist in its rebirth and contribute to human development.

Incontestably, people need to exhibit greater respect for nature than they have for some centuries, but we will also need to apply human reason to find remedies for nature's ills. Scientific research and technological innovation must accompany religious and moral responses to environmental challenges. Reverence for nature must be combined with scientific learning. In a Catholic worldview, there is no necessary clash between an environmentally responsible morality and an active application of human reason and science. Problematic uses of technology provide no excuse to retreat into prescientific attitudes toward nature. The ecological crisis heightens our awareness of the need for new approaches to scientific research and technology. Many indigenous technologies can teach us much. Such technologies are more compatible with the ecosystem, are more available to poor persons, and are more sustainable for the entire community.

C. Christian Love

At the heart of the Christian life lies the love of neighbor. The ecological crisis, as Pope

John Paul II has urged, challenges us to extend our love to future generations and to the flourishing of all earth's creatures. But neither our duties to future generations nor our tending of the garden entrusted to our care ought to diminish our love for the present members of the human family, especially the poor and the disadvantaged. Both impoverished peoples and an imperiled planet demand our committed service.

Christian love draws us to serve the weak and vulnerable among us. We are called to feed the hungry, to give drink to the thirsty, to clothe the naked, to shelter the homeless. We are also summoned to restore the land; to provide clean, safe water to drink and unpolluted air to breathe; to preserve endangered species; to protect wild places; and to help the poor help themselves. We ought to remember that Francis of Assisi, the patron saint of the environmental movement, tamed wolves and preached to the birds only after a long novitiate in which he ministered to outcasts and lepers.

Christian love forbids choosing between people and the planet. It urges us to work for an equitable and sustainable future in which all peoples can share in the bounty of the earth and in which the earth itself is protected from predatory use. The common good invites regions of the country to share burdens equitably in such areas as toxic and nuclear waste disposal and water distribution and to work together to reduce and eliminate waste which threatens health and environmental quality. It also invites us to explore alternatives in which our poor brothers and sisters will share with the rest of us in the banquet of life, at the same time that we preserve and restore the earth, which sustains us.

V. God's Stewards and Co-Creators

As others have pointed out, we are the first generation to see our planet from space—to see so clearly its beauty, limits, and fragility. Modern communication technology helps us to see more clearly than ever the impact of carelessness, ignorance, greed, neglect, and war on the earth.

Today, humanity is at a crossroads. Having read the signs of the times, we can either ignore the harm we see and witness further damage, or we can take up our responsibilities to the Creator and creation with renewed courage and commitment.

The task set before us is unprecedented, intricate, complex. No single solution will be adequate to the task. To live in balance with the finite resources of the planet, we need an unfamiliar blend of restraint and innovation. We shall be required to be genuine stewards of nature and thereby co-creators of a new human world. This will require both new attitudes and new actions.

A. New Attitudes

For believers, our faith is tested by our concern and care for creation. Within our tradition are important resources and values that can help us assess problems and shape constructive solutions. In addition to the themes we have already outlined from our social teaching, the traditional virtues of prudence, humility, and temperance are indispensable elements of a new environmental ethic. Recognition of the reality of sin and failure as well as the opportunity for forgiveness and reconciliation can help us face up to our environmental responsibilities. A new sense of the limits and risks of fallible human judgments ought to mark the decisions of policy makers as they act on complicated global issues with necessarily imperfect knowledge. Finally, as we face the challenging years ahead, we must all rely on the preeminent Christian virtues of faith, hope, and love to sustain us and direct us.

There are hopeful signs: public concern is growing; some public policy is shifting; and private behavior is beginning to change. From broader participation in recycling to negotiating international treaties, people are searching for ways to make a difference on behalf of the environment.

More people seem ready to recognize that the industrialized world's overconsumption has contributed the largest share to the degradation of the global environment. Also encouraging is the growing conviction that development is more qualitative than quantitative, that it consists more in improving the quality of life than in increasing consumption. What is now needed is the will to make the changes in public policy, as well as in life-style, that will be needed to arrest, reverse, and prevent environmental decay and to pursue the goal of sustainable, equitable development for all. The overarching moral issue is to achieve during the twenty-first century a just and sustainable world. From a scientific point of view, this seems possible. But the new order can only be achieved through the persevering exercise of moral responsibility on the part of individuals, voluntary organizations, governments, and transnational agencies.

In the Catholic community, as we have pointed out, there are many signs of increased discussion, awareness, and action on environment. We have offered these reflections in the hope that they will contribute to a broader dialogue in our Church and society about the moral dimensions of ecology and about the links between social justice and ecology, between environment and development. We offer these reflections not to endorse a particular policy agenda nor to step onto some current bandwagon, but to meet our responsibilities as pastors and teachers who see the terrible consequences of environmental neglect and who believe our faith calls us to help shape a creative and effective response.

B. New Actions

This statement is only a first step in fashioning an ongoing response to this challenge. We invite the Catholic community to join with us and others of good will in a continuing effort to understand and act on the moral and ethical dimensions of the environmental crisis:

—We ask *scientists, environmentalists, economists, and other experts* to continue to help us understand the challenges we face and the steps we need to take. Faith is not a substitute for facts; the more we know about the problems we face, the better we can respond.

—We invite *teachers and educators* to emphasize, in their classrooms and curricula, a love for God's creation, a respect for nature, and a commitment to practices and behavior that bring these attitudes into the daily lives of their students and themselves.

—We remind *parents* that they are the first and principal teachers of children. It is from parents that children will learn love of the earth and delight in nature. It is at home that they develop the habits of self-control, concern, and care that lie at the heart of environmental morality.

—We call on *theologians, scripture scholars, and ethicists* to help explore, deepen, and advance the insights of our Catholic tradition and its relation to the environment and other religious perspectives on these matters. We especially call upon Catholic scholars to explore the relationship between this tradition's emphasis upon the dignity of the human person and our responsibility to care for all of God's creation.

—We ask *business leaders and representatives of workers* to make the protection of our common environment a central concern in their activities and to collaborate for the common good and the protection of the earth. We especially encourage pastors and parish leaders to give greater attention to the extent and urgency of the environmental crisis in preaching, teaching, pastoral outreach, and action, at the parish level and through ecumenical cooperation in the local community.

—We ask the *members of our Church* to examine our life-styles, behaviors, and policies—individually and institutionally—to see how we contribute to the destruction or neglect of the environment and how we might assist in its protection and restoration. We also urge *celebrants and liturgy committees* to incorporate themes into prayer and worship that emphasize our responsibility to protect all of God's creation and to organize prayerful celebrations of creation on feast days honoring St. Francis and St. Isidore.

—We ask *environmental advocates* to join us in building bridges between the quest for justice and the pursuit of peace and concern for the earth. We ask that the poor and vulnerable at home and abroad be accorded a special and urgent priority in all efforts to care for our environment.

—We urge *policy makers and public officials* to focus more directly on the ethical dimensions of environmental policy and on its relation to development, to seek the common good, and to resist short-term pressures in order to meet our long-term responsibility to future generations. At the very minimum, we need food and energy policies that are socially just, environmentally benign, and economically efficient.

—As *citizens*, each of us needs to participate in this debate over how our nation best protects our ecological heritage, limits pollution, allocates environmental costs, and plans for the future. We need to use our voices and votes to shape a ration more committed to the universal common good and an ethic of environmental solidarity.

All of us need both a spiritual and a practical vision of stewardship and co-creation that guides our choices as consumers, citizens, and workers. We need, in the now familiar phrase, to "think globally and act locally," finding the ways in our own situation to express a broader ethic of genuine solidarity.

C. Call to Conversion
The environmental crisis of our own day constitutes an exceptional call to conversion. As individuals, as institutions, as a people, we need a change of heart to save the planet for our children and generations yet unborn. So vast are the problems, so intertwined with our economy and way of life, that nothing but a wholehearted and ever more profound fuming to God, the Maker of Heaven and Earth, will allow us to carry out our responsibilities as faithful stewards of God's creation.

Only when believers look to values of the Scriptures, honestly admit their limitations and failings, and commit themselves to common action on behalf of the land and the wretched of the earth will we be ready to participate fully in resolving this crisis.

D. A Word of Hope
A just and sustainable society and world are not an optional ideal, but a moral and practical necessity. Without justice, a sustainable economy will be beyond reach. Without an ecologically responsible world economy, justice will be unachievable. To accomplish either is an enormous task; together they seem overwhelming. But "all

things are possible" to those who hope in God (Mk 10:27). Hope is the virtue at the heart of a Christian environmental ethic. Hope gives us the courage, direction, and energy required for this arduous common endeavor.

In the bleak years of Britain's industrial revolution, Gerard Manley Hopkins wrote of urban decay wrought by industry and of Christian hope for nature's revival. His words capture the condition of today's world as it awaits redemption from ecological neglect:

> And all is seared with trade;
>   bleared, smeared with toil;
> And wears man's smudge
>   and shares man's smell:
>   the soil
> Is bare now, nor can foot feel,
>   being shod.
>
> And for all this, nature is never spent:
>   There lives the dearest
>   freshness deep down things;
>
> Because the Holy Ghost over the bent
>   World broods with warm breast
>   and with ah!
>   bright wings.

Saving the planet will demand long and sometimes sacrificial commitment. It will require continual revision of our political habits, restructuring economic institutions, reshaping society, and nurturing global community. But we can proceed with hope because, as at the dawn of creation, so today the Holy Spirit breathes new life into all earth's creatures. Today, we pray with new conviction and concern for all God's creation:

> Send forth thy Spirit, Lord
> and renew the face of the earth.

Christians and Their Duty Towards Nature

The Australian Bishops' Committee
for Justice, Development and Peace

Introduction

Since their first days on our earth human beings have looked at the world and seen that it is good. They have delighted in its beauty. They have been grateful for the good things that provide them with shelter, food and clothing. And they have been led to some crucial questions:

To what extent must the beauty we admire be left untouched, save to be nurtured and safeguarded?

How much is to be used so that we might live well upon this earth?

And how are our resources to be cared for and replenished so that our children, too, might be able to live upon the earth?

Many of us know too little about the functioning of the world and the interconnected web of life on our own planet. Therefore we can do harm without knowing what we are destroying. Large areas of the earth's desert have developed through human abuse of nature, while we Australians have destroyed large tracts of our rainforests and certain species of our fauna. With our rapidly growing technology, it has become possible for us to inflict far greater harm and to do more irreparable damage.

Fortunately, our growing technology has enabled us to understand better how to embellish our earth and how to avoid the harm that has been done to it in ignorance or greed. A widespread ecological awareness has made us more sensitive to the needs of other living things. "Ecology," from its Greek roots, signifies "The meaning of the dwelling." It refers to the study of the whole environment needed for the survival of living organisms. It studies nature in all the delicate and intricate interactions which characterise life on this planet.

Signs of the Times

Pope John XXIII called on us to look for the signs of the times. Vatican II asked us to try to discover what the Church should be in the world of our day.[1] Today, it is surely a sign of the times that many people are calling for a more enlightened care for the earth and for all living things. We give thanks for the human wisdom that has raised this cry of concern. Among the more significant actions has been that of the General Assembly of the United Nations which in 1982 adopted and proclaimed a *World Charter for Nature*. It stated its "conviction that every form of life is unique, warranting respect regardless of its worth to man." It stated a further conviction that, if we are to deal rightly with created things, we "must be guided by a moral code of action."

Here we touch on a second sign of the times, namely the widespread conviction that there is a moral dimension to questions of ecology. Increasingly Christians are rediscovering a religious character in their attitudes towards other created things. Saint Paul's words appear to be specially relevant in our times: "The whole of creation is eagerly waiting . . . creation still retains the hope of being freed, like us, from its slavery to decadence, to enjoy the same freedom and glory as the children of God (Rom 8:19-21).

We have long been familiar with the prayers of the Psalms in which all creatures are called upon to give glory to God and to bless the Lord. In our Space Age, our sense of wonder has been deepened as we increase our knowledge of the galaxies, the vast stretches of the universe, and the extraordinary way in which the earth was formed and all its varied forms of life brought into being.

We are pleased to see that Christian scholars are bringing their knowledge to bear on issues relating to our environment. We pray that, to human wisdom we may bring the riches of our Christian heritage so that all of us, enlightened by grace and nature, may work together for the good of all. To this end, in 1983 the World Council of

Churches engaged its members in a process of study of the three themes of justice, peace and integrity of creation. For the World Day of Peace, 1990, Pope John Paul II added his message "Peace with God the Creator, peace with all creation."

In February 1991 Canberra hosted the World Council of Churches' Seventh Assembly. All of us gladly joined in the prayer which expresses the theme of the Assembly: "Come Holy Spirit—Renew the Whole Creation." One of the subthemes "looked at the interrelatedness of life and what the biblical teaching of creation implies for the vocation of human beings in relation to the rest of creation." Its title, too, took the form of an intercession: "Giver of Life—Sustain your Creation."[2]

The Australian Scene

Australians have become aware of the need to treat the land with respect, and to understand its rhythms and its riches. In response to the voice of the people, portfolios for the environment have been created in our parliaments. The Australian and New Zealand Environment Council has been formed. Many Australians have come to realise that they are the possessors of an extraordinary heritage. Much of it is unique. The aboriginal inhabitants of Australia looked on this land and found it very good. For them the land was linked with the "creating spirits" still vitally present to it, and present to them who used its gifts. They enjoyed a special relationship with the earth and they possessed their own "laws" for using its resources and keeping an ecological balance between earth, plants, water, animals and people. Birds and fish, kangaroos, wallabies and other animals served as food for them as did an assortment of seeds, roots, and nuts. They felled no forests for they needed no houses, nor did they need to carve out pasture lands for animals which grazed where they pleased. However, in some areas the fire-stick was as destructive of rainforest as later the axe would be.[3]

The first white settlers looked on this land and found it very different from everything they had known and understood. If it were to provide them with permanent food and shelter, they would have to act differently from the aborigines. They introduced into the land the animals which they knew and felt they needed: cattle, pigs, sheep, horses, donkeys and cats and foxes as well. To provide themselves with shelter and to make pasture for their animals they felled tracts of forest. They planted their crops, and eventually constructed their cities. In all this they gave little thought to the rights of the aboriginal inhabitants whose land they were occupying. It seems that most gave no thought at all to the fact that their actions were destroying the aborigines' traditional way of relating to the land.

Some of the species introduced were not environmentally friendly and have done harm. While rabbits provided food, they contributed to the degradation of the soil. Athol trees were introduced for shade and shelter. But they are salt accumulators contributing to soil degradation in some areas.[4] Feral descendants of imported animals do harm to the environment and destroy some of our native fauna. In our efforts to get the land to serve us better, we can despoil the earth and even destroy forever some species of birds and animals. "At the national level, Australia has had the highest rate of mammal extinction of any nation on earth during the last 200 years. That means that the habitats of those animals and plants have been altered, degraded or destroyed."[5] Increased technological ability has brought new ways of affecting the environment adversely.

Our Call as Christians

Sometimes it is through the dark that we are brought to see the light. It is not our wish to echo cries of alarm or to repeat the well-known list of ecological disasters whether real or possible. True, the cries of alarm have drawn our attention to an urgent need. Let us profit from the dark side to look caringly for the light. Let us take this time of ecological awareness to discover in depth our Christian call to contemplate and to care for the wonders of God's created world. It is a call to discover and delight in the beauty, to care for it in an awareness that beauty is a fragile thing. It is a call to consider our relationship with other created beings and to reflect on the ways in which, as Christians, we should treat them, relate to them and use them responsibly. Recently the Pope has stated: "Christians, in particular, realise that their responsibility within creation and their duty towards nature and the Creator are an essential part of their faith."[6]

Our purpose in this statement is simply this:

To invite all Christians, Catholics in particular, to reflect on the truth that "their responsibility within creation and their duty towards nature and the Creator are an essential part of their faith."

As Catholics we should not need to ask ourselves whether we join with our brothers and sisters in trying to understand and care for our environment. We will ask, rather, how a care for the earth and its creatures can best be integrated into our Christian living. We will ask, too, whether our Christian vision can help us make enlightened choices when a love of nature seems to clash with a human need to use and consume.

In our Catholic tradition we have learned to give thanks to God for his gifts; we have called down his blessing on fields and crops and the fruits of the harvest. At the instructions of our Master we have sought the sacred through bread and wine, water and oil. The Second Vatican Council set forth the general principles of a Christian view of our place in the world—although, naturally, the Council, 25 years ago, did not share some of the more specific concerns of our day. The Council speaks of human beings as related both to God the Creator and to all of his creation: "For Sacred Scripture teaches that men and women were created 'to the image of God' as able to know and love their Creator who had set them over all earthly creatures that they might rule them and make use of them, while glorifying God."[7]

When God is not glorified, then human beings "also upset the relationship which should link them to their last end; and at the same time they break the right order that should reign within themselves as well as between themselves and other people *and all creatures.*" The source of this teaching is, of course, the Bible.

Lessons in Scripture

When we look to the word of God in the Scriptures, we do not find precise answers to every question asked in the 20th century. But we do find some norms according to which we are called to form the right human attitudes towards other created things.

Vatican II reminded us that, looking at the world through Christian eyes, we see all things touched by the redeeming action of Jesus Christ and made new in him. "Redeemed by Christ and made new creatures by the Holy Spirit, men and women can, indeed they must, love the things of God's creation: it is from God that they have received them, and it is as flowing from God's hand that they look upon them and revere them. We thank our divine benefactor for all these things, we use them and enjoy them in a spirit of poverty and freedom."[8] To this Pope John Paul II added: "In Jesus Christ the visible world which God created for the human race . . . recovers again its original link with the divine source of wisdom and love."[9]

Since the Vatican Council, a number of Catholic theologians and Scripture scholars have studied and written about our relationships with other created beings. They have invited us to look with reverence on all created things touched as they are by the redemptive love of Christ, "who is the image of the unseen God, the first-born of all creation for in him were created all things in heaven and on earth. . . . All things were created through him and for him and in him all things hold together" (Col 1:15-18). We are grateful to our own Australian scholars and writers who have written and spoken about these matters, and we commend them for their efforts. Also, Pope John Paul II has put forward some applications of the general principles enunciated by the Council. He has done this pre-eminently, in his encyclical letter *Sollicitudo Rei Socialis* (1987).

The latest and most complete papal statement regarding ecological issues is the letter which Pope John Paul II issued for the World Day of Peace, 1990, "Peace with God the Creator, Peace with all Creation." Starting from this statement we would like to stress a number of points for our Australian Catholics.

Eight Invitations

Firstly, we are invited to reflect anew on our Christian "responsibility within creation and our duty toward nature and the Creator" as "an essential part of our faith." All of us were taught that religion contained the duty of loving God and our neighbour. We were to look upon all men and women as our brothers and sisters. Now we find the Pope writing of a sense of "fraternity with all those good and beautiful things which almighty God has created, and . . . of our serious obligation to respect and watch over them with care."[10]

Secondly, an education in ecological responsibility is urgent: responsibility for oneself, for others and for the earth. The Pope says that this education must not be based on a rejection of the modern world or a vague desire to return to some "paradise lost." "Churches and religious bodies, non-governmental and governmental organisations, indeed all members of society have a precise role to play in such education." We need to acquire a sound knowledge of the environmental problems which affect the whole world, and peoples other than our own. We must know what are the special questions which Australians need to answer. Without such knowledge, fears and prejudice will harden our minds and close them to rational discussion and willing collaboration.

Thirdly, we must learn even more to appreciate the beauty of creation. A great writer has said: "Beauty will save the world."[11] Pope John Paul II says: "Our very contact with nature has a deep restorative power; contemplation of its magnificence imparts peace and serenity." And, practically, "the relationship between a good aesthetic education and the maintenance of a healthy environment can not be overlooked."

Fourthly, we must consider very carefully the ways in which we can help other nations not to harm the environment. Richer nations can criticise the poorer ones for destroying their forests and ravaging their land, even though the more affluent nations contribute to that destruction. Existing international economic structures are such that nations in the third world are forced into using up their natural resources. "The proper ecological balance will not be found without directly addressing the structural forms of poverty that exist throughout the world."[12]

Fifthly, we are all called to examine our own lifestyles. Such a serious examination is possible only through some kind of conversion. This may be conversion from ignorance to true knowledge, from selfishness to caring, from merely "using" to respecting, and, for us, to a religious awareness. For some it will be a conversion to accepting the truth that "the earth is ultimately a common heritage, the fruits of which are for the benefit of all."[13]

As the Pope says: "Modern society will find no solution to the ecological problem unless it takes a serious look at its lifestyle. In many parts of the world, society is given to instant gratification and consumerism while remaining indifferent to the damage which they cause. . . . Simplicity, moderation and discipline, as well as a spirit of sacrifice, must become a part of everyday life lest all suffer the negative consequences of the habits of a few."[14]

How many Australians would know that researchers of One World Campaign calculated, in 1989, that Australia's 17 million people have twice the impact on world resources and energy as Africa's 640 million?

Sixthly, we should all be "conscious of the vast field of ecumenical and inter-religious cooperation opening up before us." We can all profit from two excellent recent publications. The Uniting Church in Australia has produced an Australian Christian reflection on the Renewal of Creation, "Healing the Earth." The 1990 Anglican Social Justice Statement, "Justice for the Earth," is an eminently practical study guide.

The Pope has paid tribute to all men and women who "with an acute sense of their responsibilities for the common good, recognise their obligation to contribute to the restoration of a healthy environment." Uniting with them in a concern for the earth, we will not expect all of them to share our religious convictions. Some of them do not share—nor do they approve—the language of the Christian view which regards human beings as superior to other created things. They say this superiority has been understood and exercised only as exploitation of the rest of creation. Those of us who do not agree with this judgement must nonetheless recognise that, throughout history, many people have not always been attuned to what the biblical text meant by our living in the image of a life-giving God who delights in creation.

In co-operating with others in a care for the earth, we will be helped by realising that among them there will be different "models," different ways of viewing the relationships which make all creatures interdependent. We all need to listen receptively to other people's views. Members of "Greenpeace" or "Earthwatch," ecofeminists and deep ecologists will have useful things to say to all those interested in environmental issues. We will find that we share common goals and can work together for a healthy environment where all living beings can thrive and all of creation is respected.

Seventhly, let us think and act creatively as we enter a new phase of discovery both of created realities and of our own way of seeing them in God's plan for them and for us.

Eighthly, as Catholics seeking a better understanding of how a care for the earth and its creatures is a "part of our faith," we need to give careful study to the Bible and to the official teaching of the Church on these matters.

Creation Accounts

The Bible begins with two creation accounts. These are contained in Genesis 1:1–2:4, and 2:5-25. The first account makes two clear statements. Firstly, it is to the one God that all created things owe their being. Secondly God has declared that the whole of Creation is "good." It is worth noting that the Hebrew word used here for "good" *(tov)* does not mean simple "good" in a vague general kind of way. It has also a more dynamic sense of "useful," "purposeful." The whole of God's creation is good in the sense that it is fitted together and moving towards a desired goal.

"God said: Let us make man in our own image, after our own likeness; and let them have dominion over the fish of the sea, and over the birds of the air, and over the cattle, and over all the earth, and over every creeping thing that creeps upon the earth. So God created man in his own image, in the image of God he created him, male and female he created them. And God blessed them, and said to them, 'Be fruitful, multiply and fill the earth and subdue it. Have dominion over the fish of the sea, and over the birds of the air and over every living thing that moves upon the earth'. . . . And so it was. God saw everything that he had made, and behold, it was very good" (Gen 1:26-28, 31).

Two points emerge clearly from this text. One is the emphasis on the fact that human beings are created in the image and likeness of God. The other is that they are entrusted with a certain "dominion" over other created things. It should be noted that this word "dominion" gives rise to a difference of opinion. Some say that it has contributed to a selfish exploitation of the earth. They prefer "a new theology of creation (which) will reflect the broader biblical perspective in which the presence of God is immanent in nature as well as in humanity and his Spirit is constantly renewing the earth. This larger cosmic community requires a different human attitude. Instead of the instrumentality of conquering and subduing the earth, it should be one of participation and harmony."[15]

The more traditional interpretation, however, believes that "dominion," properly understood, demands a total respect for all created reality. The Bible itself rules out selfish exploitation in a passage from the Book of Wisdom: "God of our ancestors . . . in your wisdom you have fitted human beings to rule the creatures that you have made, to govern the world in holiness and saving justice" (Wis 9:2). Vatican II took up this text and said: "Men and women were created in God's image and commanded to conquer the earth with all it contains and *to rule the world in justice and in holiness;* they were to acknowledge God as maker of all things and relate themselves and the totality of creation to God, so that through the dominion of all things by the human race the name of God would be majestic upon the earth."[16]

Pope John Paul says: "Made in the image and likeness of God, Adam and Eve were to have exercised their dominion over the earth with wisdom and love."[17]

The Bible is concerned with religious truths. In this first creation account two religious truths are made quite clear. Firstly, created in God's image, human beings are able to relate to God, to enter a relationship of interpersonal communion and intimacy. This is not just an incidental feature of human nature: relationship to God enters essentially into the structure of human existence; it is a condition of life and death. In vital relationship to God human beings flourish; when the relationship breaks down they wither and die.

Secondly, being in God's image also means relationship to the rest of creation. The way human beings relate to the world and accept responsibility for it enters essentially into their relationship with God. The dominion is not one of selfish exploitation. The aim is to further the goodness, order and development of the world, to bring it to full achievement of its goal through respect for the sovereignty of God.

The relationship is also expressed in a later text from Genesis where God says to Noah: "I set my bow in the clouds and it will be a sign of the covenant between me and the earth. When I gather the clouds over the earth and the bow appears in the clouds, I shall recall the covenant between myself and you and every living creature, in a word, all living things . . ." (Gen 9:13-15).

The second creation account (Gen 2:5-25) speaks of God putting Adam and Eve "in the Garden of Eden, to till it and keep it" (v. 15). In this text, some people find the image they prefer, the task of stewardship of created realities is entrusted to human beings.

In their task of stewardship, Adam and Eve were given one commandment. We are told that they were tempted to disobey God, to use selfishly the gifts that they had received. They did so and all their relationships deteriorated. Their intimate friendship with God gave way to fear (3:8). Their own loving relationship gave way to recrimination and blame (3:12-16). Finally, their relationship to the earth was affected; the "garden" became barren, hard to cultivate, yielding a harvest only through sweat and hard labour (3:17-19).

Centuries later, Saint Paul would reflect on and write about sin and the effect that it had upon the world. Looking back to the Genesis accounts, Paul would say that sin—then and now—was "covetousness," it was perverting the goodness of things by using creation selfishly or for purposes not in the Creator's intention (Rom 3). Even concern for the environment can sometimes be selfish rather than an act of worship. For Paul, too, sin is not merely an individual matter between God and the sinner. Sin disrupts a whole pattern of right relationships that cannot flourish outside a right relationship with God.

Catholics believe that the Bible sets out to give religious truth, not exact scientific data. It does not intend to give an approved cosmology or a correct scientific account of the world's origins. We have to look to science for these. "If the cosmologies of the ancient Near Eastern World could be purified and assimilated into the first chapters of Genesis, might contemporary cosmology have something to offer to our reflections upon creation?"[18] We believe that, however the universe came into being, however the human race began, God is the Creator of the universe and of the human race. In this belief we find the origins of our conviction that, as Christians, we have an ethical duty to respect the gifts of creation, to give thanks for them, and to use them in accord with the will of God, as best we can interpret.

That interpretation depends upon the extent of our human knowledge. It is far from being perfect. Following the teaching of Pope John Paul II, we have already given some suggestions about a Christian response to our challenge to use well the goods of the earth and to treat them according to God's will. In the encyclical letter, *Sollicitudo Rei Socialis* (1987), the Pope wrote some things which merit our consideration. He spoke of "respect for the beings which constitute the natural world, which the ancient Greeks—alluding to the order which distinguishes it—called the "cosmos." Such realities also demand respect by virtue of a threefold consideration. . . ."

The three considerations were these:

First it is right that we should be ever more aware of the fact that one cannot use with impunity the different categories of beings, whether living or inanimate—animals, plants, the natural elements—simply as one wishes, according to one's economic needs. On the contrary, one must take into account the nature of each being and of its mutual connection in an ordered system, which is precisely the "cosmos."

The second consideration is "based on the realisation . . . that natural resources are limited; some are not . . . renewable. Using them as if they were inexhaustible, with absolute dominion, seriously endangers their availability not only to the present generation but above all for generations to come."

The third consideration proposed by the Pope refers to the quality of life in the industrialised zones. Here special reference is made to the pollution of the environment, with serious consequences for the health of the population. The Pope speaks of the way in which moral demands impose limits on the use of the natural world. He refers again to the proper understanding of that term "dominion." "The dominion granted . . . by the Creator is not an absolute power, nor can one speak of a freedom to "use or misuse," or to dispose of things as one pleases. The limitation imposed from the beginning by the Creator himself and expressed symbolically by the prohibition not to "eat of the fruit of the tree" (cf. Gen 2:16-17) shows clearly enough that, when it comes to the natural world, we are subject not only to natural laws but also to moral ones, which cannot be violated with impunity."[19]

The Task Ahead

In this brief message, we do not propose solutions to the problems which face us, particularly the problem of balancing a respect for all created things with the necessary development needed if human beings are to live fittingly on the face of the earth. We have proposed certain steps which we need to consider seriously if we are to work together towards a successful solution of these problems. It has been suggested that the Catholic bishops of Australia might invite all those interested to take part in a nation-wide exploration of ecological issues in a search for positive, united action. This would be by a process similar to our present enquiry into the distribution of wealth: "Common Wealth and the Common Good." That same title could well apply also to the environment. We may well respond to this request.

However, for such an enquiry to be fruitful, some preliminary steps must be taken. The first of these, we believe, is to respond seriously and with care to the eight invitations mentioned above addressed to us by the signs of the times and suggested by the message of Pope John Paul. Clearly, we must all work together for the good of the environment. However, in order that we might be able to do that effectively, there must be a meeting of minds and a common resolve.

A second task is to study and formulate the principles of a valid Christian ethic of a care for the earth. It is only recently that many Christians have considered that any ethical duty is involved here. They have not yet agreed what are common ethical grounds. The American Catholic bishops wrote, in 1986: "The resources of the earth have been created for the benefit of all, and we who are alive today hold them in trust. This is a challenge to develop a new ecological ethic that will help shape a future that is both just and sustainable."

An Ecological Ethic

Be it a new ethic or a new application of old principles, we do need to formulate a clear ecological ethic.

Pope John Paul II proposes some principles of such an ethic in the documents we have quoted. Central to his thesis is the statement: "Respect for life, and above all the dignity of the human person, is the ultimate guiding norm for any sound economic, industrial or scientific progress."[20] He does speak of "a sense of 'fraternity' with all these good and beautiful things which God has created" and also of "that greater and higher fraternity which exists within the human family."

The interaction between human population and the environment is an issue that warrants careful examination. Some advocate a reduction in population, even in Australia, to prevent what they see as an exponential growth in human numbers that would culminate in widespread famine and ecological disaster.

It needs to be said that population size in itself is not a direct cause of poverty or environmental damage, nor is its reduction a necessary solution. More direct causes are natural disasters, localized and civil wars, world trade practices that restrict food distribution, financial arrangements that lock nations into unpayable debt and the tyrannical actions of despotic rulers. Serious efforts to increase world food production, the provision of clean water and better medical services, will increase the well-being of people and lead to a stabilization of population. The direct attacks on population through international birth-control programmes are misdirected not only because they often employ immoral means and produce an anti-baby and anti-family mentality, but also because they fail to see that when food production and general well-being rise, populations look after themselves. It is surely not beyond the wit or will of the human race to solve the problems caused to the environment by modern society and to prevent future damage.

In the application of the principles outlined by Pope John Paul II, many Christians believe that "the Church's social teachings . . . need to be expanded in a new ecological age."[21] This is not surprising. We have no fund of accumulated wisdom to use in answering questions which past generations have not asked. Nor do we claim that, in searching for an expression of our Christian duty to care for created things, the Pope has found complete answers to all questions. Other issues need to be addressed, such as the effects of large populations upon the earth's resources, and an enlightened Christian approach to this question. We need to listen to new questions such as whether we should "extend our moral responsibilities vis-à-vis biocide (the killing of the life-system of the planet) and genocide (the destruction of the earth) . . . ?"[22]

We support our scholars in their attempts to develop and explain this "ecological ethic." May the Lord bless their efforts and guide us all.

Conclusion

In a Commonwealth discussion paper on "Ecologically sustainable development," June 1990, it is recognised that "most people have aesthetic and ethical reasons" for the efforts they make on behalf of our world and our environment. We believe that these are the only reasons which, in effect, will serve to "save the world."

We express our appreciation of the efforts of all who have contributed to a better understanding of environmental needs. We urge our own Catholic people to take part in the common human endeavour to care for the earth in all its beauty. We believe that reflection on our Christian faith will make us more alert and responsive to the call to care for created things "in justice and in holiness," "with wisdom and love."

Notes

1. *Gaudium et Spes.*

2. *One World* [WCC magazine] No. 158, Aug-Sept. 1990, p. 4. [See also *CI,* Vol. 1, No. 3, pp. 139ff].

3. Cf. Vincent Serventi, *Australian Native Plants,* Reld Books, Sydney, 1984, pp. 32ff; also Les Murray, *The Australian Year,* Angus & Robertson, Sydney, 1985.

4. E.g. the Finke River. Salinity is better known as a problem connected with the Murray.

5. The Hon Ms Ros Kelly, Statement for World Environment Day, 5 June 1990.

6. Pope John Paul II, 1 Jan 1990, *Peace with God the Creator, Peace with all Creation*, 15. This document will be referred to as *Peace with God*.

7. *GS*, 12.

8. *GS*, 37.

9. *Redemptor Hominis*, 8.

10. *Peace with God*, 16.

11. This is often quoted as a dictim of Dostoievsky, cf. Balthasar, *Glory to the Lord*, Clarke, Edinburgh, 1989, Vol. 3, p. 342. Cf. also *The Idiot*, Penguin, p. 420.

12. *Peace with God*, 11.

13. *Ibid.*, n. 8.

14. *Ibid.*, n. 13.

15. *Pro Mundi Vita*, Feb 1990, p. 3.

16. *GS*, 34.

17. *Peace with God*, 1.

18. Pope John Paul II, "A Dynamic Relationship of Theology and Science," *Origins* 1988, p. 377.

19. All these considerations are contained in n. 34 of the encyclical.

20. *Peace with God*, 7.

21. *Pro Mundi Vita*, Feb 1990, p. 35.

22. *Ibid.*, p. 3.

PASTORAL LETTER ON THE RELATIONSHIP OF HUMAN BEINGS TO NATURE

The Dominican Episcopal Conference

Introduction

1. On the 10th of August of 1982 on the eve of the installation of the new government, we said very clearly, "We can no longer fail to concern ourselves with the preservation and betterment of the environment in which we live. No ecological imbalance comes about by itself. The sin of humanity against nature always has its repercussions against humanity itself. The destruction of our forests, without an effective reforestation, is already bringing with it dire consequences for our rivers, our lands, and our climate. It is urgent, then, that there be a well planned and demanding policy concerning this serious national problem" (Pastoral Letter, August 10, 1982, no. 3). The situation has not only not improved but has actually grown worse and more serious.

2. Pope John Paul II in his first encyclical *Redemptor Hominis* (1979) says: "Man often seems to see no other meaning in his natural environment than what serves for immediate use and consumption. Yet it was the Creator's will that man should communicate with nature as an intelligent and noble 'master' and 'guardian,' and not as a heedless 'exploiter' and 'destroyer.'"

3. In the Dominican Republic this is not a danger that one needs to conjure up, but rather a sad reality that must be faced and drastically remedied. We find ourselves obliged to no longer postpone a promise we made sometime ago of writing of the relationship between the human person and nature, that is to say, about the national ecological problems as they actually exist today.

4. It is heartening that in recent times there have been numerous voices speaking out to draw attention to this most serious problem and to call upon everyone to assume their responsibility and to act as a united force. Voices of experts in this matter; voices of serious and conscientious persons; the angry and indignant voices of those who have been daily witnesses and have seen with their own eyes concrete crimes against nature in the very places where they have been perpetrated.

5. In the midst of these voices there has been a consensus on five points that we would like to emphasize:

— Ecological problems instead of getting better have worsened.
— The determining factor in this situation is the impunity with which the offenders have worked against nature.
— Another serious factor is the situation of poverty of many Dominicans which all but forces them to destroy nature.
— There is a need for the establishment of a high ranking office that will have authority to legislate, coordinate, and direct.
— And, above all, there is a real need for a national policy that would permit the allocation of priority funds, human resources, resolutions, and actions both legal and educational that favor this basic element of our existence, the physical environment of our nation.

6. It gives us great satisfaction and hope to see the growing consciousness of our ecological problem and the sincere preoccupation of many as well as certain concrete initiatives that are now being taken and which are being carried out amidst difficulties of every kind, and in which Church personnel is also involved.

7. Undoubtedly, when speaking on this theme, the scientific and technical aspect is most important. We bishops are not experts in this field, although it interests us greatly and we must concern ourselves with it. But together with this double aspect, there is the moral and ethical dimension of the problem that clearly enters into our mission and function. It is this aspect which we would like to develop.

I. The Disturbing and Dangerous National Reality

Land

8. There are many among us who constantly say that we are a country that is greatly endowed agriculturally. The truth is something quite different, and all of us Dominicans ought to be very aware of this.

9. According to the statistics given us by the technicians, less than 13 percent of our country is made up of arable land; another 8 percent could be cultivated, but subject to serious limitations that would require very skillful and specialized management. About 25 percent is land good only for pasture, and a little more than half the country's land is adequate only for forests. We realize also that much of our farmland remains dry awaiting a good system of irrigation.

10. The country has a population of nearly 125 inhabitants per square kilometer and about half of these live in the rural areas.

11. These figures indicate that land is a very limited resource if we are to feed our population and provide productive work for so many Dominicans who live in the rural areas. Consequently, land is a resource that must be used with the greatest possible wisdom in order to extract from it what our people need both for now as well as for the future.

Forest

12. The experts tell us that of the 53 percent of our lands classified as apt for forests and necessary in order to protect our water resources, only about 14 percent remains today as jungle.

13. The destructive action of deforestation has extended to the Jose del Carmen Ramirez Park, the East Park, the Sierra de Neiba, to the Sierra de Bahoruco, to the Haitises and only with great difficulty have they managed to arrest this in the vital J. Armando Bermudez Park in the northern sector of the Cordillera Central. There is

an urgent need for reforestation in order to stop the soil erosion, to provide firewood for cooking, to reduce the price of imported wood, and to protect our waterways.

14. The farmers who "slash and burn," the charcoal makers, and other unscrupulous people have destroyed our forests, thus exposing our major waterways to the sun, leaving the soil seriously eroded and a prey to further erosion, drying up streams and reducing the flow of rivers at an alarming rate. Of course, the damage done to dams is incalculable. In this way we have wasted our irreplaceable resources, such as reservoirs, and have ruined our hydroelectric future and hindered the reclamation of extensive areas for future agricultural production through irrigation.

15. Without putting aside our preoccupation with our marine resources, now besieged by contamination and uncontrolled fishing, and without ignoring the pollution of the atmosphere caused by heavy industry, mining, and the abuse of pesticides and insecticides, we understand that all these environmental problems of deforestation and the destruction of the land through erosion, with the constant threat to our water supply are the most urgent. Land and water are the principal mainstays of our natural life both now and in the future.

16. This situation not only threatens the possibility of the life of future generations to whom we would be bequeathing a desert as their inheritance, but it also jeopardizes any hope of using water through the construction of dams and canals to produce electrical energy so that our people might live a fairly civilized existence as well as to irrigate the land in the arid valleys so that we could produce food and other necessities, thus solving the problem of hunger among our people without having to resort to imports.

17. Human beings are born, grow, and develop within a system that is complex, closed, and interrelated. Nature is the home in which they live. They depend on her for their existence and the quality of their lives. In turn, nature depends on human beings who with their intelligence and capacity (both scientific and technical) must preserve, defend, better, and perfect it. In this system of many and varied interrelated levels, the breakdown of or interference with one of these has a negative repercussion on all.

18. The tragedy of such a system is that these interruptions and their chain reactions can be such that it becomes extremely difficult, if not even impossible, to preserve the human species in a given place. This does not refer, then, to the greater or lesser richness of the place, but rather to the quality of life, even of life itself.

19. This is already a reality in the Dominican Republic, a reality to which Paul VI adverted: "By reason of an irrational and inattentive exploitation of nature, man can destroy it and become a victim of his own depravity" *(Octogesima Adveniens, no. 21).*

20. Leading the list of causes we find ourselves confronted with is an accelerated population growth accompanied by an ever-increasing demand for food, resources, and energy, a general indolence, a lack of adequate means, the desire for luxury at any cost, and the misery of the people in areas, who are the very ones among us who are causing the impairment of the environment in which they live, so much so that the necessary balance between human beings and nature, as well as nature itself, is seriously threatened.

21. Therefore, the problem of the land and the forests is not only a technical problem but also one which has profound social and moral implications.

22. In the impairment of our natural resources, specifically the deforestation and the severe erosion of our land, it is not the impoverished campesino who has the greatest fault. There has been a great lack of vision, control, constant vigilance, and responsible and effective planning on the part of public authority. There has been negligence, complicity, and greed in many of those whom they have put in charge of overseeing this. There has been unpardonable avarice and carelessness on the part of the landowners who are unbelievably insensitive to the ecological problems.

23. It is also true, however, that there has not been lacking among us an undiscerning rural people. In most cases, nevertheless, the lack of land and technical preparation for adequate agriculture, the absence of any assistance, and the inaccessibility of necessary credit, poor living conditions, the lack of basic necessities, in a word, misery, is what has driven them to marginal lands with no other option than to make intensive use of the land without any caution, which is destroying the vegetation as well as the very soil itself.

24. If it is so that in the past lumber dealers wasted with impunity almost all the wealth of our forests which in their turn protected our lands and soil; and if it is equally certain that even in more recent times Dominicans took advantage of their influential positions in order to continue destroying nature for their own benefits; it is also true that a larger number of our own Dominican people, among them the poorest in the country, live in the forests without any other means of survival than "slashing and burning" in order to eke out their precarious living and who in this way endanger both our ecological system and our future well-being.

Fauna

25. What we have said of the forests, water, and soil can be said also of our fauna, that is, our four-footed animals, the birds, and fishes.

26. There is within us a certain destructive instinct. Any bird that flies in the air or lands somewhere is immediately threatened. We kill for the pleasure of killing.

27. On the other hand, hunting seasons are not observed. There is not the slightest scruple about violating such laws, eliminating with impunity certain species without the slightest consideration, even during the mating season. There is great negligence and thoughtlessness.

28. Thus we have arrived at a point that, in a country of such little variety in its fauna, certain species have completely disappeared and others are in imminent danger of disappearing forever.

29. Based on all that has been said, it is evident that the *recuperation* and *protection* of all the resources described is an unavoidable obligation that can no longer be postponed.

II. God's Marvelous Design on Nature

God's Plan

30. God in his wisdom and power created—brought into existence out of nothing that previously existed—the universe, and within that universe the planet earth, according to the marvelous laws which he bestowed on this universe created by him.

31. We know that on the earth the Lord created the mineral world and life: both vegetal and animal and finally, human life. To human beings he gave intelligence, the capacity to love, certain skills, and free will, and he put them in charge over the earth.

32. To this "man"—to the whole of humanity—both present and yet to come, he gave as *common patrimony* the earth and all that it contains.

33. Given this patrimony of marvelous and at times most mysterious laws that include immense possibilities for the maintenance and betterment of the quality of human life through the combination of these laws, God gave humankind the task and the obligation to "rule and govern" the earth through science and technology and in this way make it ever more useful for the perfection of human beings and of society (cf. Gn 1:26-28; Ps 8:5-9).

34. Therefore, to use human intelligence and skills (science and technology) to destroy or to threaten the earth, or not to use them when difficulties or new and varied challenges arise, is a contradiction, an abuse of the divine plan, and an affront to the will of the Creator who is absolute Lord of the earth and of humankind.

Principles

35. There are various basic principles that stem from this plan and from which we derive fundamental moral imperatives that we would like to highlight:

a) The earth with all its riches is the patrimony of humankind. It is an inheritance that we receive and which we must administer and distribute with justice and equity and which we must pass on to those who come after us, not in a deteriorated condition but rather in an improved state.

b) The earth with all its riches is a challenge to the industriousness, the ability, and the intelligence of human beings taken both individually and socially.

c) The destiny of the earth and all its riches is a universal one. The individual or group appropriation of any part of this patrimony is legitimate only if it is limited to means that are adequate for the fulfillment of the needs of an individual or a group or if it is used to bring about its true and effective fundamental universal destiny.

d) Science and technology are the product and patrimony of humankind. Each of these, as important as they might be, is an integral part of the science and technology of humankind, which is always indebted to the achievements of others who have gone before us and to those working today. This social debt must be paid by respecting and bringing to fruition the social function of science, technology and all human effort.

e) Human beings are only the users, administrators, perfecters and custodians of this common patrimony which is the earth and all its riches, functions which should be carried out with nobility and intelligence.

f) Thus we read in the Book of Wisdom: *"O God of my fathers and Lord of mercy, who has made all things by your word, and by your wisdom has formed man to have dominion over the creatures you have made and rule the world in holiness and righteousness and pronounce judgment in uprightness of soul, give me the wisdom that sits by your throne" (Wis 9:1-4).*

Nature demands from human beings wisdom, righteousness, justice and holiness and consequently forbids carelessness, ignorance, irrationality, avarice, exploitation, aggressiveness, perversity, and infidelity.

g) God made the earth a paradise for humankind. Sin is what transformed this paradise into "cursed ground." *"Because you have eaten of the forbidden tree, cursed is the ground because of you. In toil you shall eat of it all the days of your life; thorns and thistles it shall bring forth to you." (Genesis 3:17-18)*

Morality and Ecology

36. In light of the above, the duties of human beings toward God and others include very serious obligations to nature on which we depend and which depends on us. These relationships of ourselves with nature and nature with us are not arbitrary, but are determined by God. The will of God is manifested to us in the very laws of nature and in Revelation. Of course, our relationship with nature also includes our relationship with others and with God.

37. From the principles set forth we derive a series of moral criteria for reflection and lines of action which we want to explicitate:

Natural resources should never be exploited solely for the purpose of accumulating wealth rapidly, with a standard that might be called mining, without proper management and the replacement of the forests, but rather taking into consideration the needs of the whole human family both present and future. It is sad to say, but our forests, with rare exceptions, have been a typical example of this kind of abuse and depredation.

38. It is inadmissible that so many of our rural people, not having greater access to the land, find themselves permanently condemned to extreme poverty. This obliges them, on occasion, to a serious over-exploitation of the land causing deterioration and even complete destruction of the soil. Such destruction for want of arable land and the lack above all of the cultivation of the hillsides in the mountainous regions is as serious as the deforestation.

39. It is not just that those who have the highest incomes (countries, cities, groups, and individuals) tend to waste so much that, besides being an insult and a provocation to the poor, is a terrible misuse of natural resources so necessary for a dispossessed population.

40. Those who have power in society to set up guidelines for the use of natural resources cannot be influenced in their decisions by motives based on immediate economic and political benefits, without taking into account both the future and the generations to come.

41. Right ordering and the Common Good ought to lead us to establish and accept priorities in the limited resources at the disposition of the government at this time. Therefore, when reforestation is a serious national commitment, it is unjust and ab-

surd to complain and demand other works that, in the light of this national emergency, are quite secondary.

42. In the case of nonrenewable resources, the highly industrialized and developed countries may not exercise a sort of monopoly on the exploitation and use of these resources, without taking into account the present and future needs of the countries that are the suppliers of these resources. Nor can they, in their turn, for immediate economic motives, give away or misuse this present and future national patrimony.

43. Knowing that certain natural resources have taken millions of years to attain their present form, their extraction demands reflection and prudence, realizing that their re-formation will again need millions of years or perhaps will never again become available.

44. The income generated by these nonrenewable resources ought to be invested in such a way that these investments might be converted into permanent solutions to the inhuman and unjust poverty that exists and in a manner that will generate income in the future for generations to come who will not have the benefit of exploiting these resources.

45. A substantial part of the benefits derived from operations that upset the natural ecological balance ought to be used in recuperating this lost balance insofar as this is possible.

46. Renewable resources such as forests, land, and water, so necessary for life, ought to be used in such a way that respects their constant renovation and that might serve future generations to whom they also belong.

47. It is necessary to be vigilant and to employ suitable methods so that neither the overwhelming desire for wealth nor the immediate needs of the poor redound negatively on the conservation of our natural resources.

48. When there were certain elite groups who benefited greatly and irrationally from these renewable resources, it is unjust that the burden of replacing these resources fall on the poor.

49. It is so contrary to the plan of the Creator to waste or misuse natural resources, or to impede their rightful use, with certain guarantees, in order to satisfy the needs of an entire population.

50. The maintenance and defense of the necessary ecological balance is the moral obligation of all and not the exclusive function of the government. To abuse natural resources (trees, water, minerals . . .) is to act against nature, the human beings who need these resources, and God, the Creator both of nature and of human beings.

51. The most extraordinary scientific advances, the most spectacular technical feats, and the most prodigious economic growth will militate against human beings and nature if there is not at the same time a genuine moral and social progress among individuals and in society.

52. An ideology of work as an unlimited domination and exploitation of matter is false. The search for the maximum yield or production profits as an end in itself is wrong. The myth of efficiency without limits and of a hedonistic consumerism is a trap that leads to wasteful mismanagement. There is both a risk and a danger in the fascination with and idolizing of science and technology that are capable of increasing and transforming natural reserves, but which cannot create them.

Spirituality and Ecology

53. Christ to whom all things are subject and have been freed from the slavery of corruption (Rom 8:21), taught us during his earthly life to admire nature and to respect it; to use it well and enjoy it without spoiling or harming it; to be inspired by it and to love it.

54. In order to explain different aspects and conditions of the Reign of God that he had come to establish on the earth, he used as pedagogical examples certain realities such as the harvest, the drought, weeds, the mustard seed, the fig tree, the vine, the sun, the rain, the lilies of the field, the birds . . . (Mt 13:18-23; Mk 4:13-20; Lk 8:11-15; Mk 4:26-29; Mt 13:24-30; Mk 4:30-32; Lk 13:18-19; Mt 5:45; Lk 12:27; Mt 6:28; Lk 12:4-7). He always liked to go to the mountain to recollect himself and to pray (Mt 17:1; Mk 6:45), and it was from the mountainside, with no roof except the blue sky, that he proclaimed the beatitudes to the world (Mt 5:3-13; Lk 6:17-20). After having called the first disciples (Lk 5:1-11; Mk 1:19-20), he returned once again to the Sea of Galilee or the Sea of Tiberias or Lake Genesaret in order to preach, to perform miracles, and to rest (Mk 1:21-28; Mt 13:1-52; Mk 4:35-41; Jn 21:1-14).

55. The ongoing perfection of human nature includes the growing perfection of the natural environment of which human beings are, as we have said, custodians and faithful and intelligent administrators.

"AND GOD SAW THAT IT WAS GOOD"

56. The sweet and charming Francis of Assisi, patron of ecologists, always called nature "sister." And he treated her like a sister. He says in his Canticle of Sister Sun:

Blessed are you, my Lord, for our sister mother earth
which sustains and governs us
and produces different fruits
with colored flowers and herbs.

Francis of Assisi is a loud and clear call to reconciliation not only to men and women among themselves, but also between them and all of nature. For this reason, he is an extraordinary model and current figure.

57. Ignatius of Loyola, loyal servant of the Church, liked to see God in nature: "looking"—he says—"how God lives in his creatures: in the elements giving being, in the plants growing, in the animals sensing and in humans giving them understanding. And so in me giving me being, animating, feeling and making me understand" (Spiritual Exercises, no. 235), presenting in this profound way the linkage of each one with all of nature.

III. The Urgent Need for Action

58. Everything we have said will simply be like words blowing in the wind if little or nothing is done. There is a great need for effective and coordinated action.

59. The measures taken, however, must be twofold: technical and ethical. Both are necessary. Neither of these is sufficient in itself.

60. We understand the difficulties involved in reforestation and the ordered use of our land due to the present state of deterioration, the chaos that prevails in this aspect of our material life, and the social structures that have brought about this chaotic situation.

61. Let us think of the wisest efforts to completely halt deforestation as the first of a series of measures in overcoming the serious problems of our national ecological deterioration.

62. We understand, nevertheless, what caused this, and we must take into account that different groups have a negative effect on our renewable resources. It is not right to judge them all equally. Each case requires special attention. Among these groups we would like to cite:

a) Those who acquired their wealth through the destruction of nature.
b) Those who take advantage of their position and influence look for ways to reap profits for themselves from nature at any cost.

c) Those who destroy nature out of necessity, who have no other immediate option if they are not given to them.

d) Those who, even though they might not be directly involved with these natural resources, depend nevertheless, in large measure, for their livelihood on these resources, such as poor who cook with charcoal and firewood.

e) Groups of good faith who want to make a more productive use of the land through agriculture and lumber businesses that are beneficial to the country.

63. It would be unjust, in the name of assuring the physical survival of our nation, to treat all of these in the same manner. Of these, the campesino and the urban poor who depend on charcoal need special attention.

64. The margination of the campesino and his resultant poverty, the cause of many of our ecological problems, must be addressed simultaneously because it is not secondary to, but rather central to our ecological problem. The protection of nature is not an end in itself, but tends toward the balance of the relationship between the environment and humankind in order to bring about a more human world for all through a greater quality of nature.

65. Just as it is unacceptable to allow those engaged in the lumber business to continue their destructive ways, it would also be unacceptable to allow the poor campesino of the jungle to sink further into misery or those from the arid regions, to whom our society has left no other choice but nomadic agriculture or the burning and extraction of charcoal. It would be unacceptable also to cut the supply of the only fuel that the poor use to cook their food without first having sought an alternative solution.

66. It seems to us that some immediate steps that might complement the measures already taken against deforestation are the following:

a) Continue a strict surveillance of the critical regions of our national territory.

b) Organize, and this is indispensable, the production of charcoal in such a way that it might alleviate the situation of so many Dominicans who are indigent because they cannot find anything with which to cook their food, and which might also alleviate the situation of so many charcoal makers, who are amongst the poorest of our nation. This organization should be accomplished in such a way as to cause the least possible damage to our economic system, while actively looking for other alternative solutions that are more facile, viable, and economical.

c) Take a census of the campesinos who live in the jungle areas and who are most affected by the necessary restrictions on cutting down trees in these delicate areas, so as to begin the resettlement of these families on other lands or in another type of work by which they can earn a living.

d) Examine the opinions of both national and foreign technicians as well as those of the campesinos from the jungles so that the confusion that seems to us to exist as regards the seriousness of the problem and the possible solutions thereof might be clarified.

e) To restore the agricultural and tourism projects that might benefit the country and that might not adversely affect the economy.

f) Allocate each year a good part of the national budget to reforestation.

g) Not to forget to take into account the fruit trees in the reforestation project.

67. In a longer range plan, certain critical areas of reforestation must be looked at. According to the experts, we must reforest at least 600,000 hectares of the most important river banks, and preserve, among others, the two national parks of the Cordillera Central in order to assure the water needed by the nation. To do this over a prudent period of time demands the investment each year of amounts equivalent to one tenth of our national budget.

68. To prepare this work that can be delayed no longer, we would like to see a series of short term goals, among which we cite the following:

a) To determine with both national and foreign technicians how each part of Dominican land should be used and revise our laws so that regulations legislating the adequate use of the land might be established independently of those who possess the land.

b) To draw up a national plan for the reestablishment of the country's forests. This strategy as we understand it would be useless if it did not include the above measure, which would call for both specialized training of the Armed Forces and of the national police in this area and that the work of reforestation be a requisite for graduation at the secondary and university level.

c) To design programs that would guarantee a way of life adequate for those who are actually obliged by their misery to live as pillagers.

d) To educate the Dominican people in general about environmental matters by means of mass education as well as formalized education, insisting on the preparation of technicians and of campesinos who will dedicate their lives to agroforestal works.

e) To encourage and take advantage of experiments that have been carried on in the nation to educate the campesino in matters related to agroforestal subjects.

69. As for nonrenewable resources, we are also concerned about the use that has been made of the benefits derived from our mines.

70. These mineral resources have been here for millions of years and belong to the present as well as the future generations of Dominicans.

71. Consequently, it is immoral that the benefits derived from these mineral resources should go principally to international companies, or that rulers should feel obligated to invest these benefits in current needs that have no priority. The extraction of these mineral resources is only justified if the profits are used for lasting investments so that future Dominicans might find a country where they might live and work as befits human beings.

72. The benefits derived from the extraction of nonrenewable natural resources can very well be reinvested, when they are over and above the needs of the moment, to cover the costs of the ecological recuperation of the country.

73. We are aware that the recuperation and the care of our natural resources is everyone's responsibility, but the government, as administrator of the state, has the obligation to orient and coordinate this great task and all citizens should understand this.

74. The state, as the representative also of future generations, must guarantee the use of natural resources in order to satisfy the present needs while taking into account the future generations.

75. We urge the strengthening of a high level department with real authority to animate, coordinate, reflect, and manage everything related to natural resources in their ecological dimension.

76. There is much that the Church can do in the moral sphere and in actual collaboration with technology in her promotional and assistance efforts, and from now on, faithful to a multisecular tradition, she commits herself to this.

77. Pastors, presidents of the assembly, ministers, laity, pastoral agents must stress the obligations of human persons to nature. Devise a special catechesis for this. Organize days of study and reflection. Creatively adapt the ancient Ember Days, today ferias, and organize special liturgical celebrations for such occasions as Arbor Day or at the beginning or the end of the harvest of a particular product (coffee, cocoa, sugar, tobacco, etc.). In your areas see that the people become aware of their sins against the

environment and against nature. Enthusiastically support any and all efforts in defense of and/or betterment of nature. Don't be afraid to suggest to us, for these ends, some kind of "lay ministry." There are, no doubt, places, for example, the parish and the communities, that are the ideal institutions to take charge of the local "tree farm" and "nursery" etc. in their zone.

78. We congratulate those pastors who are already developing initiatives and actions among their parishioners regarding the reforestation.

79. There are five Catholic radio stations in the country that exert a strong influence in the rural areas. They have justly earned the esteem and confidence of the campesinos. They are "Radio Santa Maria" in La Vega; "Radio Seibo" in el Seibo; "Radio Enriquillo" in Tamavo; "Radio Marien" in Dajabón; and "Radio ABC" in the capital. We ask them to make this cause their own. Join forces and together plan a variety of programs. Exhort, animate, inform, instruct, denounce all negative practices, propose others that are positive and necessary, support every advantageous initiative, collaborate with each other, and always be alert. There is a great deal that can be done in the area of ecology. Do it with enthusiasm and creativity.

80. We will see that the national Catholic weekly "Camino" supports this project. We will suggest that the other Catholic publications do likewise.

81. We will also publicly call upon Caritas Dominicana, a consciousness-raising promotional organization that assists the Church at the national level, and the various diocesan and parochial centers of human promotion to make the ecological problem in all its complexity an integral part of their plans and programs. We pledge our support and encouragement in this. The majority of these programs should be carried out in coordination with the pastors of the parishes.

82. Finally, we ask all Catholic colleges and the school system in general to include instruction on ecology from the very first years. Instill deeply in future generations a profound love and respect for nature and make them aware that morality extends also to this.

83. Let us conclude with some inspiring reflections from Ecclesiasticus:

"All things are the works of the Lord, for they are very good, and whatever he commands will be done in his time." At his word the waters stood in a heap, and the reservoirs of water at the word of his mouth. At his command whatever pleases him is done, and none can limit his saving power. The works of all flesh are before him, and nothing can be hid from his eyes. From everlasting to everlasting he beholds them and nothing is too marvelous in his sight. No one can say, "What is this?" "Why is that?" for everything has been created for its use (Eccl 39:16-21).

84. Finally, we wanted to write this pastoral letter on a subject that affects every Dominican, on the Feast of Our Lady of Altagracia, protectress of our nation. She has always effectively interceded in our favor before God. She has done so, above all, in moments of crisis and in times of difficult undertakings. We ask that, once again, she might extend her maternal protection and keep this work of the reforestation of our country under her protection and care, a task of utmost importance for the Dominican people.

Santo Domingo, January 21, 1987, Feast of the Virgin of Altagracia

Cardinal Octavio A. Beras Rojas
Honorary President for life of the
   CED
Archbishop Emeritus

Nicolas de Jesús Lopez Rodriguez
Metropolitan Archbishop of Santo
   Domingo
President of the Dominican
   Episcopal Conference

Hugo E. Polanco Brito
Archbishop-Bishop of
   Our Lady of Altagracia

Thomas F. Reilly, CSSR
Bishop Emeritus

Juan F. Pepen
Titular Bishop of Arpi
Auxiliary Bishop of
   Santo Domingo

Roque Adames
Bishop of Santiago
   de los Caballeros

Juan A. Flores
Bishop of La Vega

Priamo P. Tejeda
Bishop-Elect of Bani

Renaldo Connors, CSSR
Bishop of San Juan de la Maguana

Fabio M. Rivas, SDB
Bishop of Barahona

Jesús Maria de Jesús Moya
Bishop of San Francisco de Macoris

Tomas Abreu
Bishop of Mao-Montecristi

THE CRY FOR LAND

❧

Joint Pastoral Letter
by the Guatemalan Bishops' Conference

❧

0.0   **Introduction**

0.1   *The cry for land* is undoubtedly the strongest, most dramatic and most desperate cry heard in Guatemala. It bursts forth from millions of Guatemalan hearts yearning not only to possess the land, but to be possessed by it. It is a cry from the "People of Corn" who on the one hand identify with furrows, sowing, and harvest, and who on the other hand find themselves expelled from the land by an unjust and punitive system. They are like strangers in the land which belonged to them for thousands of years; they are considered second-class citizens in the nation forged by their extraordinary ancestors.

0.2   Perhaps there is no subject which awakens more fierce passion and gives rise to more radical and irreconcilable positions than does the subject of land ownership. But it is a subject which must be dealt with in an attempt to begin to solve the great problems troubling us.

0.3   Through this Pastoral Letter, we wish to invite all Guatemalans, especially those who profess to be Catholics, to reflect sincerely and in depth on this most difficult problem, letting ourselves be enlightened by the Word of God and establishing solid foundations on which we can build a better homeland.

0.4   Our letter is made up of three large sections:
    —The Agrarian Problem in Guatemala
    —Theological Insights
    —Pastoral Conclusions

1.0   The Agrarian Problem in Guatemala

1.1   In fulfillment of our pastoral mission, we want to point out once again the critical situation of the majority of Guatemalans in rural areas. Like the Latin American Bishops at Puebla, we too feel and observe that "the most devastating and humiliating scourge" (no. 29) in Guatemala is the situation of dehumanizing poverty suffered by the campesinos (Guatemalan peasants) who painfully bring forth from Guatemalan soil a daily sustenance for themselves and their families. Rightfully called dehumanizing, this poverty is expressed by a high rate of illiteracy, by the mortality rate, by the lack of housing adequate to the dignity of the family, by unemployment and underemployment, by malnutrition and by other ills which we have carried with us for years.

1.1.1   The pitiable conditions lead us to question a system that produces inequities between those who enjoy possession of the goods of the earth even unto excess, and those who possess nothing or almost nothing. This breach between classes continues to widen, even amidst a people who profess to be Christian.

1.1.2   This is not the first time that we Guatemalan Bishops have denounced this injustice and labeled it as contrary to the Salvific Plan of God, our Father. Nor is this the first time that we have declared this the great challenge of our time in history, and that this margination endured by so many human beings is an appeal to us as people and as Christians. In our pastoral letters, we have already pointed out in the light of the Gospel that such an abysmal situation is not an accidental stage but rather the product of a sinful situation which is preventing a viable solution to the problem.

1.1.3   Gravity of the Agricultural Problem

1.1.3.1   We seriously want to invite faithful Christians and people of good will to reflect upon the critical nature of the poverty and misery endured by campesinos, because we are convinced that no situation is so painful and calls more urgently for resolution. There are many problems afflicting our brothers and sisters in the rural areas in their long calvary of suffering. However, their dispossession of the land should be considered the nucleus of the social problem in Guatemala.

1.1.3.2   It is a fact that the majority of arable land is in the hands of a privileged few, while the majority of campesinos own no plot of land on which to sow their crops. This situation, far from pointing toward a solution, becomes day by day more harsh and painful. Certainly the critical problem of land ownership is at the very heart of the propagation of injustice.

1.2   *Political System of Land Ownership from Colonial Times to Present*

1.2.1   To attempt to get to the bottom of the social problem and its roots, we must recognize that the present situation has its origins in the system of land ownership imposed in colonial times. This is preserved with many of its flaws, vices, and structures of unequal and unjust distribution even to our own times.

1.2.2   During the colonial period, the policy of land ownership was determined by a two-pronged principle. On the one hand, giving over of large land extensions to a group of colonizers favored by the Spanish crown with "encomiendas" and "royal possessions" and on the other hand by exploiting the unpaid Indian labor force for the sake of production, the people could cultivate land for themselves.

1.2.3   The period of independence, far from actually resolving these problems, accentuated by its arbitrary laws the concentration of land in the hands of the privileged few.

1.2.4   The situation was aggravated by the liberal reform of 1871 which, in order to promote coffee production, discouraged communal lands and the distributing of vast land extensions among a middle class, giving origin to a powerful class of agricultural exporters.

1.2.5   During what has been called the second revolutionary government (1950 to 1954), a careful agrarian reform process was begun which, although flawed, has been the only serious attempt to modify an unjust structure. We all know the reaction which this produced among its detractors and how it was abruptly ended.

1.3   Unequal Distribution of the Land

1.3.1   No one can deny the excessive inequality present today in regard to land ownership. The agrarian problem in Guatemala at the present time can be measured by merely considering the large landed estates and the small farms on the margin of which the great majority of campesinos who own no plot of land are situated.

1.3.2   Statistics drawn from the 1973 Agricultural Census demonstrate a dangerous concentration of land in a few hands with the majority of the population devoted to agriculture who are without adequate portions of land for tilling. The number of small landholders who own one block or less grew from 85,053 in 1964 to 247,090 in 1979. On the other hand, ever more land is concentrated in ever fewer hands, since the number of large landholders owning 855,800 acres (200 "caballerias") or more decreased from 9 to 4 between 1964 and 1979.

According to data from the Third National Agricultural Census of 1979, the distribution by number and area of farms in Guatemala is as presented in the following chart:

Number and Size of Farms in Guatemala - 1979				
Type of Farm	Number	Percent	Area (# of blocks)	Percent
Minifarms★	240,132	39.69	81,316	1.38
Subfamily farms	301,736	49.87	890,229	15.15
Family farms	79,509	8.19	1,115,739	18.98
Medium multifamily farms	13,179	2.18	2,596,551	44.18
Large multifamily farms	478	0.07	1,193,611	20.31
TOTAL	605,031	100.00	5,877,446	100.00

★Includes farms smaller than a plot of 625 square yards.

This chart shows that 39% of the mini-farms constitute but 1.38% of the total land area in farms. The situation is even more striking if it is taken into account that 89.56% of the farms (minifarms and subfamily farms) constitute but 16.53% of the land area, while 2.25% of the farms (multifamily farms and large farms) constitute 64.51% of the area.

1.3.3   Such unequal land distribution results inevitably in grave socio-economic consequences and, above all, in a situation of violence among Guatemalan farmers.

1.4   *Socio-Economic Consequences of Inequity in Land Ownership and Distribution*

1.4.1   Breach Between Rich and Poor, Between Large Landowners and Small Landowners, Between Agricultural Exporters and Campesinos

1.4.1.1   The agricultural export sector, owning huge and fertile land areas, holds the best arable lands and the means of agricultural production. This elite in Guatemala produces and sells the goods which then receive the highest prices in the international market. These include coffee, cardamon, cotton, bananas, cattle, and other traditional exports. This sector's economic solvency permits it to mechanize its cultivation process and to encounter bank credits with great facility. It must be recognized that it is the agricultural export sector which contributes most to obtaining the foreign exchange so urgently needed by Guatemala and which creates large numbers of jobs.

1.4.1.2   In contrast, there are very few campesino landowners, since the majority own no land. Those who do are devoted to subsistence farming on mini-plots where they sow only corn and beans. Large numbers find themselves obliged to rent land and are the victims of unfair speculation or are compelled to go down to the coast in unacceptable conditions. The difficulty of obtaining bank credits and the lack of adequate technical preparation leads them to exploit the land according to archaic systems, some of which are very damaging to the ecology. The majority do not benefit from any insurance system, nor do they have any possibilities of saving, so that a drought or a bad winter brings them to the brink of starvation and death.

1.4.2   Margination of the Campesino

1.4.2.1   It is no secret that the Guatemalan campesino is caught in a situation of desperate margination. The goods and services which the State is obliged to provide to all Guatemalans never reach the majority: neither do elementary school nor informal education; neither sanitary assistance nor any social security; nor any housing that has a modicum of hygiene and dignity.

1.4.2.2 Campesinos have extreme difficulty in trying to move beyond their marginalization because of scant opportunities, lack of preparation, and due to the very structure of Guatemalan society which is organized for the benefit of a minority and with no regard for the vast majority of Guatemalans. It has come to seem natural for us to see the campesino or Indian dressed in rags, sick, dirty, and despised. We call the damp, unlivable, and unsanitary shacks "folklore" and tourist attractions. We are not shocked to see tiny children trudging off with their machete or hoe early in the morning beside the men, to carry out a hard and poorly paid day's work. We fail to react before the shameful spectacle of thousands of Indian peasants transported to the coastal plantations in trucks without security or even minimal comfort. This attitude on the part of those of us who are not campesinos toward our Guatemalan brothers and sisters is but a reflection of our Nation's social and economic structure. The constitutional precept which establishes the equality of all citizens is not honored. Public funds are principally aimed for the benefit of those of us who use the highways, airports, electric lights, universities, and hospitals. There are several million Guatemalans who don't benefit from these services, although they have contributed their share of taxes, have been obliged to do military service and to lose millions of work-hours in the Civil Defense Patrols. A huge social debt weighs upon the entire Nation.

1.4.3   Exploitation of Campesinos

1.4.3.1   In our society the campesino is frequently exploited in a ruthless and inhumane way. The campesino continues to be the cheapest and most cruelly exploited labor force. It is obvious that the legal minimum wage of Q4.50 ($1.50) is insufficient nowadays, given the high cost of living. And, although there are some employers who pay more than the minimum legal wage and organize a system of loans and benefits, many still resist paying even the minimum wage. Then there are those who find a way to get around it, taking advantage of the extreme need in which the campesinos find themselves. To argue these cases for the law of supply and demand is, from every point of view, unjust and inhumane. Human work is not a marketable item!

1.4.3.2   Some people's attitudes toward campesinos are so harsh that in order to increase their profits, they go as far as eradicating the "mozo colono" tradition (one's right to work a given piece of land on a plantation or farm because one's family has served the plantation/farm for generations). This pre-capitalist, anachronistic and paternalistic relationship provides the campesino, who has lived for generations on a particular plantation, a certain statute guaranteeing him a kind of stability and right to work on that property and to continue cultivating certain strips of land for his own use. Certainly this represents a burden to the employer or owner, because it carries with it some minimal social responsibilities and honors certain rights. Even this, miserable and imperfect as it is, they seek to wipe out. Many landowners exert pressures and resort to clever tricks, not excluding armed violence, to discourage the "mozos colonos" and to force these campesinos to leave the farm in which they and their parents and grandparents were born and where they have established their home. It just so happens that it is easier and less complicated to bring in work crews each year at harvest time in a system which adds to the impoverishment of campesinos.

Over the course of many decades, a grave problem has been generated in Guatemala by those who work as intermediaries and/or negotiators of legal-administrative matters before government institutions, as by middle-men in agricultural commerce, those who hire or bring in laborers. These, too, participate in the exploitation of campesinos and in their impoverishment. It can be said that this is an institutionalized problem, since it is commonly accepted by the society. It is sad to see that even liberal professionals, unscrupulous businessmen, and landowners participate in these schemes which deepen the wounds of their own people.

1.4.4   Dirth of Legal Help for Defending the Campesino's Rights to Land

1.4.4.1 We should not be surprised that this unjust social situation is one of the reasons why campesinos flee from their places of origin and migrate to the city, seeing it as a refuge from their misery and as a possible solution to their extreme poverty. The campesino thus arrives in town or city, swelling the ranks of the unemployed, multiplying the slum areas, and many times falling into the webs and vice of delinquency. It is not unusual that campesinos also lose the only possession they have left, their Catholic faith. In this way millions of campesino families have been violently forced to flee their lands to seek refuge beyond their own homeland. The grave problems which municipalities face in providing indispensable public services will continue to increase daily as campesinos abandon their "trabajaderos" (workplaces). Simultaneously hospital health service, educational service in government schools, and all public services generally will become more inadequate and insufficient.

1.4.5   Growing Violence in the Countryside

1.4.5.1 Violence in the rural area is common. The very situation of desperation is a source of many tensions that are a shout of protest and a cry of desperation from hundreds of thousands of people. Nothing is solved if we merely try to place blame on agitators or leaders, since the root of the evil is in the social situation itself. All of us inhabitants of our country must open our eyes to the gravity of the problem.

1.4.5.2   We observe joyfully that the campesinos are daily reaching a greater awareness of their rights and of their own dignity. This is an irreversible move forward and, despite the continuing and brutal repression to which they have been subjected, theirs is a legitimate cry and action in defense of the land.

But we fear that without proper accommodation for these hopes and if mechanisms are not established for responding quickly and effectively to their request, an outburst of violence may result with unforeseen consequences. We have in mind the painful case of Panzos in Alta Verapaz. It is a tragedy and a crime which we still remember and condemn, since we know well that just ten years ago more than a hundred Kek'chi Indians were massacred over land problems. This could happen again in any place and at any moment. The multitudinous demonstrations held in many parts of Guatemala are an indication of the troublesome situation in the rural area. Because of it, we repeat again with Pope John Paul II: "To forestall any extremism and to consolidate an authentic peace, there is no better way than to return their dignity to those who suffer injustice, contempt and misery" (John Paul II, Homily at Campo de Marte, March 7, 1983, 6).

In the light of God's Word and the Church Magisterium, we want to offer to the faithful and to all people of good will a word of guidance regarding the Christian meaning of land ownership.

2.0   Theological Insights

2.1   *Sacred Scripture*

2.1.1   The Earth, a Gift of God

In the Bible the subject of land is important, because from the dawn of creation to the Apocalypse the human person develops in a particular land, God's gift and the habitation of God with people.

Scripture describes for us the origin of humanity, saying that it was created in the image of God (Gn 1:26). This is the theological basis for human dignity. God also blessed that humanity created as man and woman (Gn 1:27) that it might multiply, filling and submitting the earth. The fruits of the earth were given them as food (Gn 1:27). The earth is, then, according to God's plan, humanity's world.

Man and woman belong to the earth (Gn 2:7) and it belongs to them because right after creating them God charges them with tilling and caring for the earth (Gn 2:15). Thus farmwork appears as the essential task defining and situating the human person in the world and before God.

2.1.2 Shared Joy

Many Scripture texts express humanity's joy at the fruit of their labors on the earth and their gratitude to God for the divine blessing. When the earth gives its harvest, men and women know that God is blessing them (Ps 67:7; 85:13).

The joy with which people gather up the first fruits and conclude the harvest was in the ancient people of God an occasion for the family to make a pilgrimage to the sanctuary of the Lord and to celebrate there a fiesta in God's honor (Dt 16:1-15).

These agricultural feasts, continued now in the completely new light of our Christian Easter and Pentecost feasts, teach us to rejoice before the Lord for the goods of the earth, and show us that we should share with those who have less the abundance with which God has blessed us.

2.1.3 The Earth a Sign of Covenant Between God and Humanity

The Lord promises his oppressed people in Egypt that God will guide them to a good and spacious land yielding milk and honey (Ex 3:8). Thus the promise made to Abraham is gathered up again (Gn 12:1).

When the Israelite offered the first fruits of the earth, he remembered that the earth and those fruits were a gift from God (Dt 26:9-10). When the people came into possession of the earth, each tribe was assigned its territory according to its inhabitants: "You shall increase the legacy of the numerous and reduce that of the meager" (Nm 26:54). In this way no individual nor tribe will come into possession of the land by depriving others of their livelihood.

The earth does not belong to men but to the Lord, and what each one calls his property is in reality the portion to which he is entitled in order to make a living. The earth is the Lord's and the bounty thereof, the world and those who inhabit therein (Ps 24:1).

2.1.4 A Prophetic Denouncing of Sin

The voice of the prophets was raised to denounce those who hoarded the earth with greed to the detriment of the poor and destitute: "Woe unto you who gather house upon house and field upon field, annexing until you occupy the whole place and are the sole inhabitants of the country! Thus has the Lord of hosts sworn to my ears: "Many great and beautiful homes shall be left abandoned, without inhabitants" (Is 5:8-9). "Woe unto those who meditate upon evil. They covet fields and steal them, homes and usurp them, they do violence to a man and to his house, to an individual and his inheritance. Behold I am preparing an hour of misfortune against you who do this from which you shall never escape" (Mi 2:1-2).

The prophet's voice was also raised against those who did not pay or who gave unjust wages to their workers: "Woe unto the one who builds his house without justice and his foundations without righteousness! He takes advantage of his neighbor and does not pay the neighbor for his work" (Jer 22:13). These are those who, "resting upon marble beds, lounging upon their couches, drink wine from large cups, anoint themselves with the best of perfumes, but care nothing for the ruin of my people" (Am 6:4-6).

This denunciation of avarice and of the excessive wealth attained by the hoarding of land and by the paying of unjust wages is also repeated in the New Testament writings. "You rich, weep and cry out over the disgraces which are about to fall upon you! Look, the salary you have not paid to the workers who harvested your fields is shouting, and the cries of the harvesters have reached the ears of the Lord of hosts. You have lived in luxury upon the earth and given yourselves over to pleasures" (Jas 5:1, 4-5).

2.1.5   Jesus the Poor Points Out to the Wealthy Their Responsibility

Jesus, the Son of God, Lord of heaven and earth, has nowhere to lay his head (Lk 9:58). He being rich, became poor for our sake. This poverty freed him to carry out his mission: "To evangelize the poor" (Lk 4:18).

Jesus does not present himself as a judge or arbiter in the distribution of legacies. On one occasion he rejects such a request in order to make evident that earthly goods do not guarantee one's existence.

Then he tells the parable of the man whose fields gave forth such an abundant harvest that he had to put up new, much larger grain bins in order to store it. He thought that with this he would have enough to live for many years, but that night he died (Lk 12:13-21). This is why Jesus also calls down woe upon the rich and upon those who are full (Lk 6:24-25). And he describes money as "unjust" (Lk 16:9) when there is at the origin of great wealth the exploitation of the weak. That is why Jesus commands the rich who want to follow him to place their wealth at the service of the needy: *"Sell what you have and give alms"* (Lk 12:33).

The concept of "alms," so frequent in the New Testament, should be correctly understood. It was an ancient practice by which the most powerful members of a population took charge of the neediest in the community—the orphans, widows, strangers—providing for them a means of subsistence. The concept, then, expresses the moral responsibility of one who has more toward those without possessions (Dt 15:7-8; 10, 11).

2.1.6   The Paschal Mystery of Christ Transforms Creation

The New Testament affirms that the world was created by the One who is the Word of God and that without Him nothing of what exists was created (Jn 1:3). This Word of God became flesh, truly a human being in Jesus (Jn 1:14). In such a way Jesus can be called the "first-born of all creation." It is not that He was the first of creatures, but that all that exists finds its meaning in Him, "because in Him were created all things and everything was created by Him and for Him" (Col 1:15, 16).

Because of this, Christ's redeeming work affects not only the group of believers of humanity alone; but rather by his death and resurrection, Christ reconciled all things with God, "pacifying, by the blood of His cross, everything on earth and in the heavens" (Col 1:20). Christ's Paschal Mystery has transformed human beings from sinners to the just who live for God (Rom 6:11). But creation has been redeemed, too, together with people, and groans in "the hope of being freed from its servitude to corruption in order to participate in the glorious freedom of the children of God" (Rom 8:20-21). This liberation begins for creation when the goods of the earth cease to be instruments of human rivalry and exploitation in order to become a means of friendship and communion.

2.1.7 The Earth and Wealth at the Service of Friendship

The effect of the transformation brought about by Christ's Paschal Mystery is palpable in the first Christian community called together by the Risen Lord in the power of the Spirit. It is true that in this community there is deceit and sin, as in the case of Ananias and Safira (Acts 5:1-11); however, the testimony of friendship prevails, a friendship which unites all the believers: "the multitude of believers had but one heart and a single soul. No one called their belongings their own, but rather everything was held in common among them. . . . There was in their midst no one in need, because all those who had fields or homes sold them, brought in the money from the sale and set it at the feet of the apostles, and they distributed it to each one according to their need" (Acts 4:32-35).

Faith in the Risen Lord and the friendship which thus results lead to a new earth in which justice is at home (2 Pt 3:13). "At that time there will be a new heaven and a new earth where there shall be no death nor tears, nor cries nor fatigue, because the old world shall have passed away" (Apoc 21:1-4).

That hope should encourage our awareness today so that in the meantime we may make of this earth a place of togetherness in justice and equity.

2.2   *Fathers of the Church and the Magisterium*

2.2.1 The Social Purpose of Property

The biblical teaching concerning land ownership has been studied and reflected upon in depth since the Church began. The Holy Fathers have left us an impressive wealth of thought and examples of action on topics such as the meaning of property, the role of earthly goods, and the demands of social justice.

The Church has always recognized the right of all people to own property sufficient for themselves and for their family (PP 22). However, this right to property "constitutes for no one an unconditional and absolute right. There is no reason to reserve for one's own exclusive use that goes beyond our need while others are lacking essentials" (PP 23).

This is the teaching which, like a river of pure water, flows through the history of the Church and which, in the recent period of Vatican Council II and under recent popes in their social encyclicals has been repeated tirelessly. "God has destined the earth and everything she contains for the use of all human beings and all people" (GS 69).

There is special vigor in the thought expressed by John Paul II during his inaugural address at the Third General Conference of Latin American Bishops: "Upon all private property there is a grave *social responsibility*" (literally, a social *mortgage*) (III, 4). Because of this, the right to private property is not an absolute right, but rather a conditional one, limited by a broader and more universal principle: God has created all things for the use and benefit of all human beings, with no distinction whatsoever.

2.2.2   Land for All

The Holy Fathers have also referred directly to land distribution. Thus, for example, St. Ambrose declares: "It is not part of your (own) goods that you give to the poor, but rather what belongs to them. Because you have appropriated to yourself what was given for the use of everyone. The earth has been given for the whole world and not merely for the wealthy" (From Nabuthe, ch. 12, no. 53: P1 14, 747, cit. PP 23). St. John Chrysostum is even more explicit: "God never made some rich and others poor. God gave the earth to everyone. The whole earth belongs to the Lord, and the fruits of the earth should be available (lit. "common") to all. "The 'mine' and 'thine' are motive and cause for discord. Community of goods is therefore a form of existence more adequate to our nature than is private property itself.

During his apostolic trips to Latin America, Pope John Paul II has been able to see and touch our reality and, since having this direct experience, he has strengthened Church doctrine on the subject of land.

When he experienced personally that a timid application of doctrinal principles resulted in conflictive social situations in which a large number of people had no access to the goods necessary for their human fulfillment, he expressed to the campesinos in Cuilapan, Mexico, the need for profound reforms: "As for you who are responsible for (whole) peoples, you powerful classes who sometimes hold uncultivated the land that hides a daily bread needed by so many: the human conscience, the conscience of nations, the cry of the destitute, and above all the Voice of God, the voice of the Church repeat with me: It is not just, nor is it human, nor Christian to continue on with certain situations which are clearly unjust" (no. 9).

In Recife, Brazil, John Paul II said to the farmers: "The earth is a gift from God, a gift God makes to every human being, men and women, whom God wants gathered together in a single family and related to one another with a spirit of friendship. It is not right, therefore, because it is not in harmony with God's plan, to use this gift in such a way that the earth's benefits favor just a few, leaving others, the immense majority, excluded" (Homily at the Mass celebrated for farmers, no. 4).

Today Guatemalan campesinos have an ever clearer awareness that they live in what Leo XIII and Paul VI called *undeserved misery* (9, 67). Because of this, they are raising their voices from all over the country, urging those responsible for the nation to "put into effect daring and profoundly innovative transformations . . . to bring about, without further delay, urgent reforms" (John Paul II to the campesinos in Cuilapan, no. 6) so that the goods created by God may reach everyone with equity, according to the rule of justice, inseparable from charity.

3.1   Pastoral Conclusions

3.1.1   Throughout these reflections we have reviewed the injustices the unequal land ownership in Guatemala engenders. We also have tried to sketch in the light of scriptural reflection and Church teaching, the divine plan for God's children. As shepherds of the Church in Guatemala, we have the grave obligation given us by our ministry to denounce the situation which is at the root of our dehumanizing poverty. We Christians should not only concern ourselves with the problems of our nation, but above all "involve ourselves" in them. The first step will be to become aware of the situation suffered by our campesino brothers and sisters.

3.1.2   Repetition of a Pastoral Denunciation
As we pointed out in 1984: "An evil distribution of property, immense extensions of uncultivated or insufficiently cultivated land make of our people a hungry, sickly people with a high mortality rate" (Message of the Guatemalan Episcopate, May 9, 1984).

3.1.3   In Pope John Paul II's Encyclical "Laborem Exercens," we read a description/denunciation which finds in Guatemala a desperate case in point: "In some developing countries, millions of people find themselves obliged to cultivate others' land and are exploited by large landowners, with no hope of managing to own some day even a tiny plot of land of their own. Long working days of heavy physical labor are paid miserably. Cultivated lands are abandoned by their owners, legal titles for possession of a small plot, cultivated over many years are not taken into account or are without defense in the face of the 'hunger for land' of more powerful individuals and groups" (LE 21).

3.1.4 Futile Cry of the Campesino

All these situations naturally provoke the outcry of the campesinos for their rights; but we know (because we have such recent experience that we cannot forget it) that the campesinos' cry has been stifled by the power of arms. Thousands of campesinos have been killed in Guatemala merely for having attempted a change of structure. Since then, as a result of this terrible repression suffered by Guatemalans, campesino organizations of whatever type are viewed with suspicion and there are no lack of coercive measures to suppress them. At this level there should be mentioned the role—forced (compliance) in practice—of the Civil Defense Patrols which enormously limit the campesinos' right of association. It is not unusual to learn that campesinos have been hunted down or "disappeared." This list has become by now one of the most shameful and tragic in our history.

3.1.5 Dirth of Legal Backing

Unfortunately, as we pointed out above, there is a painful lack of legislation when it comes to defending the campesino and his rights or to really promoting them effectively. On the contrary, Guatemalan legislation seems designed to maintain a system of land ownership which benefits the large landowner and those who control economic and military power to the detriment of the campesinos and Indians. This legislation forms the basis and the legal framework for the unjust situation experienced in Guatemala, as we already stated several years ago in our Pastoral Letter, "United in Hope."

3.2 Episcopal Guidelines

3.2.1 This entire list of negative circumstances cannot cause us as Christians to remain passive out of disappointment or discouragement. Our response must be a positive one. Evil and all its consequences have been overcome by Christ, who triumphed over sin and death. It is up to us to take this redemption to the sinful structures of our national situation.

3.2.2 Invitation to Solidarity

3.2.2.1 But this is a task that can only be carried out effectively if all of us do our part generously. Because of this, the first requirement is *solidarity*. Only insofar as we feel ourselves brothers and sisters in solidarity with one another can such a critical problem as the ownership and exploitation of land in Guatemala find channels for solution. Solidarity is the opposite of egotistical individualism, since it makes us think

"AND GOD SAW THAT IT WAS GOOD"

of others at the same time as we think of our own needs. It makes us seek a solution to the problems of our neighbors. It has its basis in the Christian meaning of friendship, since solidarity is based precisely on a fundamental truth of Christianity: we are all brothers and sisters because we are children of the same God, we are gifted with the same dignity, we enjoy the same rights, and we are called to the same glorification with God.

3.2.2.2   At times of crisis, such as the one we are living in Guatemala, there is a tendency to forget everyone else and just try to save ourselves ("salvese quien pueda") which kills all sense of solidarity and throws people into a frenetic search for egotistical satisfactions leading to extremes of consumerism. We must react against such an orientation in our life and action, appealing to the great principles of our faith.

3.2.3   Integral Development

3.2.3.1   Another important aspect in the search for genuine and adequate solutions to the grave problems of land ownership is the effort to reach a high degree of development. But this will be not merely an economic development. Rather, it should be an authentic integral human and social development as expressed by Pope Paul VI in his encyclical "The Progress of Peoples," no. 35.

We should struggle so that this development may reach everyone, not just a privileged group. Development should reach the entire people.

3.2.3.2   If any sector should be privileged, let it be the campesino or Indian people, not simply because it is the majority of the Guatemalan population, but also because of a basic sense of justice, in order to compensate in some way for the centuries of abandonment they have endured, as if they were citizens of a second or inferior class. Guatemala will not progress as it should as long as, with inconceivable myopia, it tries to keep marginated the campesino and worker sectors, "the dynamizing force in the building up of a more participative society" (Puebla, 1245).

In effect, this has been one of the causes of Guatemala's greatest tragedy; preventing, out of egotism and irrational fear, the full use of the campesino potential to make the land produce abundantly.

If this sleeping giant is not invited and prepared to participate in the building up of a better Guatemala, it will awaken embittered by the contempt heaped upon it over many centuries and may become a source of even more painful and violent conflict.

3.2.4 Justice, Change of Social Structure

3.2.4.1 The Need and Urgency of Social Change

Nothing we have spoken of can come about unless we accept the idea that a change of sinful and obsolete social structures is necessary and urgent in Guatemala. We want to make our own the strong words of John Paul II in his historic message at Oaxaca, Mexico in 1979: "Real, efficacious measures must be put in practice at the local, national, and international levels along the broad lines set out in the Encyclical *Mater et Magistra.*"

3.2.4.2 The pope invites us to follow the broad guidelines set out by John XXII's encyclical *Mater et Magistra* which has been called the campesinos' "Magna Carta." This encyclical, in effect, highlights the emphasis that should be given to the agricultural sector when it says: "Now in order to attain a proportionate development among the different sectors of the economy, it is also absolutely essential [that there be] an economic policy in regard to farming, followed by public, political, and economic authorities, who must deal with the following areas: fiscal responsibility (taxation), credits, social security, prices, publicity, and complementary industries and, finally, the perfecting of the farming enterprise structure" (MM 131).

3.2.4.3 In harmony with Church doctrine and with the needs of Guatemala, the following measures, urgently needed to improve the situation, may be highlighted:

1. To legislate in view of an equitable land distribution, beginning with the vast government properties and "properties insufficiently cultivated, in favor of those able to make them fruitful" (GS 71).

2. To facilitate the presenting of additional titles for lands which the campesinos have been cultivating for years.

3. To guarantee legally the defense of campesinos and refugees so that they will not be stripped of their lands.

4. To defend the campesinos against speculation in the renting of lands to be cultivated.

5. To assure that campesinos receive a just and equitable price, protecting them from voracious and unscrupulous middlemen.

6. To give an adequate farming education to the greatest possible number of campesinos, so that they may improve their methods of cultivating and may be able to diversify their crops.

7. To grant the greatest possible facilities for bank credits and for acquiring seeds, fertilizers, and other materials and farming tools needed.

8. To increase the salary of the campesinos in accord with human dignity and their family responsibilities.

9. To open up channels and to create mechanisms so that the campesino can participate actively and directly in the local, regional, national, and even international marketplace.

10. To diminish the indirect taxes on the purchasing of products for farmwork.

11. To create direct taxes for large land extensions proportionate to the size of the lands.

12. To organize some kind of protective measures for campesinos against poor harvests and work accidents.

13. To stimulate and protect campesino organizations in defense of their rights and to increase their farm production.

3.2.5   Christian Characteristics in the Change of Structures

3.2.5.1   Nonviolence

We cannot resort to violence because it is neither evangelical nor Christian, but rather generates further violence in an endless spiral. As Christians, we have more confidence in the power of those who are nonviolent than in the brute force of those who place all their trust in armed homicides.

3.2.5.2   Legal Framework

A second characteristic is that the change of structures should be brought about legally. We advocate an adequate legislation which takes as its goal the common welfare and defense of the campesino who, as we have pointed out repeatedly, is in practice the weakest, poorest, and most defenseless sector in our society. We are convinced that measures which are in fact outside the law aggravate the problem (like invading land—far from solving the agrarian problem, increase it) and lead to explosions which are impossible to control.

3.2.5.3   The Urgency of Change

We Christians are peaceful and builders of peace. We trust in the foundation of the law, in the value of what is reasonable, and above all, in the transforming power of love. And based upon this conviction, we demand that the changes which are indispensable for seeking adequate solutions to such an enormous problem be carried out urgently though without the haste which might diminish the reasonableness, efficacy, and credibility of the measures. We are aware that something which has been structured over the course of many centuries cannot be changed overnight. However, it is essential to delay no longer than necessary, as delay might aggravate the agrarian problem even further.

4.0   Conclusions

4.1   We have tried to promote a reflection which is deep, serene, sincere, and constructive on one of the most serious and complex problems in our Guatemalan panorama. In our judgment, this is the fundamental problem in the social structure of Guatemala. To solve it will mean having achieved, through a difficult but patriotic process, a basic change in Guatemalan history.

4.2   We have thus shed light on this reality with the Word of God and the teaching of the Church, demonstrating that it is not something foreign to our pastoral mission, but rather something that falls within the lines of our work as shepherds of the Church. Neither the sufferings nor the errors of the people entrusted to us can be beyond our concern.

For all these reasons, we have the hope that our faithful will read this Pastoral Letter attentively and will study it, trying to discover the very positive perspective that it offers for the future of our Guatemala. We also have the hope that everyone will commit themselves with a fraternal spirit to carrying out the tremendous task implied in finding an adequate and peaceful solution to such a grave problem.

Our pastoral invitation is sent with great hope to the government, to political parties, to Guatemala's productive forces, to the means of social communication, and to the private sector; also to Catholic lay movements and to the Indians and campesinos, inviting them to join forces fraternally and peacefully in an effort which calls for the commitment of every Guatemalan.

4.3   We recognize that in the final analysis the most difficult thing is personal conversion. Conversion means a "turning around," a radical change. As long as one's only goal is profit, to grow rich, ambition for money or power, it is impossible to understand these truths which we have desired to bring to mind, and to see with Christian eyes the reality which must be transformed.

4.4   We have presented the human and moral aspects of the problem rather than delving more deeply into the technical and practical aspects which go beyond our mission. Our pastoral service is limited to a posing of the problem in the light of human dignity, the common good, and Christian love.

4.5   In concluding this letter, we ask God, through the intercession of the Virgin Mary, mother of all people, who moves our hearts and illumines our understanding, that setting aside every violent, revengeful, and biased attitude, we may give a worthy, courageous, and Christian response to the tremendous *"cry for land."*

Guatemala de la Asuncion, February 29, 1988

(Followed by the signatures of **Próspero Penados del Barrio,** Archbishop of Guatemala, **Rodolfo Quezada Toruño,** President of the Guatemalan Episcopal Conference, and the Bishops of Guatemala.)

ECOLOGY:
THE BISHOPS
OF LOMBARDY
ADDRESS
THE
COMMUNITY

The Catholic Bishops of Northern Italy

Introduction

Every human being has the fundamental right to live in an environment suitable to his health and well being.[1] This declaration of basic human right shows the importance that must be attributed on a global scale to the environmental question. The problem of the relationship between man and the environment, presented to public understanding as "the ecological crisis," is one of the most acute and well publicized in modern society.[2] It involves scientists, economists, social workers, and scholars of ethics; governments and international organizations. It has extended beyond the confines of narrow, specialized circles of scientific experts and special interest groups to become an issue of interest, of criticism, and of evaluation throughout the population.

As it has occurred with many other themes of an ethical and social nature—such as the problems of peace, of disarmament, of the development and liberation of third world countries, of the status of young people, of the emancipation of women, and so forth—the environmental issue is also imposing itself on Christian reflection and upon ecclesiastical sensibility; it has once and for all entered the centers of theological research and absolutely can not be separated any longer from pastoral practice.

The environmental movements then, in noteworthy manner, stir up a resounding consensus in the circles of Catholic associations, often involving the young, who are encouraged by the example of Saint Francis and the Franciscan tradition, which is interpreted as a Christian contribution toward a more ecologically oriented culture.

The pontifical teaching of John Paul II has often touched on the theme of the relationship between man and the environment, consistently emphasizing the protection and defense of human life. Here we can recall two texts which seem especially significant: the one found in no. 15 of the *Redemptor Hominis* (The Redeemer of Man), and the longer and more elaborate text of no. 34 in *Sollicitudo Rei Socialis* (Concern for Social Matters).

In this broader ecclesiastical horizon, as Bishops of the Churches of Lombardy, we believe it is opportune to make a statement in order to aid and sustain the conscience of Christians in a dutiful effort of discernment. This will also submit the grave problem of the environment's decline to critical evaluation in light of the Christian vision, which situates man at the center of the world and the environment.

With this perspective, the attentive Christian conscience becomes important for the ecological cause. The Christian conscience must assume a critical and culturally informed view, equally avoiding quick cliches from the mass media or stereotyped assumptions about the religious texts typically associated with a Christian vision of creation.

Despite the simplifications in the mass media, the issues of ecology show themselves to be of great complexity. The seriousness of the ecological predicament leads discussion toward a reevaluation of the form of Western civilization, and it opens the door to a critique of society, both theoretical and practical, which seeks to find alternative ways of living.

The complexity of this question can be compared to a variety of topics which can be considered theoretically and addressed practically. Let us focus in particular upon areas of social and political activity, of moral conscience for the individual person, and of the perspective of the Church itself. Among these diverse areas, one senses that an active discussion should occur, but without blurring or neglecting necessary distinctions.

In the framework of such a complexity to the problems of the environment, this intervention in a Pastoral Letter by the Bishops of the Lombard Church is necessary; it is clear in its objective; and it is required by the pastoral nature of the ecological problem.

"AND GOD SAW THAT IT WAS GOOD"

The ecological problem does not require immediate political solutions. Neither are theological theses necessary on the relationship between man and nature. What is needed is to strengthen the conscience of Christians to develop personal reflection, while at the same time maintaining a historically and socially grounded understanding of our region, and maintaining a consistent tradition of faith.

The Threatened Environment: Symptoms and Causes

1. Resource Depletion and Pollution

Man's activity often produces obvious damage to the environment. Nevertheless a false belief persists in public thinking that the environment is a fountain of almost unlimited resources. This misconception does not respect, conserve or protect nature from an arrogant exploitation by society. This belief, more or less conscious, is nonetheless operative. It is, however, confronted by the emergence of threats of impoverishment, and, in some cases, the depletion of natural resources (some non-renewable), and also by the danger in which we place numerous living species, hundreds of thousands of plants and animals, and countless micro-organisms, many of which have not yet even been studied.

This depletion affects resources that are diverse and of varied economic importance. This should be considered in relation to the real damage caused by the impoverishment of the life forms existing on the planet. This is true, not only for ecosystem equilibrium, but also for the benefits that society derives from them.

The prospect of energy resource depletion, even though it is a different situation, does not make it a problem of minor significance as it relates both to the quality of human life and to its appropriate development.

The problem of pollution or environmental deterioration is linked to the previous considerations, relating to natural resources, to existing plant and animal species, and to energy resources. This problem of pollution involves the essential components of human life—air, water and soil. Here the deteriorating and ruinous consequences are macroscopic (i.e., regional or global in effect). It is sufficient just to consider the increase of carbon dioxide in the atmosphere, the acid rain, the reduction of the ozone layer, and the pollution of surface waters, lakes and rivers. The waters of the rivers which border our land of Lombardy, beginning with the Po, are in various stages of degradation and despoilment, from poisoned to at least seriously deteriorated from severe environmental breakdowns.

Among the causes that have disturbed the equilibrium of the environment, three seem the most prominent: the implications of agricultural production, the increases in industrial production and the specialized trades, and the demand for energy.

Agriculture constitutes a primary influence on the environment, and in its turn, depending on circumstances, could be considered either a victim or a cause of the environmental decline.

The growth of world population has undoubtedly posed problems for the development of agriculture. For rich countries the demands of agriculture mean increasing and improving the food supply and providing greater consumer and social benefits. For poor countries, it is a problem of satisfying a basic right to a food supply, which not only allows for survival but provides for growth in a harmonious manner.

The agriculture of Lombardy can be characterized as one of high yield and high specialization. It needs however to rely upon an ever increasing use of chemical fertilizers to improve soil fertility and in some cases upon pesticides. These chemical additives have their own rationale and are understandable, but they do not succeed because they contaminate the underground aquifer and they constitute a grave hazard to our health through the food chain.

Throughout Lombardy, and not just in the centers of high productivity, there can be noted a growing industrial and service presence. This, on the one hand, indicates the industriousness of the Lombardian people, but on the other hand, it shows the necessity that capital investment cannot focus solely upon increased production because it must also combat the risks of pollution.

The demand for energy is connected to the quality of human life as a primary need. However secondary needs cannot be ignored or underestimated which are connected to the structure of society. What is necessary, therefore, is to discern among the diversity of human values placed upon energy and to determine the actual energy costs that are the result of so many different uses of energy. Thus, it becomes necessary to decide at the social and political level which types of production should be discouraged, beginning with those that constitute a source of atmospheric pollution or some other serious danger to the health of man.

With environmental questions, it is also necessary to recognize population pressures and their distribution within a region. Production levels (whether industrial or agricultural), the standard of living (level of consumption), and, consequently, the effects of waste accumulation in relation to population density are proportionate to the number of inhabitants and businesses of the area.

From these different perspectives (as indicated above), Lombardy presents a conspicuously intense picture of environmental diversity. In the past twenty years our region has been at the center of a vast influx of immigration which has caused a significant increase in population. This has brought about a notable increase in housing, new businesses, automobile traffic, means of communication, and population density, all of which is significantly greater than the Italian national average. This translates into a greater pollution risk which calls us to a major responsibility and imposes the duty of an adequate grasp of conscience.

2. Ecology, Environment, Ideology

Faced with the gravity and complexity of the problems raised by environmental destruction, one naturally turns to the practices and methods appropriate to ecological action. Such a mandate brings us back to the needs of a healthy environment.

On the other hand, the environmental problem does not have only a scientifically measurable aspect because it also presents profound economic, social and ethical implications. For this reason, a global awareness of progress and development is inherent in a complete perspective on the relationship between man and the environment and this requires stringent and genuine discernment.

We recognize the important contribution that the scientific, ecological model offers for comprehension of the environment and its relation to human existence. From the perspective of methodology, this contribution of science requires a holistic view that does not reduce the significance of man and his destiny. The relationship between man and the environment, however, cannot be understood only through its biological dimension. Human life ultimately has a spiritual quality. Expression of this spiritual quality is liberty, which establishes man in a position of dominion over nature. The exercise of this dominion (or lordship) is not expressed only in the technical dimension, but also through safeguarding human dignity as a goal which concerns all of creation. As it proclaims in the Bible, *With glory and honor you have crowned him. . . . All things you have put under his feet.*[3]

These few insights are sufficient to exhort the Christian conscience to an attentive discernment of the issues amidst the multiplicity of ecological ideologies.

The urgent need for discernment manifests with particular clarity when the intricacies of politics are considered. In the first place it should be emphasized that ecological issues are not only embraced by political and environmental organizations, but they have become in varying degrees a common position of all the parties and political organizations.

On the other hand it is difficult to determine how much attention to environmental issues constitutes an appropriate amount and how much instead overemphasis risks reduction of this issue to a favorite rhetorical expedient of the mass media.

In any case it is necessary to make a careful distinction between the general approval that must be accorded to many of the social and political appeals put forth from different environmental organizations, and the disapproval that must be declared against those who attempt to use the urgency of our ecological predicament as an appeal for what are complex global, civil and political schemes.

The Relationship Between Man and the Environment

The human-environmental relationship presents complex situations to which the Christian conscience is called first to provide a clarifying principle, and then the practical responsibilities which are the consequences of those principles.

This question, when reduced to its essential elements, becomes, "In what manner should human activity alter the dynamic ecological balances so as to guarantee the survival of both the biosphere and the resources essential for human life?"

Beyond this basic question of appropriate resource utilization, the environmental crisis should be seen not just as a crisis of the land and its resources, but it should also be seen as a crisis of the underlying spiritual values.

In these days when we're accustomed to seeing only the material side of human activity, the transparency of the spiritual and eternal reality to life has become obscured. Material or economic views of nature condition a worldly attitude, both in theory and practice, about the events of society. To point out and denounce such a situation, without descending to a renewed pagan deification of nature, it is pertinent to recall briefly the Christian point of view about nature that puts faith in the teachings of the Bible.

The Blessed Earth and the Cursed Soil

O Lord, my God, how great art thou![4] The exclamation of awe, of admiration, of gratitude, bursts from the mouth of the psalmist in consideration of the cosmic spectacle. *You have established the earth on its foundations; it cannot be moved.*[5]

The stability of the earth appears as a primary and fundamental promise of God, through which is assured his faithfulness for the sake of human life. More than just stable, the earth is ordered and arranged in a manner suited for human needs. *And He molded it so that it would be inhabited,*[6] so that the psalmist could exclaim, *You have made all things in wisdom, the earth is full of your creatures.*[7]

Besides the awed voice of the psalmist, we find in the Bible voices with a different emphasis. Among these, in particular it is worth remembering the curse of the soil pronounced following the sin of Adam: *Cursed be the soil for your sake! With the sweat of your brow you shall bring forth food all the days of your life.*[8] Is this the same earth that was praised in the Psalm? How can these situations which are so different be reconciled? Perhaps the earth and all of creation show a different and contradictory face according to the times and places in which man comes to find himself? In our present time, the earth seems to be cursed in its stability and in its astonishing order and equilibrium because of the indiscriminate and arrogant proliferation of man's technological activities.

Technology pertains to those resources which man has acquired down through history as part of his dominion over nature—which corresponds to God's plan: *You have given them power over the works of thy hands; you have placed everything under their feet, all the flocks and herds, all the beasts of the field, the birds of the sky, and the fish of the sea, those that traverse the ways of deep.*[9]

The benefits that have been obtained for human life by technology and scientific research are undeniable. It is, however, necessary to be clear about the ambiguous aspects of technology. To see this clearly, one needs to correctly understand and coordinate between two different perceptions of the world that natural reality presents to human understanding: There is on the one hand that view which sees the world as a divine and God-given dwelling place, predisposed to the sustenance of human life, and on the other there is that which sees the earth as a simple inventory of material resources that awaits human enterprise to employ them effectively for the construction of a comfortable dwelling place.

To establish and clarify a few general principles, it is legitimate either to diagnose the serious dangers that threaten the environment and to itemize possible remedies to these dangers, or to itemize some ethical, cultural and political conditions for realizing solutions in practice.

Life is More than Food and Clothing

The fundamental misunderstanding that threatens the relationship between man and the resources of the earth has been denounced in a concise and penetrating manner by the Sermon on the Mount. Here the attention of the disciples is called to the model of life offered by the birds of the sky and the lilies of the field.

Concern for life, says Jesus, cannot be exchanged for the more lowly care for food, nor concern for the body with the lesser care of clothing. Is not life worth more than food and the body more than garments? This is like saying that concern for human life cannot be reduced to care for simple needs, even though gratification of those needs is an essential requirement for survival.

The gratification of bodily needs is not adequate for the fulfillment of human life. *For man does not live by bread alone; to live, man has need for the Word,*[10] and therefore for a sense of hope—which modern society earnestly seeks and which the Word of God reveals in its fullness. Yet when man exhausts this yearning for the fullness of life in a pagan preoccupation with food, clothing and many other concerns, then that pure yearning is inevitably degraded into interminable anxiety, stress and unending toil.

Of greater importance than concern for food, the Sermon on the Mount points to this further consideration: the kingdom of God and its righteousness. For whoever seeks first the kingdom of God, to him shall all other things be added. *For your heavenly Father already knows your need.*[11] In other words, he who seeks first the kingdom of God and its righteousness shall also receive a way to take care of food and clothing in accordance with methods and means capable of accommodating and caring for the transcendence of life as primary in respect to all things.

The so-called material wealth must be recognized as real wealth only on the condition that it becomes for man's conscience a symbol and token of hoped for spiritual wealth.

Take Dominion Over the Earth and Steward It

In light of the structure for human life which biblical revelation proposes, the affirmations of Genesis, which are frequently quoted but easily misunderstood when one discusses the relationship of man with the earth, need to be restated.

God creates man in his own image, so that he might *have dominion over the fish of the sea, over the fowl of the air, and over the cattle and all the wild beasts and over every creeping thing that creepeth upon the earth.*[12]

Then blessing man and woman, God entrusts them with the task of "ruling" over the earth.[13] This is a trust assigned to every generation in which man is called upon, not only to harvest the fruits of the earth, but to take care of it and to share its wealth with all peoples. The stewardship of the earth which is alluded to here must not be too quickly interpreted, almost as though it corresponded to the mastery which is realized through the power of technology. This "dominion" is laborious to accomplish, it is a "blessing," and therefore it is a gift which should inspire gratitude.

However, according to biblical tradition, the mediation of human liberty is essential in order that God's creation should realize the destiny assigned to it. But such a mediation cannot be understood in terms of the scientific-technological undertaking to have dominion over nature. Rather, this understanding consists in the ethical dimension with which man lives in relationship to nature. Further still this understanding consists in the promise of salvation which is inscribed in the earth and which God entrusts to man, and in the correspondence of his life with such a promise depending upon his obedience to His commandments.

On this point, we must conclude with the words of John Paul II: *The dominion accorded to man by the Creator is not an absolute power, nor can one speak of freedom to 'use and abuse' nor to utilize things as one pleases. The limitation imposed by the Creator from the very beginning and expressed symbolically with the prohibition against 'eating of the fruit of the tree'* (Genesis 2:16) *shows with sufficient clarity that in the relationship with visible nature, we are subject to laws which are not only biological, but also moral, and they may not be transgressed with impunity.*[14]

The Ethical Requirements in the Relationship Between Man and Nature

1. Respect, Moderation and Attention to the Quality of Life

Faced with the well-documented prospect of an earth with limited resources, emotional reactions, the condemnation of progress, birth control, or the unrealistic "sylvan-pastoral" (ed. note: a "return to nature" proposal) solutions are not adequate.[15]

The basic principles which we have simply pointed out allow us to achieve a clearer picture of the so-called ecological crisis. The world, as it is inhabited today by Western man, appears in many ways to be a treasure in peril. The reasons for this crisis should be sought by searching much more deeply than simply by analyzing the ecosystem and its degradations. These reasons should be sought in the crisis of conscience and in the acceptance of ambiguous ethical values and the failure to fulfill the Lord's commandments. Therefore in the crisis of the environment, it is the moral certainties alone that can authorize (spiritually direct) a behavior which leads to a grace-filled and truly free way of life.

This does not involve a renunciation of development as pursued by industrial societies. What is needed is that the moral character of the relationship between man and the environment becomes recognized and that "ethically qualified" development be promoted. Appropriate development and environmental quality depend upon the exercise of ethical responsibility, as John Paul II reminds us in *Sollicitudo rei socialis*.

It is necessary therefore to remember several ethical principles which must guide the interaction of man with the environment:

The first is respect. To respect the natural environment means to steward the potential which the Creator has infused into it and out of which human interaction proceeds. The natural environment is an ordered whole, and upon this order it is willed by God that man establish his civilization. It is essential that every type of activity and alteration of the environment becomes carefully evaluated, not only on the basis of economic considerations, but also with attention to the possible risks of destruction to the environment. Respect for the environment is a gratitude toward God, and activities concerned with preserving the beauty of the natural environment are not far from being a form of praise and worship.

A second criterion is moderation. Many natural resources are nonrenewable and therefore not subject to indiscriminate exploitation. This criterion of moderation is demanded by the necessity of the common good of all humanity and particularly by concern for the developing countries, which are economically poorer. Ecological concern must become a firmly and universally embraced practice and moderation in consumption must become a sharing. It must not be forgotten that the current generation is responsible for the possibility of development by future generations and this potential would become compromised by the lack of those resources which today are improvidentially consumed.

Finally, a third criterion is attention to the quality of life. Human activity must not merely be respectful to the natural environment, but also toward the everyday living environment. Particular attention must be paid to the unrestrained urbanization of the metropolitan periphery, to the areas with high population density, and to those which are heavily industrialized. In these areas where the highest levels of environmental pollution are caused, effluents or other ecological impacts should be measured, taking account of the consequences for the health of the population.

Now we open a vast and complex subject concerning the safety and the use of certain types of energy such as coal and nuclear power. Although judgment regarding the risks associated with these sources of energy are complex and sensitive, involving many factors of a technical and economical nature, nevertheless the morally stringent duty remains to make every effort to reduce to a minimum the possible risks. Since the health of thousands of human beings is at stake, and the integrity of future generations, prudence demands that no motive have priority over that of human safety.

2. Evangelical Conversion and the Courage of Bearing Witness

The criteria that we have indicated should inform the decisions and choices of the individual. Believers are called into this direction by the way of life which the Gospel itself demands. Faith calls for conversion and in this case, we must speak of an "ecological conversion." The degradation of the environment, as seen in light of the Word of God, is shown to be the fruit and the sign of sin. The sins against God include defiling nature which of itself also aspires to the liberty of the sons of God, which only Christ can give.

The exemplary life of Jesus in his evangelical radicalness is therefore the way which leads to a reconciliation between man and his threatened environment. The kingdom of God which Christ came to bring is also the fulfillment of a world that becomes totally transparent to its Creator. Ecological awareness, correctly understood, is no less than a dimension of Christian asceticism. It requires that individuals become aware of the problems of the environment and of the values connected to ecological healing. If necessary, it requires that they change their thinking as regards attitudes toward nature. This will lead to a style of life that is more sober, more attentive to the use of appropriate products, and more concerned about waste and the excesses of consumerism. If necessary, we should eventually accept voluntary limitations or surcharges tied to the use of certain products. Above all a sense of personal responsibility should emerge in the human community which grows in individuals and widens to worldwide proportions.

The ecological problem demands choices which lead to a global task for society. At the same time the success of this task will not be possible if individuals do not develop a new style of life. Resignation or pessimism must not be a factor. To hope is connected the courage of testimony (bearing witness). In this endeavor, Christian communities, especially the parishes, have a great responsibility: to promote and sustain ecological choices, ecological commitment, and authentically evangelical choices. This response confronts a consumerism which leads to a suffocation of even the most developed consciences. By their nature these choices for an ecologically appropriate style of life, even if they only produce limited changes, will act as courageous and prophetic stimuli which will shake increasing levels of people and invite them to reflect on the seriousness of this situation.

Next, the Christian communities can accomplish a vital and irreplaceable mission in the education of younger generations, through the parish congregations, which are enjoying a season of renewal in our Lombardian dioceses. Through youth associations linked to nature (for example, scouting), young people can be taught about nature. More than just discussions, the very lifestyle of those youth-oriented organizations constitutes an effective means for teaching respect, care and protection of our God-created inheritance.

3. Cultural, Social and Political Responsibility

Finally, the ecological problem must bring about a commitment for a massive effort of ecological renewal with elaborate cultural, social and political ramifications. What is required is to promote a whole series of scientific research efforts which would allow us to evaluate and to foresee adequately the extent of human impact upon the natural environment and to assess the possibility of promoting alternative methods which do not threaten the ecological equilibrium. Research dedicated to the discovery and efficient use of alternative energies and to "clean" energy sources is of great importance. So is the restoration and protection of the already damaged countryside. These are only examples.

Perhaps the crucial factor in this predicament is the progressive establishment of a new global economic order. This would be founded on the mutual willingness and the conscience of the people in a common knowledge of the interdependence that binds together the natural environment and the future of humanity through what would be an authentically human form of development.

Conclusion

As we declared at the beginning, the purpose of this document is not to provide a global and comprehensive statement for the solution of the ecological problem. That is beyond our competence and, in any case, that is not our task. Nor did it seem useful to repeat here a detailed inventory of the degradations which the natural environment has suffered from human life as a consequence of many technologically caused abuses—or to cite the corresponding list of possible solutions, which we might anticipate from political authorities responsible for this region.

It has rather been our intention to draw attention to the many forms and the integrated character of the environmental problem, as well as to correct the simplistic views which have wide circulation in society and among the faithful themselves.

It is necessary to emphasize the most fundamental perspectives of this critical reflection on the destiny of our civilization—which are ethical and religious perspectives. Only within the framework of such perspectives is it possible to articulate in appropriate terms the ecological question itself. Or, better still, the many questions implicit in the relationship between man and nature.

A suitable habitat for human life is certainly not the "virgin forest" nor is it any other ecosystem achieved solely through the forces of nature. The appropriate setting can only be a civilized habitation built through the work of man. The real challenge is not to preserve nature from the work of civilization, but to design civilization with an appropriate quality so that it verifies and maintains the balance of nature.

An essential factor which contributes to the appropriate quality to this work must be a knowledge both of the delicate and marvelous balances within the entire ecosystem, brought about by the forces of nature on our small planet, and of the responsible behavior which respect for this balance requires.

Even more fundamental, the appropriate quality of this work must stem from listening to the voice of the earth: for the earth has a voice. This voice speaks a language which re-echos the very Word of God.

The following passages from the Book of Wisdom are valuable for inspiring even today such a realization:

For creation in obedience to you its Maker, exerts itself to punish the wicked and sweetens itself for the benefit of those who trust in you.

Thus it becomes, by adapting itself to every situation, the agent of your all-nourishing bounty, conforming to the wish to those in need;

So that your beloved sons, O Lord, might understand that what nourishes man are not the various foods, but your Word which preserves all who trust in You.[16]

Notes

1. Cf. *The Future of All of Us. A Report of the World Commission on Environment and Development,* Milan, 1988, p. 421.

2. It seems useful to recall here that in scientific terms, the term "environment" may be considered the sum total of animate and inanimate factors, organized into systems of varying complexity, regulated by certain energy cycles, in which participate biological and chemical phenomena, linked to vegetable and animal life and geochemical phenomena, dependent on modifications which come about in the soil and the atmosphere and in surface waters. Within the environment are observed a series of balances which tend to maintain their composition as consistently as possible.

"AND GOD SAW THAT IT WAS GOOD"

The term "nature" is used to indicate the natural environment, that is, that part of the environment not substantially modified by man (cf. Giovanni Battista Marini Bettolo, "Relations on the Theme of the Environment made to the Synod of Laymen," *L'Osservatore Romano,* October 10, 1987, p. 3).

3. Psalm 8:6b–7b

4. Psalm 104:1b

5. Psalm 104:5

6. Isaiah 45:18

7. Psalm 104:24b

8. Genesis 3:17b

9. Psalm 8:7–9

10. Cf. Matthew 4:4; Deuteronomy 8:3

11. Matthew 6:32

12. Genesis 1:26

13. Cf. Genesis 1:28

14. John Paul II, *Sollicitudo rei socialis,* p. 34.

15. Giovanni Battista Marini Bettolo, *op. cit.*

16. Wisdom 16:24–26

Authorized by:

Cardinal Carlo Maria Martini, President
+ Bernardo Citterio, Secretary
+ Giulio Oggioni, Vice President
Milan, Italy, September 15, 1988

WHAT IS HAPPENING TO OUR BEAUTIFUL LAND?

A Pastoral Letter on Ecology
from the Catholic Bishops of the Philippines

Introduction

The Philippines is now at a critical point in its history. For the past number of years we have experienced political instability, economic decline and a growth in armed conflict. Almost every day the media highlight one or other of these problems. The banner headlines absorb our attention so much so that we tend to overlook a more deep-seated crisis which, we believe, lies at the root of many of our economic and political problems. To put it simply: our country is in peril. All the living systems on land and in the seas around us are being ruthlessly exploited. The damage to date is extensive and, sad to say, it is often irreversible.

One does not need to be an expert to see what is happening and to be profoundly troubled by it. Within a few short years brown, eroded hills have replaced luxuriant forests in many parts of the country. We see dried up river beds where, not so long ago, streams flowed throughout the year. Farmers tell us that, because of erosion and chemical poisoning, the yield from the croplands has fallen substantially. Fishermen and experts on marine life have a similar message. Their fish catches are shrinking in the wake of the extensive destruction of coral reefs and mangrove forests. The picture which is emerging in every province of the country is clear and bleak. The attack on the natural world which benefits very few Filipinos is rapidly whittling away at the very base of our living world and endangering its fruitfulness for future generations.

As we reflect on what is happening in the light of the Gospel we are convinced that this assault on creation is sinful and contrary to the teachings of our faith. The Bible tells us that God created this world (Gen 1:1); that He loves His world and is pleased with it (Gen 1:4, 10, 12, 18, 21, 25, and 31); and that He created man and woman in His image and charged them to be stewards of His creation (Gen 1:27-28). God, who created our world, loves life and wishes to share this life with every creature. St. John tells us that Jesus saw His mission in this light. "I have come that they may have life and have it to the full" (John 10:10).

We are not alone in our concern. Tribal people all over the Philippines, who have seen the destruction of their world at close range, have cried out in anguish. Also men and women who attempt to live harmoniously with nature and those who study ecology have tried to alert people to the magnitude of the destruction taking place in our time. The latter are in a good position to tell us what is happening since they study the web of dynamic relationships which supports and sustains all life within the earthly household. This includes human life.

A Call to Respect and Defend Life

At this point in the history of our country it is crucial that people motivated by religious faith develop a deep appreciation for the fragility of our islands' life-systems and take steps to defend the Earth. It is a matter of life and death. We are aware of this threat to life when it comes to nuclear weapons. We know that a nuclear war would turn the whole earth into a fireball and render the planet inhospitable to life. We tend to forget that the constant, cumulative destruction of life-forms and different habitats will, in the long term, have the same effect. Faced with these challenges, where the future of life is at stake, Christian men and women are called to take a stand on the side of life.

We, the Catholic Bishops of the Philippines, ask Christians and all people of goodwill in the country to reflect with us on the beauty of the Philippine land and seas which nourish and sustain our lives. As we thank God for the many ways He has gifted our land we must also resolve to cherish and protect what

"And God Saw That It Was Good"

remains of this bounty for this and future generations of Filipinos. We are well aware that, for the vast majority of Filipinos, the scars on nature, which increasingly we see all around us, mean less nutritious food, poorer health and an uncertain future. This will inevitably lead to an increase in political and social unrest.

We See the Beauty and the Pain of the Earth

As you read this letter or listen to sections of it being read, scenes from your barrio may come to mind. In your mind's eye you may see well laid out rice paddies flanked by coconuts with their fronds swaying in the breeze. Or you may hear the rustle of the cogon grass on the hills behind your barrio. These scenes mean so much to us and are beautiful. Yet they do not represent the original vegetation with which God has blessed our land. They show the heavy hand of human labor, planning and sometimes short-sightedness.

For generations the hunting and food gathering techniques of our tribal forefathers showed a sensitivity and respect for the rhythms of nature. But all of this has changed in recent years. Huge plantations and mono-crop agriculture have pitted humans against nature. There are short-term profits for the few and even substantial harvests, but the fertility of the land has suffered and the diversity of the natural world has been depleted. So our meditation must begin by reflecting on the original beauty of our land, rivers and seas. This wonderful community of the living existed for millions of years before human beings came to these shores.

The Forests

When our early ancestors arrived here they found a country covered by a blanket of trees. These abounded in living species—over 7,500 species of flowering plants, not to mention animals, birds and insects. These were watered by the tropical rains which swept in from the seas and gradually seeped down through the vegetation and soil to form clear flowing rivers and sparkling lakes which abounded in fish and aquatic life before completing the cycle and returning in the sea. An incredible variety of insects lived in the forest and were busy with all kinds of tasks from recycling dead wood to pollinating flowering plants. The community of the living was not confined to creatures who walked on the Earth. Birds flew through the air, their bright plumes and varying calls adding color and song to the green of the forests. Birds are also great sowers. They contributed greatly to the variety of plant life which is spread throughout the forest. Finally small and large animals lived in the forest and feasted on its largesse. Our land born out of volcanic violence and earthquakes brought forth a bounty of riches. We stand in awe at the wisdom of our Creator who has fashioned this world of life, color, mutual support and fruitfulness in our land.

Our Seas

The beauty did not end at the shoreline. Our islands were surrounded by blue seas, fertile mangroves and enchanting coral reefs. The coral reefs were a world of color and beauty with fish of every shape and hue darting in and out around the delicate coral reefs. *Perlas ng Silanganan* was an appropriate name for this chain of wooded islands, surrounded by clear seas, studded with coral reefs.

Creation Is a Long Process

You might ask: Why is it important to remember the original state of our land? First of all, it reminds us how God, in his wisdom and goodness, shaped this land in this part of the world. It did not happen overnight. It took millions of years of care and love to mould and reshape this land with all its beauty, richness and splendor, where intricate pathways bind all the creatures together in a mutually supportive community. Human beings are not alien to this community. God intended this land for us, his special creatures, but not so that we might destroy it and turn it into a wasteland. Rather He charged us to be stewards of His creation, to care for it, to protect its fruitfulness and not allow it to be devastated (Gen 1:28, 9:12). By protecting what is left of the rainforest we insure that the farmers have rain and plants for the food that sustains us.

Our Forests Laid Waste

How much of this richness and beauty is left a few thousand years after human beings arrived at these shores? Look around and see where our forests have gone. Out of the original 30 million hectares there is now only 1 million hectares of primary forest left. Where are some of the most beautiful creatures who used to dwell in our forests? These are God's masterpieces, through which he displays his power, ingenuity and love for His creation. Humans have forgotten to live peacefully with other creatures. They have destroyed their habitat and hunted them relentlessly. Even now many species are already extinct and the destruction of species is expected to increase dramatically during the next decade as few remaining strands of forest are wiped out by loggers and *kaingineros*. What about the birds? They used to greet us each morning and lift our spirits beyond the horizons of this world. Now they are silenced. In many places all we hear now are cocks crowing. Where is the soaring eagle circling above the land or the colorful kalaw (hornbill)?

The Hemorrhage of Our Life Blood

After a single night's rain look at the chocolate brown rivers in your locality and remember that they are carrying the life blood of the land into the sea. The soil, instead of being the seed bed of life, becomes a cloak of death, smothering, retarding and killing coral polyps. Soil specialists tell us that we lose the equivalent of 100,000 hectares of soil one meter thick each year. We are hardly aware of this enormous loss which is progressively eroding away our most fertile soil and thus our ability to produce food for an expanding population. Any comprehensive land reform must address this most serious threat to our food supply.

Deserts in the Sea

How can fish swim in running sewers like the Pasig and so many more rivers which we have polluted? Who has turned the wonderworld of the seas into underwater cemeteries bereft of color and life? Imagine: only five per cent of our corals are in their pristine state! The blast of dynamite can still be heard on our coastal waters. We still allow *muro-ami* fishing methods which take a terrible toll both on the young swimmers and the corals. Mine tailings are dumped into fertile seas like Calancan Bay where they destroy forever the habitat of the fish. Chemicals are poisoning our lands and rivers. They kill vital organisms and in time they will poison us. The ghost of the dreaded Minamata disease hangs over towns in the Agusan river basin and the Davao gulf.

Recent Destruction Carried Out in the Name of Progress

Most of this destruction has taken place since the beginning of this century, a mere wink of an eye in the long history of our country. Yet in that time we have laid waste complex living systems that have taken millions of years to reach their present state of development.

We often use the word progress to describe what has taken place over the past few decades. There is no denying that in some areas our roads have improved and that electricity is more readily available. But can we say that there is real progress? Who has benefited most and who has borne the real costs? The poor are as disadvantaged as ever and the natural world has been grievously wounded. We have stripped it bare, silenced its sounds and banished other creatures from the community of the living. Through our thoughtlessness and greed we have sinned against God and His creation.

One thing is certain: we cannot continue to ignore and disregard the Earth. Already we are experiencing the consequence of our short-sightedness and folly. Even though we squeeze our lands and try to extract more from them, they produce less food. The air in our cities is heavy with noxious fumes. Instead of bringing energy and life it causes bronchial illness. Our forests are almost gone, our rivers are almost empty, our springs and wells no longer sparkle with living water. During the monsoon rain, flash-floods sweep through our towns and cities and destroy everything in their path. Our lakes and estuaries are silting up. An out-of-sight, out-of-mind mentality allows us to flush toxic waste and mine tailings into our rivers and seas in the mistaken belief that they can no longer harm us. Because the living world is interconnected, the poison is absorbed by marine organisms. We in turn are gradually being poisoned when we eat seafood.

We Can and Must Do Something About It

It is already late in the day and so much damage has been done. No one can pinpoint the precise moment when the damage becomes so irreversible that our living world will collapse. But we are rapidly heading in that direction. Even now there are signs of stress in every corner of our land. As we look at what is happening before our eyes and think of the horrendous consequences for the land and the people, we would do well to remember that God, who created this beautiful land, will hold us responsible for plundering it and leaving it desolate. So will future generations of Filipinos. Instead of gifting them with a fruitful land, all we will leave behind is a barren desert. We, the Bishops, call on all Filipinos to recognize the urgency of this task and to respond to it now.

As Filipinos we can and must act now. Nobody else will do it for us. This is our home; we must care for it, watch over it, protect it and love it. We must be particularly careful to protect what remains of our forests, rivers, and corals and to heal, wherever we can, the damage which has already been done.

The task of preserving and healing is a daunting one given human greed and the relentless drive of our plunder economy. But we must not lose hope. God has gifted us with creativity and ingenuity. He has planted in our hearts a love for our land, which bursts forth in our songs and poetry. We can harness our creativity in the service of life and shun anything that leads to death.

Signs of Hope

Despite the pain and despoliation which we have mentioned, there are signs of hope. Our forefathers and our tribal brothers and sisters today still attempt to live in harmony with nature. They see the Divine Spirit in the living world and show their respect through prayers and offerings. Tribal Filipinos remind us that the exploitative approach to the natural world is foreign to our Filipino culture.

The vitality of our Filipino family is also a sign of hope. Parents share their life with their children. They protect them and care for them and are particularly solicitous when any member of the family is sick. This is especially true of mothers; they are the heartbeat of the family, working quietly in the home to create an atmosphere where everyone is accepted and loved. No sacrifice is too demanding when it comes to caring for a sick member of the family. The values we see in our families of patient toil, concern for all and a willingness to sacrifice for the good of others are the very values which we must now transfer to the wider sphere in our efforts to conserve, heal and love our land. It is not a mere coincidence that women have been at the forefront of the ecological movement in many countries. The tree planting program of the Chipko in India, popularly known as the "hug a tree" movement and the Green belt movement in Kenya spring to mind.

We call to mind that, despite the devastation which has taken place in our forests and seas, we Filipinos are sensitive to beauty. Even in the poorest home parents and children care for flowers. We are also encouraged by the growth in environmental awareness among many Filipinos. Small efforts which teach contour plowing, erosion control, organic farming and tree planting can blossom into a major movement of genuine care for our Earth. We are happy that there have been some successes. Both the Chico dam project was suspended and the Bataan nuclear plant mothballed after massive local resistance. This year the people of San Fernando, Bukidnon and Midsalip, Zamboanga del Sur defended what remains of their forest with their own bodies. At the Santa Cruz Mission in South Cotabato serious efforts are underway to reforest bald hills and develop ecologically sound ways of farming. The diocese of Pagadian has chosen the eucharist and ecology as its pastoral focus for this year. These are all signs for us that the Spirit of God, who breathed over the waters, and originally brought life out of chaos is now prompting men and women both inside and outside the Church to dedicate their lives to enhancing and protecting the integrity of Creation. In order that these drops and rivulets will join together and form a mighty stream in the defense of life we need a sustaining vision to guide us.

Our Vision

We will not be successful in our efforts to develop a new attitude towards the natural world unless we are sustained and nourished by a new vision. This vision must blossom forth from our understanding of the world as God intends it to be. We can know the shape of this world by looking at how God originally fashioned our world and laid it out before us.

This vision is also grounded in our Faith. The Bible tells us that God created this beautiful and fruitful world for all his creatures to live in (Gen 1:1-2:4) and that He has given us the task of being stewards of His creation (Gen 2:19-20).

The relationship which links God, human beings and all the community of the living together is emphasized in the covenant which God made with Noah after the flood. The rainbow which we still see in the sky is a constant reminder of this bond and challenge (Gen 9:12). This covenant recognizes the very close bonds which bind living forms together in what are called ecosystems. The implications of this covenant for us today are clear. As people of the covenant we are called to protect endangered ecosystems, like our forests, mangroves and coral reefs and to establish just human communities in our land. More and more we must recognize that the commitment to work for justice and to preserve the integrity of creation are two inseparable dimensions of our Christian vocation to work for the coming of the kingdom of God in our times.

Christ Our Life (Col 3:4)

As Christians we also draw our vision from Christ. We have much to learn from the attitude of respect which Jesus displayed towards the natural world. He was very much aware that all the creatures in God's creation are related. Jesus lived lightly on the earth and warned his disciples against hoarding material possessions and allowing their hearts to be enticed by the lure of wealth and power (Matt 6:19-21; Luke 9:1-6). But our meditation on Jesus goes beyond this. Our faith tells us that Christ is the center point of human history and creation. All the rich unfolding of the universe and the emergence and flowering of life on Earth are centered on him (Eph 1:9-10; Col 1:16-17). The destruction of any part of creation, especially the extinction of species, defaces the image of Christ which is etched in creation.

Mary, Mother of Life

We Filipinos have a deep devotion to Mary. We turn to her for help and protection in time of need. We know that she is on the side of the poor and those who are rejected (Luke 1:52). Our new sensitivity to what is happening to our land also tells us that she is on the side of life. As a mother she is pained and saddened when she sees people destroy the integrity of creation through soil erosion, blast-fishing or poisoning land. Mary knows what the consequences of this destruction are. Therefore as Mother of Life she challenges us to abandon the pathway of death and to return to the way of life.

Taken together the various strands of our Christian vision envisage a profound renewal which must affect our people, our culture and our land. It challenges us to live once again in harmony with God's creation. This vision of caring for the Earth and living in harmony with it can guide us as, together, we use our ingenuity and many gifts to heal our wounded country.

This Is What We Suggest

In the light of this vision we recommend action in the following areas.

What Each Individual Can Do

Be aware of what is happening in your area. Do not remain silent when you see your environment being destroyed. Use your influence within your family and community to develop this awareness. Avoid a fatalistic attitude. We are people of hope, who believe that together we can change the course of events. Organize people around local ecological issues. Support public officials who are sensitive to environmental issues. Become involved in some concrete action. There is much that can be done by individuals to reforest bald hills and prevent soil erosion.

What the Churches Can Do

Like every other group, the Church as a community is called to conversion around this, the ultimate pro-life issue. Until very recently many religions, including the Catholic Church, have been slow to respond to the ecological crisis. We, the bishops, would like to redress this neglect. There is a great need for a Filipino theology of creation which will be sensitive to our unique living world, our diverse cultures and our religious heritage. The fruits of this reflection must be made widely available through our preaching and catechetical programs. Our different liturgies must celebrate the beauty and pain of our world, our connectedness to the natural world and the ongoing struggle for social justice. We would like to encourage the administrators of our Catholic schools to give special importance to the theme of peace, justice and the integrity of creation in their schools.

Since programs, however laudable, will not implement themselves, we suggest the setting up of a Care of the Earth ministry at every level of Church organization; from the basic Christian communities, through the parish structure and diocesan offices right up to the national level. This ministry could help formulate and implement policies and strategies which flow from our new and wider vision. The idea is not so much to add another activity to our pastoral ministry, but rather that this concern should underpin everything we do.

What the Government Can Do

We ask the government not to pursue short-term economic gains at the expense of long-term ecological damage. We suggest that the government group together into an independent Department all the agencies which deal at present with ecological issues. This Department should promote an awareness of the fragility and limited carrying capacity of our islands' eco-systems and advocate measures designed to support ecologically sustainable development. Obviously the Department should have an important contribution to make to related Departments like Education (DECS), Health, Natural Resources (DENR) and Agriculture. There is also a need to encourage research into the eco-systems of our land and the problems they face in the future. The Department should publish a state of the environment report for each region and for the country as a whole each year. Above all the Department needs legislative teeth to insure that its policies and programs are implemented.

Non-governmental Organization

NGOs have a very important role to play in developing a widespread ecological awareness among people. They can also act as a watch-dog to ensure that the government and those in public office do not renege on their commitment to place this concern at the top of their list.

Conclusion

This brief statement about our living world and the deterioration we see all around us attempts to reflect the cry of our people and the cry of our land. At the root of the problem we see an exploitative mentality, which is at variance with the Gospel of Jesus. This expresses itself in acts of violence against fellow Filipinos. But it is not confined to the human sphere. It also infects and poisons our relationship with our land and seas.

We reap what we sow; the results of our attitude and activities are predictable and deadly. Our small farmers tell us that their fields are less productive and are becoming sterile. Our fishermen are finding it increasingly difficult to catch fish. Our lands, forests and rivers cry out that they are being eroded, denuded and polluted. As bishops we have tried to listen and respond to their cry. There is an urgency about this issue which calls for widespread education and immediate action. We are convinced that the challenge which we have tried to highlight here is similar to the one which Moses put before the people of Israel before they entered their promised land: "Today I offer you a choice of life or death, blessing or curse. Choose life and then you and your descendants will live" (Deut 30:19-20).

Approved at Tagaytay, 29 January 1988

"AND GOD SAW THAT IT WAS GOOD"

REPRINT
OF
ARTICLES
FROM PARISH
RESOURCE MATERIALS

⸕

Introduction

⸕

THE UNITED STATES CATHOLIC CONFERENCE ENVIRONMENTAL JUSTICE Program has produced several parish resource materials to help Catholics integrate a concern for ecological and environmental issues into their faith life. We reprint here several helpful and popular articles from the first and second resource kits.

The first article is by Most Rev. James T. McHugh, Bishop of Camden, who explores the Church's concern for this issue, providing a broad contextual view and linking major themes from Catholic theology and social teaching. Bishop McHugh served on the Vatican delegations to the United Nations Conference on Environment and Development in Rio de Janeiro in 1992 and the Conference on Population and Development in Cairo in 1994.

Monsignor Charles Murphy, a pastor in Portland, Maine, and author of *At Home on the Earth: Foundations for a Catholic Ethic of the Environment,* examines the problem of materialism and overconsumption and their environmental effects in light of Catholic teaching.

The editors have included an article on how science goes about its work and the difficulty the public often has in interpreting the scientific debate.

STEWARDS
OF LIFE,
STEWARDS
OF NATURE

❧

Most Rev. James T. McHugh
Bishop of Camden

❧

OVER THE PAST TWO DECADES, THERE HAS BEEN A GROWING AWARENESS OF the need to protect and enhance the environment. But this increasing awareness is far from a comprehensive understanding. And despite new and urgent concerns about specific ecological problems (e.g., acid rain, deforestation, and global warming) most people tend to think of the environment as something "out there," something detached from their everyday lives and personal behavior patterns.

Earth Day 1990 attempted to foster public understanding of environmental problems and point to the progress, or lack thereof, in meeting such problems since Earth Day 1970. Some progress has been made. In 1969, the National Environmental Policy Act was adopted, giving us a national charter for the environment, and in 1975, the Environmental Protection Agency was established. Since the 1970s, legislation has been adopted to protect our rivers and lakes, to control automobile emissions, and to prohibit certain types of noxious chemicals used in pesticides. There are now courses in ecology in our schools and colleges, and nationwide public advocacy organizations mobilize public sentiment and political support.

Ecology: An International Concern

The 1992 United Nations Conference on Environment and Development (UNCED) held in Rio de Janiero focused international attention on environmental issues. The conference addressed a wide range of environmental issues, such as protection of the atmosphere, planning and management of land resources, deforestation, the impact of pollution on fragile ecosystems, desertification, biological diversity, and biotechnology. It also discussed protection of the oceans and seas, fishing rights, freshwater resources, and reserves. Further, it attempted to deal with problem areas such as sound management of toxic chemicals and hazardous wastes and sewage-related issues.

But overshadowing these weighty discussions was the inevitable tension between the developed nations of the world pushing for more control and legal restrictions to decrease pollution and safeguard natural resources, and the developing nations that do not possess and cannot presently afford the technology necessary to meet all the demands of the environmental advocates in the industrialized nations. Development was the central concern, and this escalated the economic disparities between nations and peoples and the continued presence of hunger, disease, and poverty. The conference also pointed to the patterns of production, consumption, and waste that prevail in the developed nations and the dependence of developing nations, not always acknowledged, on new patterns of international assistance and cooperation. Thus, despite the agreements and forward-looking strategies of the Rio conference, there remains the difficulty of establishing international agreements and policies to which we all subscribe.

In *Making Peace with the Planet,* Barry Commoner describes the situation in terms of a war between the ecosphere and the technosphere. Tragedies like Bhopal, Three Mile Island, Chernobyl, and the Alaskan oil spill remind us of the damage done to the ecosphere when we ignore or fail to control properly the technosphere. Commoner maintains that peace can be achieved only through understanding and negotiation, not by a proliferation of battles or small wars.

Environmental degradation is often claimed to be a natural consequence of population growth. It is important to realize that the greatest abuse of the environment takes place in the least populated industrialized nations of the world. It is not the number of people, but the processes of industrial production that create the greatest problem. As Commoner observes:

In sum, the data from an industrial country like the U.S. and from developing countries show that the largest influence on pollution levels is the pollution-generating tendency of the system of industrial and agricultural production, and the transportation and power systems. In all countries, the environmental impact of the technology factor is significantly greater than the influence of population size or affluence.

In surveying the recent literature on ecology and the environment, one notes a growing recognition that protecting and properly using the goods of creation is fundamentally a moral issue.

The goods of the earth are part of the heritage of the entire human family. They are held in common across national boundaries and continental divides. They belong to the poor and developing nations as well as to the rich and successful. Indeed, many of the untapped resources of the world—very likely beyond our present estimation—are in Africa and South America. Add to this the resources in our oceans and the undiscovered treasures of outer space. A collective sense of stewardship and worldwide recognition of common needs and the common good—including proper use of all resources now and in the future—will enable us to exercise proper self-restraint in the use of natural resources.

Integrity of Creation

In his 1990 World Day of Peace message, *Peace with God the Creator; Peace with All Creation,* Pope John Paul II addressed the ecological question. The Holy Father placed this discussion in the context of humanity's quest for peace—peace among nations, peace among peoples, peace within nations and families. True solutions to environmental problems, he said, will be based on a morally coherent world view.

The Holy Father begins with the account of creation in the Book of Genesis, noting that the creation events are always followed by the refrain "And God saw that it was good." When human beings reject the Creator's plan, or recklessly ignore it, they provoke "a disorder which has inevitable repercussions on the rest of the created order." This leads us, says the Holy Father, to look at the ecological crisis as a moral issue.

Two fundamental principles should guide our moral consideration: *the integrity of all creation* and *respect for life.*

Pope John Paul II's description of environmental problems is similar to those described by Barry Commoner and others. Ozone depletion, "greenhouse effect," the unregulated dumping of industrial waste, the burning of fossil fuels, the unrestricted sacking of the forests—all of which damage the atmosphere and the environment.

But environmental problems are not only these massive problems over which the ordinary person has little or no control. Ride along our city streets and country roads and see the old tires and abandoned cars, the empty cans, the paper and plastic refuse from "fast-food" stores, the abuse of trees and shrubs, and the omnipresent broken glass on sidewalks and streets. All of these are part of the assault on the environment, and they result from personal carelessness, negligence, and arrogant wastefulness. With minimum attention and effort, they can be corrected and our daily environment vastly improved.

The Dignity of the Human Person

The second principle the Holy Father points to is respect for life and for the dignity of the human person. Too often, increased productivity overshadows a concern for the worker's safety or long-range well-being. And in the United States, a libertarian approach to the use of drugs, alcohol, and tobacco endangers health. Add to this the consumerist mentality and the emphasis on personal comfort and convenience, and we see an erosion of respect for life, health, and well-being. The Holy Father also notes the disruption of ecological balances by the uncontrolled destruction of plant and animal life. Much of this results from the dumping of industrial wastes into our local streams and rivers and from a reckless use of aerosol products.

John Paul II also warns against indiscriminate biological and genetic research and experimentation. This is already underway in plants and animals, and we are constantly faced with proposals for genetic experimentation on humans. The whole debate about government funding of fetal research is a signal of real danger.

In search of a solution, the Holy Father points to a harmonious universe or "cosmos" endowed by God with its own integrity, its own internal dynamic balance. This order must be respected and protected. The earth and its natural resources are "a common heritage, the fruits of which are for the benefit of all."

The New Solidarity

Protection of this common heritage demands a more internationally coordinated approach to the management of the earth's goods, not only to serve the wealthy, industrialized nations of the world but to meet the needs and legitimate aspirations of the people of the developing nations. In United Nations debates, Third World representatives are often suspicious of environmental strategies that may have the tragic effect of retarding or nullifying the development process. A truly responsible global worldview must meet the problems of the developing nations.

The urgent moral need for a new solidarity is a first step toward global cooperation, says John Paul II. This need presents new opportunities for strengthening cooperative and peaceful relations among states. But it must also include a worldwide effort to address the structural forms of poverty that exist throughout the world, especially in the poorer nations. Many ecologists remind us that the greatest threat to the environment comes from the life-styles of the wealthy and affluent who consume far more per capita than do the populations of the developing nations.

Pope John Paul II also warns of the threat posed to the environment by modern war and the arms race. Granted that the present world situation is promising for peace, there are still local and regional conflicts that damage land, rob the workforce of farmers, and often destroy the systems that protect the environment. Witness conditions in Bosnia, Somalia, Burundi, and Bangladesh.

The principles enunciated in the 1990 World Day of Peace Message were restated and applied in the interventions of the Holy See's Delegation to the Rio Conference. Cardinal Angelo Sodano, Vatican Secretary of State, emphasized again the need and duty for international solidarity. While recognizing some of the failures or omissions to take proper action on the part of developing nations, he also noted a growing isolation on the part of developed nations and a tendency to ignore, often for selfish reasons, their duty and responsibility to assist the developing nations and to spearhead new strategies to alleviate global suffering and human misery. Cardinal Sodano urged that "humanity discover its common roots and that our awareness of being brothers and sisters give rise to a great creative effort aimed at the effective exercise of solidarity." Cardinal Sodano also called upon the developed nations to address the structural forms of poverty, "by ensuring employment, education and primary health care for parents and children, with special attention for overcoming infant mortality."

Population growth has frequently been pinpointed as a major cause of pollution and resource depletion. The Holy See has consistently argued that population growth, of and by itself, is not the primary cause of environmental degradation, and even as a contributing cause, it must be seen in a larger context. In addressing population issues, respect for the dignity of the person, recognition of the family as the basic social unit, and protection of the inherent right of parents to decide freely and responsibly on the number of children and the spacing of births are the guiding principles. Alleviation of poverty and disease, improvement of living conditions and wider educational opportunities, as well as recognition of women's rights and potentialities, contribute to responsible decision making regarding childbearing and parenting.

Stewardship: An Action Plan

The Holy Father calls on modern society to take a serious look at its lifestyle—particularly the demand for instant gratification and unlimited consumption. He also calls for education in ecological responsibility—responsibility for oneself, for others, and for the earth.

In this regard, there are simple things we can all do to lessen environmental damage. We can trim our consumption patterns, especially in terms of convenience goods. We can conserve water and energy. We can cooperate with local recycling programs by tying up old newspapers and by separating glass and cans from other trash. In sum, we can make some small personal sacrifices that cost little more than convenience and comfort, and thereby safeguard and enhance the treasures of God's creation.

Pope John Paul II concludes his message by repeating that care of the environment is the responsibility of everyone. Similarly, Barry Commoner concludes that making peace with the planet demands an appreciation of our common concerns and responsibilities. The U.S. bishops, in *Economic Justice for All,* noted that

> No one can ever own capital resources absolutely or control their own without regard for others and society as a whole. . . . Short-term profits reaped at the cost of depletion of natural resources or the pollution of the environment violates this trust.

The basic message is that protecting the environment protects the common good of humanity—now and for untold centuries to come. And the common good supersedes individual comfort and convenience, for when the common good is ignored or denied, the good of the individual is likewise endangered.

"And God saw everything that he had made, and behold it was very good" (Gn 1:31). God entrusted all creation to the man and woman. We inherit the goods of creation and the responsibility of stewardship. We must pass on all that is good to generations yet to come.

THE GOOD LIFE FROM A CATHOLIC PERSPECTIVE: THE PROBLEM OF CONSUMPTION

⁂

Msgr. Charles Murphy

⁂

LAST YEAR AT A MEETING OF THE DIRECTORS OF PERMANENT DIACONATE programs, one of the prayer experiences was a paraliturgy involving the sharing of bread. The meeting was in San Francisco and apparently the bread was freshly made sourdough. The participants expressed a common satisfaction with this ritual of sharing modeled on the eucharist—until a telling theological comment. In a session immediately following, theologian Megan McKenna commented, "That was all very beautiful, but what did you do with the leftovers?"

"Christianity is not about feeding yourself. Christianity begins with what people do with the leftovers." Professor McKenna, whose field is social ethics, alluded to the biblical miracle of the sharing of the loaves and the admonition that the leftover fragments be gathered (Mt 14:20).

Faces fell. A certain religious complacency was pierced, giving way to a degree of consciousness raising. It is startling to be told, in a culture as wasteful as ours, that Christianity begins with what we do with our leftovers. Just visit a typical school lunch program and see the mounds of garbage. "Waste not, want not" means little to children brought up to believe that if something does not meet your taste or adhere to the current fashion, toss it.

A familiar statistic in this context begins to ring true: The industrialized countries, with only one-fifth of the world's population, consume two-thirds of the world's resources and generate 75 percent of all the pollution and waste products. The disparities between human beings who live in squalor and those who have everything money can buy are glaring in a world brought closer together through amazing advances in communication. This great disparity denies social justice, leads to ecological tragedy, and, most of all, creates a misperception of what the good life really is, which ultimately makes excessive consumption a religious question.

What and how much we consume manifests our conception of who we are and why we exist. The spiritual and cultural impoverishment that are the natural byproducts of consumerism are evident everywhere. Money talks, but, as they say, "it has such a squeaky voice and has so little to say." How can our Catholic faith help us to find a more satisfying life for ourselves and at the same time make us more socially responsible in achieving it? I suggest three ways: the cultivation of the natural virtue of temperance; the gospel admonitions about the dangers of over-consumption and the fundamental requirement of love of neighbor; and, finally, the recent social teachings of the Church based upon both the order of nature and the higher demands of gospel living. I will also provide some indications of what the good life might be like for us all.

Temperance as a Virtue for Living

More and more ethical theorists give credence to the role virtues play in building character. Virtues are being seen and appreciated anew because their cultivation can provide the inner strength needed to live happily and successfully. Without these well-established habits we are at the mercy of external stimuli, and we become victims of our own disordered needs and passions. To be creative and contributing members of society we need a structure that allows us to use our gifts in a sustained way; the virtues provide such a structure. They are a wisdom for living that was recognized as far back as the ancient Greeks and beyond. The virtues are honored in the Scriptures as part of a household code for living on earth and were incorporated by the church fathers in their syntheses of Christian life.

Among the four "cardinal," or "hinge," virtues that humans find essential is the virtue of temperance; with prudence, justice, and fortitude, temperance is regarded as one of the hinges on which hangs the gate to a happy life.

In his classic study of the cardinal virtues, Josef Pieper is quick to point out that the rich meaning of temperance is not captured by the concept of moderation. Moderation is only a small part of temperance, the negative part. According to St. Thomas Aquinas, temperance gives order and balance to our life. It arises from a serenity of spirit within oneself. This reasonable norm allows us to walk gently upon the earth. Temperance teaches us to cherish and enjoy the good things of life while respecting natural limits. Temperance in fact does not diminish but actually heightens the pleasure we take in living by freeing us from a joyless compulsiveness and dependence. Temperance therefore means a lot more than the so-called "temperance movement" regarding the consumption of alcohol!

E. F. Schumacher, in his most influential book, *Small is Beautiful: Economics as if People Mattered*, contrasts the consumerist way of life which multiplies human wants with the simple life whose aim is to achieve maximum well-being with the minimum use of the earth's resources. The "logic of production" that demands more and more growth in consumption is a formula for disaster, he argues. "Out of the whole Christian tradition," Schumacher concludes, "there is perhaps no body of teaching which is more relevant and appropriate to the modern predicament than the marvelously subtle and realistic doctrines of the Four Cardinal Virtues" and in particular temperance that means knowing when "enough is enough."

The Gospel and Wealth

When Pope John Paul II paid his first visit to the United States in 1979, he delivered one of his most memorable homilies on the subject of consumption. Speaking to a congregation gathered in New York City at Yankee Stadium, the Holy Father said:

> Christians will want to be in the vanguard in favoring ways of life that decisively break with the frenzy of consumerism, exhausting and joyless. It is not a question of slowing down progress, for there is no human progress when everything conspires to give full reign to the instincts of self-interest, sex and power. We must find a simple way of living. For it is not right that the standard of living of the rich countries would seek to maintain itself by draining off a great part of the reserves of energy and raw materials that are meant to serve the whole of humanity. For readiness to create a greater and more equitable solidarity between peoples is the first condition for peace. Catholics of the United States, and all you citizens of the United States, you have such a tradition of spiritual generosity, industry, simplicity and sacrifice that you cannot fail to heed this call today for a new enthusiasm and a fresh determination. It is in the joyful simplicity of a life inspired by the Gospel and the Gospel's spirit of fraternal sharing that you will find the best remedy for sour criticism, paralyz-

ing doubt and the temptation to make money the principal means and indeed the very measure of human advancement.

As the basis of his teaching, the Holy Father drew upon the parable in St. Luke's Gospel regarding Lazarus and the rich man. The Lukan Gospel is particularly harsh regarding the hazards of wealth. The parable may be read as another illustration of the biblical saying that it is easier for a camel to pass through the needle's eye than for a rich person to enter God's kingdom (Lk 18:25). What is notable in the parable is that the rich man is condemned because he is rich. Enclosed in his world of wealth and self-sufficiency that wealth brings, he simply failed to notice Lazarus begging at his gate, much less help him. Even the natural world, symbolized by the dogs licking Lazarus' sores, displayed more sympathy. The rich man's incurable spiritual condition continues into eternity; he continues to regard Lazarus as a social inferior and begs Abraham to dispatch Lazarus with a message of warning to his brothers. Abraham explains that this is impossible: the "abyss" between Lazarus and the rich man is "too great" (Lk 16:19ff).

St. Matthew tempers the first of Jesus' beatitudes with the qualifying "Blessed are the poor in spirit" (Mt 5:3); in Luke Jesus boldly declares, "Blessed are you who are poor, for the kingdom of God is yours" (Lk 6:20). Why are the poor in such an advantageous position? It is because in the Bible the poor ones have only Yahweh to look to for their help; thus they are able to recognize the radical human dependency that is the condition of every creature before God. Wealth, on the other hand, creates the illusion of independence and self-sufficiency, a dangerous posture.

Going beyond human virtues like temperance, the Gospel demands a "higher righteousness." Jesus tells the rich young man who says he has observed all the commandments since childhood, "There is still one thing left for you: sell all that you have and distribute it to the poor, and you will have a treasure in heaven. Then come, follow me" (Lk 18:22). Jesus demands detachment from wealth and prescribes the just use of monetary resources. As later church teaching highlights, he asks that our preferential love go particularly to the poor. Included today with the poor and the exploited must be the whole natural world.

When the church fathers take up the same theme of personal consumption, they not only have the spiritual dangers of wealth in mind but also the idyllic common life that Luke describes in the Acts of the Apostles. There all things were held in common and distributed according to everyone's need (Acts 2:44-45). In his 1967 encyclical letter on the development of peoples, *Populorum Progressio*, Pope Paul VI drew upon St. Ambrose to emphasize the universal purpose of all created things, a purpose not abrogated when certain things become someone's private property. St. Ambrose wrote:

You are not making a gift of your possessions to the poor person. You are handing over to him what is his. For what has been given in common for the use of all, you have abrogated to yourself. The world is given to all, and not only to the rich.

St. Basil, in a much-quoted homily, once declared that the bread we clutch in our hands belongs to the starving, the cloak we keep locked up in our closet belongs to the naked, the shoes that we are not using belong to the barefooted. In these ways in the post-biblical age Christians strove to keep a religious perspective on their use of material things.

Consumption in Light of Church Social Teaching

Part of the background of Pope Paul VI's encyclical *Populorum Progressio* was a journey he made to India where he saw firsthand its wretched poverty. In that encyclical he proposed a fundamental human right to development, a right he saw as impeded by the phenomenon of "overdevelopment" in some parts of the world. But even as he advocated the cause of development, Pope Paul was careful to give a distinctively Christian interpretation to what desirable development might be: it is, he said, the right not to "have" more but to "be" more.

Pope John Paul II built upon these insights when in 1991 he wrote *Centesimus Annus*. Although the occasion for this encyclical was the 100th anniversary of Pope Leo XIII's *Rerum Novarum* that started the whole modern phase of the Church's social teaching, John Paul focused on the new opportunities and dangers accompanying the collapse of the communist ideology. With market forces now unleashed across the world, he cautioned about consumer attitudes and lifestyles that could be improper and also damaging physically and spiritually. "It is not wrong to want to live better," he writes; "what is wrong is a style of life which is presumed to be better when it is directed towards 'having' rather than 'being,' and which wants to have more, not in order to be more but in order to spend life in enjoyment as an end in itself" (no. 36). "Equally worrying," he goes on, "is *the ecological question* which accompanies the problem of consumerism and which is closely connected to it. In his desire to have and to enjoy rather than to be and to grow, man consumes the resources of the earth and his own life in an excessive and disordered way" (no. 37).

Consumer choices and consumer demands are moral and cultural expressions of how we conceive of life. Is life all about working and spending and working more to have more to spend? Could not it rather all be about contemplation, what the pope calls a "disinterested, unselfish and aesthetic attitude that is born of wonder in the presence of being and of the beauty which enables one to see in visible things the message of the invisible God who created them" (no. 37)?

The Good Life

The question of defining more accurately what the good life is has become especially acute. In her helpful book, *The Overworked American: The Unexpected Decline in Leisure,* Juliet Schor documents how American households find themselves locked into an insidious cycle of work and spend. Households go into debt to buy products they do not need and then work longer than they want in order to keep up with the payments. She makes the telling observation that "shopping is the chief cultural activity in the United States."

The good life should allow people to work at things that are personally satisfying and expressive of themselves. In his encyclical on the subject, *Laborem Exercens*, Pope John Paul calls this the "subjective" value of work. The good life should include also a certain leisure for, as Josef Pieper wrote, leisure is the basis of human culture. There should be opportunities to contribute to the common good as well as to pursue personal happiness. There should be time for family and friends, for worship and prayer. There also should be a certain asceticism to include a rediscovery of the benefits of fasting.

Fasting is part of the Gospel. It helps us to focus on the nourishment that can only come from God. It encourages good health and enhances our enjoyment of the good things of life, freeing us from a certain deadness in spirit. A reemphasis on fasting may not only put us in touch again with a gospel ideal but also increase our ecological awareness as we sparingly use scarce earthly resources. Fasting in the modern world can have a strong social justice meaning.

Thomas Merton in his *Thoughts in Solitude* raises the specter of the desertification of life on this planet. The desert, he writes, once was a privileged place for the encounter with God because there humanity could find nothing to exploit. "Yet look at deserts today. What are they?" He says they have become testing grounds for bombs as well as the locations for glittering towns "through whose veins money runs like artificial blood." "The desert moves everywhere. Everywhere is desert," Merton concludes.

In her enlightening book, *Ancient Futures, Learning from Ladakh*, Helena Norbert-Hodge offers hopeful patterns for future living from the ancient ways of a once-isolated Himalayan village. In Ladakh she encountered a society "in which there is neither waste nor pollution, a society in which crime is virtually non-existent, communities are healthy and strong, and a teenage boy is never embarrassed to be gentle or affectionate with his mother or grandmother."

Perhaps we cannot save pockets of ancient wisdom like Ladakh from modern influence. What we can do is discover "ancient futures" in the abundant resources of Catholic social teaching and make our own choices for living based upon its wisdom.

NAYSAYERS
AND
DOOMSAYERS:
HOW DO WE
SORT OUT THE
DIFFERENCES
IN THE ONGOING
ENVIRONMENTAL
DEBATE?

IT SEEMS THAT EVERY WINTER WE HEAR ABOUT "UNUSUAL" WEATHER patterns in the news. Sometimes we have an unusually mild winter or lack of snowfall in the Northeast. More ominously, we see pictures of the devastating floods in California and Europe and watch in horror as lives are disrupted and towns are covered by rampaging rivers.

If these sorts of unusual climate events continue, we are very likely to start seeing interviews on television news programs with two types of scientists. The first will look serious, intelligent, and concerned as he or she explains that mild winter temperatures are consistent with scientists' theories of global warming and that some scientists believe extreme weather events are likely to become more frequent as the earth becomes warmer.

The second type of scientist will appear equally credible and knowledgeable but have a very different story to tell. He or she will explain that any unusual weather patterns are well within normal weather cycles and have nothing to do with global warming.

Whom do we believe? Our first reaction might be to say: "If the experts can't sort it out, how can I?" The problem with this perspective, understandable as it may be, is that it leads to apathy or noninvolvement. To be a responsible citizen requires us to make moral, civic, and political choices based on our assessment of whether we think threats to the environment are real or not.

Before trying to sort out the conflicting statements from scientists, let's first ask the question, why do scientists disagree? The short answer is that disagreement is an intrinsic part of science. Scientists are taught to question, to be skeptical, to theorize based on current data but then change their theories as they obtain new or better data. Think of it as a debate with logical arguments on all sides.

The short answer invites two more questions: How can both sides have logical arguments and how is it that the data can conflict? When scientists study the environment they are not studying something controlled, something in a test tube or laboratory where variables can be isolated. The environment (our world) is made up of elements that change constantly and affect each other. These elements weave together like the threads in a blanket—though their interaction is infinitely more complex.

Natural ecosystems are complex for reasons other than just having many elements. A jar with 100 jelly beans is no more complex than a jar with 50. On the other hand, a meadow can include wild roses, other wildflowers, shrubs, small sedges, hedges, many kinds of insects, birds that feed on the insects and have nesting sites, small animals, and predators. The chemical composition of the soil can vary from location to location while worms and insects live in the soil and help modify its texture. Given this tremendous complexity in the natural world, it is remarkable that any two scientists who approach an environmental problem from different vantage points ever reach an agreement at all.

Causality and Gradualism

The complexity of the environment is also linked to two objective factors that further cloud debates over environmental issues and cause scientists to disagree: causality and gradualism.

Causality is defined as "the relationship between a cause and its effect." In the case of global warming, many scientists believe increasing concentrations of certain gases in the atmosphere will cause rising temperatures in some regions of the world and increased violent storms in others. But other factors like cloud formations and the length of time specific molecules remain in the air also play a role. As soon as you throw these extra elements into the mix, it becomes much harder to determine cause and effect or to predict the results of a change in any single variable.

Let's examine a less well-publicized subject than global warming. Some scientists now speculate that a complex series of components may conspire to cause potentially dangerous developments in some of the world's coastal waters. The theory runs like this: Climatic changes are combining with the influx of sewage and fertilizer washed from farms into streams and rivers, the overharvesting of fish and shellfish, and the loss of wetlands to produce an explosion in coastal algal blooms (small, single-cell plants that live in the water). The algae, in turn, harbor microorganisms or bacteria. Scientists think elevated temperatures along with the pollution and other factors causes a thick algal soup with new forms of this small plant or more frequent occurrence of specially noxious plants.

In addition, scientists believe that the warmer water with extra amounts of nitrogen or phosphorous and other nutrients may either promote mutation or select bacterial species harmful to humans and nourish algae lethal to fish and marine mammals. Among the new bacterial forms arising from the algal soup may be a unique variant of cholera based on a newly discovered association between the cholera bacteria and very small animals called copepods that feed on algae. The more algae, then, the more copepods and the more chance for this new cholera to spread, especially in warmer waters that have been enriched. This new version of the cholera bacteria has a devastating effect on the people of India and the subcontinent. To understand the origin of this form of cholera bacteria, scientists need to study a long, convoluted set of causes—not obvious by any stretch of the imagination—leading to an adverse effect.

In addition to causality, gradualism adds to the confusion over the changes in the environment. Our actions alter the global environment slowly or gradually rather than dramatically or abruptly. For instance, compare human-induced air pollution with the eruption of the Philippines' Mount Pinatubo in 1991. The volcanic blast spewed 20 million tons of sulphur dioxide (SO_2) more than 15 miles into the atmosphere; scientists labeled it possibly "the largest climate perturbation of the century." The SO_2 was photochemically transformed into sulfuric acid, which in turn formed a global layer of small droplets known as aerosols. These aerosols temporarily altered the climate around the world by cooling the lower atmosphere and warming the stratosphere.

The eruption and its results were dramatic and quick. In contrast, the emissions from factories, power plants, and cars seem more routine and their impact is far more gradual. Compared to the abrupt eruption of a volcano, the human factor is glacial. People and industries do not usually pollute a harbor all at once or wipe out a fish species or destroy a rainforest with the speed and drama of volcanic eruption. Scientists have much more difficulty identifying, sorting out, and reaching agreement about such slow-moving changes. However, in the long run, these gradual changes can have just as large an impact on the environment and the quality of life on the planet. When one person takes a walk across a lawn, the grass can recover; when one hundred people follow, they create a trail.

Models and Uncertainty

Scientists use models to help them understand complexity in nature. Models help them make predictions, not only over short time periods, but also over much longer periods where changes occur so gradually that they are not observable in a day or week or even a year.

A model seeks to clarify the relationships among the known variables under study. Since a model is based on complex mathematical formulas, scientists rely on computers to do the calculations. These computer models do not portray every part of the real world. Scientists do not know everything about every process. So models can never be perfect.

Yet, part of the scientific method is to find out how to deal with uncertainty. Using models, scientists produce results that are probably true, but can also be wrong in some cases. Scientists continually debate among themselves how to improve the models. As they gain greater knowledge or alter their assumptions, they increase the reliability of their predictions.

We should not therefore be surprised just because someone says a model prediction is uncertain. Rather, we should be cautious and ask the result if the outcome were correct. Also, we need to remember that if the model has an uncertain outcome, it does not mean the opposite is more certain. It means every prediction has elements of uncertainty, so we must look to the entire scientific community for guidance.

Environmental Science in the News

So, for these reasons, the science of global environmental change will inevitably be confusing and involve considerable debate and disagreement among intelligent, sincere scientists. That does not mean that the scientific community as a whole is unable to reach any conclusions or provide any useful guidance about what society needs to do to protect the environment and the earth's life-support systems. Unfortunately, the way the media cover environmental issues often makes it hard for the average person to know when the scientific community has reached such conclusions or has such advice to impart.

Professionally, reporters and newscasters seriously seek to report what they believe is the truth. Nevertheless, they have difficulty covering science issues since many reporters have little scientific background or write about an area of science they have not studied. It can be difficult for them to learn a subject well enough to tell good from bad science or to detect when data are being manipulated.

"AND GOD SAW THAT IT WAS GOOD"

As important, the journalists' normal method of operation is not always well suited to covering science. They are trained to be balanced in their coverage and to present both sides of an issue. However, achieving balance can be harder when covering science than, for example, politics. News sources in politics express opinions that deserve coverage just as much as another source expressing an opposite view. On the other hand, in science some views are more valid than others because they represent a consensus—the agreement of the vast majority of scientists in the scientific community. Scientists reach consensus through studies conducted by many researchers evaluating facts, gathering data, and—most important—acting independently. Through the process of replication, or the rerunning of the same experiment by many different scientists, they reach agreement that a theory is solid.

Once scientists reach a consensus, the views of the few remaining skeptics do not deserve equal weight. Nevertheless, the media continue to give equal attention to both sides—even if one of the viewpoints no longer has enough weight or substance to receive such prominence. The media and politicians have made sound bites seem as significant as rigorous scientific discourse, but in truth their simplification does not always do justice to complex environmental issues.

Knowing this quirk of the media, you can read news stories on environmental issues more critically. We can ask whether the exponent of a particular point of view speaks only for him or herself or whether the position was reached after work by a large number of researchers at varied institutions. When a major scientific society or association—such as the National Academy of Sciences, the Ecological Society of America, or the Pontifical Academy of Sciences—endorses or adopts a scientific position, it deserves greater consideration than if only a few isolated individuals promote it. The number of experiments carried out to reach a conclusion and the length of time scientists study a particular subject also help indicate how much we can trust a particular conclusion.

But sometimes factors other than the scientific value of a particular theory or point of view help determine how much attention it receives in the media. Many individuals, groups, and organizations have a stake in the outcome of debates over environmental science. For example, when scientists concluded that CFCs, or chlorofluorocarbons, were destroying the ozone layer, certain manufacturers had to take their products off the market while some producers of alternative technologies benefited.

Because the stakes are high, various people and organizations try to influence the outcome. These groups and organizations therefore often recruit scientists to promote their point of view and employ public relations experts to publicize it. Before we come to any judgments regarding a particular scientific debate, we should first scrutinize which organizations fund and support the opposing scientists' research. Is there a well-funded, well-organized campaign to promote a particular point of view or to give the impression that a fringe, minority viewpoint is commonly held by a majority of scientists?

Whom Should We Believe and What Should We Do?

Even if we become critical readers and news watchers, it will remain difficult to evaluate the conflicting reports from scientists on environmental issues. On some occasions, scientists who have predicted serious dangers from human-induced environmental changes have later been proven right, while in other cases impacts have turned out to be less serious than scientists expected. For example, the predictions of atmospheric chemists Mario Molina and Sherwood Rowland in 1973 that CFCs threatened the ozone layer turned out to be borne out over time, while estimates of the amount of damage the Exxon Valdez oil spill would do to whale and bird populations off the coast of Alaska turned out to be exaggerated.

While the debate continues over the degree of seriousness of environmental problems, there is ample evidence of environmental problems with negative impacts on people's quality of life. In many of the United States' coastal waters, fish stocks have fallen dramatically. The famous Chesapeake Bay crabs, for example, are at their lowest levels in recorded time. In parts of the country, groundwater is being withdrawn through irrigation faster than it can be replenished. Many rivers and streams are still polluted.

In other parts of the world, the impacts of environmental problems on people's lives are often more dramatic. The people of Mexico City suffer greatly from significant air pollution. In the Philippines, more than two-thirds of the mangroves (trees or shrubs that grow along the tidal shores) have been lost, reducing the nation's fisheries. Many of the poor residents of Bombay, India, get their water from a river that includes the wastes of industrial plants. Worldwide, millions of children die from water-related diseases that have mostly been eliminated from the United States.

No scientist can know exactly where the world is heading, but we should keep this in mind: When all factors are considered, if enough evidence is given to create reasonable doubt and indicate that society's present course could threaten the quality of life for our descendants, it is justifiable and prudent to throw our weight on the side of those predicting severe environmental harm. If you were told that you had a 75 percent chance, or even a 50 or 30 percent chance, of breaking your leg if you skied down a particularly treacherous trail, you would probably stay off the mountain even though there is a good chance that you would not be hurt. When presented with a potentially serious environmental threat, the responsible course is to act to reduce the threat rather than sit back and wait for conclusive proof that scientists' worst predictions of disaster will be realized.

ABOUT
THE
AUTHORS

Deborah D. Blake is an associate professor of religious studies at Regis University in Denver, Colorado. She received her undergraduate degree in biological sciences—ecology and botany—from the University of California, Santa Barbara. Her doctoral studies in theological ethics were completed at the Graduate Theological Union, Berkeley. Her publications address issues of genetics, creation theology, and ethics in education. Professor Blake recently presented a paper at the *Evangelische Akademie Loccum,* Germany, entitled "U.S. Concerns about the Ethical and Social Issues Linked to the New Genetics." In summer 1995, she held an NIH fellowship in "Clinical and Molecular Genetics" at the School of Medicine, University of Iowa, Iowa City.

Reverend Drew Christiansen, SJ, is the director of the Office of International Justice and Peace at the United States Catholic Conference. Before coming to the

USCC, he served as Bannan Scholar at the Santa Clara University in the 1990-1991 academic year. From 1986-1990, he served with the founding team of the University of Notre Dame's Kroc Institute for International Peace Studies and is co-editor with George A. Lopez of *Morals and Might: Ethics and the Use of Force in Modern International Affairs*. Presently, he is co-editor with Gerard F. Powers and Robert T. Hennemeyer in *Peacemaking: Moral and Policy Challenges for a New World*. He has also published "Moral Theology, Ecology, Justice and Development," in *Covenant for a New Creation*, ed. Carol Robb and Carl Casebolt, and "The Common Good and the Politics of Self Interest: A Catholic Contribution to the Practice of Citizenship" in *Beyond Individualism*, ed. Donald Gelpi, SJ.

Anne M. Clifford, CSJ, earned her Ph.D. in theology at The Catholic University of America in 1988. She is an assistant tenured professor of theology at Duquesne University, where she teaches a variety of systematic theology and religious studies courses in the graduate and undergraduate programs. She is currently a member of the board of directors of the College Theology Society and of the editorial advisory board for the Fundamental Theology Section of Concilium. In 1995, she received the "Presidential Award for Excellence in Teaching" at Duquesne University and the College Theology Society Award for the "Best Scholarly Essay of the Year" for "Postmodern Scientific Cosmology and the God of Creation," published in *Horizons* (1994). Her essays have also appeared in *Systematic Theology, Roman Catholic Perspectives, Vol. 1; The Struggles over the Past, Fundamentalism in the Modern World; The Journal for Feminist Studies in Religion;* and *A Handbook of Catholic Theology*.

Reverend Hugh Bernard Feiss, OSB, became of monk of Mount Angel Abbey in 1960 and was ordained a priest in 1966. He received his Ph.L. from The Catholic University of America in 1972. He is a scholar in medieval spirituality and has done additional studies at Pontificum Athenaeum Anselmianum in Rome, as well as at Harvard University and Georgetown University. He is currently a lecturer at the Trappist Abbey in Lafayette, Oregon, and is the director of the Mount Angel Abbey Library. He has written numerous articles on the history of monasticism and medieval spirituality.

Walter E. Grazer is the director of the Environmental Justice Program for the United States Catholic Conference. Formerly, he served as deputy director for Migration and Refugee Services and as policy advisor for food, agriculture, and rural development at the Conference. Prior to his fifteen-year service at the USCC, he directed the social ministry program of the Diocese of Richmond after working for the City of Richmond's Commission on Human Relations and the Richmond

"And God Saw That It Was Good"

Community Action Program. Mr. Grazer holds a B.A. in philosophy, an M.A. in international relations, and an M.S.W. in social work.

John F. Haught is a professor of theology at Georgetown University. His area of specialization is systematic theology, with a particular interest in issues pertaining to science, cosmology, ecology, and religion. He is the author of numerous books including *Science and Religion: Conflict or Conversation?*, *The Promise of Nature: Ecology and Cosmic Purpose*, *Mystery and Promise: A Theology of Revelation*, *What is God?*, and *Nature and Purpose*.

Christine Firer Hinze received her bachelor's degree in religious studies (1974) and later a master's degree in theology (1978) from The Catholic University of America. Before earning a Ph.D. in Christian Social Ethics at the Divinity School of the University of Chicago (1989), she spent two years in full-time inner-city pastoral ministry at St. Dominic's Parish, Detroit, and another three years teaching high school religious studies. From 1986-1990 she served on the faculty of religious studies at St. Norbert College, DePere, Wisconsin. Since 1990, she has been assistant professor in the Department of Theology, Marquette University, Milwaukee, Wisconsin.

Reverend Kevin Irwin, a priest of the Archdiocese of New York, is ordinary professor of liturgy and sacramental theology and director of the liturgical studies program in the School of Religious Studies at The Catholic University of America in Washington, D.C. He also serves as advisor to the National Conference of Catholic Bishops' Committee on the Liturgy. He is the author of *Context and Text: Method in Liturgical Theology* and co-editor of *Preserving the Creation: Environmental Theology and Ethics*.

Reverend David S. Toolan, SJ, is an associate editor of *America* magazine. Formerly, he was associate editor of *Commonweal* magazine, 1970-1979, and taught at Canisius College, 1974-1979. He received his Ph.D. in philosophical theology from Southern Methodist University. He has published in the fields of Jesuit spirituality and the new physics, *Nature as Heraclitean Fire*, and *Facing West*, in which he explores the American consciousness movement.

INDEX

Baptism
    former Roman vs. post–Vatican II,
        133n.7
    water symbolism in, 119–22, 135n.19
Barfield, Owen, 75–76, 79
Barney, Gerald, 50
Barrow, John D., 83
Basil, St., 331
Bataan nuclear plant, 315
Beaubien, Carlos, 209n.21
Bede, St., 153
Bellah, Robert, 197
Benedictine order, 148–52, 157–60
    agricultural practices of, 161n.12
    balanced understanding of human
        well-being by, 185–86
    environmental responsibility and, 12–13,
        158–60
    greed avoided by, 150–51
    reverence displayed by, 126–27, 149
    stability of, 148–49
Benedict, St.
    life of, 152–53
    Rule of, 12–13, 126–27, 148–52, 155,
        161n.12
Bennett, William, 197
Berry, Thomas
    on ecological change, 99
    on environmental loss as spiritual loss, 55
    human being defined by, 84
Biblical interpretation
    contemporary, 22, 23
    literal vs. historical, 25
    religious truth and, 253–54
Big bang theory, 80–82
Binkman, Martin E., 138n.45
Birth control, 236, 255–56
Bishops, United States Catholic
    call to environmental action by, 2, 3, 255
    on consumption of resources, 326
    God-centered ecological approach of, 7
    see also Renewing the Earth
Blake, Deborah D., 13, 16–17, 197–210
Bombay, India, 338
Book of Virtues, The (Bennett), 197
Brief History of Time, A (Hawking), 84
Bright, John, 137n.39
Brundtland Commission, 191
Bukidnon, Philippines, 315

Bustos, Patrick, 205–6

Caeli Deus sanctissime, 115
Cahill, Thomas, 74
Calendar, Roman
    births commemorated in, 112
    northern vs. southern hemisphere, 131
Camino (periodical), 273
Campaign for Human Development, 226
Campbell, Joseph, 70
Campesinos
    exploitation of, 280–81
    governmental suppression of, 288
    land distribution amongst, 279, 286–87,
        290
    legal defense of, 290–92
    poverty suffered by, 276, 279–80
Canberra, Australia, 247
"Canticle of Sister Sun" (Francis of Assisi),
    74, 269
Caritas Dominicana, 273
Carolingian dynasty, 162n.17
Cassino, Monte, 148, 152
Catechism of the Catholic Church, 5
Catholic community
    ecological organizations, cooperation
        with, 251
    growing ecological awareness of, 185,
        225–26, 240
    scientific community, relationship with,
        2, 65–66, 70–73, 241
Catholic Relief Services (CRS), 226–27
Causae et Curae (Hildegard), 155, 156
Causality, 334–35
Cellarer, task of, 150
Celtic Christianity, oral culture of, 74–75
Centessimus Annus (Pope John Paul II),
    195n.33, 226, 233, 331
CFCs. See Chlorofluorocarbons
Chaos theory, 90–91
Charcoal, 270
Charity, 203
Chauvet, Louis Marie, 108
Chico dam project, 315
Chipko, 315
Chlorofluorocarbons, 337, 338
Cholera, 335
Christiansen, Drew, 1–18, 170, 180n.21,
    183–95, 333–38

Christmas, euchology of, 113-14
City of God (Augustine), 70
Civil Defense Patrols, 288
Clifford, Anne M., 9-10, 19-46
Clifford, Richard J., 27, 44n.21
Climate, unusual patterns in, 333-36
Colossians, Book of, christological creation
    hymn in, 35-36, 118
Commoner, Barry, 322-23, 326
Common good
    authentic development and, 15, 185-88,
        189-90
    historical development of, 183-84
    as ideal, 192-93
    meaning of, 15, 184-85
    moderation and, 15, 187-88, 303
    solidarity and, 233, 326
    universal, 190-92, 232-33
Common ownership, 201
Communication, nature and, 88-89
Communitarian vision as ecological virtue, 207
Community of Character, A (Hauerwas),
    197-98
"Concern for Social Matters." *See Sollicitudo*
    Rei Socialis
Confessions, The (Augustine), 70
Consensus, scientific, 337
Consistent ethic of life, 3
Consumerism. *See* Materialism
Consumption
    as religious question, 327-28
    of resources, 235, 251, 297, 326
Control vs. service, 149-50
Conversion
    examination of modern lifestyles and,
        250, 304-5
    personal goals and, 292-93
Cooperation as ecological virtue, 207
Copernicus, 65
Cordillera Central, 261, 271
1 Corinthians, Book of, liturgical symbolism
    in, 111
Cosmology
    Catholic theology, interactions with,
        10-11, 70-73
    premodern, 69, 70
    scientific vs. visionary, 70
Costillo Estates Land Development
    Company, 209n.21

Covenant, Noachic, 29-30, 232, 253, 315-16
Cowdin, Daniel M., 168-70, 179n.17
Creation
    aesthetic value of, 145n.99, 221
    contemplation of, 186-87, 221, 237-38
    God-centered approach to, 7
    God, leading to knowledge of, 137n.41
    Hildegard's theology and, 155-56
    in liturgical worship, 11, 12, 108, 111-19,
        124-28
    as long process, 312
    neglect (theological) of, 21-22
    redemption, dichotomy between, 10, 20,
        29-37
    sacramentality of, 51-52, 94-99,
        145n.101, 231-32
    see also Genesis, Book of; Nature
Creationism, 21-22
Crick, Francis, 71
Crows, 159-60
Cuilapan, Mexico, 286
Cuthbert, St., 153-54

Daniel, Book of, 115
Dawkins, Richard, 71
"Deer Cry, The." *See* "St. Patrick's
    Breastplate"
Deforestation. *See* Forests
Dei Verbum (Vatican II), 22, 23, 44n.12
Democritus, 86
Denver, Colorado, 204-7
De operatione Dei (Hildegard), 155, 156
Deserts, 157-58
Determinism, open thermodynamic systems
    and, 91
Deuteronomy, Book of
    God praised in, 228
    Promised Land described in, 28
Development
    authentic, 15, 185-88, 189-90, 234-35
    integral, 289
    Paul VI on, 331
    sustainable, 191
Dignity, 14, 168-71, 176, 187, 324
District Court, United States, 209n.21
Ditmanson, Harold, 136n.26
Divino Afflante Spiritu (Pope Pius XII), 22
Dominican Republic
    agriculture in, 261

deforestation in, 261–62, 263, 266,
  269–71
population of, 261
radio stations (Catholic) in, 273
Dominion
  in Biblical creation account, 21, 24–27,
    252
  human exercise of, 299, 302, 312
Donne, John, 76, 77
Doxology, Trinity in, 119
Dualism of Gnostics, 37
Duran, Josephine, 205, 206

Earth Day, 321
Earthwatch, 251
Easter vigil, 117, 120, 129
East Park, Dominican Republic, 261
Ecclesiastes, Book of, 273–74
Eckhart, Johannes, 75
"Ecological Crisis: A Common
  Responsibility." See World Day of
  Peace Message
Ecology
  defined, 43n.1, 246
  economy and, 14, 171–72, 175–77
  growing awareness of, 185, 225–26, 240,
    314–15, 321–22
  as international problem, 219–20, 221–22,
    232–33, 322–23, 324–25
  as moral problem, 199–201, 217–18,
    302–4, 323
  as religious issue, 300
  scientific method and, 334–36, 337
Economic Justice for All, 326
Economism, 186
Economy, ecological ethics and, 14, 171–72,
  175–77
Ecophilia, 186
Ecumenism, 17, 251
Education
  in agricultural techniques, 291
  in ecological responsibility, 221, 241, 250,
    271, 273, 305
Egypt, 227
Einstein, Albert, 85, 86, 87
Eliot, Thomas Stearns, 72
Ember days, 129–30
Energy, 4
  alternative, 200

in Dominican Republic, 270
evaluating sources of, 298
Enuma elish, 25–26
Environmental crisis
  complexity of, 296
  ethical responses to, 199–201, 302–4
  growing awareness of, 185, 225–26, 240,
    314–15, 321–22
  international response needed for,
    219–20, 221–22, 232–33, 322–23,
    324–25
  as religious issue, 4–5
Environmental Justice Program (United
    States Catholic Conference), 3, 6, 319
Environmental Protection Agency, 321
Epiphany, euchology of, 113, 114
Equity as ecological virtue, 207
Erosion
  in Dominican Republic, 262
  in Philippines, 312–13
Escamilla, Margaret, 205
Eschatology
  as ecological menace, 53
  personal destiny within, 60–63
  as promise, 10, 49–50, 52, 54–59
Ethicists, environmental
  anti-Christian sentiments amongst, 50–51
  naturalism endorsed by, 50, 56
Ethics
  consistent, 3
  environmental crisis, in relation to,
    199–201, 302–4
  liturgy and, 107–8
  materialism and, 173–75
  natural resource usage and, 266–68, 272
  Thomistic, 172–73
Eucharist
  dialogic character of, 110–11, 128–29
  gifts presented at, 131–32
  hymns during, 130, 132
  symbolism of, 109–10, 122–24, 129
Euchology
  natural phenomena in, 112–14
  northern vs. southern hemisphere, 131
Evangelical Environmental Network, 4
Eve, 216, 252, 253
Everett, Hugh, 80–81
Evolutionism vs. creationism, 21–22
Export sector, agricultural, 279

Faith
as center of Catholic community, 2
eschatological, 49-50, 54
life of, and the environment, 2
as theological virtue, 203
Farms. *See* Agriculture
Faroe Islands, 163n.28
Farsightedness as ecological virtue, 207
Fasting, 332
Feiss, Hugh, 12-13, 147-64
Feminist theology, 178n.6, 179n.17
Fertilizers, 298
Firer Hinze, Christine, 13-14, 165-82
Flood story. *See* Great Flood
Florentius, 152
Flores, Emma, 205
Forests
destruction of, 200, 246, 261-62, 263,
266, 269-71, 312
of Philippines' early ancestors, 311
reforestation, 271
Fortitude as moral virtue, 203, 207
Franciscan order, liturgical tradition of, 128
Francis of Assisi, St., 239
"Canticle of Sister Sun," 74, 269
as patron saint of the environment, 7,
127, 222
White, Lynn, Jr., on, 44n.14
Freedom, 201
Friendship, 285
solidarity and, 289
Frye, Northrop, 81

Galileo Galilei, 66
Gallegos, Angelina, 205
Gaudium et Spes (Vatican II), 184, 199, 218.
*See also Pastoral Constitution on the
Church in the Modern World*
Gell-Mann, Murray, 85
General Instruction on Christian Initiation,
142n.79
General Instruction on the Liturgy of the
Hours, 139n.50
General Norms for the Liturgical Year and
the Calendar, 129-30
Genesis, Book of
creation stories in, 9, 19, 21-22, 23-28,
95, 216, 228, 251-54
Great Flood in, 27, 229, 232

original sin in, 265-66
Gifts presented at eucharist, 131-32
Global warming, 333-34
Globeville community (Denver, Colorado),
16, 204-7
Gnosticism, 37
God
as Creator, 5, 19-20, 25-28, 30-35,
155-56, 216, 228-29, 251-54, 264-65
in gnosticism, 37
kingdom of, 301
reverence for, 231, 237-38, 249
as Sustainer, 31, 34
in Thomism, 39-40
Good, common. *See* Common good
Goodness
in Biblical creation account, 251-52
virtue and, 202-3
Goodpaster, Kenneth, 179n.15
Government. *See* State
Gradualism, 335-36
Granados, Lorraine, 206
Grand unified theories, 72
Grants, land. *See* Land grants
Grazer, Walter E., 1-18, 333-38
Great Flood, 27, 29-30, 135n.19, 229
Greed, Benedictines and, 150-51
Green belt movement, 315
Greenhouse effect. *See* Global warming
Greenpeace, 251
Gregory the Great, St., 152
Guardini, Romano, 198
Guatemala
agrarian problem in, 276-81, 290-92
violence in, 281-82
Gula, Richard, 179n.14
Gustafson, James M., 170

Habits of the Heart, 197
Haeckel, Ernst, 43n.1
Hardin, Garrett, 201
Hauerwas, Stanley, 197
Haught, John F., 10, 47-64
Hawking, Stephen W.
"good scientific theory" defined by, 70
on improbability of life in universe,
82-83
on quantum mechanics, 86
questions raised by, 84

on self-contained universe, 81
    "theory of everything" sought by, 71–72
"Healing the Earth," 251
Health, Department of (Colorado), 206
Hegel, Georg Wilhelm Friedrich, 85
Heisenberg, Werner, 83, 86
Hermits. *See* Monasticism
Hildegard, St., 154–57
Himes, Kenneth R., 51–52
Himes, Michael J., 51–52
Hispanic culture, communal ownership in, 201
Hollenbach, David, 179n.14
Holy Spirit
    ecological hope and, 243
    in liturgical worship, 118–19
Hominis supernae Conditor, 115
Hope
    as ecological virtue, 50, 243
    eschatological, 10, 53–54, 55
    as theological virtue, 203
Hopkins, Gerard Manley, 243
Hosea, Book of
    creation's suffering in, 229
    Noachic covenant in, 29–30
Hubble, Edwin, 79–80
Hubble Space Telescope, 70
"Hug a tree" movement, 315
Humility
    Benedictine emphasis upon, 149–50
    Hildegard on, 156
Hunting, 264, 312
Hymns
    at eucharist, 130, 132
    offertory, 132
    vesper, 114–15

Iam sol recedit igneus, 115
Ideals, function of, 192–93
Ignatius of Loyola, St., 269
Immense coeli Conditor, 115
Immortality of soul, ecological responsibility and, 60
Industrialization, future approaches to, 219
Information physics, 87–89
Inner Farne, 153
Innocent XI, Pope, 182n.36
Integral development. *See* Development, authentic

Irenaeus, St., 37
Irwin, Kevin W., 11–12, 105–46
Isaiah, Book of, creation in, 28–29

Jakowska, Sophi, 198
Jeremiah, Book of, creation in, 30
Jersey City, New Jersey, 226
Jesus Christ
    creation faith and, 34–36, 118, 284–85
    in gnosticism, 37
    as model for ecological action, 62, 98, 316
    nature admired by, 268
    present in needy people, 151
    on proper concerns for life, 301
    reconciliation with nature and, 229–30, 249, 285, 304
    wealth denounced by, 284, 330
John the Baptist, St., 112
John Chrysostum, St., 286
John, Gospel of, Prologue, 34–35, 95, 113, 114, 118
John Paul II, Pope, 6–7, 215–22, 249, 251, 252, 255, 282, 323
    on aesthetic value of creation, 7, 145n.99, 221
    class separation and, 195n.33, 234
    consumerism discouraged by, 188, 234, 329–30, 331
    on economism, 186
    on education in ecological responsibility, 250
    on Francis of Assisi, 127, 222
    on human dominion over nature, 302
    on land distribution, 286–87
    Mater et Magistra and, 290
    on population growth, 236
    on respect for nature, 1, 20, 185, 190, 218, 254, 260, 324
    on responsibility for ecological crisis, 219–20, 221–22, 233
    on world peace (threats to), 1, 198, 218, 220
Johnson, Elizabeth, 179n.17
John XXIII, Pope
    agricultural sector emphasized by, 290
    common good and, 184, 190, 199, 232
Jose del Carmen Ramirez Park, Dominican Republic, 261

temperance and, 329
Molina, Mario, 338
Moltmann, Jürgen
    on Christian eschatology, 53
    on creation, 118
    on God's essence, 58–59
    pneumatology of, 55
Monasticism
    Easter vigil and, 129
    locations for, 157–58
    nature and, 12–13, 152–54, 157–60
    reverence and, 126–27
    see also Benedictine order; Franciscan
    order
Monod, Jacques, 78
Monte Cassino, 148, 152
Montoya, Al, 206
Morals. *See* Ethics
Moses, 318
Mozo colono tradition, 280–81
Murnion, Philip J., 145n.101
Murphy, Charles, 319–20, 327–32

Narrative as clarifier of virtues, 204–7
Nash, James A., 170, 176, 182n.39
National Catholic Rural Life Conference,
    226
National Council of Churches in Christ, 4
National Environmental Policy Act, 321
National Religious Partnership for the
    Environment (NRPE), 3–4, 6
Naturalism, 50
Nature
    as communication system, 88–89
    defined, 307n.2
    historical character of, 57
    in oral cultures, 73–76
    as promise, 55–59
    respect for, 1–2, 6, 20, 185, 190, 218, 232,
    254, 303
    sacramental character of, 51–52, 94–99,
    231
    social teaching and, 168–70
    textualization of, 76–77
    see also Creation
Newman, Cardinal, 155
News. *See* Journalism
Newtonian mechanics, 72–73, 86
Nicene Creed, 38, 119

"Ninth Duino Elegy" (Rilke), 97
Noah, 27, 154, 229, 232, 253
Noble, David, 162n.17
Nonviolence. *See* Peace; Violence
Norbert-Hodge, Helena, 332
NRPE. *See* National Religious Partnership
    for the Environment

Oakland, California, 226
Oaxaca, Mexico, 290
O'Connell, Timothy, 179n.14
Octogesima Adveniens (Pope Paul VI), 184–85,
    199
One World Campaign, 251
Ong, Walter, 78
Open thermodynamic systems. *See* Chaos
    theory
Oral cultures, creation experienced by, 73–76
Origen, 46n.43
Othmar, St., 162n.21
Our Common Future (World Commission on
    Environment and Development),
    191
*Overworked American: The Unexpected Decline
    in Leisure* (Schor), 332
Ownership, common. *See* Common
    ownership

Pacem in Terris (Pope John XXIII), 190, 199,
    232
Pagadian, Philippines, 315
Paganism, ecological ethics and, 56
Pannenberg, Wolfhart, 64n.14
Panzos, Guatemala, 282
Pasig River, 313
Passmore, John, 50
*Pastoral Constitution on the Church in the
    Modern World* (Vatican II), 8, 184. *See
    also Gaudium et Spes*
Paul, St.
    creation faith of, 35–36, 237, 246
    on sin, 253
Paul VI, Pope, 178n.10, 184–85, 263
    development desired by, 331
    on population growth, 236
    on sacrifice of goods, 188, 199
Peace
    as environmental priority, 236–37
    threats to, 198, 218, 220

"Peace with God the Creator, Peace with All Creation." *See* World Day of Peace Message

Peasants (Guatemalan). *See* Campesinos

Penzias, Arno, 80

Peru, 227

Pesticides, 298

Philippines
deforestation in, 312
growing ecological awareness in, 314-15
original environmental state of, 311-12

Physics
potential paradigm shift in, 84-85
theological reflection and, 11, 62-63, 69, 83-84, 88-89
theories of, 71-73, 80-82, 85-91
time variable in, 71

Physiologus, 159

Pieper, Josef, 329, 332

Pinatubo, Mount, 335

Pius XI, Pope, 173

Pius XII, Pope, 22

Planck, Max, 86

Plants in Thomistic hierarchy, 40-41

Pneumatology
of Moltmann, Jürgen, 55
see also Holy Spirit

Pollution
causes of, 297-99
pervasiveness of, 324
respect for life and, 218
of seas, 312-14, 335

Poor, 1, 3, 8
access to land and, 266, 278-79, 286-87
environmental justice and, 5, 6, 220, 225
option for, 234
see also Campesinos

Population, world, 235-36, 255-56, 322-23, 325

Populorum Progressio (Pope Paul VI), 188, 330, 331

Po River, 297

Porter, Jean, 197, 198, 204

Poulos, Susan, 206

Power, David, 108

Prayers
Celtic, 74
creation in, 112-14, 115-18, 128
eucharistic, 116, 128, 131, 140n.55

Pride, Benedictine suspicion of, 149-50

Prigogine, Ilya, 78

Promised Land, 27-28, 283

Property
common ownership of, 201
private, 285-86

Prosper of Aquitaine, St., 105

Protestantism, commitment to ecological activities by, 4

Proverbs, Book of, creation in, 32-33

Prudence as moral virtue, 203, 207

Psalms, Book of, creation in, 31-32, 300

Quadragesimo Anno, 199

Quantum mechanics, 72, 86

Racism, 3, 207

Radio stations, 273

Rahner, Karl, 58, 61

Ramshaw-Schmidt, Gail, 141n.69

Raymo, Chet, 79

RCIA. *See* Rite of the Christian Initiation of Adults

Recife, Brazil, 287

Recovery of Virtue, The (Porter), 197, 198

"Redeemer of Man." *See Redemptor Hominis*

Redemption
of Christ, 230, 249
creation, dichotomy between, 10, 20, 29-37
in liturgical worship, 115-16

Redemptor Hominis (Pope John Paul II), 199, 260, 296

Reductionism. *See* Scientism

Relationality. *See* Communitarian vision

Religious community
qualifications for engaging ecological issues, 4-5
scientific community, relationship with, 65-66, 70-73, 241

Renewing the Earth: An Invitation to Reflection and Action on the Environment in Light of Catholic Social Teaching, 6, 15, 167-68, 223-43
on Christian way of life, 148
on common good, 190
on environmental crisis as moral challenge, 154
on hope, 50

"Renewing the Earth: the Environmental Justice Program," 3

Rerum Novarum (Pope Leo XIII), 165, 198, 331

Rescher, Nicholas, 184

Resources
  consumption of, 235, 251, 297, 326
  ethical use of, 266–68, 272

Respect for nature, 1, 20, 185, 190, 218, 232, 254, 303

Responsibility for ecological crisis, 219–20, 221–22, 233, 241–42, 248, 263, 269–70

Resurrection, 60–61, 216–17

Reverence
  for Creator, 231, 237–38, 249
  St. Benedict's call for, 126–27, 149

Rilke, Rainer Maria, 93, 97, 99

Rio de Janiero, 322

Rite of the Christian Initiation of Adults (RCIA), 119–22

Rocky Mountain News (newspaper), 204–6

Rogation days, 129–30

Rolston, Holmes, III, 48

Romans, Book of, creation in, 36, 137n.41

Rouillard, Philippe, 122–23

Rowland, Sherwood, 338

Ruether, Rosemary, 179n.17

Rule of the Master, 148

Ryan, John A., 173–76, 181nn.29, 33, 34, 182nn.36, 37

Sabbath, 229

Sacramentalism
  creation and, 3, 5, 51–52, 94–99, 145n.101, 231–32
  eschatology, independent of, 64n.12
  premodern roots of, 66–67, 73–79
  two senses of, 67–68

Sacred, sense of, 5

Sacrifice of goods, 15, 188

Sagan, Carl, 71, 81–82

Saints, 147

Salvation
  liturgy, articulated by, 110, 126
  as theology's main concern, 71

San Fernando, Philippines, 315

Sangre de Cristo land grant, 209n.21

San Luis, Colorado, 201, 209n.21

Santa Cruz Mission, 315

Sartre, Jean-Paul, 78

Schaefer, Jamie Ehegartner, 172–73, 176, 181n.28

Schor, Juliet, 332

Schumacher, E. F., 329

Science
  in divine plan, 264–65
  media coverage of, 336–38
  methodology of, 334–36, 337
  new approaches needed in, 238
  perceptions of nature changed by, 77–78
  religion, relationship with, 2, 65–66, 70–73, 241

Scientism, 71

Scivias (Hildegard), 155–56

Scotus Ereuigena, 75

Scripture
  attitudes toward creation derived from, 249, 300–301
  critics' interpretations of, 9
  land stressed in, 282–84

Seas, pollution of, 312–14, 335

Sermon on the Mount, 301

Serres, Michel, 89, 92–93, 94

Service vs. control, 149–50

Sierra de Bahoruco, 261

Sierra de Neiba, 261

Simon, Richard, 22

Simon, Yves, 198

Sin
  Hildegard on, 156
  Paul on, 253
  as ruination of paradise, 265–66

Small is Beautiful: Economics as if People Mattered (Schumacher), 329

Snow, C. P., 84

Social teaching, Catholic, 165–77
  common good and, 184–93
  human dignity and, 14, 168–71, 176, 187
  private property and, 285–86
  recent history of, 165–66
  see also Development, authentic

Sodano, Angelo, 325

Solemnity of the Birth of John the Baptist, 112

Solidarity, 233, 288–89, 324–25

Sollicitudo Rei Socialis (Pope John Paul II), 178n.10, 190, 195n.33, 236, 249, 254, 296

War, 220, 325
Washington state, 226
Water
    as liturgical symbol, 109, 119-22
    pollution of, 312-14, 335, 338
Wealth
    excessive consumption and, 329-31
    prophetic denunciation of, 283-84
Weather. *See* Climate
Westermann, Claus, 25
Whitehead, Alfred North
    on fourth-century theologians, 68
    on science's effect upon nature, 77
    on scientism, 71
White, Lynn, Jr.
    on Christian creation doctrine, 24
    on Francis of Assisi, 44n.14
Wilson, Robert, 80
Wisdom. *See* Sophia

Wisdom, Book of
    on godliness of nature, 94-95, 306
    rule of creation in, 252, 265
Women, contributions to ecological
    movement by, 315
Worcester, England, 154
Word. *See* Logos
World Charter for Nature (General Assembly
    of United Nations), 246
World Council of Churches, 246-47
World Day of Peace Message (Pope John
    Paul II), 1, 6, 20, 145n.99, 198,
    215-22, 233, 249-50, 323
Wulstan, St., 154

Youths, ecological education of, 305

Zamboanga del Sur, Philippines, 315
Zimmerli, Walter, 32